D0454888

U.S. Trade Policies in a
Changing World Economy

U.S. Trade Policies in a
Changing World Economy

edited by Robert M. Stern

The MIT Press
Cambridge, Massachusetts
London, England

Second printing, 1988

This book was set in Apollo by Asco Trade Typesetting Ltd., Hong Kong, and printed and bound by Halliday Lithograph in the United States of America.

Library of Congress Cataloging-in-Publication Data

U.S. trade policies in a changing world economy.
  Includes bibliographies and index.
  1. United States—Commercial policy.   I. Stern, Robert Mitchell, 1927–
II Title: US trade policies in a changing world economy.
HF1455.U548   1987   382′.3′0973   86-10553
ISBN 0-262-19253-5

Contents

Foreword

During the 1980s it became apparent to many observers that the state of Michigan was passing through a period of difficult economic adjustment. Further, it seemed clear that the adjustment was more basic than the typical cyclical movements that had long characterized Michigan's durable goods—based economy. In addition, many believed that the new era of international economic competition and changing consumer tastes had permanently changed the near monopoly of domestic motor vehicle manufacturers and labor unions that had so effectively represented industry workers.

Whatever the causes, economic activity in Michigan was experiencing a sharp recession. As president of the state's flagship public university, I asked myself what helpful role the University of Michigan might play in helping the citizens of the state deal effectively with the economic challenges before them. As I thought about the issue, I became convinced that the university should take special advantage of the expertise that resided in our faculty and do what it could to take a responsible part in the formation of public policy. As a result the regents of the University of Michigan and I undertook a number of initiatives designed to bring faculty expertise to bear on some of the economic and social challenges facing Michigan. The Conference on U.S. Trade Policies is one of the outcomes of these initiatives. Although the university provided the financial support for this conference, our faculty had full and complete autonomy in the designing of the conference, and the content of this book is the result of their efforts.

On behalf of the regents of the university, I want to express my thanks to our faculty colleagues and staff in the Institute of Public Policy Studies who organized the conference and to the many distinguished participants who contributed to its success.

Harold T. Shapiro

Preface

The idea of a conference dealing with international trade and trade policies was first broached by University of Michigan president Harold T. Shapiro to a group of interested university faculty members in January 1984. An organizing committee was established, with Robert M. Stern as chairman. Other members were Alan V. Deardorff, John H. Jackson, and Gary R. Saxonhouse.

The planners decided to focus the conference along analytical lines, with academic papers to be prepared on designated topics and with discussants and a limited number of invited participants to be drawn from universities, government agencies, research organizations, and the corporate sector. Our hope was that the papers and comments would be informative on the current issues of trade policy and at the same time provide analytical insights and perspective of lasting value.

A great deal of advance planning was necessary to secure commitments from the authors and discussants, extend invitations to other participants, and make all the logistical arrangements. I would like to thank the administrative staff of the Institute of Public Policy Studies—especially Helene McCarren, Judith Brown, and Judith Jackson—for their unflagging attention in helping to organize the conference and taking care that everything ran smoothly. Filip Abraham, Deb Clark, and Bernard Hoekman of the Department of Economics also lent a helping hand. Finally I am grateful to President Harold T. Shapiro and the regents of the University of Michigan for their interest, encouragement, and financial support for the conference and preparation of this book, and to Jaime de Melo for useful comments on several of the conference papers.

1

Introduction

Robert M. Stern

1.1 Overview

Issues of international trade and trade policy have been at the center of the U.S. political system in recent years. There has been growing concern and even alarm at the size of the U.S. trade deficit and the associated difficulties being experienced by U.S. import-competing and export industries. Most economists would attribute this state of affairs in large measure to the substantial appreciation of the U.S. dollar that occurred between 1980 and 1985 in response to the sizable and continued flow of foreign financial capital into the United States. It is not surprising in these circumstances that the trade and current accounts would go into deficit to accommodate the capital inflow.

At the political level it is probably understood, though not always acknowledged in public statements, that the source of the foreign imbalance is a macroeconomic phenomenon. It is another matter altogether, however, to devise changes in macroeconomic policies that could relieve the pressures on trade-affected sectors. Although the Reagan administration and the Congress have taken some steps to reduce the existing and prospective future government budget deficits, the measures have not been decisive at the time of writing (January 1986). Since the trade effects are very real to the firms and workers involved, this failure of macroeconomic policy has been translated into a heightened sensitivity to trade issues in the Congress. Congress has been deluged in 1985 and 1986 by a spate of legislative proposals to assist trade-sensitive sectors of the economy.

These events must be seen in the broader and long-run context of a world economy that is experiencing structural adaptation. In particular the United States is now much less dominant than previously, and its traditional comparative advantage in resource-based and especially in manufacturing industries has been eroded by foreign competition. Japan and the newly industrializing countries (NICs) of Asia and Latin America have been at the forefront of the new wave of international development and competition. These long-term changes provide the basis for improvements in economic welfare in the countries undergoing structural transformation, although there may be some asymmetries involved in the process of change, especially in importing countries. Thus to the extent that import-competing firms find it difficult or impossible to withstand the pressures of increased foreign competition and workers become unemployed and experience problems in obtaining new and comparably paid jobs, this will give rise to efforts to restrict imports. These efforts will be magnified in circumstances like those experienced in the United States when dollar appreciation has resulted in unprecedented trade account deficits. For similar reasons U.S. export interests will be motivated to seek government assistance to sustain their foreign market shares.

The decline in U.S. economic predominance has resulted in greater parity between the United States and the other major nations in the industrialized world, especially Japan and the European Economic Community (EEC). The period of greatest strength and influence of the United States can be dated approximately from World War II to the late 1960s. During this time the United States took the initiative first in aiding the reconstruction of Western Europe and Japan and then fostering the liberalization of world trade and investment. The United States was also the major force in promoting political stability internationally in the Western world through its economic policies and its assumption of the greatest share of expenditures on defense. During this phase of world leadership, the United States was a strong (though not always consistent) supporter of the principles of nondiscrimination and multilateralism in world trade. Although these principles still provide the foundation for most U.S. trade policies, they have been criticized on the grounds that they encourage free riders and in themselves cannot be used as a disciplining mechanism for limiting the use of foreign government restrictions and subsidies that work to the disadvantage of U.S. producers. The United States therefore now appears more inclined than previously to pursue selective trade policy arrangements both within the General Agreement on Tariffs and Trade (GATT) and on its own. It has also adopted a somewhat more aggressive stance in threatening and actually taking actions designed to encourage or force foreign governments to change policies deemed detrimental to U.S. interests.

As the world's international economic and political relationships have been changing, the adequacy of the rules of international trade as embodied in the GATT has come under question. Important sectors like agriculture and textiles and clothing have long been exempt from GATT rules, and there has been an increasing resort by the U.S. and other major countries to nontariff restrictions, particularly voluntary export restraints (VERs), which have an ambiguous status in the GATT. All of this is evidence that the GATT is not functioning effectively since its most important members feel that they can bypass or ignore GATT authority and obligations when their national interests are on the line. The international trading system thus appears to be in disarray as the example and influence of the GATT have been eroded and the United States and other countries have become increasingly inclined to take unilateral policy actions.

There are numerous other aspects of government policies that may impinge upon trade. These include policies to correct distortions, achieve noneconomic objectives such as national defense, and influence the behavior of other nations for political purposes. The traditional analysis of distortions suggests that trade intervention is not optimal to correct distortions, except when a government has monopoly power and can impose an optimum tariff without incurring foreign retaliation. The same conclusion holds when there are noneconomic objectives, although trade intervention may be optimal when the objective is to affect trade directly. While the foregoing presumptions about optimal policies are well established theoretically, the presence of institutional and political constraints and rent-revenue–seeking behavior by different interest groups may alter the outcome and thus affect the choice of optimal policies in certain circumstances.

Trade policy may be an objective of foreign policy when international economic and political interests coincide. Trade policy may also be used as an instrument of foreign policy in order to achieve some international political objective. Both uses of trade policy have a long history in the United States and other major countries, but views differ especially on whether trade policy has been effective when used as an instrument of foreign policy. The problem is in defining criteria to evaluate effectiveness since the goals of foreign policy may be complex and therefore difficult to relate directly to specific measures of trade policy. This appears to be the case with respect to the use of economic sanctions and embargoes by the United States and other countries.

1.2 Summaries of Chapters

The preceding discussion was intended as an introduction to the range of issues of trade policy confronting the U.S. Although many of these issues have been analyzed at length over the years and are well understood at least conceptually, the changing circumstances of the United States in the world economy require a refocusing and consolidation of analytical perspective. The papers commissioned for the conference, now the chapters in this book, were designed accordingly to provide insight into current issues. Although the individual papers and the discussants' comments were not intended to pursue new directions in international trade theory and policy, readers will find ample reference to and evaluation of current developments in research.

Each chapter is summarized briefly below. The papers were revised after the conference to take into account the comments of discussants and other questions raised in the floor discussion. The discussants' comments following each chapter in this book are not included in the summaries. These comments, which were also revised after the conference, deal with both particular points and broader issues considered germane to the topic.

Deardorff and Stern: "Current Issues in Trade Policy: An Overview"

In their overview chapter Deardorff and Stern first provide information on the broad movements of global trade aggregates, the commodity and sectoral composition of net exports of merchandise and services for the United States, Japan, and the EEC, changes in exchange rates, and recent changes in protectionist pressures and actions in the United States and other industrialized countries. They note that the expansion of world trade slowed considerably beginning in the mid-1970s and that there was actually a decline in 1982 due to world recession. In the United States the post-1980 appreciation of the dollar exacerbated the structural adjustment problems that many import-competing industries were already experiencing. It is not surprising therefore that protectionist pressures have become more acute in recent years, particularly in the United States and the EEC.

Following their presentation of developments in trade and protectionism, Deardorff and Stern review the case for free trade and then address arguments in favor of trade intervention. Although some of their discussion covers familiar ground, it is nonetheless worth repetition because it focuses on optimality conditions and how various types of trade intervention may be detrimental to economic welfare. Deardorff and Stern classify the optimum tariff argument as an exploitative policy, given that the country imposing the tariff benefits at the expense of the rest of the world. They consider recent arguments for trade intervention in imperfectly competitive markets, which are designed to enable a country to appropriate monopoly profits or to achieve strategic advantage, as also being exploitative in nature rather than representing genuinely new arguments. The same is true for the use of countervailing policies, which can benefit a country only when it is able to influence its terms of trade. They note further that the classic problem of the Prisoners' Dilemma arises in strategic trade intervention when various exploitative policies are being considered. This suggests that the world might benefit if governments were precommitted to retaliation in response to exploitative policies used by others.

The final issues considered relate to trade intervention for domestic political reasons. To the extent that government officials take the interests of the nation as a whole into account, the arguments for and against trade intervention are highly pertinent. Moreover, in deciding which instruments of protection to use, there is something to be said for choosing the mildest form of intervention, which might arguably be a tariff. Unfortunately the use of the tariff instrument is subject to national and international legal constraints, and the result has been to choose much more costly measures of trade intervention such as the VER.

Dornbusch and Frankel: "Macroeconomics and Protection"

Dornbusch and Frankel begin their chapter with a factual and interpretive analysis of the macroeconomic setting in which changes have been made in U.S. tariffs and NTBs, ranging from the Smoot-Hawley tariff legislation of 1930 to the Tokyo Round negotiations of the late 1970s and events of the early 1980s. They classify the macrocyclical determinants of protectionism into those associated with aggregate demand and micro-supply variables. The variables affecting aggregate demand are domestic or foreign, and these will vary in importance depending on cyclical factors. The effects of the substantial real appreciation of the U.S. dollar since 1980 are judged to be especially important in explaining the upsurge of U.S. protectionism. They note, however, that the depreciation especially of the European currencies did not mitigate protectionist pressures there, so that the role of the exchange rate is by no means obvious in all circumstances. This is borne out in regression analysis of the determinants of employment in the U.S. auto, steel, textiles and apparel, and metal fastener industries. Although the exchange rate is important for steel and metal fasteners, the most significant variable in each case is a simple time trend. This suggests that long-run structural considerations rather than macroeconomic influences may be the root causes of changes in U.S. protection in these industries.

They identify four key micro-structural reasons for protection: (1) shifts in productivity in domestic or foreign industry, (2) sectoral imbalances that arise when favorable events in one sector put pressure on another sector through wages and/or exchange rates (the Dutch disease), (3) wage misalignments, and (4) transfer difficulties arising from the need of debtor countries to generate foreign exchange by means of increased exports and/or reduced imports.

Dornbusch and Frankel note that U.S. protectionist sentiment is directed especially against Japan, yet they find little factual reason for this sentiment since the dollar has not appreciated significantly against the yen in comparison to the major European currencies, and Japan has not increased its own trade barriers. The explanation presumably lies more in productivity differentials and wage misalignments between the United States and Japan.

Dornbusch and Frankel conclude by arguing in favor of a change in the U.S. policy mix to permit fiscal tightening and monetary expansion and to have the opposite policy changes carried out in Europe and Japan. This would result in lower real interest rates in the United States and depreciation of the dollar. Such coordinated action would serve to correct the existing U.S. trade imbalance and bring about a realignment of the tradable sector. It is to be preferred to other, possibly ill advised, measures such as a U.S. import surcharge or a tax on international capital movements.

Magee and Young: "Endogenous Protection in the United States, 1900–1984"

In their chapter Magee and Young develop a model of endogenous protection and use it to search for variables that may help empirically to explain changes in protection in the United States since 1900. The essential idea is that trade policies lie outside the control of policymakers, who function as intermediaries between the narrow interests of protectionist and proexport groups, on the one hand, and the broad interests of voters (consumers) on the other hand. Protectionism is thus regarded as the equilibrium outcome of the interactions involving political parties (Democrats and Republicans), lobbying groups (representing labor and capital), and voters. The demand for protection will depend on the importance of labor relative to capital (endowment effect), the relation between product and factor prices (magnification effect), and changes in the terms of trade (compensation effect). There will be macroeconomic influences on protection as well, stemming from changes in the rates of unemployment and inflation. Voters may oppose protection especially during inflationary periods. Since labor is the scarce factor in the United States, it will favor protection, while capital interests will oppose protection. The Democrats, whose main constituents are labor, can be expected to be more inclined toward protectionism than the Republicans.

In observing changes in protection since 1900, Magee and Young note a paradox in the way that the political parties have behaved, with prolabor Democratic administrations promoting freer trade and Republican administrators being more protectionist. They attribute this paradox to the macroeconomic policies that the two parties have used to serve their constituencies, with the Democrats choosing lower unemployment and higher inflation and Republicans the opposite.

Magee and Young fit a series of regressions in which the average tariff levels for sixteen presidential administrations (four prior to 1932 and twelve thereafter) from 1905 to 1980 are to be explained by various microeconomic and macroeconomic influences. Even taking account of the limited degrees of freedom in these regressions, Magee and Young interpret their empirical results as providing broad support for their model. In comparing the actual and predicted values of the changes in tariffs based on their preferred equation, they would expect the first Reagan term to be characterized by considerable protectionist pressure and, if unemployment were to fall and inflation rise in Reagan's second term, the protectionist pressure could be expected to abate. Magee and Young also analyze nontariff protection as provided by the U.S. antidumping statutes, and they conclude that special interest variables are the dominant influences involved.

Krugman: "Strategic Sectors and International Competition"

Krugman deals with the question of identifying strategic sectors and the extent to which international competition and national government policies may affect the returns to such sectors under conditions of imperfect competition or when externalities are present. Although the concept of strategic sectors is not meaningful when there is perfect competition because the returns to equivalent factors are equalized, particular sectors may realize excess returns when competition is imperfect. Governments may therefore be motivated to engage in international rent seeking in an effort to capture some portion of these returns for their domestic firms or residents. In exploring this possibility, Krugman cites the work of Brander and Spencer, who show in the context of a Cournot duopoly model that there may be an optimal export subsidy that will benefit a country and in effect substitute for the strategic commitment that the country's firms cannot make themselves. Krugman notes, however, that this possibility seems remote on theoretical grounds since it does not survive any of a number of changes in assumptions: if the firms compete in terms of price rather than quantity, if factors of production are in inelastic supply, if there is a significant degree of competition among domestic firms and substantial exports, and if entry barriers are potentially or actually low. He argues further that the possible gains from international rent seeking may in fact be rather limited since excess profits of firms may not translate into large gains for a nation, especially in the case of the United States where most production is domestic rather than trade oriented, and also the benefits may be once and for all rather than continuing. Finally he notes that it is not clear that the excess profits would in fact be diverted to domestic residents when account is taken of diverse ownership patterns and differences in tax regimes.

The case for identifying strategic sectors may be more compelling when there are externalities that are country or location specific. But to the extent that the products involved can be traded, Krugman notes that it may not matter where the industry is located. There is no necessary connection therefore between the availability of technology and the production of goods in a given country. Accordingly Krugman is doubtful that there is much to be gained by governments seeking to identify and capture the returns associated with strategic sectors.

Dixit: "How Should the United States Respond to Other Countries' Trade Policies?"

Dixit notes that the response that the United States might make to other countries' trade policies requires prior consideration of how these policies affect U.S. real national income and national security. The effects on real income work primarily through changes in the terms of trade and the division of excess profits between the United States and foreign countries. There may also be domestic considerations involving the distribution of income between gainers and losers from the policies of foreign countries.

If changes in the U.S. terms of trade occur because of foreign export subsidies, the United States will benefit nationally, although it may be necessary in the process to compensate any losers. Foreign restrictions on U.S. goods may be damaging, however, and the United States might consider responding with restrictions of its own, in which case both countries would be worse off. In any event the empirical evidence suggests that U.S. terms of trade movements are fairly small and probably not greatly influenced by foreign countries' policies. The existence of excess profits under imperfect competition raises the question of whether the government can employ better strategies to capture these profits than the strategies available to firms. This is the Brander-Spencer type of situation, and Dixit is doubtful that there is much to be gained here.

Foreign countries may impose embargoes or sanctions on their trade, which may threaten U.S. national security. The impact of such policies may be limited, however, if there are alternative sources of supply available, if the U.S. economy can adjust or if stockpiles can be built up for later use in time of emergency.

The United States can react to foreign countries' policies, develop precautionary policies to deal with trade disruptions, and employ or promise to introduce strategic measures in order to deter or compel changes in foreign government behavior. In designing strategic policies, Dixit stresses the importance of maintaining credibility, which may require taking action quickly, irreversibly, and automatically, being clear on what is at stake, and perhaps resorting to brinkmanship and suggestion of irrationality. He concludes that the United States is poorly situated for successful strategic use of threats and also that the United States has not had much success with threats. By the same token he notes that the United States has a good record in fostering cooperation with other countries, and accordingly it could beneficially use strategic advance responses to alter other countries' trade policies in a mutually beneficial way.

Cooper: "Trade Policy as Foreign Policy"

Cooper divides U.S. history into three periods: (1) 1765–1820, when boycotts and embargoes were instrumental in seeking to achieve independence and national sovereignty, (2) 1820–1934, when tariff policy was almost exclusively governed by domestic political considerations and the promotion of U.S. exports was a principal aim of foreign policy, and (3) 1934–1985, when trade policy has been directed in large measure to overcoming the economic and political disasters of the Great Depression by fostering an environment conducive to full employment, growth, and stability within and among nations in the world economy. In the third period trade policy has also been used on occasion to achieve other foreign policy objectives.

Cooper points out that the international trading system after World War II was premised on the ideals of nondiscrimination, multilateralism, and international dispute resolution. Foreign trade was thus intended to be insulated from domestic economic and foreign policy pressures. There have been exceptions, however, with the U.S. denial of most-favored-nation treatment to communist countries, preferential arrangements such as the U.S.-Canadian Auto Pact, the Generalized System of Preferences, the Caribbean Basin Initiative, and the U.S.-Israel free trade arrangement, and the manipulative use of trade policy, mostly by means of export controls, with the intention of influencing the behavior of other countries. The range of manipulative trade policy includes full embargoes and partial embargoes or restrictions on arms exports, strategic materials, and defense-related technologies. U.S. trade actions have been guided by a variety of foreign policy objectives, including a desire to curb nuclear proliferation, encouragement of human rights, discouragement of international terrorism, and encouragement of political and military restraint by the Soviet Union around the world.

In evaluating trade policy as foreign policy, Cooper asks what the world would be like if the action had not been taken and what other courses of action were available to achieve the particular objective of foreign policy. It seems clear in this regard that U.S. support of multilateral trade liberalization has been enormously successful in terms of foreign policy. It is more difficult, however, to evaluate the use of manipulative trade policy. Here Cooper is more convinced than many other observers that trade sanctions have been successful in achieving the desired foreign policy objective, although he cites some historical examples to illustrate how difficult it may be to evaluate particular measures when there are manifold objectives in complex situations.

Srinivasan: "The National Defense Argument for Government Intervention in Foreign Trade"

The use of trade policy for national defense objectives may involve assistance to particular industries or factors of production deemed vital to defense, as well as strategic measures designed to respond to foreign actions or to affect the behavior of foreign governments. National defense can be treated as a noneconomic objective or as an externality. Srinivasan demonstrates the familiar conclusion that a domestic tax-subsidy is optimal when the objective of policy is to increase the production, consumption, or employment involved in defense goods, while a trade tax may be optimal when the objective is the restriction of trade for defense purposes. This conclusion abstracts from the use of resources in carrying out the intervention or the diversion of resources to lobbying activities. Examples of (dynamic) externalities are that private capital accumulation may increase the need for defense expenditures in order to deter potential aggressors from seeking to acquire the nation's capital stock, a larger private capital stock may increase a nation's defense capacity, and underinvestment is possible because private investors may anticipate the imposition of controls during times of emergency. Corrective fiscal measures will be justified in these circumstances.

If a nation's security is threatened by trade restraints, embargoes, or sanctions imposed by foreign governments, the appropriate policy response will depend on whether private agents anticipate and allow fully for the time interdependence of their actions in present and future periods. In case the private decisions do not anticipate and make appropriate allowance for the relevant effects, a corrective tax-subsidy will be in order.

Srinivasan also analyzes the strategic use of policies to affect the behavior of foreign countries. He considers the case for strategic stockpiles, noting that intervention may be justified if there is an externality but not necessarily when the private agents and governments have perfect foresight and strategic interactions are taken into account. Issues of national security and global political influence are analyzed in the context of the gains from trade. Empirical evidence suggests that there is an inverse relationship between international trade and political conflict. Yet in the context of East-West relations, there is a perception, especially in the United States, that restrictions on trade and related transactions may impose substantial costs on and elicit more cooperative behavior from the Soviet Union and its satellites. Srinivasan cites a number of studies that offer conflicting conclusions in this connection, and he develops a formal model of the relation between national security and the gains from trade that permits a variety of possible outcomes in response to the imposition of trade controls. Finally Srinivasan reviews embargoes and sanctions in a historical context and concludes that they have had limited effectiveness, especially since 1973.

Jackson: "Multilateral and Bilateral Negotiating Approaches for the
Conduct of U.S. Trade Policies"

Issues of alternative negotiating approaches for the conduct of U.S. trade policies must be seen in the wider context of the institutions and principles that form the basis for the international trading system. Jackson notes that although the United States had ambivalent attitudes toward GATT as an international organization during much of the postwar period, it was nonetheless a strong proponent of the GATT principles of nondiscrimination and multilateralism. At the same time, however, it appears that U.S. support of these principles has been eroding, as evidenced by the conditionality attached to the nontariff codes negotiated in the Tokyo Round, U.S. preoccupation with its trade imbalance with Japan, implementation of selective VERs and related policies designed to restrict U.S. imports, and the adoption of a more pragmatic approach to trade policy and willingness to pursue bilateral arrangements and to reward friendly countries.

Although the GATT has played a vital role in fostering trade liberalization multilaterally, its institutional structure is hampered because it is difficult to amend the articles of agreement, the EEC is able to exercise undue and often negative influence on GATT matters, the GATT secretariat is small, and its dispute settlement procedures have not been operating effectively. Further some important substantive problems have been abdicated or remain muddled within GATT because of national pressures. These include the exemption of

agriculture and textiles from GATT discipline, the ambiguous rules that
countries exploit in their use of VERs and other protectionist measures, and
the ambiguities that limit the effectiveness and coverage of the Tokyo Round
codes.

Despite these problems the principles of nondiscrimination and multilateralism are of fundamental importance. As Jackson notes, the most-favored-
nation (MFN) obligation of nondiscrimination serves to minimize distortions in
market principles, facilitates the formation of rules, reduces transactions costs,
and limits the political side effects of policies. There are, of course, problems
of foot dragging and free riders, which may counteract these benefits and
therefore have to be addressed. The use of conditionality is only one way to
respond to these problems. Preferential arrangements and selectivity are other
options.

Trade policies in the United States are the joint responsibility of the
executive branch and the Congress, and there has often been an uneasy
tension on these matters. The legislative procedures of the Congress and the
domestic pressures to which elected officials are subjected raise important
questions about the desirability and efficacy of conducting U.S. trade policies
along bilateral lines. There is a need for international rules and international
institutions to help manage interdependence among nations. As Jackson
concludes, the pursuit of multilateralism may certainly be frustrating. Maybe
what is needed are certain tactical departures from MFN, or what Jackson calls
a minilateral approach to trade liberalization.

Corden: "On Making Rules for the International Trading System"

Corden notes that a rules-based system governing international trade economizes on negotiations and power play among nations. Rules provide the benefit
of certainty to transactors, although they may also entail a loss of flexibility if
they cannot be readily changed. In making rules, countries should take a long
view since they cannot be sure about their eventual situations. The greater is
the investment in terms of negotiations concerning rules at a given time, the
less need there may be for negotiations in the future. It is often argued that
rules may protect relatively small and weak nations. But as Corden points out,
this is not necessarily the case since nations that are weak currently and will
remain so in the future are not likely to have a substantial impact in the making
of rules.

In judging economic policies and systems of rules, Corden stresses the
traditional criterion of Pareto efficiency and the long-term mutual gains from
free international trade. There is a difficulty, however, since compensation

of those harmed by changes in policies may not be possible or may be incomplete. One way to deal with this situation is to attach different welfare weights to different income recipients, as, for example, in the case of an egalitarian social welfare function that gives more weight to the poor than the rich or a conservative social welfare function that is designed to maintain the status quo. Corden also notes that rules may be justified as a means of restraining governments for the good of their countries, especially to resist pressure groups that seek to advance their narrow interests at the expense of general welfare. The problem is that governments may be the best judges of the national interest, in which case there is an argument to be made in favor of decentralized national decision making. The final point made is that rules should be devised to promote harmony in the international system, minimize costly negotiations and conflict, and yet not place unnecessary restraints on governments.

The United States has a special role to play, according to Corden: to set an example for other nations and to spread belief in the efficacy and desirability of efficiency-oriented and market-based policies while recognizing national differences concerning intervention and distributional objectives. Corden addresses two issues of current importance in the trading system: discrimination and subsidies. He notes that discrimination may be beneficial if it results in a movement toward free trade but not if it produces continuous and therefore costly opportunities for bargaining and if it works against the interests of the developing (poor) countries. The opposition to subsidies comes mainly from sectoral interests, although there may be problems when there are sudden or severe changes in trade associated with subsidies. It is difficult nonetheless to envisage comprehensive rules restraining the use of subsidies without impinging on national sovereignty.

Corden offers a package of rules for the international trading system that he believes would be desirable, though not probable, overall but with some elements that may nonetheless be possible to attain. The package includes complete free trade; a safeguards code that permits temporary, nondiscriminatory use of tariffs; restriction of the benefits of free trade and safeguards only on a reciprocal basis; subsidy freedom; complete transparency of policies; and allowance for exceptions by developing countries in transition.

2

Current Issues in Trade Policy: An Overview

Alan V. Deardorff and
Robert M. Stern

2.1 Introduction

Issues of international trade policy have increased in number and importance in recent years as the United States and other countries have struggled to deal with inflation, recession and recovery, and the substantial changes that have taken place in international relative prices and international competitiveness. These pressures have led to the proposal and occasional use of new forms of trade policy for intervening in world markets. There has also been renewed interest in older policy alternatives that seem to offer some hope of protecting against the vicissitudes of domestic and world economic events. Informed discussion of both the old and the new issues of trade policy is crucially important, lest the world sink inadvertently into a quagmire of protectionism and distorted trade that could limit economic progress for years to come.

It is the purpose of this chapter to provide empirical and theoretical background for such a discussion. On the empirical level, the subject of section 2.2, dramatic changes have taken place in world economic activity and trade in just the last few years, and there has been an accompanying increase in protectionist sentiments and actions in the United States and Western Europe especially. We call attention to some salient features of these developments in world trade and protectionism to provide a factual setting, which is essential to put the discussion of trade policies in perspective.

There have also been notable developments in recent years in the theoretical arguments advanced for and against trade intervention. The classic case for the gains from trade continues to dominate the views of most international economists, but it is increasingly being realized that these longs-held views are overly simple. The analysis of trade policy has been broadened considerably to encompass the realities of imperfect markets, monopolistic and oligopolistic competition, political considerations, and the possible need to anticipate or respond to the trade policies of foreign governments. In section 2.3 we discuss these developments after reviewing the classic argument for free trade and the well-established optimal tariff and second-best arguments of trade intervention. A number of general principles can be identified that should be kept in mind in any detailed discussion of specific trade policies.

We do not address, except tangentially, any of the specific trade policy proposals and initiatives that have come to the fore in recent years, such as the strategic dumping of surplus agricultural goods, other special retaliatory measures, content protection, embargoes and export controls, and numerous other policies used or suggested in such sectors as textiles and clothing, steel, automobiles, and high-technology goods. Each could and should be the subject of separate theoretical and empirical analysis. Our purpose is rather to identify the important principles that need to be kept in mind in all such analyses.

The underlying question to which we seek an answer is, What should we as international trade economists be advising policymakers to do? The classical case for the gains from trade is not very helpful in this regard since it posits a world so far removed from the reality within which policymakers have to operate. Yet the data on changes in trade and protection in section 2.2 indicate a growing need for responsible trade policy advice, and the theoretical developments in section 2.3 indicate that our profession is beginning to confront many of the complexities of the real world. The answers are only beginning to emerge, but the progress being made is encouraging nonetheless.

2.2 Recent Developments in Patterns of Trade and Protectionism

2.2.1 Global Changes in Merchandise Trade

There have been sizable increases in world merchandise trade since the end of World War II. Total world exports increased in value terms twelve-fold between 1963 and 1983 (table 2.1). When the value figures are corrected for changes in prices (unit values), the volume of trade can be seen to have tripled overall, with a relatively much greater expansion of trade in manufactures as compared to agricultural products and minerals.[1] If earlier data were reported, they would reveal growth tracing back to the postwar years once reconstruction was completed and recovery underway.

These changes in world trade reflect the currents of economic activity, especially in the advanced industrialized countries and, to a lesser extent, the major developing countries. Prior to the first oil shock of 1973–1974, there was rapid and sustained growth in world income and trade. The expansion of trade was fostered by a liberal environment in which barriers to trade and

Table 2.1
World exports and production, 1963–1983

	1963	1973	1979	1982	1983
World exports					
Total value ($ billions)[a]	154	574	1,635	1,842	1,807
Agricultural products	45	121	262	271	269
Minerals**	26	96	400	490	452
Manufactures	82	347	945	1,051	1,057
Total unit value (1963 = 100)	100	161	354	400	380
Agricultural products	100	185	300	288	283
Minerals[b]	100	192	780	1,232	1,140
Manufactures	100	152	303	314	300
Total volume (1963 = 100)	100	231	300	300	306
Agricultural products	100	147	196	209	211
Minerals[b]	100	195	201	153	152
Manufactures	100	280	382	410	429
World production					
Total, all commodities (1963 = 100)	100	180	220	223	230
Agriculture	100	128	147	154	154
Mining	100	171	199	183	184
Manufacturing	100	197	249	249	259

Source: Adapted from GATT, *International Trade 1983/84*, table A1.
a. Including unspecified commodities.
b. Including fuels and nonferrous metals.

international factor movements were progressively liberalized in many countries. There has occurred as well a remarkable increase in the degree of economic interdependence since World War II. This is evident in table 2.1, which indicates that trade in agricultural products and especially manufactures has increased considerably more than world production. The result has been to spread the benefits of increased specialization and trade over a wide spectrum of countries and income groups. Although interrupted by the first oil shock and the onset of world recession in 1974–1975, world production and trade continued to expand for the remainder of the decade. Following the second oil shock of 1979–1980 and the introduction of contractionary domestic policies in the United States and elsewhere in the industrialized world, the growth process was halted and thrown into reverse gear, especially in 1981–1982. Associated with these developments, there was an upsurge of protectionist pressures in many countries, and trade restrictions were measurably increased in some important instances. Recovery and expansion have since occurred, particularly in North America and Japan but to a noticeably lesser extent elsewhere. There has also been considerable turmoil in the foreign exchange and international credit markets in the wake of the real shocks and changes in policies.

2.2.2 Merchandise Trade of the United States, Japan, and the European Community

It may be useful to disaggregate some of the information in table 2.1 by commodity and geographic groupings in order to highlight recent developments. Table 2.2 lists the values of exports and imports for 1973 and 1983 for the major commodity subgroups comprising primary products and manufactures for the United States, Japan, and the European Community (EC). The trade balances are also shown for each subgroup and overall.

The trade balance data are significant in drawing attention to the factors that shape the comparative advantage and trade policy of each country-region. Thus U.S. net exports of food and raw materials reflect to a large extent the U.S. relative abundance of land, other natural resources, and the associated investments in physical capital. Similarly U.S. net imports of fuels, metals, and other semimanufactures reflect the U.S. relative scarcity of the associated factors. The net exports of chemicals, machinery, and equipment reflect U.S. comparative advantage in high-technology industries. These industries combine especially the services of the most highly educated, technically trained, and experienced members of the work force and business management with the services of the physical plant and equipment that embody the most recent technological innovations. Finally the net imports of automotive vehicles, household appliances, clothing, and other consumer goods are indicative of a shift in comparative advantage that has taken place over the years from the United States to other producing countries. Because most of these goods can now be produced with relatively standardized production methods, it has become cheaper to produce them in countries with lower wage costs. This also means that these U.S. industries will be increasingly subjected to competitive pressures from abroad and are likely therefore to seek protection from imports. This will be all the more true to the extent that these industries may be adversely affected by the significant appreciation of the dollar that has occurred since 1980.

The data for Japan indicate a substantial trade deficit due to net imports of primary products, which is more than offset by a trade surplus in net exports of manufactures. The EC also has significant net imports of primary products, but these are greater than its net exports of manufactures. In both Japan and the EC therefore, agriculture and other natural resources sectors are import-competing industries and will solicit government assistance to mitigate compe-

Table 2.2
Total merchandise exports, imports, and trade balances, by commodity groups, for the United States, Japan, and the European Community, 1973 and 1983 (billions of dollars)

Commodity group	Year	United States			Japan			European Community		
		Exports	Imports	Balance	Exports	Imports	Balance	Exports	Imports	Balance
Primary products										
Food	1973	16.6	10.3	6.3	0.9	7.2	−6.3	25.2	38.4	−13.2
	1983	34.7	21.0	13.7	1.5	17.1	−15.6	63.6	75.4	−11.8
Raw materials	1973	4.0	3.4	0.6	0.6	6.6	−6.0	5.5	14.4	−8.9
	1983	8.6	6.8	1.8	1.1	8.5	−7.4	10.5	22.1	−11.6
Ores and other minerals	1973	1.5	1.8	−0.3	0.1	4.5	−4.4	2.3	6.7	−4.4
	1983	3.3	2.7	0.6	0.1	7.5	−7.4	5.2	12.4	−7.2
Fuels	1973	1.7	9.2	−7.5	0.1	8.3	−8.2	8.8	25.4	−16.6
	1983	9.6	60.0	−50.4	0.4	58.9	−58.5	53.5	124.9	−71.4
Nonferrous metals	1973	1.0	2.5	−1.5	0.3	1.7	−1.4	5.4	8.4	−3.0
	1983	2.3	7.6	−5.3	1.6	4.1	−2.5	12.5	15.0	−2.5
Total primary products	1973	24.7	27.0	−2.3	2.0	28.3	−26.3	47.2	93.3	−46.1
	1983	58.5	98.1	−39.6	4.7	96.1	−91.4	145.3	249.8	−104.5
Manufactures										
Iron and steel	1973	1.3	3.3	−2.0	5.3	0.2	5.1	14.2	10.2	4.0
	1983	1.5	7.4	−5.9	12.8	1.4	11.4	24.4	16.9	7.5
Chemicals	1973	6.2	2.7	3.5	2.2	2.0	0.2	23.3	16.8	6.5
	1983	21.4	12.9	8.5	8.2	7.5	0.7	74.3	55.5	18.8
Other semimanufactures	1973	2.4	4.6	−2.2	1.2	1.3	−0.1	12.9	14.2	−1.3
	1983	6.1	12.6	−6.5	4.6	2.6	2.0	31.2	32.4	−1.2
Total semimanufactures	1973	9.9	10.6	−0.7	8.7	3.5	5.2	50.4	41.2	9.2
	1983	29.0	32.9	−3.9	25.6	11.5	14.1	129.9	104.8	25.1
Machinery	1973	7.8	3.2	4.6	3.0	1.1	1.9	25.1	14.5	10.6
	1983	18.1	11.5	6.6	15.0	2.0	13.0	54.2	29.3	24.9

Table 2.2 (continued)

Commodity group	Year	United States			Japan			European Community		
		Exports	Imports	Balance	Exports	Imports	Balance	Exports	Imports	Balance
Office and telecommunications equipment	1973	4.0	2.4	1.6	1.9	0.8	1.1	7.0	6.6	0.4
	1983	19.1	17.0	2.1	13.6	2.3	11.3	22.2	25.0	-2.8
Road-motor vehicles	1973	6.0	10.6	-4.6	4.9	0.2	4.7	20.2	11.8	8.4
	1983	14.2	37.0	-22.8	31.6	0.6	30.0	51.7	36.8	14.9
Other machinery and transportation equipment	1973	11.5	5.8	5.7	7.9	1.3	6.6	25.6	18.1	7.5
	1983	38.3	21.6	16.7	24.8	5.4	19.4	74.3	52.2	22.1
Household appliances	1973	1.1	3.3	-2.2	3.9	0.3	3.6	5.8	5.6	0.2
	1983	2.5	11.4	-8.9	18.4	0.7	17.7	11.2	15.3	-4.1
Total engineering products	1973	30.4	25.4	5.0	21.6	3.7	17.9	83.7	56.6	27.1
	1983	92.2	98.5	-6.3	103.4	11.0	92.4	213.6	158.6	55.0
Textiles	1973	1.2	1.7	-0.5	2.4	1.1	1.3	11.2	9.1	2.1
	1983	2.4	3.3	-0.9	5.3	1.5	3.8	19.6	18.1	1.5
Clothing	1973	0.3	2.3	-2.0	0.3	0.6	-0.3	5.0	5.8	-0.8
	1983	0.9	10.4	-9.5	0.7	1.5	-0.3	12.6	16.4	-3.8
Other consumer goods	1973	1.2	4.7	-3.5	1.5	1.0	0.5	12.0	9.6	2.4
	1983	6.2	18.9	-12.7	5.5	2.4	3.1	35.3	28.8	6.5
Total consumer goods	1973	2.7	8.7	-6.0	4.2	2.7	1.5	28.2	24.5	3.7
	1983	9.5	32.6	-23.1	11.5	5.4	6.1	67.5	63.3	4.2
Total manufactures	1973	43.0	44.8	-1.8	34.5	9.9	24.6	162.3	122.3	40.0
	1983	130.7	164.0	-33.3	140.5	27.9	112.6	411.0	326.7	84.3
Total trade[a]	1973	70.2	73.6	-3.4	36.9	38.3	-1.4	212.0	217.8	-5.8
	1983	194.6	268.0	-73.4	146.8	125.0	21.8	570.0	584.9	-14.9

Source: Adapted from GATT, International Trade, 1981/82 and 1983/84.
Note: Totals may not agree due to rounding; exports f.o.b.; imports c.i.f.
a. Including unspecified commodities.

tition from imports. At the same time these countries will be concerned to sustain their net exports of manufactures.

Some additional insight into the factors affecting comparative advantage and trade policy is provided in table 2.3, which contains a breakdown of total exports and imports by region for 1973 and 1983 for the United States, Japan, and the European Community. In 1983 the United States had an import deficit with all of the countries-regions indicated, except for the other industrial countries and the socialist countries. Japan had an import deficit in 1983 with Canada and the oil-exporting countries and an export surplus with all the other countries-regions shown. Finally the EC had an import deficit in 1983 with the United States, Canada, Japan, the oil-exporting countries, and the socialist countries and an export surplus with the other industrial and other developing countries. Although these patterns of regional trade balances may be influenced by ongoing changes in exchange rates, they may nonetheless serve to demonstrate the multilateral nature of the trade of each country-region. Thus, for example, in the case of Japan, its import deficit with respect to oil is compensated in large measure by its export surplus with the United States and the EC. This suggests that it may be inappropriate for the United States and the EC to focus attention on bilateral trade imbalances with Japan without recognizing Japan's dependence on imports of oil and other natural resource products.

We have already made reference to the significant appreciation of the U.S. dollar that has occurred since 1980 and to the associated effects on the trade of the United States and its major trading partners. Thus in table 2.4 we list the weighted average effective (nominal) exchange rate for the dollar and the average bilateral (nominal) rates for the Japanese yen and German mark on an annual basis for 1975–1984 and by quarter for 1981–1984. The effective exchange rate for the dollar appreciated by 43.5 percent on an annual basis from 1980 to 1984. The dollar appreciated by 56.6 percent in relation to the German mark during this same period. The quarterly data for 1981 and 1982 disclose the rapid appreciation of the dollar over the yen that occurred. This movement was reversed from the first quarter of 1983 to the second quarter of 1984, and the dollar resumed its appreciation in the last half of 1984. Exchange rate changes of this order of magnitude are bound to have substantial effects on U.S. trade, both overall and bilaterally.[2]

In assessing U.S. trade performance, it is thus necessary to distinguish changes due to exchange rate movements and relative changes in income from the long-run or structural changes in comparative advantage that may occur. These distinctions are especially important since a substantial part of the adjustment problems being experienced by import-competing sectors in the

Alan V. Deardorff and Robert M. Stern

Table 2.3
Merchandise exports, imports, and trade balances, by region, for the United States, Japan, and the European community, 1973 and 1983 (billions of dollars)

	1973			1983		
	Exports	Imports	Balance	Exports	Imports	Balance
United States						
Industrial countries	46.6	50.9	−4.3	118.6	156.7	−38.1
Canada	14.8	18.0	−3.2	36.0	51.6	−15.6
Japan	8.2	10.5	−2.3	21.5	43.5	−22.0
European Community	16.8	16.6	0.2	43.0	45.8	−2.8
Other industrial countries[a]	6.8	5.8	1.0	18.1	15.8	2.3
Developing countries	20.6	22.0	−1.4	70.8	107.4	36.6
Oil exporters	3.7	5.4	−1.7	16.6	26.5	−9.9
Other developing countries	16.9	16.6	0.3	54.2	80.9	−26.7
Socialist countries	3.1	0.6	2.5	5.1	4.0	1.1
Total[b]	70.2	73.6	−3.4	194.5	268.1	−73.6
Japan						
Industrial countries	19.2	19.8	−0.6	77.2	48.1	29.1
United States	9.6	9.3	0.3	43.3	24.7	18.6
Canada	1.0	2.0	−1.0	3.6	4.4	−0.8
European Community	4.8	3.2	1.6	18.5	7.6	10.9
Other industrial countries[a]	3.8	5.3	−1.5	11.8	11.4	0.4
Developing countries	13.6	16.2	−2.6	58.3	69.9	−11.6
Oil exporters	2.7	7.0	−4.3	19.1	42.2	−23.1
Other developing countries	10.9	9.2	1.7	39.2	27.7	11.5
Socialist countries	2.0	2.3	−0.3	8.9	6.9	2.0
Total[b]	36.9	38.3	−1.4	144.4	124.9	19.5
European Community						
Industrial countries	173.3	169.4	3.9	443.1	447.7	−4.6
United States	15.8	18.3	−2.5	44.3	46.6	−2.3
Canada	2.4	3.5	−1.1	4.8	5.7	−0.9
Japan	2.8	4.4	−1.6	6.4	18.8	−12.4
European Community	113.6	113.2	0.4	298.9	295.0	3.9
Other industrial countries[a]	38.7	30.0	8.7	88.7	81.6	7.1
Developing countries	27.2	39.5	−12.3	101.9	108.0	−6.1
Oil exporters	8.1	19.1	−11.0	45.9	53.9	−8.0
Other developing countries	19.1	20.4	−1.3	56.0	54.1	1.9
Socialist countries	9.1	8.2	0.9	20.6	27.4	−6.8
Total[b]	212.0	217.8	−5.8	565.6	583.1	−17.5

Source: Adapted from GATT, *International Trade, 1981/82* and *1983/84*.
a. Includes other Western Europe, Australia, New Zealand, and South Africa.
b. Includes unspecified trade; totals may not agree due to rounding; exports f.o.b.; imports c.i.f.

Table 2.4

U.S. average effective and selected bilateral exchange rates, 1975–1984 (1975 = 100)

Period	Effective exchange rate (foreign currencies/$)	Japan (yen/$)	Germany (DM/$)
Year			
1975	100.0	100.0	100.0
1976	105.2	99.9	102.3
1977	104.7	90.5	94.3
1978	95.7	70.9	81.6
1979	93.7	73.8	74.5
1980	93.9	76.4	73.9
1981	105.6	74.3	91.9
1982	118.0	83.9	98.6
1983	124.8	80.0	103.8
1984	134.7	80.0	115.7
Year and quarter			
1981–I	98.5	69.3	84.8
1981–II	105.4	74.1	92.5
1981–III	111.2	78.1	98.9
1981–IV	107.4	75.7	91.2
1982–I	111.6	78.7	95.4
1982–II	115.7	82.3	96.7
1982–III	121.3	87.2	100.8
1982–IV	123.3	87.5	101.7
1983–I	119.9	79.4	97.9
1983–II	123.3	80.0	101.0
1983–III	127.7	81.7	107.4
1983–IV	128.1	78.9	108.8
1984–I	129.0	77.8	109.8
1984–II	130.2	77.4	110.1
1984–III	138.0	82.0	118.6
1984–IV	141.7	82.9	124.1

Source: Adapted from IMF, *International Financial Statistics*, country tables, line am x and rf.
Note: Exchange rates are period averages. Effective exchange rates are based on weights from the International Monetary Fund multilateral exchange rate model. A year-to-year increase in the index indicates dollar appreciation; a fall indicates dollar depreciation.

United States may be due to the rapid and sizable appreciation of the U.S. dollar. Also the large bilateral trade imbalances that the United States has been running, especially with Japan, are attributable to an important extent to exchange rate movements rather than Japan's commercial policies and related inducements to production and trade.

2.2.3 Trade in Services and Investment Income of the United States, Japan, and EC

Although exports and imports of merchandise still account for a large proportion of the foreign transactions of the United States and other industrialized countries, trade in services and investment income flows have become increasingly important.[3] Thus, for example, in 1983 the United States had net receipts of $7.4 billion for fees and royalties, $2.9 billion for other private services, and net payments of $4.6 billion for travel and transportation. Its net receipts of investment income were $23.5 billion. In 1983 Japan had net payments of $6.9 billion for travel and transportation and $7.2 billion for other private services as compared to net receipts of $3.1 billion for investment income. The EC had net payments for travel and net receipts for all other services as well as investment income.

It is interesting to relate the foregoing to the merchandise trade position of each country-region. The United States had sizable net receipts on services and investment income that offset a considerable portion of its merchandise trade deficit. The opposite was the case in Japan, where the deficit on services and investment income was offset against the merchandise trade surplus. The position of the EC resembled that of the United States, with a merchandise trade deficit offset in part by a surplus in services and investment income.

The patterns of trade in services are broadly indicative of underlying comparative advantage, while the investment income flows reflect in large measure the returns to international direct investment and to private and government asset portfolios. Although the United States and the other major industrialized countries have an important stake in trade in services and in international investment, these activities lie mainly on the future agenda for policy discussion rather than on the current agenda.[4] We shall concentrate our attention therefore on issues involving merchandise trade, although some of our remarks and analysis may carry over to services as well.

2.2.4 Recent Developments in Protectionism

As Corden (1984b, p. 1) has remarked and as many other observers would agree, there has been a definite revival of protectionist sentiment or attitudes since the mid-1970s, especially in the United States and the EC. There are probably many reasons for this, including the perceived and real difficulties that some important import-competing sectors have had in the United States and elsewhere in adjusting to long-term changes in comparative advantage, as well as the short-term disruptions arising from the sharp downturns in economic activity in the recessions of the mid-1970s and 1981–1982. Sizable movements in exchange rates have also compounded adjustment problems. Since many of these problems were viewed as being caused by external factors, it was perhaps inevitable that national governments would turn increasingly to the use of trade policies to help improve their domestic situation.

As these various developments were unfolding, the role and authority of the GATT have become increasingly circumscribed. This is due in part to the success of GATT, which served as a vehicle to reduce tariff barriers in the major industrialized countries in the periodic rounds of multilateral trade negotiations that have taken place since World War II. At the same time as adjustment problems have become more difficult and governments have sought ways to alleviate these problems, the consensus underlying the GATT has been eroded. In particular there has been increasing resort to trade policy measures that seem to have an ambiguous status within the Articles of Agreement of the GATT or lie outside its purview. The most prominent of these measures are VERs, subsidies of various kinds, and a host of discretionary policies designed to limit imports. It is these nontariff measures that constitute what many observers have called the new protectionism.

Because many of these measures are framed in terms of changes in administrative guidelines and practices, which may vary by type of product, industry, and country, it is difficult to determine precisely how prevalent these barriers to trade are, how they have changed, and especially what impact they may have on international trade and economic welfare.[5] In the case of the United States, for example, administered protection can take a variety of forms depending on which of the existing grievance mechanisms may be invoked under U.S. trade legislation. The main alternatives include the escape clause, complaints directed at foreign government practices, countervailing duty actions against foreign subsidies, and antidumping. Table 2.5 summarizes the various actions filed under the 1974 and 1979 Trade Acts by year from 1972 to 1984. It can be seen that escape clause actions have declined in number since the late 1970s, while actions involving foreign government practices and especially countervailing duty and antidumping actions have increased greatly. These latter actions reflect the large number of separate filings by the steel industry in the United States between 1982 and 1984.

Table 2.5
Trade actions brought in the United States under the 1974 and 1979 Trade Acts, 1972–1984

Type of action	1972	1973	1974	1975	1976	1977	1978	1979	1980	1981	1982	1983	1984	Total
201														
Escape clause	na	na	na	14	5	12	7	4	2	1	3	1	5	54
(steel actions)	na	na	na	(4)	—	(2)	(1)	—	—	—	(1)	(1)	(1)	(10)
301														
Foreign government practices	na	na	na	5	5	3	2	5	1	5	12	7	2	47
(steel actions)	na	na	na	—	(1)	—	—	—	—	—	(6)	(1)	—	(8)
701														
Countervailing duty														
1974 Trade Act	2	1	6	27	14	13	24	17	—	—	—	—	—	104
1979 Trade Act[a]	—	—	—	20	—	1	2	39	6	18	114	9	26	235
(steel actions)	—	—	—	—	—	—	—	(1)	(1)	(3)	(103)	(5)	(17)	(130)
731														
Antidumping														
1974 Trade Act	4	22	6	10	12	17	34	15	—	—	—	—	—	120
1979 Trade Act	—	—	—	—	—	—	—	16	21	15	65	46	72	235
(steel actions)	—	—	—	—	—	—	—	(1)	(8)	(5)	(49)	(14)	(53)	(130)

Source: Adapted from Jackson (1985).

Note: The section numbers (201, etc.) refer to the 1974 and 1979 Trade Acts.

a. Under the 1974 Trade Act, the president could grant a waiver of countervailing duty actions until 1979 if certain circumstances were met. The entries prior to 1979 thus represent actions taken under the 1979 Trade Act that had been waived previously.

Table 2.6 summarizes the outcomes of the various actions. It is evident that nearly two-thirds of the total actions filed were terminated or unsuccessful and that about 20 percent were successful. Despite this large proportion of terminated and unsuccessful actions, the ease with which actions can be filed may well act as a deterrent to foreign exporters insofar as it increases their uncertainty over continued and unimpeded access to the U.S. market. There may be added costs as well to the extent that bonds have to be posted pending the outcome of particular cases. But even more important the system of investigation can be subjected to great stress when an important industry like steel decides to file numerous separate actions. Indeed this could be done for tactical reasons to put pressure on the executive branch to seek a political solution, as was done in the case of steel in the fall of 1984 when the Reagan administration decided to negotiate VERs with the major foreign steel-exporting countries.

Although information on the number and types of trade actions filed may be useful as an indication of protectionist pressures, we would like to know something about the actual measures that have been adopted. The best that we can do in this connection is to use information on existing NTBs in terms of their unweighted or trade-weighted frequency by commodity and country. The most comprehensive available study is by Nogues, Olechowski, and Winters (1985), based on the inventory of NTBs maintained by the United Nations Conference on Trade and Development (UNCTAD).[5] Their results for sixteen major industrial countries are shown in table 2.7 for 1983. The coverage ratio was calculated using the value of own-country (1981) imports that were subject to any (1983) NTB at the detailed tariff line level and then aggregating across product categories.[7] Omitting fuels, the coverage ratio for all industrial country markets of 18.6 suggests that more than $100 billion of trade in agricultural products and manufactures was subject to NTBs in 1983. In terms of individual countries, column 2 of table 2.7 indicates that Belgium-Luxembourg, France, Australia, and Switzerland had the highest coverage ratios. It is also noteworthy that the coverage ratios are considerably higher for agricultural products as compared to manufactures. Among manufactures, textiles, iron and steel, and vehicles have relatively high coverage ratios. Nogues, Olechowski, and Winters further distinguish industrial country NTBs by product groups according to imports from the industrial countries themselves and from the developing countries. Their results in table 2.8 show that the NTB coverage ratio for agricultural products is higher for the industrial countries, while the coverage ratio for manufactures is higher for the developing countries.[8] There is evidently also considerable dispersion of the ratios among the countries listed.

Table 2.6
Summary of outcomes of U.S. trade actions under the 1974 and 1979 Trade Acts, as of December 31, 1984

Type of action	Filed since	Terminated	Unsuccessful	Successful	Pending	Total
201						
Escape clause	1974 Trade Act	—	35	18	1	54
(steel actions)		—	(5)	(5)	—	(10)
301						
Foreign government practices	1974 Trade Act	12	2	17	16	47
(steel actions)		(7)	(1)	—	—	(8)
406						
Nonmarket economy	1974 Trade Act	—	8	2	—	10
(steel actions)		—	—	—	—	—
701						
Countervailing duty	1979 Trade Act	64	125	27	19	235
(steel actions)		(37)	(57)	(21)	(15)	(130)
731						
Antidumping	1979 Trade Act	51	76	48	60	235
(steel actions)		(43)	(25)	(16)	(46)	(130)
Total		127	246	112	96	581
(steel actions)		(87)	(88)	(42)	(61)	(278)

Source: Adapted from Jackson (1985).
Note: The section numbers (201, etc.) refer to the 1974 and 1979 Trade Acts.

Table 2.7
NTB coverage ratios by product category for the major industrial countries, 1983

Industrial country markets	All products	All, less fuels	Agriculture	Manufactures	Textiles	Footwear	Iron and steel	Electrical machinery	Vehicles	Rest of manufactures
EEC	22.3	21.1	36.4	18.7	52.0	9.5	52.6	13.4	45.3	10.3
Belgium-Luxembourg	26.0	33.9	55.9	33.6	38.2	12.3	47.4	19.5	54.3	30.6
Denmark	11.7	15.9	28.5	13.2	46.5	13.6	49.9	6.7	35.0	5.4
France	57.1	28.1	37.8	27.4	48.4	6.6	73.9	41.7	42.9	19.4
West Germany	12.4	18.3	22.3	18.5	57.0	9.7	53.5	6.8	52.0	6.6
Greece	13.4	23.2	46.4	20.4	21.8	22.8	54.5	13.5	65.5	8.5
Ireland	13.4	15.0	24.8	13.8	31.7	8.8	23.0	0.5	65.8	6.6
Italy	6.9	14.6	39.9	9.3	37.2	0.2	48.6	7.1	10.2	2.6
Netherlands	25.5	28.0	51.9	17.8	57.3	12.0	35.5	4.0	49.7	10.7
United Kingdom	14.3	17.5	34.9	14.8	59.6	12.2	42.1	12.7	44.3	6.7
Australia	34.1	24.1	36.1	23.6	30.9	50.0	55.6	48.7	0.7	21.6
Austria	4.9	6.0	41.7	2.4	2.2	0.1	0.0	0.0	2.9	3.0
Finland	34.9	9.2	31.5	6.7	31.0	68.8	43.9	0.0	0.0	0.4
Japan	11.9	16.9	42.9	7.7	11.8	34.1	0.0	0.0	0.0	7.7
Norway	5.7	5.8	24.2	4.1	42.9	5.4	0.1	0.0	0.2	0.4
Switzerland	32.2	23.6	73.4	17.6	57.4	0.0	3.9	28.1	1.1	14.6
United States	43.0	17.3	24.2	17.1	57.0	11.5	37.7	5.2	34.2	6.1
All industrial country markets	27.1	18.6	36.1	16.1	44.8	12.6	35.4	10.0	30.4	8.8

Source: Nogues, Olechowski, and Winters (1985, p. 43).

Table 2.8
Differential impact of major industrial country NTB coverage ratios, by product category for developing and industrial countries, 1983

Industrial country markets	All products	All, less fuels	Agriculture	Manufactures	Textiles	Footwear	Iron and steel	Electrical machinery	Vehicles	Rest of manufactures
EEC	25.4	26.9	26.9	29.9	68.0	9.9	31.9	7.0	8.4	14.7
	18.6	18.9	47.7	15.2	15.6	0.6	51.8	15.8	49.9	9.3
Belgium-Luxembourg	38.1	45.1	35.1	54.7	43.5	5.6	40.2	0.2	0.1	58.1
	25.7	27.1	72.0	22.5	30.4	6.5	43.4	21.4	56.5	13.5
Denmark	29.5	35.8	36.3	36.7	72.3	16.3	34.4	0.0	0.5	5.4
	9.5	10.9	20.9	9.8	11.1	0.2	48.5	5.9	38.0	5.0
France	50.1	28.6	28.1	33.0	64.6	11.3	35.1	35.5	29.0	21.3
	31.3	27.4	53.3	25.0	21.9	0.3	78.1	42.8	45.6	18.3
West Germany	18.1	23.9	16.6	30.2	71.9	2.9	32.2	0.2	0.0	3.5
	13.7	14.5	28.5	13.3	8.8	0.5	51.6	8.8	56.2	7.2
Greece	6.2	12.9	20.1	11.8	33.5	41.2	43.6	6.9	41.9	2.9
	26.1	26.4	61.8	22.6	4.4	0.1	50.4	16.5	71.9	10.2
Ireland	19.6	19.9	21.2	19.5	55.5	10.5	4.4	0.0	0.0	9.3
	13.4	13.8	29.1	12.8	17.6	0.0	19.2	0.3	67.9	6.3
Italy	7.3	16.2	32.1	12.0	49.0	0.3	33.8	0.1	0.0	1.0
	11.0	11.9	47.6	6.0	4.4	0.2	47.0	6.9	16.8	3.1
Netherlands	29.3	32.3	38.3	28.0	72.4	8.9	15.9	0.0	0.2	8.7
	25.8	27.1	68.8	15.3	6.7	1.7	35.7	6.8	53.3	11.6
United Kingdom	23.3	27.4	24.4	30.4	78.6	18.0	26.8	5.8	0.0	5.0
	15.4	17.0	44.5	13.2	26.0	0.6	40.4	16.7	46.7	6.8
Australia	43.7	27.9	21.6	28.6	29.1	48.5	42.5	62.5	0.0	22.3
	23.6	23.4	47.7	22.7	28.1	51.6	57.8	46.8	0.7	21.7
Austria	13.8	19.2	40.5	6.1	15.1	0.0	0.0	0.0	1.9	0.0
	4.5	4.7	39.9	2.4	0.0	0.0	0.0	0.0	3.0	3.3
Finland	38.4	26.9	28.7	27.5	63.0	56.2	15.8	0.0	0.0	0.6
	10.9	7.4	32.6	5.5	23.5	72.0	42.8	0.0	0.0	0.5

Japan	12.1	17.5	53.3	4.4	13.0	36.3	0.0	0.0	0.0	1.3
	21.4	16.9	36.8	9.7	11.0	27.9	0.0	0.0	0.0	10.6
Norway	16.8	18.2	15.4	20.9	59.5	20.5	20.6	0.0	43.9	5.0
	4.3	4.9	27.0	3.2	39.5	0.1	0.0	0.0	0.2	0.2
Switzerland	43.4	34.5	67.3	19.5	45.8	0.0	7.7	10.1	0.0	3.6
	27.2	22.4	74.9	17.4	60.9	0.0	3.8	28.9	1.1	15.1
United States	54.0	18.9	25.1	18.6	64.0	16.7	48.9	5.3	0.0	5.4
	26.0	16.6	23.5	16.5	31.1	0.0	35.6	5.2	34.7	6.4
All markets	34.3	22.5	31.2	21.3	57.2	17.3	31.4	6.1	5.0	11.0
	21.0	17.1	40.5	14.5	23.3	3.5	34.3	11.8	31.4	9.8

Source: Ibid.

Note: The top figure in the table body represents developing countries and the bottom figure industrial countries.

Table 2.9
Percentage changes in the prevalence of NTBs as measured by the NTB coverage ratios for all products for the major industrial countries, 1981–1983

Industrial country markets	Coverage ratio		
	All countries	Industrial countries	Developing countries
EEC	2.5	4.5	1.2
Belgium-Luxembourg	1.9	3.5	0.8
Denmark	2.9	3.8	1.0
France	2.7	5.1	2.1
West Germany	2.8	5.5	0.8
Greece	4.0	10.2	0.9
Ireland	3.8	4.5	2.3
Italy	1.0	2.6	0.7
Netherlands	2.0	4.3	0.8
United Kingdom	3.6	4.2	1.4
Australia	2.5	2.7	2.7
Austria	0.1	0.0	2.1
Finland	−3.8	−5.5	−1.4
Japan	0.0	0.1	0.0
Norway	−0.3	−0.4	1.0
Switzerland	2.5	2.7	1.2
United States	1.3	1.6	1.4
All industrial country markets	1.5	2.2	1.1

Source: Ibid. (1985, p. 61).

The study by Nogues, Olechowski, and Winters permits some assessment of whether protectionism has been growing in recent years. Unfortunately the UNCTAD inventory of NTBs does not extend readily to years prior to 1981, and information for 1984 is not yet available. Nonetheless there has been a noticeable increase in the extent of NTBs between 1981 and 1983 (table 2.9). Measured in terms of 1981 values, an additional $13 billion of trade was subjected to new restrictions, for an increase of about 6 percent. The underlying calculations suggest that the new restrictions were placed especially on products of interest to the industrial countries (such as iron and steel, electronic products, and vehicles) that had large trade flows. There were more numerous restrictions affecting developing countries, but they were smaller in terms of trade coverage.

These results are by no means definitive because they do not reflect the economic impact of the NTBs on the prices and quantities of the goods produced and traded and how the economic welfare of the individual nations and the world may be affected. It appears nonetheless that a substantial proportion of world trade has been distorted by NTBs, and there is reason to believe that this proportion has been rising in recent years.[9]

2.3 Free Trade and Arguments for Trade Intervention

With the expansion in the volume and the volatility of trade, there have been
introduced not only new actual measures of trade intervention but also a
variety of new arguments from economists providing possible reasons to
justify such intervention. At the same time many older arguments have been
revived, and there is sometimes the impression that the traditional theoretical
case for free international trade has become outmoded and obsolete. We do not
share that view, though we recognize that a number of legitimate arguments
for trade intervention exist, and it may be useful to review some of them. We
will try especially to clarify the circumstances under which trade intervention
may be justified, with particular attention in each case to additional reasons
why intervention may not be desirable after all. Our discussion will be
somewhat abstract, but this is necessary to avoid becoming bogged down in
the specifics of particular cases and circumstances of intervention.

We begin by briefly considering the classic argument for free trade. The case
for free trade rests on a model of a world in which there is assumed to be
perfect competition, absence of market impediments, ample time for markets
to adjust, and given technology. It is by relaxing some of these idealized assumptions that various cases for trade intervention have been developed.
Still, the model of free trade is important because it provides a standard or
frame of reference against which reality can be compared. It also serves as a
guide to the formulation and assessment of trade and other government
policies.

We will then address various arguments for trade intervention. We will
begin with the optimal tariff argument, which until recently has been regarded
as the only first-best argument for trade intervention in the national interest.
Although this is an old argument, many of the principles involved are of
renewed interest since they also apply to some of the more recently developed arguments for intervention in imperfectly competitive and strategic
environments.

Next we will look at second-best arguments for trade intervention. These
arguments have been the subject of the bulk of the literature on trade
intervention for the last thirty years at least and need not be addressed in too
much detail. The principles, however, like the arguments themselves, continue to belong near the forefront of the policy debate, and it is on these
principles that we will focus.

Having attended to these well-established elements of the literature on trade
intervention, we will turn to arguments raised in the last few years. Many of
these arguments have been couched in terms of models of trade with imperfect

competition, and we will look first at how the more traditional arguments fare in such a model. Then we will examine the idea of profit-seeking intervention, which lies at the core of many of the new arguments for intervention in monopolistic and oligopolistic environments. This is indeed a novel and important idea, though we will argue that the principles that should guide decisions as to whether to pursue such intervention are really the same as were already met in the optimal tariff and second-best arguments for protection.

A similar conclusion emerges when we consider arguments for trade intervention motivated by the trade policies of other nations. Such trade policies may either be intended to countervail against policies undertaken abroad or may have the more subtle intent of leading strategically to changes in the policies themselves. With some exceptions, these uses of policy, though different on the surface from more traditional arguments, are also subject to many of the familiar objections to trade intervention.

Our last topic in this section will have to do with various politically motivated arguments for trade intervention. These include trade intervention intended to achieve certain political objectives abroad and intervention motivated by political considerations at home. To some extent such arguments do not suggest the desirability of trade intervention but only its practicality or even inevitability in a world where policymakers must accommodate the political forces that would otherwise remove them from office. But even here traditional arguments against intervention can and should play a role in directing policymakers toward those uses of policy that will be the least harmful to the general interest, within the constraint of accommodating the necessary special interests.

Thus although recent arguments for trade intervention have been diverse, we do not consider them as sufficient grounds for seriously compromising or rejecting outright the principles of free trade as the basis for trade policy. These well-established principles continue to be relevant, though the case for free trade no longer has the simple force of a textbook theorem.

2.3.1 Classic Argument for the Gains from Trade

The argument that there are gains from international trade is too old and well established to require much attention here. And it is generally understood that under certain idealized conditions, which include perfect competition, these gains are maximized with free trade. The core of the argument may be said to rest on two principles. First, consumers are made better off by the opportunity to exchange the goods that are available in their domestic market for other goods that can be obtained abroad, since this enlarges the set of consumption

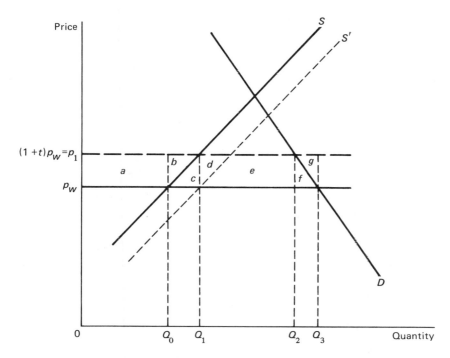

Figure 2.1
Effects of a tariff and production subsidy under conditions of competition.

opportunities. Second, the greatest benefits from this exchange of goods will
be possible if domestic producers first produce a bundle of goods that is worth
as much as possible on world markets, which they too will do if they are free to
trade their products in pursuit of profits. Departures from free trade are
therefore undesirable since they distort the decisions of both producers and
consumers.

All of this is familiar from decades of theoretical refinement in the literature
of international trade.[10] As a prelude to later discussion we will illustrate the
proposition in the simple form of the standard supply and demand, consumer
and producer surplus diagram of figure 2.1. The figure illustrates the domestic
market for a good that is available also from abroad at a fixed price p_w. With
free trade, domestic suppliers produce Q_0 while consumer demand Q_3, importing the difference. Trade intervention in the form of a tariff, t, raises the
domestic price to p_1, causing domestic supply to rise and domestic demand to
fall. Producers benefit in the amount given by the area $a + b$, while consumers
lose the larger area $a + b + c + d + e + f$ and the government collects a tariff
revenue of $d + e$. The net welfare effect for the country as a whole is therefore

a loss equal to $c + f$, where area c can be attributed to the distortion of producer decisions and area f can be attributed to the distortion of consumer decisions.

This familiar analysis suggests two qualifications to the argument for free trade that should be kept in mind, since it is easy to lose sight of them in the heat of the debate between free traders and protectionists. First, the mere removal of policies that interfere with trade is most unlikely to benefit all residents of a country. That there are gains to be had from free trade means that free trade makes available, to the economy as a whole, enough to make everyone in it better off than they are without free trade. But mere removal of a tariff or other trade impediment will normally benefit only some members of society and harm others. Thus in figure 2.1, the removal of the tariff would certainly hurt those who contribute to production of the import-competing good (the lost producer surplus, area $a + b$), the bulk of the gain in consumer surplus being enjoyed by others spread throughout the economy. The gains from trade make it economically possible to redistribute income from the gainers to the losers so that all are made better off. But there is often no reason to expect, from a political point of view, that policies designed to accomplish such a redistribution will ever be used. If redistribution is not effected, then the advantages to a country of a move to free trade may be suspect, especially from the standpoint of those who lose. For them, the gains from trade mean only that those who benefit from free trade gain more than is lost, collectively, by those who are hurt, and that is small comfort. Even under ideal conditions, therefore, a case can be made for government to compensate individuals whose economic welfare may be lowered by removing impediments to trade.[11]

A second qualification is also implicit in analyses like those of figure 2.1 and needs to be stressed. When we say that a country benefits most from free international trade, the emphasis should be on the word *free* much more than on *trade*. The point is that there is nothing inherently desirable about trade per se if that trade is not an appropriate response to market forces. If two countries were completely identical in all respects, then barring such complications as economies of scale and preference for variety, it would be optimal for them not to trade with each other at all, and that is exactly what they would do if trade were free. In general, it is just as distortionary to interfere with trade by artificially promoting it as by artificially restricting it.[12] There is therefore nothing in the classic argument for the gains from trade that supports the use of export subsidies or other policies of export promotion. This too has long been recognized in the academic literature, but it is again a distinction that can be lost sight of in the heat of debate between protrade and antitrade constituencies.[13]

2.3.2 National Monopoly Power and the Optimal Tariff

The idealized assumptions of the classic argument for free trade imply the optimality of free trade only for the world as a whole. For individual countries the optimality of free trade requires the additional assumption that the country is too small to have any influence, through its policies, over the prices at which it trades. Without that assumption it is well known that free trade is not optimal from a national perspective and instead that there exists an optimal degree of trade intervention, known as the optimal tariff, that works by turning the country's terms of trade in its favor.

This too is easily illustrated in figure 2.1. If the imported good is supplied less than infinitely elastically from the world market, then the reduction in the country's demand for imports will cause the world price to fall. A domestic price at the level p_1 can still be achieved, but it requires a tariff larger than t. As a result the tariff revenue that accrues to the government is larger than the area $d + e$ and includes another rectangle extending down beneath e to the new lower world price (not shown). If this rectangle is larger than the combined areas $c + f$, the country as a whole gains by levying the tariff. Furthermore if the world price falls for any reduction of demand, no matter how small, then such a gain must be possible for a sufficiently small tariff.

This argument is sometimes thought to require that the country in question be large and therefore to apply only to such large, industrialized countries as the United States; however, the argument applies to some extent to any country that is not insignificantly small. Furthermore the size that is important is not the size of the country as a whole but rather its share of world trade in markets in which it exports and imports. Since many countries tend to specialize their exports in a fairly small range of goods—exactly as trade theory predicts they should—even quite small countries may have enough market power over the prices of their exports for the optimal tariff argument to apply.[14]

The optimal tariff argument has the important feature that it involves a benefit for the intervening country only at the expense of the country's trading partners. Indeed since free trade is known to be optimal for the world as a whole, it must be true that the rest of the world loses more than the tariff-levying country gains. Furthermore the rest of the world, were it able to act collectively, would have the same sort of power over the terms of trade as does the original country, and it is therefore quite inappropriate to think of a single country as levying an optimal tariff in isolation. The possibility that other countries may do the same, either in retaliation or because they too think they recognize an opportunity for gain, must surely be considered.

This feature of the optimal tariff argument—that it involves gain by one country at other countries' expense—is one that we will meet again in some of the newer arguments for trade intervention. To address such arguments in a common framework, we will refer to such trade policies as being exploitative intervention. Such policies typically are available to more than one country (and even many), each of which can have adverse effects on the others and therefore require that strategic issues be considered. Like other forms of exploitative intervention, the optimal tariff argument is likely to find countries in the classic position of the Prisoners' Dilemma; that is, each country has available a policy that will benefit itself at the expense of others, but if all countries simultaneously pursue that policy, all are likely to lose.[15]

Exploitative intervention policies, like the optimal tariff argument, place economists in a dilemma too. First, any policy that depends for its effect on hurting others can hardly be recommended as socially desirable. If economists view their role as promoting world welfare, they should surely not be advocating the use of such a policy. But whether or not they take the world view, the advice they should give to policymakers is still far from clear. The appropriate policy in either case depends on what policies will be undertaken abroad, on how those policies may depend on the policies that we ourselves pursue or claim that we will pursue, and so forth. Thus exploitative intervention policies, even without the complications of imperfect competition, inevitably raise the complicated and perhaps unsolvable strategic issues that we will be considering more directly below. For the moment, the only conclusion we can draw from the optimal tariff literature is that although the optimal tariff argument is valid, it would be best if no country were to try to take advantage of it.[16] How to get countries to follow this advice and what to tell them if they do not may be another question altogether, however.

2.3.3 Second-Best Arguments for Intervention

A crucial assumption underlying the classic gains-from-trade proposition is that everything within the domestic economy is working properly: all domestic markets are perfectly competitive, prices and wages adjust freely so that markets clear, and there are no externalities in production or consumption. If any of these conditions fails to hold, there exists a domestic distortion, and the first-best optimal results of free trade are no longer assured. Instead the distortionary effects that trade interventions are known to have could conceivably be used to offset the domestic distortion and make the economy better off.

A simple illustration of this possibility is again shown in figure 2.1. Suppose that the supply curve, S, reflects only the private marginal cost of producing the good and that production of the good also generates a positive external benefit that, if it were deducted from private marginal costs, would yield the social marginal cost curve S'. The area between these two curves then measures an additional benefit to society of increasing the output of the good. In this situation a tariff that raises output from Q_0 to Q_1 creates an additional external benefit equal to area $b + c$. Thus if $b > f$, a tariff's net effect is beneficial.

Such use of trade intervention is said to be second best for a reason that is also clear from figure 2.1. Because a tariff always distorts both producer and consumer behavior while the externality in question concerns only one of these groups, a better policy is possible that addresses the original distortion more directly. Thus, for example, a production subsidy could be used instead of the tariff to shift the private marginal cost curve down to S'. This would raise output to Q_1, generating the desired external benefit while leaving consumers free to consume at Q_3. A check of the welfare effects of such a policy yields a gain to producers of $a + b$, a gain due to the externality of $b + c$, and a cost to the government of $a + b + c$, for a net gain of b. This is superior to the possible gain of $b - f$ that was yielded by the tariff.

The general principle is that trade intervention, by introducing two distortions rather than one, may succeed in solving one problem but only at the same time that it causes another. Trade policy is like doing acupuncture with a fork: no matter how carefully you insert one prong, the other is likely to do damage.

Such examples are rife in the theory of protection. The classic example is the infant industry argument where a tariff is said to protect a young industry while it learns to be efficient. The assumption here is that some market failure—such as an imperfection in the loan market or the impossibility of keeping new technical knowledge from being copied—makes it impossible for competitive firms to take advantage of what would otherwise be a profitable opportunity. A tariff or other import restriction can therefore be used temporarily to make the operation profitable even in the short run while the learning process is underway. Naturally, though, the success of such a policy depends crucially on a correct diagnosis of which industries offer the potential for such improvement over time. Also it may be difficult politically to remove protection once it has been put in place, though this particular rationale for protection is explicitly temporary.

As in the case of the externality discussed above, the infant industry argument may be valid in the sense that a tariff may be beneficial, but it is also true that some other policy would be superior. Once again a production subsidy, equal in size to the tariff, would yield exactly the same benefits to producers as the tariff without causing the additional costly distortion of consumer choice. Even better might be a policy that subsidizes or guarantees loans to the industry, if the capital market was the real source of the distortion, or a policy that permits firms to appropriate technology if that was the problem. The general principle is that first-best policies deal directly with the distortions involved, and distortions rarely involve the double effect on both producer and consumer choice that would be best addressed with trade intervention.

Many other arguments for intervention can similarly be traced to the presumption of a distortion somewhere in the domestic economy. Tariffs to protect essential industries, for example, depend on the private sector's being unable to perceive or take advantage of the fact that these industries are essential, which often means that they confer social benefits on others in society. Tariffs designed to discourage consumption of undesirable goods similarly assume an undesirable social effect of such consumption or else that consumers themselves have a distorted view of their own welfare. And finally tariffs for employment and balance-of-payments purposes assume rather obviously that certain markets—labor and foreign exchange—are failing to adjust to equilibrium.

All of these arguments may be valid if the distortions on which they rest are correctly diagnosed, but they could be better dealt with by means of some other policies that deal more directly with the distortions in question. Production taxes or subsidies, consumption taxes or subsidies, analogous policies in labor and foreign exchange markets: each in the individual cases mentioned has a better chance of being optimal. This kind of reasoning has been used extensively over the years in defending against arguments for trade intervention, and it has become almost a matter of professional pride among trade theorists to be able to pass the buck in this way.[17]

Still, to argue against trade intervention on the grounds that some other policies would be preferable sounds weak. Practical policymakers can be excused from shrugging such reasoning aside. After all they are in the business of trying to make only marginal improvements in the economic environment, and if they can find some feasible policy that will work, they are unlikely to worry that some other policy might have worked a bit better.

It is here that trade economists need to go beyond the simple argument that better policies are available and point out other implications of the second-best result that cast further doubt on the desirability of trade intervention. For example, the first-best policies that economic theory suggests for dealing with distortions often turn out to involve either subsidies or the taxation of politically sensitive activities. Thus it may be argued that first-best policies are politically unacceptable and therefore that trade interference, though only second best in economic theory, may be first best in terms of political reality. This may be true, but it is a dangerous argument, for the following reason. If trade intervention is politically more acceptable than domestic taxes and subsidies, it is probably because its true effects are less well understood by the electorate. If the public would not approve a direct subsidy to an industry, for whatever reason, then that fact should perhaps be taken as evidence that protection of that industry through trade intervention is also socially undesirable, for we know from the second-best property of protection in this case that protection has exactly the same effects on the industry itself as does a subsidy, while at the same time it inflicts further damage elsewhere in the economy.

Yet another implication of the second-best argument is that despite the name *second best*, there is no assurance that the use of remedial trade intervention is desirable at all. This is already evident in the externality example, where the tariff would have made matters worse had the area f been greater than the area b. It is always a very difficult empirical question whether the benefits of offsetting a domestic distortion exceed the costs that arise from the second distortion caused by trade intervention. Estimates of these costs and benefits are notoriously difficult and unreliable. Therefore there is always a good chance that the net effect of a trade policy is adverse, even when it does act in the direction of offsetting a domestic distortion.[18] Since first-best policies are not subject to this uncertainty, their use in preference to trade policies represents more than just a marginal improvement.

It is not inevitable that trade intervention is only second best as a means of dealing with a distortion, since it is conceivable that a distortion might arise in trade itself. The near consensus among economists opposed to trade intervention reflects in part their view that most distortions are not of this type, but there is one area that may require special consideration. In recent years especially, economies have been buffeted by changes in trade that seem to have arisen from changes in exchange rates that many view as inappropriate. This has led to demands, in the United States especially, for some sort of import surcharge that would offset the effects of dollar appreciation on U.S. trade. It is appropriate to ask whether such a surcharge could in fact be a first-best response to an appreciated dollar.

The answer is surely that a surcharge is not first best, but the reason is in a sense the opposite of what occurs in the usual second-best situation. In the usual case a tariff is suboptimal because it entails more distortions than one is trying to correct. A tariff is second best for dealing with an incorrect exchange rate, however, in part because the tariff entails fewer distortions than the exchange rate. An appreciation of a country's currency reduces the domestic prices of both exports and imports, a fact that is relevant only if there is something else, such as a nontraded good, to which these prices can be compared.[19] A tariff, on the other hand, raises the domestic price of only imports. Thus a tariff seems to do too little, rather than too much, as a means of dealing with an appreciated currency. It is only second best and may not be beneficial at all since at the same time that it restores the original price of imports relative to nontraded goods, it also distorts the price of imports relative to exports. A better policy in this case would be a combination of an import tax and an export subsidy, since the two together would mimic exactly a devaluation in terms of its effects on relative prices.

Even this would probably not be first best, however, since an overvalued currency—if that concept is meaningful at all—is more likely a symptom than the primary cause of the problem. It would be better to identify the reason for the exchange rate change that has taken place and address's policy directly to that. This might mean a change in monetary or fiscal policy, or it might mean accepting the exchange rate as either correct or inevitable and addressing one's policies toward imperfections in the economy's means of dealing with it.

Whatever the answer, it seems clear that some recognition of the problems associated with exchange rate changes is necessary. Exchange rates have fluctuated a great deal in recent years, as we documented in section 2.2, and these fluctuations have had significant effects on the real behavior in the economy. Whether these effects are inappropriate, they have certainly generated strong political pressures for action, and these pressures will show up in policy.

2.3.4 Trade Intervention in Imperfectly Competitive Markets

Recognizing that many markets, domestical and international, are imperfectly competitive, a number of trade theorists have begun to analyze trade and trade policy in an imperfectly competitive world. It is clear that the classical case for the gains from trade does not apply directly in such a world; however, we do not yet have a very clear understanding of the alternatives. Instead we have several suggestive ideas about the role of trade policy in particular situations that have not yet been established with any generality.

The first such idea is probably also the most important and is also very simple. If a domestic market is not competitive, competition can be fostered by removing barriers to trade. Often a major reason that domestic markets are dominated by a small number of producers is that these producers are protected from foreign competition by tariffs or other trade restrictions. If given a choice, producers for the domestic market will opt for quantitative import restrictions, since these reduce the elasticity of demand for the domestic product and thus increase the profit that can be made by monopoly pricing in the domestic market. The trade policy that will best improve this situation does not require any subtle effort to offset the effects of monopoly power. Instead a simple opening of markets to free international trade will remove the market power itself and restore the benefits of competition.[20] A domestic market with only a few domestic firms may therefore approximate free competition if those few firms must compete with a larger number of foreign producers.

Unfortunately there is sometimes no assurance that even worldwide free trade will confer the benefits of perfect competition in all markets. Some products are not tradable or are not available as perfect substitutes from abroad. In addition the world market itself may be imperfectly competitive, due perhaps to the historical dominance of a few firms or the nature of the product. Many products in today's international trade more and more seem to lend themselves to product differentiation and the use of large-scale and aggressive marketing techniques. In such cases, while free trade still increases competition, the nature of that competition is sufficiently imperfect that the benefits from it are no longer assured.

Two issues need to be addressed here. First, to what extent are our earlier arguments undermined by the persistence of imperfect competition even under free trade? In particular, is it still true that trade intervention constitutes only a second-best means of dealing with domestic distortions? Second, do imperfect market structures give rise to any new arguments for trade intervention other than the traditional ones? We will examine these two issues in turn.

Second-Best Principle with Imperfect Competition

This is not an issue that we can resolve definitively since there is no single model of imperfect competition that can provide the basis for a conclusive proof. We can, however, look at an example and attempt to infer whether the existence of at least one form of imperfect competition seems to cast doubt on the principle that trade intervention is a suboptimal means of dealing with a domestic distortion.

Consider the case of the production externality that we looked at with perfect competition, but suppose now that the industry in question is a monopoly. In order to ensure that the monopoly can continue to exist even with free trade, assume that the good it produces is a differentiated product and that only an imperfect substitute for it is available from abroad. For simplicity suppose that the good cannot be sold abroad. We wish to determine

Alan V. Deardorff and Robert M. Stern

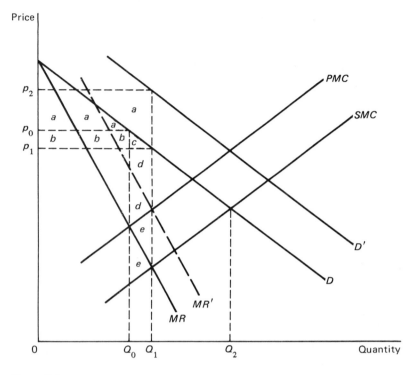

Figure 2.2
Effects of a tariff and production subsidy under conditions of domestic monopoly.

the relative merits of a production subsidy and an import tariff as means of offsetting the distortion caused by the externality. There is also another distortion present since the industry is a monopoly, but we are taking that as given.

Figure 2.2 illustrates the case. With free trade the monopolist faces the demand curve, D, and the corresponding marginal revenue curve, MR. The private marginal cost perceived by the monopolist is PMC, while because of the assumed externality, the social marginal cost is the somewhat lower curve, SMC. With free trade and no production subsidy, the monopolist produces Q_0 and sells at price p_0. This output is lower (and the price higher) than would have been the case if the monopolist had itself confronted the true cost curve, SMC, in which case it would have produced Q_1. In addition both outputs are lower than the competitive, no-distortion output of Q_2 that would obtain if a competitive industry's marginal cost curve were also SMC.

Now suppose that a tariff were levied on imports of the imperfect-substitute competing good. This would shift the demand curve for the monopolist's product up to D', and the corresponding marginal revenue curve would likely also shift up.[21] Suppose that the size of the tariff can be selected so that the new marginal revenue curve, MR', crosses PMC at Q_1. Then one could say that the tariff has undone the effect of the externality since it has led the monopolist to produce as it would have with the externality internalized.

Whether this tariff is in fact beneficial is hard to determine since the figure does not contain information directly about the imported good. However, we can still make the case that, whether good or bad, the tariff is inferior to a production subsidy. Consider such a subsidy that shifts the private marginal cost curve down to coincide with SMC. This too would raise the monopolist's output to Q_1 and thus have the same external benefits as the tariff.

To compare the production subsidy and the tariff, it is convenient to compare them both to yet a third policy of a consumption subsidy applied directly to the output of the monopolist. Such a consumption subsidy can also be used to shift the demand curve facing the monopolist to D' and is therefore entirely equivalent to the production subsidy. In figure 2.2, then, either subsidy raises the price received by the monopolist to p_2, raising profit by the area $a + c + d$ while costing the government area $a + b + c$. At the same time, price to consumers falls to p_1, increasing consumer surplus by the area $b + c$. Including also the gain from the externality of area e, the net effect of either the production or consumption subsidy is $c + d + e$.

Now compare the consumption subsidy to the tariff that we mentioned originally, noting that the tariff was also set so as to raise demand for the good to the level Q_1. It can easily be shown that to generate a given change in quantity demanded of a good, the best policy is always to tax or subsidize the good itself rather than attempt to get the same result from a subsidy or tax on consumption of some other good. In this case, since the imported good is not produced domestically, a tariff on it is just a consumption tax and is therefore inferior to a consumption subsidy as a means of raising demand for the monopolist's output to Q_1.

Thus in this particular case at least, a tariff is still an inferior means of offsetting the effect of a domestic distortion, even when there is domestic imperfect competition. Perhaps an example can be found in which this is not the case, but we would expect the general principle to continue to be valid.

Profit-Seeking Motives for Protection

Free trade may fail to ensure perfect competition even in traded goods if world markets are not perfectly competitive. If world markets are monopolistic or oligopolistic and monopoly profits are being made at the expense of either

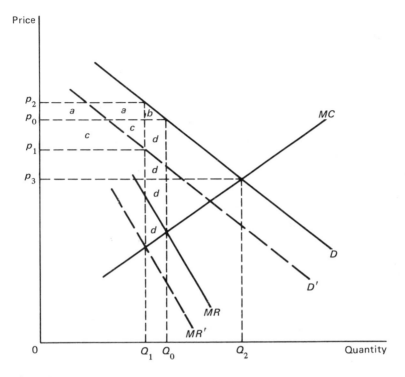

Figure 2.3
Effects of a tariff under conditions of foreign monopoly.

foreign or domestic consumers, then trade intervention may benefit a country by capturing for it a larger share of these monopoly profits.

The idea has considerable appeal. Certainly politically if you must be exploited, it is better to be exploited by your own kind than by foreigners. Even economically there may be a valid case for trade intervention. Arguments of this sort have become quite common in the recent literature of international trade, many of them associated with the works of James Brander and Barbara Spencer.[22] We will look at two relatively simple examples of arguments of this type.

To see first how trade intervention can capture a portion of foreign monopoly profits, consider a country that imports a good from a foreign discriminating monopoly. Figure 2.3 illustrates the case, in which the domestic demand for the imported product is initially D, with corresponding marginal revenue MR, and the marginal cost of the foreign monopolist for supplying the domestic market is MC. Output is initially therefore at Q_0 with price p_0.

Output is well below the competitive optimum Q_2, and the monopolist is charging well above marginal cost and presumably profiting as a result.

A tariff in this case can benefit the importing country, even though it moves the equilibrium further from the competitive norm. A tariff shifts the demand curve faced by the monopolist down to D' and the marginal revenue curve down to MR'. Output falls to Q_1 while the price received by the monopolist falls to p_1. Consumers, however, pay a higher price, p_2, the difference going to the government as tariff revenue. Examining the effects on welfare, the monopoly's profit falls by the area $c + d$, domestic consumers lose the area $a + b$, and the domestic government gains tariff revenue of $a + c$. The net effect on the world is negative, but the importing country gets a net gain of $c - b$, which as drawn in the figure can easily be positive.

On the face of it, this seems to constitute a distinctly different argument for trade intervention than those we have already dealt with. Certainly the interpretation as an exercise in profit seeking could find no place in the competitive world. On reflection, however, what is happening here is not so novel.

Notice first that the importing country gains from the tariff only if the price paid to the monopolist does in fact fall. Otherwise area c is zero, and there is only a loss. Thus like the optimal tariff argument in a competitive world, the tariff here is working by improving the importing country's terms of trade. That this should be possible even with imperfect competition should not be surprising, since even monopolists can be expected to respond to a decline in demand for their product. On the other hand, the gain from the tariff is less assured when imports are supplied by a monopolist, as can be verified in figure 2.1 by changing to a sufficiently downward-sloping marginal cost curve.

Even more important than the price change is the size of the effect on the monopoly's profits. These must fall by more than the gain to the importing country, implying that the tariff has not merely redistributed profits but has introduced additional inefficiency as well. It also implies that, again like the optimal tariff argument, this profit-seeking tariff is an exploitative one and is subject to all of the strategic concerns associated with a Prisoners' Dilemma. Indeed the only difference in principle between this and the optimal tariff is that there may be less ethical reluctance to attempt to turn the terms of trade against a foreign monopolist than against the residents of a foreign competitive economy.

Finally, it should be noted that this policy is far from first best as a means of dealing with this situation. A price ceiling at the level of the competitive price p_3, if that were feasible, would restore the benefits of the competitive optimum.

Now if, as this example suggests, the access to domestic markets benefits foreign companies in a way that is reasonable to resist, then it may also seem similarly beneficial to subsidize the access of domestic firms to foreign markets. Many countries behave as though they believe that their domestic firms need help in penetrating foreign markets. Presumably they also believe that the profits from these activities are an addition to the national welfare. Even if this is true, however, intervention in the form of export or credit subsidies or the like will be desirable only if there is some reason why the firms on their own cannot pursue profit opportunities optimally. Recent literature on trade with imperfect competition has succeeded in identifying a reason why this might be the case.

A simple example, due to Brander and Spencer (1985), illustrates the case and has also been discussed insightfully by Dixit (1984), Grossman and Richardson (1985), and Salant (1984). It consists of two firms from two different countries producing the same product for export to yet a third country where they interact as a Cournot duopoly. Assuming that its competitor's output will remain constant at its current level, each firm acts as a monopolist with respect to the market demand curve shifted inward by the amount of the other firm's output. This leads each to select an optimal output that depends negatively on the other firm's output, as shown by the reaction curves R and R^* in figure 2.4. The Cournot equilibrium is at E_0, with the domestic and foreign firms producing Q_0 and Q_0^*, respectively.

Implicit in the locations of the reaction curves are isoprofit loci for each firm such as the broken curve I_0 that is drawn through the equilibrium for the domestic firm. It is horizontal where it crosses R and is part of a family of curves that indicates larger profits for the domestic firm as one moves down in the figure. From the way that this curve crosses R^*, it follows that the domestic firm could earn a greater profit at a point like E_1 along the foreign reaction curve. Such an equilibrium cannot be attained as long as both firms continue to act freely under the Cournot assumption. But it is possible for the domestic government to move the equilibrium there by subsidizing the exports of the domestic firm. An appropriate subsidy will shift the domestic firm's reaction curve to the right to R' and will move the equilibrium to E_1. Since the subsidy payment itself is only a redistribution between the domestic government and the domestic firm, the fact that domestic profits would have been larger at E_1 even without the subsidy ensures that the gain to the country as a whole from the subsidy is positive.

This, then, gives a simple case for an export subsidy. The crucial question is why the domestic firm could not have moved to E_1 on its own. The answer is that it could have done so, but if it had and if the foreign firm had moved as

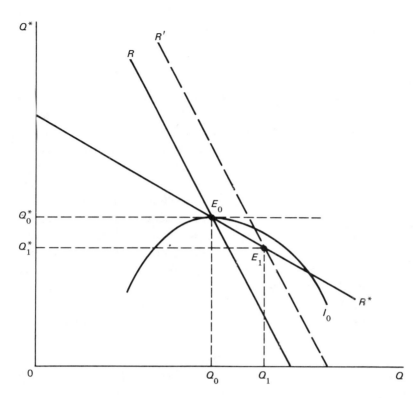

Figure 2.4
Effects of an export subsidy in the two-trading-firm Cournot duopoly model.

expected to Q_1^*, then the domestic firm would have been unable to resist raising its profits still further by returning to its own reaction curve. Under the Cournot assumption it would not expect any subsequent reaction by the foreign firm. The subsidy, on the other hand, precommits the domestic firm to remaining at Q_1, since in the presence of the subsidy it is optimal for it to do so.

This argument has been elaborated in a number of other contexts. The common thread is the ability of government to use its policy to precommit firms to behavior that would otherwise appear to be—and be known by their competitors to be—suboptimal. In this fashion trade intervention and other policies can be used to alter the outcomes of strategic games played by firms so as to increase the profits that can be shared by them with their sponsoring governments.

This particular case of a third market export duopoly, perhaps because it is so simple, has been subject to a number of criticisms. Dixit (1984) and Salant (1984), for example, have examined extensions of the model to larger numbers of firms in each exporting country and have found the desirability of an export subsidy disappearing rather quickly as the number of firms grows beyond two.

Another criticism, due to Eaton and Grossman (1983), recognizes an inconsistency in the behavior being assumed in the Cournot model. This inconsistency is important for our purposes here since it helps to put in perspective the reason that trade intervention can play a role in this model. Each firm expects the other's output to remain fixed when it changes its own, though the reaction curves dictate that this will not happen. According to the model, if the domestic firm expands its output, the foreign output will drop, and the demand curve facing the domestic firm will shift out. But the domestic firm does not recognize this. There is in a sense a distortion here, each firm perceiving that the benefit from expanding exports will be less than it in fact will be. It is no wonder, then, that there is scope for government intervention to correct that distortion. Of course, this is true only if the firms in fact behave in Cournot fashion. Eaton and Grossman try out a range of other conjectural variations and find that the case for an export subsidy reverses and becomes a case for an export tax as the conjectural variations become closer to the Bertrand assumption that each firm expects the other's price, rather than output, to be held fixed. Indeed their most interesting result is that if two firms have consistent conjectures, each conjecturing that the other would do what it would in fact do, then no trade intervention is desirable in either direction. This is understandable since their conjectures then involve no distortion that requires correction.

Clearly these contributions to the trade literature, and others like them, have broadened our understanding in useful ways. But have they added to the arsenal of reasons for trade intervention in ways that should alter the trade theorists' bias in favor of nonintervention? We think not.

Even in the two-firm Cournot model of figure 2.4, the case for intervention is once again exploitative, and though the mechanism is different, our reservations are the same that we expressed for the optimal tariff argument. It is clear from the figure that if both governments try to play this game, both exporting countries will be worse off.[23]

Furthermore as we move beyond the simple model to more firms and less simplistic behavioral assumptions about the firms, the case for export subsidies disappears and is replaced by a case for export taxation. The latter is intervention, certainly, but the gains to the countries now are the straightforward terms-of-trade gains that one would expect in any case to result from restricting supply to the third country.

2.3.5 Countervailing and Strategic Intervention

However one may feel about the case in economic theory for free trade, the fact remains that countries do make extensive use of policies that interfere with trade, perhaps for the reasons we have been discussing. This fact raises the question of whether the cases for and against intervention are altered at all for countries whose trading partners use such policies. We have already encountered cases in which trade policies may be used in response to the policies of other countries. This was the case noted of retaliation against an attempt to levy an optimal tariff, and the same motivation is likely to operate for any of the exploitative forms of trade intervention that we have discussed. Other cases are sometimes suggested, and some are even a formal part of national as well as GATT rules.

There seem to be two distinct rationales for responding to the trade policies of other countries. One is to try to neutralize, offset, or countervail the presumed adverse effects of a foreign country's trade policies.[24] The other is to try strategically to discourage the use of such policies by foreign countries by threatening, or actually implementing, policies that will affect them adversely. The difference between these two approaches is the following. In the former case the policy should be chosen with a view to benefiting the domestic economy directly. In the latter case since the purpose of the policy is to alter behavior abroad, a policy might be chosen in spite of having adverse direct effects domestically.

Countervailing Intervention
Countervailing intervention makes sense only if it benefits the domestic economy on its own account. It is not enough that it partially undoes the effect of the foreign country trade policy to which it responds. An obvious though hardly realistic example of this problem would be use of an export subsidy to offset the effects of a foreign tariff. Such a subsidy restores the equality between domestic prices at home and abroad and can restore almost exactly the pattern of trade that would have occurred if trade had been free in both countries. But it leaves the subsidizing country even worse off than with the foreign tariff alone since the subsidy becomes essentially a transfer payment to the foreign government.

The scope for successful use of a countervailing trade policy is limited by another consideration. Generally although trade intervention by other countries can certainly affect trade and the welfare of the domestic country, such intervention typically does not alter the policy options available to the domestic government or the ability of these policies to benefit the domestic economy.

Thus at least in a competitive environment, a so-called countervailing trade policy can be beneficial only if it would have been desirable anyway, without the excuse of any foreign government action. That being the case, one may wonder why the policy should not have been in place already, and if it was not, why it is a good idea now. In the end the fact that another country is intervening in trade may not in itself provide a separate reason for intervening ourselves but perhaps only a pretext for intervening for one of the reasons already discussed.

The familiar example of this use of trade policy is the national and GATT-sanctioned use of countervailing duties to offset the effect of foreign export subsidies. Just the opposite of the case described above, this countervailing policy normally does benefit the country using it, but only to the extent that the importing country is large enough to alter the terms of trade by using the duty. This is illustrated in figure 2.5, both panels of which show the market for an imported good under two different assumptions about its supply from abroad. In both cases a supply curve, S_M, has been shifted downward to a position S'_M by a foreign export subsidy. These subsidized supplies intersect domestic demand for imports, D_M, in an initial equilibrium with quantity of imports Q_0 and price p_0. When a countervailing duty is levied by the importing country, the demand curve shifts down to D'_M, reducing the quantity of imports to Q_1 and raising the price of imports on the domestic market to p_2. The difference between the two panels is that in A, the foreign supply of imports slopes up, while in B it is infinitely elastic.

In the former case analysis of the welfare effects of the countervailing duty yields a tariff revenue of area $a + c$ and a net loss of surplus for domestic residents of area $a + b$. The net effect on the importing country is $c - b$, which may well be positive as shown. The reason for the gain here, however, has nothing to do with the subsidy that initiated the action but rather is the familiar result of using a tariff to influence the terms of trade. This is clear by comparison with panel B where the infinite supply elasticity keeps the price paid to the foreign country constant. Here there is no counterpart to area c in panel A, and the country suffers a net loss due to the countervailing duty of area b.

Thus in this competitive framework a countervailing duty benefits a country only where it has enough market power to influence its terms of trade. Where this is the case, it could have benefited from a duty even had there been no foreign subsidy, assuming that it could have avoided retaliation. The question then is whether the fact of the subsidy, together perhaps with the official sanctioning of a countervailing duty, reduces the likelihood of retali-

A

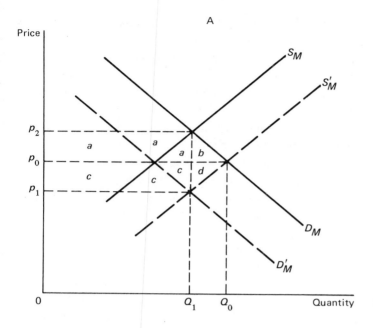

B

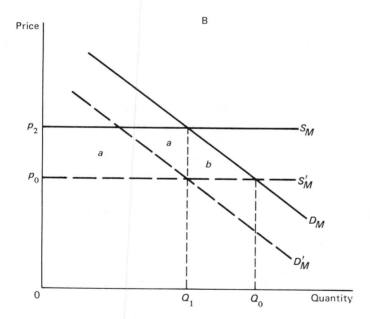

Figure 2.5
Effects of a countervailing duty with rising and infinitely elastic foreign supply of imports.

ation. Only if this is the case does it appear that the use of a countervailing duty is responsible policy in a competitive environment.

Countervailing duties require a demonstration of injury before they can be used. This presumes that there is a domestic distortion present (for example, a difficulty of adjustment in the labor market). But if such a distortion exists, then it would be better dealt with directly by domestic policy in its own right rather than by a countervailing duty. The fact that the source of disturbance to the labor market is an increase in imports brought on by a foreign government subsidy may provide a political reason for giving it special treatment, but that is no reason to deal with it then with a less than optimal policy.

All of this does, however, presume perfect competition. In an imperfectly competitive world subsidies may be used to give a country's producers a competitive edge in a foreign market. In that case a countervailing duty of some sort may be an optimal response on the part of the importing country's government as it tries to balance the gain from cheaper subsidized imports against the loss of monopoly profit earned by its domestic firms. Dixit (1984) has examined this possibility and found in one special case that the optimal countervailing duty is equal to one-half of the subsidy. This is an interesting result but is still somewhat tentative since it is derived in a model of Cournot behavior similar to the one we criticized.

There is, however, one role for countervailing duties that strikes us as undoubtedly legitimate: as a means of discouraging the use of export subsidies in the first place. This takes us, though, into the topic of strategic intervention.

Strategic Intervention

A number of arguments suggest that trade intervention may benefit one country at the expense of others. Such exploitative trade intervention is not new, having always been the core of the optimal tariff argument. But analyses of trade with imperfect competition especially have seemed to expand the scope for such intervention. This in turn has led to new interest in the strategic issues of how countries may use intervention to exploit others and to keep from being exploited by them. Johnson's (1954) early analysis of optimal tariffs and retaliation has become the starting point for a variety of game-theoretic analyses of this issue.

An excellent survey of this literature is available in Grossman and Richardson (1985), and we have little to add beyond citing a number of the points they make. This does not mean that we dismiss these issues as unimportant. On the contrary it is our view that the question of how policymakers should act in a world of exploitative trade intervention may well be one of the great unresolved questions in the trade policy field today. It is because we see so few convincing answers to this question that we encourage trade economists to consult with colleagues in other fields who face similar problems in an effort to come up with policy advice that will be both credible and useful.

The problem at issue is hardly unique to international trade. In simple terms it is the classic Prisoners' Dilemma game, in which each player has an incentive to act at the other's expense, and both lose if both act. Although it is clearly optimal for them collectively to refrain from acting (from intervening in trade), each has an incentive to depart from that optimum if it is ever reached.

As a matter of positive economics, the solution that is likely to be reached in a game of this sort is a suboptimal one in which both players act or both countries intervene in trade. Since trade intervention can take on a variety of forms and intensities, this has led to an interesting literature in which the nature of the solution is examined to see how it depends on various behavioral parameters. Thursby and Jensen (1983), for example, have examined how the outcome depends on the conjectural variations of the players—that is, the extent to which each government expects that its own trade intervention will be retaliated against. They find that the greater is the perceived likelihood of retaliation, the closer will the solution lie to free trade. This suggests that although trade intervention itself is harmful, it may be quite desirable that countries expect intervention by other countries in response to intervention they themselves may undertake. A country that is known to be ideologically committed to free trade at all costs may actually contribute to a world in which there is greater trade intervention.

A similar conclusion emerges from another strand of literature that is only now beginning to be recognized by trade theorists. Axelrod (1983) has examined repeated Prisoners' Dilemma games, pitting various strategies against one another in computer simulations. He finds that the tit-for-tat strategy, in which a player acts exploitatively only in response to exploitative action by its opponent on a single preceding play of the game, tends to dominate other strategies as a means of winning the game. Translated to the trade context, this too seems to suggest that some regular policy of intervening temporarily whenever one's trading partner intervenes may be desirable. This is precisely the use of the countervailing duty that we have alluded.

Alternatively one could attempt to pursue negotiated solutions to games of this sort. Such negotiations, however, pose the well-known problem of enforcing whatever agreement is reached. On the other hand, the incentives to enter into such negotiations are strong, even if one has no intention of abiding by their outcome. It is therefore not surprising that the trade policy community has managed to keep such negotiations going during a large part of post–World War II history.

Much work needs to be done to find solutions to these problems, both in the abstract context of game theory and in adapting any solutions that are found to international trade and policy. International trade policy poses some especially difficult problems here for a number of reasons. Trade policy, even if conducted bilaterally, is a multilateral issue. One cannot neglect the effects, positive or negative, that policies between two countries will have on others. Trade policy can assume a multitude of forms. Negotiations that cover only some of these forms may be severely limited if they merely lead to other and perhaps more pernicious forms of trade intervention. Even within a country, trade policy affects a multitude of individuals in many different ways. The players in trade policy may therefore find themselves being drawn toward different and often conflicting objectives. And finally trade policies and other trade-related domestic policies may be used for a variety of legitimate objectives that have nothing to do with exploiting other countries. Thus for policymakers in their negotiations and in their responses to policies abroad, to disentangle exploitative foreign policies from legitimate ones may be next to impossible.

2.3.6 Trade Intervention for Foreign Policy Reasons

The strategic uses of trade intervention that we just discussed were focused specifically on influencing analogous policies abroad. But trade intervention is sometimes also used as a means of influencing foreign policies that have nothing to do with trade. Because countries depend on and gain from trade, policies that interfere with trade can serve as weapons and can be used for a variety of aims. Still, one must ask whether trade intervention can succeed in changing foreign country policies and, if so, whether it is worth the cost.

To take the second issue first, trade as a political weapon makes sense only if it is capable of inflicting relatively a lot of harm abroad compared to any disruption it causes at home. For too small a country this would clearly not be the case, but for a large country like the United States, it does seem likely that we could do rather severe damage to at least some of our smaller trading partners at relatively little obvious cost to ourselves. Indeed if we have nobly refrained until now from levying an optimal tariff or using some other form of exploitative trade intervention, then we might actually be able to harm others while benefiting ourselves by doing so now. Thus there does appear to be some scope for trade policies in large countries to be sufficiently damaging to others to make them potentially useful as instruments of foreign policy.

One must be careful, however, even here. Markets often work far better than anyone expects.[25] Even the United States might find that long-run effects of its policies will go against it in ways that would be hard to predict. When foreign markets and foreign suppliers are lost to us, either because we accidentally hurt them more than intended or because they look elsewhere for a more certain trading environment, our claim that we were only manipulating trade to promote the general welfare will fall on deaf ears.

Finally, there is real doubt in our minds that even draconian trade policies such as embargoes can ever be very effective in changing the behavior of foreign governments and their constituencies. Trade can have powerful effects. But when used as a weapon, it seems more likely to generate resistance, rather than fear, in the hearts of its victims. The world's considerable experience with the use of embargoes does not suggest to us that they have been very successful in drawing concessions from those they were intended to influence.

On the other hand, it is conceivable that trade policy might be more successful in influencing policies abroad if it were oriented toward providing positive rather than negative incentives. As an example, Salant (1984) suggests an ingenious use of a subsidy on exports of drilling equipment to the Soviet Union. In his model such a subsidy induces the Soviets to procure more of their oil at home rather than using military intervention for that purpose in the Middle East. His proposal may not be appropriate for actual conditions in the oil market and in the Eastern bloc, but the idea of using trade policy to provide positive rather than negative incentives in the political sphere strikes us as one that may be worth pursuing.

2.3.7 Trade Intervention for Domestic Political Reasons

In actuality most trade intervention is not intended to benefit the intervening country as a whole but only particular groups within the country whose interests are most clearly affected by trade and whose political influence is great enough to make itself felt in the formation of policy. This has led to a number of attempts in recent years to explain the formation of trade policy in terms of the interests of those who benefit from it and the political power they represent.[26]

Particular interests within a country can benefit from protection applied to their own activities.[27] These interests include most obviously firms in import-competing industries. But protection may also be sought by unions in these industries and by members of other industries that supply inputs to them or otherwise depend on them for their own economic well-being.[28] All of these groups can be viewed as demanders of protection. They make their demands felt by voting, lobbying, and otherwise using their resources to influence the political process.

The suppliers of protection are the government officials and legislators who have the power, variously circumscribed, to enact protective legislation, implement protective regulations, and negotiate trade concessions with other governments. They are restrained from yielding to demands for protection by the opposing political forces of those who stand to benefit from trade, by the fact that any political action entails a political cost, and also, one hopes, by the desire to represent the interests of society as a whole. Thus these policymakers yield to the demands for protection only if these demands are argued sufficiently forcefully and with sufficient use of resources, and a balance is struck in which the actual level of protection is determined. This level depends positively on the resources expended by the demanders of protection and negatively on the costs to the trade policy decision makers of yielding to those demands.

For our purposes, one thing that is interesting about this view of trade policy formation is that it seems explicitly to reject as irrelevant all of the arguments that we have discussed so far. It seems not to matter whether trade intervention is desirable. It only matters whether sufficiently powerful special interest groups benefit from trade intervention or its absence. This conclusion is too harsh, however. Government policymakers can and do seek to act in the national interest. Their view of where the national interest lies provides an important determinant of their willingness to supply protection. Thus arguments such as those about the relative merits of trade intervention can influence policy. But they must be balanced against opposing political forces. Neither the special interests nor the national interest, whatever that may be, will ever be the sole determinant of international trade policy.

This political view does, however, suggest one additional reason why trade intervention might be in the national interest. Given that political forces will lead to some intervention anyway, policymakers might be able to minimize the harm done by that intervention by selecting comparatively mild intervention policies and implementing them before the demands for protection become so strong as to require more drastic measures. Thus the point is to use trade policies that will distort only a little in order to avoid using policies that will distort a lot.[29]

This is surely a valid argument. Unfortunately it is often used to defend policies that are more harmful than the alternatives rather than less. The case in point is the increasing use of VERs by the United States and others on the grounds of resisting protectionist pressures in lieu of supposedly more drastic measures such as import quotas and tariffs. For a variety of reasons VERs are the worst of these three alternatives rather than the best when viewed from the national interest. VERs are quantitative restrictions, and, like quotas, they limit the market's ability to adapt to changing conditions much more than would a tariff. Further, by protecting domestic producers from price competition, both VERs and quotas enhance their market power and permit greater monopolistic distortion of the domestic market. Finally, VERs, unlike tariffs and quotas, are implemented by the foreign exporters. Whatever revenues or increased profits arise because of the restrictions are therefore likely to be captured by foreigners rather than by domestic residents or the domestic government. For all of these reasons, a strong case can be made that equivalent restriction of trade could be achieved at less cost to domestic welfare by simply levying a tariff.[30]

There are two likely reasons why policymakers have shown a preference for VERs over quotas and tariffs, aside from the fact that the economic differences among policies have apparently not always been well understood. The first is that the legal institutions of trade policy, both within the United States and internationally in the GATT, have severely constrained the use of tariffs and to a lesser extent quotas. VERs, on the other hand, have an unclear legal status especially in importing countries, and it appears therefore that their use is unconstrained. Policymakers may perhaps be forgiven for interpreting these institutional circumstances as indicating that VERs are less onerous than other trade restrictions.

The second reason for the popularity of VERs is that the very features that distinguish them from other policies also make them more attractive to those whose interests must be accommodated by trade policy. Domestic producers stand to benefit more from VERs than from tariffs since VERs enhance their domestic market power. Foreign producers too should prefer VERs to both alternatives since they are at least permitted to keep for themselves the higher prices for the limited quantities they are allowed to sell. Indeed the administration of a VER may well accomplish what foreign producers would like to have done on their own but could not: restriction of their collective sales and prevention of new entrants, both of which raise their monopoly profits. Thus it is not surprising that these arrangements are often negotiated with comparative ease.

All of this suggests that some trade intervention may indeed be defended as averting further and more drastic intervention. But the intervention called for is not the kind that is most often justified and used for this purpose. Instead it may be argued that a certain amount of protection in the form of tariffs may be desirable after all.[31] A moderate level of tariffs might placate protectionist interests without conceding them the use of policies that would benefit them more and the rest of us less.

2.4 Conclusions

Our purpose here has been twofold. First, we wanted to provide some factual material relating to global trade, the trade of the major industrialized countries, and recent changes in protectionism. In this connection, the following points deserve emphasis.

1. After many years of continuous and rapid growth in the period following World War II, expansion of world trade slowed considerably beginning in the mid-1970s and actually declined in 1982 due to the worldwide recession in the major industrial and developing countries. The ensuing economic recovery and expansion have been uneven among the major countries, and there has been a notable increase in protectionist pressures and actual protection in recent years, especially in the United States and EC.

2. The commodity and sectoral composition of net exports of merchandise and services for the United States and other major countries is broadly reflective of the factors that determine comparative advantage. In the case of the United States, the important factors include the relative abundance of land, certain other natural resources, human and physical capital, and the availability of advanced technology.

3. The major countries and regions of the world are involved in a network of multilateral trade relations, which reflects national differences in comparative advantage and policy. It may be inappropriate therefore to focus attention on bilateral trade imbalances, as, for example, between Japan and the United States and EC.

4. The rapid and sizable appreciation of the U.S. dollar since 1980 has resulted in a significant deficit on U.S. merchandise trade, compounding the structural adjustment problems being experienced in many import-competing sectors in the United States.

5. It is widely acknowledged that there has been an increase in protectionist sentiment or attitudes in the United States and elsewhere since the mid-1970s. In the United States this has been manifested especially in the number of countervailing and antidumping actions filed under U.S. trade law. Such actions may increase the uncertainty facing foreign exporters and add to their costs. The available procedures in the United States may also be used for tactical reasons by particular industries (such as steel) to overload the system and to bring added pressure on the executive branch to seek political solutions to trade complaints.

6. There was a noticeable increase in the extent of NTBs maintained by the major industrial countries between 1981 and 1983. The new restrictions were applied especially on products with large trade flows (such as iron and steel,

electronic products, and vehicles), which were produced and traded primarily among the industrial countries themselves.

Our second purpose was to review the case for free trade and the various arguments for trade intervention that may arise when one or more of the assumptions of the model of free trade do not hold. Several points emerged in our discussion.

1. In a world of perfect competition and no distortions, free trade will result in an optimal allocation of resources and maximization of consumer welfare, subject to compensating individuals whose welfare might be reduced if trade were free. Trade intervention has a double distortionary effect because it leads, first, to a misallocation of productive resources and, second, to a welfare-reducing diversion of consumer expenditure. This is true of interventions that expand trade and those that contract trade, it being just as distortionary to promote trade artificially as to restrict it.

2. If a nation has monopoly power in trade, it can impose an optimal tariff to improve its terms of trade. This is an exploitative policy in that it benefits the country at the expense of the rest of the world. Thus it may lead to retaliation, in which case all countries are likely to lose.

3. Trade intervention may be used to offset domestic distortions; however, trade intervention is only second best for this purpose and may not be desirable at all since it adds a second distortion that may outweigh any benefits of offsetting the initial distortion. A domestic tax-subsidy targeted on the domestic distortion is optimal or first best.

4. If markets are imperfectly competitive, opening them to free trade is likely to increase competition and be beneficial. If competition continues to be imperfect even with free trade, trade intervention is still likely to be only second best as a means of dealing with other domestic distortions.

5. With imperfect competition in world markets, trade intervention may have the additional capability of appropriating a larger share of monopoly profits for a country's firms or government. Such profit-seeking intervention is another example of exploitative intervention and, like the optimal tariff, is subject to retaliation.

6. If world markets are oligopolistic, trade intervention may be used as a means of precommitting a country's firms to follow strategies that would otherwise not appear to be in their interest. This can alter the outcome of oligopolistic competition in the firms' and the country's favor under certain assumptions about behavior in these markets. This too is exploitative intervention and is subject to retaliation.

7. Countervailing trade intervention, if intended to offset the effects of policies abroad, has limited justification, since under perfect competition, the

benefits it generates are independent of the foreign intervention being coun-
tervailed. Recent work suggests, however, that this may not be the case with
imperfect competition.

8. Strategic trade intervention, consisting of the use of any of several
exploitative trade policies in order to preempt or discourage other countries
from doing the same, poses for trade policy the classic problem of the Prisoners' Dilemma. Work on this problem suggests the desirability of being
committed to retaliation.

9. Trade intervention as a tool to achieve foreign political objectives is likely
to be ineffective if used primarily as a negative incentive since it often leads to
resistance by those it intends to influence.

10. Trade intervention may be a result of a political process in which various
interest groups make their demands felt through lobbying and other means of
influencing government officials. If these officials also attempt to pursue the
national interest as they perceive it, the resulting trade policies will strike a
balance between special interests and those of the nation as a whole. Arguments for and against trade intervention can influence policy by altering
policymakers' perception of the national interest.

11. Mild forms of trade intervention may be desirable as a means of
satisfying domestic political forces that would otherwise lead to more costly
forms of intervention. VERs have been justified on these grounds in preference
to import quotas and tariffs, but in fact VERs may be the worst of the available
alternatives.

12. A strong case can be made for using tariffs as the preferred policy for
intervention, but the tariff alternative is unfortunately constrained by the
national and international legal institutions of trade policy.

Notes

1. As noted in GATT (1984, pp. 191–192), the existence of floating exchange rates
creates some difficulty in converting transactions values from foreign currencies to
domestic currency and in converting national trade data to a single reference unit.
Because of the dollar appreciation since 1980, the unit value indexes of world exports
show a decline. When the special drawing right (SDR) is used as the reference unit, the
indexes behave similarly but are less affected by the dollar appreciation.

2. For a disaggregated, multicountry computational analysis of how exchange rate
changes can affect trade and employment in the United States and the other major
industrialized countries, see Deardorff and Stern (1985b).

3. The discussion in this section is based in part on Stern (1985b).

4. For a treatment of current issues and problems involving trade and foreign direct
investment in goods and service industries in the context of U.S.-Canadian bilateral and
global relations, see Stern (1982, 1985a) and Fretz, Stern, and Whalley (1985).

5. See Deardorff and Stern (1985a) for an analysis of alternative methods of measuring the effects of NTBs.

6. They consider five major types of NTBs that impinge directly on imports at national borders: (1) measures increasing the landed price of imports (tariff quotas, seasonal tariffs); (2) measures for enforcement of decreed prices (variable levies, minimum price systems, voluntary export price restraints); (3) quantitative import restrictions (prohibitions, quotas, discretionary import authorizations); (4) voluntary export restraints; and (5) other import management measures (price-volume surveillance, antidumping and countervailing duties).

7. Nogues, Olechowski, and Winters also calculate unweighted frequency measures of NTBs as well as measures using world imports as weights. These produce different levels as compared to using own-country imports as weights, but all three measures are similar qualitatively.

8. Separate calculations suggest that major borrowing developing countries are strongly affected by NTBs. Also, the NICs apparently have higher coverage ratios than developing countries on average. Finally, Nogues, Olechowski, and Winters show that of all the NTBs considered, VERs have a predominant impact on the coverage ratios for manufactures with respect to the developing countries especially.

9. A similar conclusion is reached in Balassa and Balassa (1984) and in USTR (1984, esp. pp. 53–58 and 119–125). Bergsten and Cline (1983, esp. pp. 70–72) consider the path of NTB protection in the United States from 1967 to 1982. They note that import quotas on steel, oil, meat, and sugar were phased out after 1974, and restrictions on television sets and footwear were lifted after 1981. After 1980, however, protection was increased in automobiles, textiles, sugar, and steel. They conclude (p. 72): "Overall, the trend in protection over the last several years has been at best ambiguous, and more probably toward intensification. . . . Nonetheless, it would appear that the pressures for protection since the mid-1970s have increased relatively more than has actual protection."

10. See the classic contribution of Samuelson (1939) and abundant other literature surveyed in Corden (1984a).

11. The need for such compensation has been well understood throughout the development of the theoretical case for free trade by Samuelson (1939) and others. It is only in the less formal context of debate over particular trade policies that this need is often forgotten.

12. This can be illustrated in figure 2.1 by reversing p_w and p_1 and letting the now lower p_1 represent the effect of an import subsidy that raises imports from Q_2 to Q_3. The welfare effects would be analogous to removing a tariff, except that the cost of the subsidy to the government would now include triangles b, c, f, and g, as well as the rectangle $d + e$.

13. See, for example, Bhagwati (1967, pp. 11–12).

14. Estimates of optimal tariffs for industrialized countries have been calculated using a computable general equilibrium model by Hamilton and Whalley (1983). Their results are surprisingly large. Brown (1985) has pointed out that this is due to their use of the Armington assumption that all products are differentiated by country of origin. This

assumption in effect gives each country a 100 percent share of the market for what it exports.

15. The outcome that all lose is not inevitable in the optimal tariff and retaliation situation, as shown by Johnson (1954). For more on this subject, see Thursby and Jensen (1983).

16. One recent theoretical development should be mentioned since it bears a resemblance to the optimal tariff argument though it involves the use of an export subsidy. In a model with trade in more than two goods, Feenstra (1986) has shown that optimal use of trade policy to manipulate world prices need not lead exclusively to tariffs. In certain circumstances an export subsidy can be desirable if it causes price changes in other markets that benefit the country. Salant (1984) has presented a simple example of this in which a country exports two goods in exchange for a third. The two goods are perfect complements in foreign demand, and one is supplied infinitely elastically while the other is available only in fixed supply. For the particular preferences assumed by Salant, he shows that a subsidy on the export of the elastically supplied good, by raising demand for the other export, can cause the price of the latter to rise sufficiently to make the country better off. This idea is intriguing, and it certainly complicates the interaction among governments that may occur as they try strategically to manipulate the terms on which they trade, but it otherwise shares the same properties as the traditional optimal tariff argument.

17. See Bhagwati (1971) and Corden (1984a) for quite general treatments of this topic.

18. Empirical studies of trade intervention do not always address the costs of the intervention itself and the benefits that it might provide in offsetting distortions, though it is not uncommon to measure benefits in terms of jobs saved or earnings of workers. Our impression from this literature is that trade intervention is seldom warranted on cost-benefit grounds. See, for example, Morkre and Tarr (1980), Tarr and Morkre (1984), and Crandall (1984) for cost-benefit studies of particular cases of trade intervention in the U.S.

19. See Jones and Corden (1976) for an analysis of how exchange rates may operate in a model with a nontraded good.

20. This idea can be stated as a theorem analogous to the usual gains from trade result in a small country. If a country is a price taker on world markets for all goods, then there must be gains from free trade, for if the country is a price taker on all world markets, every individual in the country will be too, once trade is free, and competition will therefore be perfect regardless of how imperfect it may have been initially. Thus free trade adds together the benefits of moving to perfect competition with the classical benefits, under perfect competition, of moving to free trade. Unfortunately this result is not as useful as it sounds since it requires that the country be a price taker on all markets, ruling out nontraded goods and even nontraded factors.

21. If the demand curve changes slope as well as position, then the shift of the marginal revenue curve is uncertain.

22. See, for example, Brander and Spencer (1981) and Spencer and Brander (1983). Excellent critical reviews of this literature are also available in Dixit (1984) and Grossman and Richardson (1985).

23. Though interestingly the third country, which imports the good, gains from the intervention in this case.

24. One should be sure, of course, that the foreign country's policies are in fact causing, not correcting, a distortion. This is especially important in responding to the domestic policies of foreign countries that may be their first-best means of dealing with domestic distortions.

25. Baldwin (1982) has provided an excellent discussion of reasons why trade policy in particular may be less effective than expected.

26. Models of this sort have been surveyed in Baldwin (1984).

27. This is certainly true. On the other hand, Mayer and Riezman (1985) have argued that even the interest of particular factors and/or industries could be better served by direct subsidies, much as in the second-best discussion above. Thus one cannot explain trade intervention per se in terms of the political power of these special interests alone. Something else must be keeping them from lobbying for their first-best policy.

28. See Deardorff and Stern (1979) for a discussion of the various channels through which individuals may find their interests tied positively or negatively to trade.

29. In a slightly different vein, Rodrik (1986) has pointed out that trade intervention might even be preferable to domestic policies if the equilibrium that will be struck between policymakers and special interests turns out to imply a sufficiently smaller dose of trade policy than of domestic policy.

30. Some would argue, on the other hand, that VERs have the advantage of being easier to remove than tariffs. The evidence on this, however, is at best ambiguous. Another argument in their favor is that VERs, by securing the cooperation of foreign governments, are less likely to induce retaliation than are tariffs. This is true, but if tariffs were used primarily for defensive purposes, as in a safeguard action, then retaliation should not be a problem anyway.

31. Cooper (1983, p. 738) has suggested that if we cannot make progress in truly liberalizing trade, then it might be desirable to "impose a uniform minimum tariff of 5 percent or even 10 percent and treat this tariff as the basic protection that domestic economic activity would have from the actions of foreign firms and governments." The hope is that one could then require a "very heavy burden of proof" before providing additional protection of any kind to anyone.

References

Axelrod, Robert. *The Evolution of Cooperation*. New York: Basic Books, 1983.

Baldwin, Robert E. "The Inefficacy of Trade Policy." Essays in International Finance, no. 150. Princeton: Princeton University Press, 1982.

Baldwin, Robert E. "Trade Policies in Developed Countries." In Ronald Jones and Peter Kenen, eds., *Handbook of International Economics*. Vol. 1. New York: North-Holland, 1984.

Balassa, Bela, and Carol Balassa. "Industrial Protection in the Developed Countries." *World Economy* 7 (1984): 179–196.

Bergsten, C. Fred, and William R. Cline. "Trade Policy in the 1980s: An Overview." In William R. Cline, ed., *Trade Policy in the 1980s*. Cambridge: MIT Press, 1983.

Bhagwati, Jagdish. "The Theory and Practice of Commercial Policy: Departures from Unified Exchange Rates." Special Papers in International Economics, no. 8. Princeton: Princeton University Press, 1967.

Bhagwati, Jagdish. "The Generalized Theory of Distortions and Welfare." In Jagdish Bhagwati, Robert Mundell, Ronald Jones, and Jaroslav Vanek, eds., *Trade, Balance of Payments and Growth: Papers in International Economics in Honor of Charles P. Kindleberger*. Amsterdam: North-Holland, 1971.

Brander, James, and Barbara Spencer. "Tariffs and the Extraction of Foreign Monopoly Rents under Potential Entry." *Canadian Journal of Economics* 14 (1981): 371–389.

Brander, James, and Barbara Spencer. "Export Subsidies and International Market Share Rivalry." *Journal of International Economics* 18 (1985): 82–100.

Brown, Drusilla. "A Theoretical and Computational Evaluation of Commercial Policies in a Model in Which Imports Are Disaggregated by Place of Production." in process, 1985.

Cooper, Richard N. "Toward a Policy Synthesis: Panel Discussion." In William R. Cline, ed., *Trade Policy in the 1980s*. Cambridge: MIT Press, 1983.

Corden, W. Max. "The Normative Theory of International Trade." In Ronald Jones and Peter Kenen, eds., *Handbook of International Economics*. Vol. 1. New York: North-Holland, 1984a.

Corden, W. Max. "The Revival of Protectionism." Occasional Papers 14. New York: Group of Thirty, 1984b.

Crandall, Robert W. "Import Quotas and the Automobile Industry: The Costs of Protectionism." *Brookings Review* 2 (1984): 8–16.

Deardorff, Alan V., and Robert M. Stern. "American Labor's Stake in International Trade." In Walter Adams et al., *Tariffs, Quotas and Trade: The Politics of Protectionism*. San Francisco: Institute of Contemporary Studies, 1979.

Deardorff, Alan V., and Robert M. Stern. "Methods of Measurement of NTBs." United Nations Conference on Trade and Development, UNCTAD/ST/MD/28. Geneva: United Nations, 1985a.

Deardorff, Alan V., and Robert M. Stern. "The Effects of Exchange-Rate Changes on Domestic Prices, Trade, and Employment in the U.S., European Community, and Japan." In Douglas Hague and Karl Jungenfelt, eds., *Structural Adjustment in Developed Open Economies*. London: Macmillan, 1985b.

Dixit, Avinash. "International Trade Policy for Oligopolistic Industries." *Economic Journal*, supplement 94 (1984): 1–16.

Eaton, Jonathan, and Gene M. Grossman. "Optimal Trade and Industrial Policy under Oligopoly." 1983.

Feenstra, Robert. "Trade Policy with Several Goods and Market Linkages." *Journal of International Economics*. Forthcoming, 1986.

Fretz, Deborah, Robert M. Stern, and John Whalley, eds. *Canada/United States Trade and Investment Issues*. Toronto: Ontario Economic Council, 1985.

General Agreement on Tariffs and Trade (GATT). *International Trade 1983/84*. Geneva: GATT, 1984.

Grossman, Gene M., and J. David Richardson. "Strategic U.S. Trade Policy: A Survey of Issues and Early Analysis." Special Papers in International Economics, no. 15, Princeton: Princeton University Press, 1985.

Hamilton, Bob, and John Whalley. "Optimal Tariff Calculations in Alternative Trade Models and Some Possible Implications for Current World Trading Arrangements." *Journal of International Economics* 15 (1983): 323–348.

Jackson, John H. *Trade Action Inventory*. 1985.

Johnson, Harry G. "Optimum Tariffs and Retaliation." *Review of Economic Studies* 21 (1954): 142–153.

Jones, Ronald, and W. Max Corden. "Devaluation, Non-Flexible Prices, and the Trade Balance for a Small Country." *Canadian Journal of Economics* 9 (1976): 150–161.

Mayer, Wolfgang, and Raymond Riezman. "Endogenous Choice of Trade Policy Instruments." In process, 1985.

Morkre, Morris E., and David G. Tarr. *The Effects of Restrictions on United States Imports: Five Case Studies and Theory*. Washington, D.C.: Federal Trade Commission, 1980.

Nogues, Julio J., Andrzej Olechowski, and L. Alan Winters. "The Extent of Non-Tariff Barriers to Industrial Countries' Imports." Discussion Paper, Report DRD 115. World Bank, 1985.

Rodrik, Dani. "Tariffs, Subsidies, and Welfare with Endogenous Policy." *Journal of International Economics*. Forthcoming, 1986.

Salant, Stephen W. "Export Subsidies as Instruments of Economic and Foreign Policy." Note N-2120-USDP. Rand, 1984.

Samuelson, Paul A. "The Gains from International Trade." *Canadian Journal of Economics and Political Science* 5 (1939): 195–205.

Spencer, Barbara, and James Brander. "International R&D Rivalry and Industrial Strategy." *Review of Economic Studies* 50 (1983): 707–722.

Stern, Robert M. ed. *Proceedings of the First Annual Workshop on U.S.-Canadian Relations*. Ann Arbor: Institute of Public Policy Studies, 1982.

Stern, Robert M. "Global Dimensions and Determinants of International Trade and Investment in Services." In Robert M. Stern, ed., *Trade and Investment in Services: Canada/U.S. Perspectives*. Toronto: University of Toronto Press, 1985a.

Stern, Robert M., ed. *Trade and Investment in Services: Canada/U.S. Perspectives*. Toronto: University of Toronto Press, 1985b.

Tarr, David G., and Morris E. Morkre. *Aggregate Costs to the United States of Tariffs and Quotas on Imports: General Tariff Cuts and Removal of Quotas on Automobiles, Steel, Sugar, and Textiles.* Washington, D.C.: Federal Trade Commission, 1984.

Thursby, Marie, and Richard Jensen. "A Conjectural Variation Approach to Strategic Tariff Equilibria." *Journal of International Economics* 14 (1983): 145–161.

U.S. Office of the U.S. Trade Representative. *Annual Report of the President of the United States on the Trade Agreements Program, 1983.* Washington, D.C.: Government Printing Office, 1984.

Comment on "Current Issues in Trade Policy"

Ronald W. Jones

Deardorff and Stern seem less concerned with the details of the recent drift toward protection in U.S. commercial policy than with the burgeoning theoretical literature discussing normative and positive aspects of tariffs and quotas. As a theorist I find this emphasis unobjectionable. As well I tend to agree with what I consider is a basic proposition they advance: many of the traditional arguments concerning protection in a competitive world survive, albeit somewhat altered, in a trade setting characterized by elements of imperfect competition. Nonetheless there are differences that perhaps merit more explicit attention than they give.

The basic concession to protectionist sentiments that economists are likely to make when private markets are perfectly competitive is that countries large enough to influence world prices may gain by levying an optimal tariff. In addition, in the event that domestic distortions exist, impediments to trade may be rationalized, although they often prove second best compared with direct measures aimed at countering the distortions. The optimal-tariff argument casts the government in the role of being aware that prices paid and received for the items that a country trades may depend on the volume of such trade and thus imposing tariffs or quotas so that competitive price-taking firms and consumers alter their choices and obtain better prices. The government thus behaves as a monopolist or monopsonist, although private firms do not. Deardorff and Stern are at pains to point out that some of the recent arguments supporting protection, such as the concept of profit-seeking intervention when markets are imperfect, are basically optimal-tariff arguments in disguise.

If producers operate in a setting of imperfect competition, can they be expected to behave in their trading relationships much like the government levying an optimal tariff when firms are competitive? The hallmark of monopolistic behavior is awareness that decisions made concerning sales have an effect on market price. To ascertain the extent to which private maximizing behavior is a substitute for traditional government policy, suppose that a country's export sector comprises a single monopolist. Furthermore, to replicate the traditional setting of the optimal-tariff argument, let the rest of the world be competitive and passive, so that the home monopolist faces a downward-sloping net demand curve for its product.

Simple monopoly behavior cannot imitate the optimal tariff unless it can charge different prices in different countries. The optimal tariff implies discrimination between home and foreign markets, and the private monopolist may have no way of keeping these markets separate. There is no obvious private analog to the customs inspector. Overruling these objections, even in the case that the home export firm is a discriminating monopolist, there is no guarantee that it will charge a higher price abroad for its exports than it does in the home market. Price differentials for the discriminating monopolist depend sensitively on the difference between demand elasticities in various markets. Some of the recent literature stresses that a home monopolist may well face a more elastic demand response abroad, in which case foreign price might be lower than home price—the analog of an export subsidy, which is not typically an optimal instrument of commercial policy in the competitive setting. If the monopolist cannot discriminate among markets, the gains to home country residents (including the monopolist) may not be as great as under an optimal tariff.

Optimizing behavior on the part of a private monopolist also differs from the behavior of a government's levying an optimal tariff in that the private firm is solely interested in its own profits, not the real income of the community. An example of the consequences of such a difference is provided by Berglas and Jones (1977) in their discussion of a multinational firm headquartered at home and capable of locating some of its capital (and technology) abroad at a higher rate of return (it could successfully discriminate). Such a multinational could well export more capital than would be in the home country's interest since it would not be concerned with the deleterious effect of such transfer on wage rates at home. In general, if the government is levying an optimal tax or tariff, a further small increase leaves aggregate home real incomes unchanged. But if it alters the distribution of income among home claimants, the optimal rate for any subgroup would be different from that for the aggregate.

In discussing the optimum tariff argument, Deardorff and Stern underscore the possible retaliation that any country faces when using aggressive commercial policy. To the extent that the private sector can succeed in manipulating prices to the home country's advantage, such action might avoid official retaliation abroad. Alternatively governments may be bound by tariff agreements so that home monopolistic behavior may be a useful substitute in getting some of the gains associated with the optimal tariff.

A free trade equilibrium in which elements of imperfect competition exist is one in which private profits appear, a spread between price and cost that is absent in free trade equilibria when competition is perfect. As the authors point out, these profits seem to suggest a new role for government intervention: profit seeking (shades of rent seeking or revenue seeking). They continue, however, that seeking such profits is in reality trying to obtain better prices, an argument that finds its analogy in the traditional competitive literature. I am tempted to put the point more strongly. If we focus on autarky comparisons instead of free trade, potential profits abound, even with competition ruling in each country's markets. Government taxes on trade and factor flows are instruments whereby particular countries can attempt to grab for themselves at least some of the spread between autarky prices. The logic of the optimal tariff argument in a setting in which one country is active and all others passive is not that the active country should try to get the lowest price for its imports. Instead optimal strategy balances the benefits from a low price with the costs of forgoing purchases when home value (price) exceeds costs (foreign price). The concept that governments might intervene in trade in order to capture monopoly profits is a variation on an old argument.

The power to tax coupled with the existence of factor inputs that possess international markets sets the stage for governmental rivalry of a form not matched in private markets. Suppose a country with a slight competitive disadvantage offers tax concessions or subsidies to attract production of a commodity it would otherwise import. Such a policy has little merit if it results only in production levels matching local demand. But if an export base is established, the commonly held convention whereby host countries have first rights at taxing incomes and profits suggests that net tax revenues could be substantial for countries willing to bid for such footloose factors. Models allowing trade among many countries emphasize the potential gains from such tax rivalry.

There are limits to the argument that trade policy in an imperfectly competitive setting involves little that differs from that in a competitive world. Thus Deardorff and Stern point at the outset to the extra potential gains that trade introduces if in autarky domestic markets are highly imperfect. Earlier Caves (1974) explicitly focused on two additional ways in which the effect of trade differs when there is imperfect competition: trade may actually increase a country's production of importables (by lessening local monopoly power) and/or force a reduction in the price of exportables (if that sector is monopolized).

In conclusion I find little with which to quarrel or comment concerning the Deardorff-Stern remarks on the second-best nature of arguments for protection, regardless of the state of local competition. The vision they conjure of a fork as a second-best instrument for acupuncture will long remain. The spirit of second best is somewhat ironically reflected in their concluding paragraph in which they support tariffs as a preferred device to VERs and quotas if a country must protect. Negotiated tariff reductions of the Kennedy and Tokyo rounds perhaps proved counter productive in that now "the tariff alternative is unfortunately constrained by the national and international legal institutions of trade policy." In second-best theory it often pays to raise some forms of taxation to balance others more stubbornly in place.

References

Berglas, Eitan, and Ronald W. Jones. "The Export of Technology." In K. Brunner and A. Meltzer, eds., *Optimal Policies, Control Theory and Technology Exports*. Amsterdam: North-Holland, 1977.

Caves, Richard. "International Trade, International Investment, and Imperfect Markets." Special Papers in International Economics, no. 10. Princeton: Princeton University Press, 1974.

Comment on ''Current Issues in Trade Policy''

Ronald Findlay

Deardorff and Stern have written an excellent survey of the theory and practice of commercial policy as it stands today, against the background of long-term trends in the volume and pattern of world trade and recent protectionist threats. I agree with their analysis, judgment, and sentiments regarding the issues to such an extent that I am unable, despite diligent search, to find any bone of contention. Deardorff and Stern have also provided a succinct summary of their work, so I am precluded from even that humble role.

The most useful thing I can do, in the light of my own recent interests, is to expand on their brief discussion of trade intervention for domestic political reasons. The implicit model that the authors use can perhaps be described more formally in terms of figure 1. It is a demand and supply model in which the level of protection is the commodity considered as a function of the price that the recipient industry (or associated factors of production) is prepared to pay, on the demand side, and the dispensing authorities (politicians or bureaucrats) receive on the supply side. The loss to consumers, and to non-import-competing industries, is a cost in terms of goodwill to the politician-bureaucrats and is what determines the amount of protection they are willing to supply at each price. Equilibrium is best thought of as resulting from a Marshallian, rather than Walrasian, process. Given an arbitrary level of protection, it will rise or fall over time depending on whether the demand price exceeds the supply price, or vice-versa. Changes in exogenous data, such as technological progress or underlying political variables, would shift either or both of the curves and thus lead to new levels of protection and the associated implicit price.

Suppose there is a shock such as a sharp improvement in the terms of trade. With a given level of protection, this will result in a contraction of the import-competing industry, with associated reduction of real income and perhaps unemployment. Feelings of altruism and solidarity on the part of the general public may reduce the cost of protection in political terms, thus resulting in a

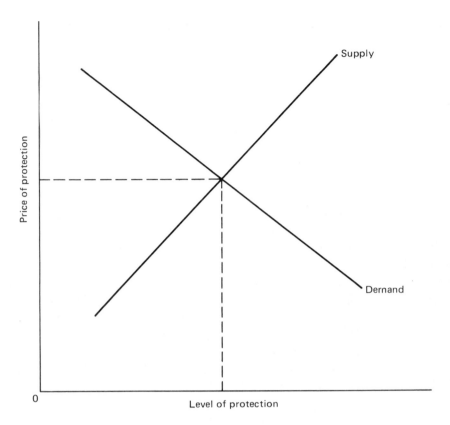

Figure 1
Demand and supply of protection.

shift of the supply curve to the right. At the same time the loss of real income to the import-competing industry may make it more willing to seek protection by incurring further lobbying costs, thus shifting the demand curve to the right. Both shifts therefore result in a higher level of protection triggered by the cheapening of imports.

A more explicit model of an endogenous tariff is provided in Findlay and Wellisz (1982), drawing on earlier contributions by Tullock (1967) and Brock and Magee (1978). The tariff-determination process is embedded in a Ricardo-Viner general equilibrium model, with two outputs and three inputs, capital and land, each specific to one of the sectors and labor, which is perfectly mobile between the two. Each of the specific factors behaves atomistically in the goods and factor markets but acts collectively in the political sphere. The political system is a black box that is, however, responsive, in a systematic fashion, to economic pressures from the interest groups. We postulate a tariff formation function

$$t = F(L_K, L_T) \quad \text{with} \quad \partial F/\partial L_K > 0, \partial F/\partial L_T < 0$$

where L_K and L_T are the political inputs deployed by capital (which is protariff) and land (which is antitariff). This adds one equation and three unknowns to the general equilibrium system. The two additional equations are provided by the optimizing behavior of each of the interest groups that determines L_K (or L_T) for any choice by the other party of L_T (or L_K). Thus we get reaction functions for each group and a Cournot-Nash equilibrium for the three-equation political subsystem to determine the equilibrium levels t^*, L_K^*, and L_T^* of the tariff and the lobbying inputs of each interest group. Subtraction of $(L_K^* + L_T^*)$ from the fixed labor endowment determines the labor available for goods production, and t^* determines the domestic price ratio as $(1 + t^*)\bar{p}$ where $\bar{p}$ is the exogenous international terms of trade. Factor prices, output levels, and resource allocation are simultaneously determined as well in the Walrasian competitive economic subsystem adjoined to the cournot-Nash equilibrium of the political subsystem.

The determinants of the degree of protection in this model are therefore the exogenous political and ideological circumstances subsumed in the form of the tariff formation function and the endogenously determined lobbying inputs of the two factions, which depend in turn on such factors as the cohesion and organization of each of these interest groups. The more prevalent a free trade ideology is on the part of the government and public opinion in general, the more difficult will be the task of the protariff faction and the easier that of the antitariff faction. The cost of protection in this model is not simply the misallocation of given resources due to the deviation of domestic from world prices but also, and perhaps more important, the diversion of resources from production of useful goods and services to such directly unproductive uses as lobbying by both factions.

The model could be extended to a two-country context, with the terms of trade as well as the tariff endogenous. The structure of the factions, however, would now have to be altered, with exporters in each country pushing for free trade and import-competing sectors in each country for protection. The black box would now comprise both governments, as well as relevant international bodies such as GATT. It could be shown that VERs could emerge as the mutually preferred outcome of such a process, though they are inferior on welfare grounds to tariffs.

The effects of a shock such as an improvement in the terms of trade can be carried out as a comparative statics exercise for the model, given the tariff formation function. Without further restrictions on this function, however, it would be difficult to make any firm predictions. Political scientists are not confident of their ability to provide any intuition, not to speak of empirical evidence, of relationships such as this. Furthermore the function itself might shift with a change in exogenous factors such as the terms of trade, with a greater public willingness to support injured industries and factors. The formalism that I have presented, however, has the merit of at least pointing out what we need to know before we can have a well-established political economy of trade restrictions.

References

Brock, W. A., and S. P. Magee. "The Economics of Special Interest Politics: The Case of the Tariff." *American Economic Review* 68 (1978): 246–250.

Findlay, R., and S. Wellisz. "Endogenous Tariffs, Trade Restrictions and Welfare." In J. N. Bhagwati, ed., *Import Competition and Response*. Chicago: University of Chicago Press, 1982.

Tullock, G. "The Welfare Costs of Tariffs, Monopolies and Theft." *Western Economic Journal* 5 (1967): 224–232.

3 Macroeconomics and Protection

Rudiger Dornbusch and Jeffrey A. Frankel

The United States is facing an unprecedented crisis in international trade. Over the last four years, U.S. exports have dropped and imports of foreign products have soared. The sharp deterioration of the international economic position of the United States has had a profound and negative impact on scores of domestic industries and millions of American workers. Left unchecked, this trade crisis poses a serious threat to the industrial base of the United States and the standard of living of all Americans.
Mark Anderson, AFL-CIO, 1984.

Not only has our trade performance been much better than widely perceived, it has gained almost unwarranted importance in economic policy discussions. It has become almost as though a booming trade sector is an end unto itself, when in reality it is merely a stepping stone to the overall goals of strong economic growth, low unemployment and stable prices.
New York Stock Exchange, 1984.

3.1 Introduction

Twenty years ago protection among industrial countries was almost a thing of the past. Tariff rates had been whittled down in successive rounds of multilateral bargaining, and, with well-defined limitations, most notably in agriculture, the world was heading fatally toward free trade. But in the past fifteen years, not a year has passed without a crisis in world trade diplomacy. And each time the crisis is said to be more acute, more definitive, and more threatening to the postwar liberal framework of world trade that is credited with the prosperity of these years. Multilateral negotiations toward trade liberalization continue, but now they are awkwardly supplemented by vows of abstention from protectionist moves, the frequency and urgency of which highlight that protectionism is on the move.

As a sectoral issue, protection never quite died. Agricultural protection had been there from the start, textiles came as early as the 1960s, and automobiles, radios, and televisions followed. Sectoral protection has become common, but the big change underway now in the United States is the quest for much more comprehensive protection, perhaps in the form of a uniform import surcharge. Macroeconomics is now the issue. The strong dollar, high interest rates, the collapse of debtor country markets, and their own export surge are the arguments supporting the broad-based reach for protection. This chapter investigates the impact of macroeconomic disturbances on international trade flows and the linkages that exist between macroeconomics and protection.

Macroeconomics is here interpreted widely so as to encompass a general equilibrium view of the economy. In that perspective two propositions are central. First, at full employment, protection for one sector means a tax on the remaining sectors. Lerner's symmetry theorem in some cases goes further, to apply even under conditions of unemployment. The second proposition is that we cannot export unless we are also willing to import. This proposition, however, is less tight. There are third-country effects that may be significant in that extra foreign exchange earned by a country in the U.S. market may be spent elsewhere. Furthermore, at least in the short run, borrowing and lending provide another way of circumventing an exact link between exports and imports.

3.2 Trends and Patterns of Macroeconomics and Protection

3.2.1 Tariff Levels

Any discussion of protection runs into the overwhelming problem that there is no simple, unambiguous statistic measuring the degree of protection a country is imposing at any time. By some measures protection in the United States is at an all-time low. The average import duty has fallen to a level lower than any other time in the past one hundred years. Table 3.1 shows average tariff rates for three product categories in the major industrialized countries.

Table 3.1
Average Post–Tokyo Round tariff rates

	United States	Japan	Canada	EEC
Finished manufactures	6.9	6.4	8.1	7.0
Semifinished manufactures	6.1	6.3	6.6	6.2
Raw materials	1.8	1.4	2.6	1.6

Source: GATT, unpublished data.

There are caveats that apply to the averages, but when everything is said and done, these low rates of duty convey nothing but a dramatic reversal from the high levels of the interwar period. Even taking effective protection effects into account, there is no indication of severely restrictive tariffs on any broad scale.

High effective protection rates do exist in a few sectors, but it would be an exaggeration to say that they represent a trade impediment for a significant volume of trade. In textiles or rubber, there is significant escalation by stage of processing, thus implying effective rates of protection that may reach perhaps as much as 30 or even 50 percent in some industries. But these high rates do apply to very small sectors. Of course, one might be fooled by the fact that actual trade in categories affected by high tariff rates is relatively small. The very fact of tariffs restricts trade below what it otherwise would be, and therefore low trade volumes may be a reflection of the protection, not of its irrelevance.

The low tariff rates in table 3.1 convey, however, a very partial picture of the protection issue. While trade liberalization has been proceeding actively in respect to tariffs, there has been a growing tendency to restrict trade, or at least the growth of trade, in sensitive sectors such as textiles, steel, and automobiles. These trade restrictions have taken the form of VERs, which essentially amount to officially sanctioned or even promoted cartelization. Other nontariff barriers to trade vastly amplify the range of protective measures already in place.

Tariffs and nontariff barriers represent actual protection in place. What is more worrying is that protectionist sentiment is running strong. The sharp real appreciation of the U.S. dollar since 1980 has given protectionist sentiment a strong boost to the point where across-the-board import surcharges or other drastic departures from postwar trade philosophy are being promoted in Congress. This protectionist sentiment is an issue of concern because it may prove the vehicle for a quantum jump in trade barriers in the United States and, without much delay, abroad.

Figure 3.1 shows the ratio of duties to dutiable imports, as well as dutiable imports as a fraction of total imports. Because of the Laffer curve effect, these are imperfect measures of the impact of protection. Where the former schedule reflects reduced tariff rates, the latter reflects the growth of trade in manufactures that has come in part as a consequence of reduced protection and because of structural change in the world economy.

3.2.2 Smoot-Hawley

The outstanding event in protection history and macroeconomics is often thought to be the 1930 Smoot-Hawley tariff that, in the midst of a disintegrat-

Percentage

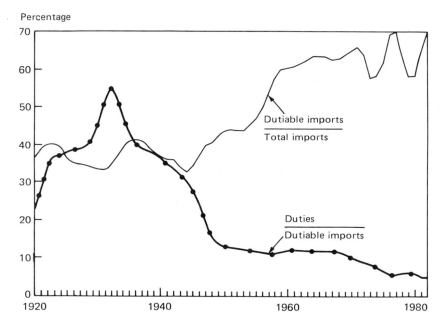

Figure 3.1
Dutiable imports and import duties. Source: Adapted from U.S. Department of Commerce, *Historical Statistics of the United States*, and *Statistical Abstract for the United States*.

ing world payments system, increased tariff rates, which were already at very significant levels. The Smoot-Hawley tariff is often represented as a key event not only in spreading the world recession from the United States abroad but in aggravating the depression. Meltzer (1976, p. 460) argues:

The tariffs restricted their operation of the price specie flow mechanism and the adjustment of the U.S. and the world economy. In the absence of the tariff prices in the U.S. would have fallen relative to prices abroad, and the change in relative prices would have increased foreign demand and net exports. . . . This argument assigns a large role to the Smoot-Hawley tariff and subsequent tariff retaliation in explaining why the 1929 recession did not follow the path of previous monetary contractions but became the Great Depression.

At the time it was perceived by the profession as a dramatic mistake, leading 1,028 economists to sign a declaration of opposition that included the following language:[1]

The undersigned American economists and teachers of economics strongly urge that any measure which provides for a general upward revision of tariff rates be denied by Congress, or if passed, be vetoed by the President. . . . Our export trade in general would suffer. Countries cannot permanently buy from

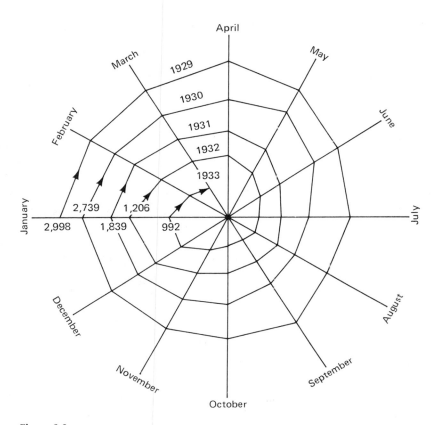

Figure 3.2
Kindleberger spiral (world trade, millions of U.S. dollars). Source: Kindleberger (1973, p. 172).

us unless they are permitted to sell to us, and the more we restrict importation of goods from them by means of even higher tariffs, the more we reduce the possibility of our exporting to them.

The Smoot-Hawley tariff retains as a special significance the fact that it is widely associated with causing the Great Depression. The famous Kindleberger spiral in figure 3.2 certainly is suggestive of the spreading of recession worldwide. Table 3.2 shows some of the relevant data.

Despite this consensus on the role that the Smoot-Hawley tariff played in aggravating the Great Depression, the conclusion does not follow from standard macroeconomic models. If one country unilaterally cuts its imports M and its trading partner unilaterally cuts its imports X, there is no net effect on $X - M$, and therefore no net effect on aggregate demand. There is no presumption in standard macroeconomic models that protection should reduce world aggregate demand, thus causing a depression.

Table 3.2
Great depression and world trade (index 1929 = 100)

	Total Price	World trade Volume	Manufactures Price	World trade Volume
1930	87.1	93	94	88
1931	67.7	85.5	78	76
1932	52.4	74.6	64	59
1933	46.7	75.4	56	61
1937	47.5	96.8	52	86

Source: Adapted from Hilgerdt (1945).

There are at least four approaches one could take to bring output-reducing effects of a tariff into standard models. First, the tariff causes welfare losses. Although we do not have a well-developed body of theory that integrates aggregate spending and distortions, there is no reason to reject this possibility out of hand. Second, the fiscal effects of a tariff can be brought into play to argue for a depressive effect of tariffs on aggregate demand. A tariff, just like any indirect tax, represents a reduction in disposable income. Setting aside the expenditure-switching effects that might cancel on a world scale, the expenditure-reducing effect of the fiscal measure would reduce world aggregate demand.

Although this argument can stand on theoretical grounds, the more plausible channels are probably the following two. To achieve the link to world demand, one of two channels of reasoning might be engaged: one is to argue that liquidity-constrained countries reduce their total spending as their ability to export vanishes. Alternatively there might be linkages to financial markets involving loss of market access and export earnings and thus an inability to service external debts. The delinquency in debt service in turn spreads to financial difficulties in the creditor countries. This is exactly the story of debtor countries in the 1930s.

3.2.3 Liberalization, Trade, and Growth

The Reciprocal Trade Agreements Act of 1934 started a reversal of restrictive trade legislation. By granting the president authority to negotiate multilateral tariff concessions, it was the chief instrument of tariff cuts for the following fifty years. The impetus for these tariff cuts was above all the recognition that protection breeds retaliation and worse. An open trading system (no politician would be caught saying "free trade") by contrast is thought to be an important reason for the sustained growth of the world economy in the postwar period. Table 3.3 shows the facts.

Table 3.3
World economic growth and trade (average annual growth, volume)

	1953–1963	1963–1973	1973–1983
World trade	5.6	8.5	3.0
Output	4.1	6.0	2.0

Source: GATT, *International Trade*, various issues; *Network of World Trade* (Geneva 1978); IMF, *International Financial Statistics Yearbook*, various issues; and Maddison (1964).

The relation between trade and growth is interesting in view of the different emphases placed by various authors. In the studies on U.S. growth accounting, international trade receives no credit.[2] The same is true in the work of Simon Kuznets. But there is a different tradition exemplified by the work of Haberler and Nurkse and that is a central tenet in the more recent studies of Anne Krueger and Bela Balassa, dealing with developing countries, where opening to trade is hailed as the sine qua non of satisfactory growth. Failure to open the economy in this tradition is said to provoke a foreign exchange bottleneck that sooner or later chokes off the scope for expansion. The same thinking is reflected in the criticism of growth through import substitution that the Economic Commission for Latin America had recommended in the 1950s.

The trade and growth linkage arises in another perspective. Strong growth in the center countries, and spilling over into import growth and growth in world trade, is thought to be the engine of transmission that links less-developed countries (LDCs) to economic progress in the center. Arthur Lewis in particular has documented this linkage, and two-gap models of growth with their emphasis on import requirements also make growth of real export revenue central to the growth equation. In a Schumpeterian vision of the growth process as promoted by Giersch, trade becomes even more central.

The general trend toward import liberalization has continued throughout the postwar period. In particular it is worth noting that in the early 1960s when the dollar was already perceived as overvalued, this was not an obstacle to the Kennedy Round tariff cuts. The Tokyo Round of trade liberalization of the 1970s took place in the midst of the most severe macroeconomic shocks of the past fifty years, suggesting that macroeconomics is no longer, unlike in the 1930s, an important consideration in trade policy. But that is certainly contradicted by the surge of complaints by U.S. manufacturing where, the recovery notwithstanding, exchange appreciation is blamed for a lack of competitiveness, import growth, and poor export performance.

Certainly in addition to exchange rate issues, the debt crisis has raised the question of protection as a macroeconomic issue. Debtor LDCs have had to bring about dramatic swings in their trade balances. They have done so in good part by reducing imports by means of tariffs, quotas, regulation, and real depreciation, but they would have surely preferred to make the adjustment with increased exports of manufactures, semimanufactures, and commodities. Trade restrictions in these areas barred what could have been (in some sectors) easy expansion.

3.2.4 Nontariff Barriers and Other Restrictions

Accompanying the broad trend toward tariff liberalization, there has been in the past twenty years a serious move toward trade restriction. This has been concentrated in key sectors: first in textiles and then in a growing range of goods that includes steel, rubber footwear, leather products, television sets, motorcycles, and automobiles. Interestingly this shift toward trade restriction is common to most, if not all, major industrialized countries except Japan (despite popular conceptions to the contrary). Figure 3.3 shows the pattern of this North Atlantic protectionism and makes the point that nontariff barriers, the active instrument of trade restriction, are very sector specific. Figure 3.3 also shows clearly the increasing intensity and spread of this new protectionism in the 1970s.

From the perspective of our topic—macroeconomics and protection—this is a particularly interesting problem: are textiles especially macrosensitive, or is steel, or are automobiles? And does this sensitivity arise from particular policy mixes reflected in output–interest rates–exchange rates patterns? Alternatively are the sectors that receive protection primarily determined by structural factors and/or their industrial organization and location that make them particularly effective at lobbying for relief? The legal framework that grants protection under the escape clause may in fact be strongly biased against protection. Since relief is conditional on demonstration that imports are the most important source of injury—though in fact macroeconomics may be a larger factor—the test is hard to establish. But that may also open the door to more protection by the political route; the tariff quota on motorcycles, VERs with Japan, and the steel cartel are important recent moves to opt out of a basically free trade system and accept industry protectionism or cartelization.

Protectionist moves across the board for all imports or all of manufacturing have been extremely rare and temporary. Their motivation appears to date to have been the trade balance and the currency, not employment. The case that comes to mind is the 1971 U.S. import surcharge. But while across-the-board protection for employment reasons has not taken place so far, protectionist sentiment is running high. The distinction between actual protection and protectionist sentiment is difficult to make because one would expect the two to be correlated. Sustained, increasing protectionism is likely to spark off actual legislation under the right conditions.

There is certainly evidence that protectionism is particularly active. In the Ninety-eighth Congress, as Czinkota and Kollmer (1984) show, in the House the average congress person sponsored five trade restriction bills for every one trade liberalization bill. In the Senate there were two trade restriction bills for every trade liberalization measure. Even with a protectionist bent of trade initiatives in Congress, there has so far been little congressional action in favor of sweeping protection. The local content bill has not passed, nor has any other measure that would comprehensively restrict imports.

What has grown, however, is the willingness of the executive to negotiate trade restrictions using VERs and orderly marketing arrangements, as well as activity under the escape clause. That may have been high activity during an election year, but it may also be an indication that the promise of an open trading system is wearing thin in the face of a structural and macroeconomic testing of a weak manufacturing sector.

The winter 1985 decision by the Reagan administration to lift the automobile VERs with Japan, however, is promising. Here the choice to exercise trade restriction was shifted to Japan, and perhaps there will be less of it. In exchange the administration has gained a better negotiating position on the issue of access to the tradeproof Japanese market.

3.3 Macroeconomics and Trade Flows

Trade flows are principally affected by two variables: relative levels of activity in the home country and abroad, and international competitiveness. Figure 3.4 shows the U.S. trade balance as a fraction of GNP.

3.3.1 Trade Balance Equation

The question we address here is whether relative activity and competitiveness provide a significant explanation for the large swings in trade flows.

$$RAT = 111.8 \quad -7.44 \; RMERM \quad -15.1 \; ACT \quad -2.01 \; ROIL$$
$$(7.4)(-5.05) \qquad\qquad (-5.78) \quad (-6.06) \tag{3.1}$$

$$R^2 = 0.75 \qquad rho = 0.28 \qquad DW = 2.07 \qquad SER = 0.44$$

Equation 3.1 reports a regression where the trade deficit as a fraction of GNP (RAT) is explained by activity levels in the United States relative to the major non-U.S. industrial countries, the real oil price and the real exchange rate. The relative activity level (ACT) is measured by relative indexes of industrial

	1973	1974	1975	1976	1977	1978	1979	1980	1981	1982	1983	1984	Termination date
Automobiles													
United States									VER/Japan: 1.68M cars (increased to 1.85M)				February 1986
European Community													
West Germany										VER/Japan: growth limited to 10%/year	VER/Japan		June 1984
France					VER/Japan: 2.5–3.0% of domestic market								
Italy													
United Kingdom			Monitor imports/Japan:						Prudent market agreement: set at 1977 level–11% domestic market				
Canada									VER/Japan: varying units permitted				April 1984
Japan													
Steel													
United States		VRA/Japan, EC: (carbon)				OMA/Japan, Quotas/Sweden, EC, Canada, other: (specially)				US/EC arrangement: (carbon)	Addt t & q (specialty)		October 1985
European Community						BPS or VER: 14 major suppliers (carbon) / BPS or VER: 14 major suppliers (specially)							July 1987
Textiles													
United States	Multi-fiber arrangement, as extended												
European Community	Multi-fiber arrangement, as extended												
Canada	Multi-fiber arrangement, as extended												

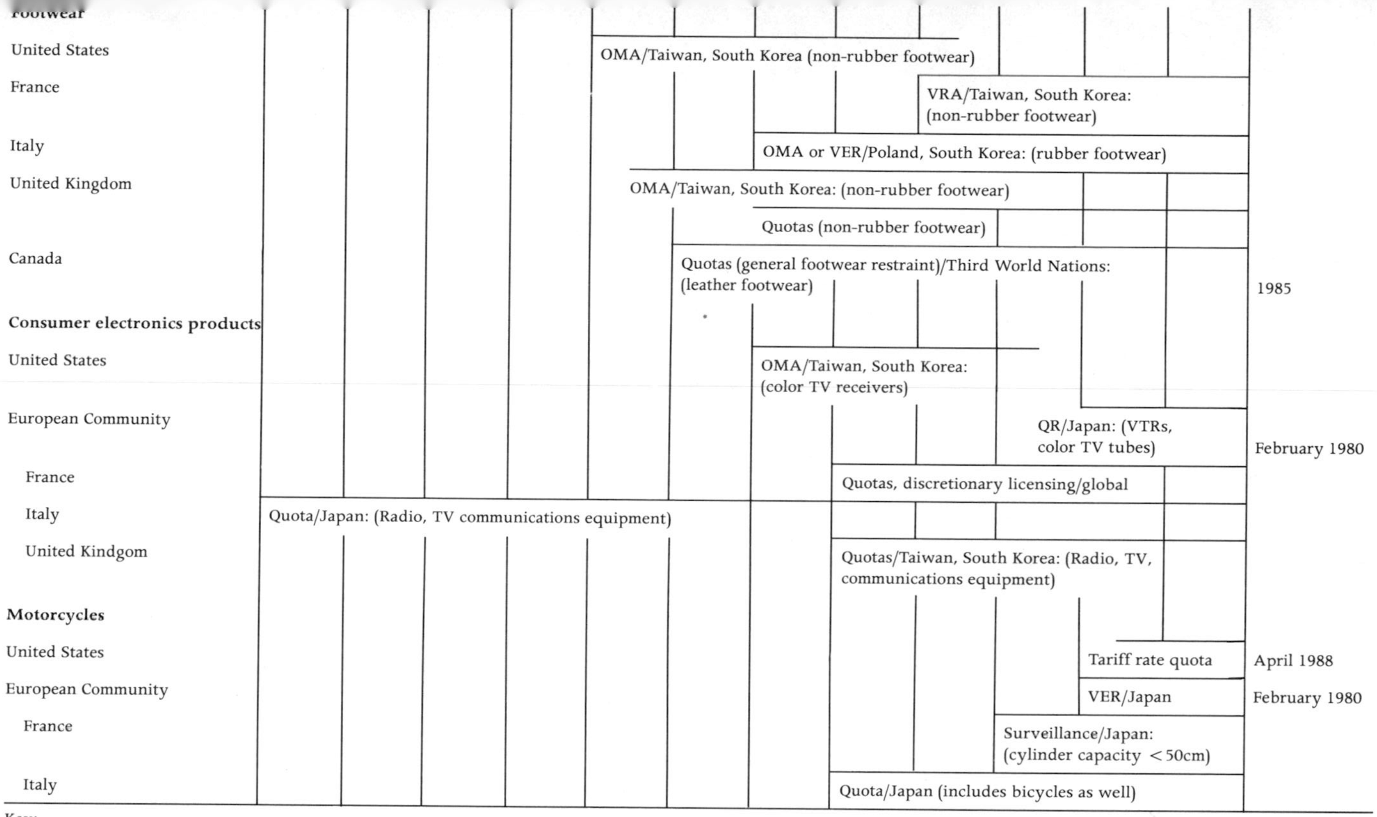

Figure 3.3
Trade restrictions of industrialized countries. Source: *Annual Report of the President on the Trade Agreements Program* (Washington, D.C., 1983).

The figure contains the following content:

Footwear

			1985	February 1980
United States	OMA/Taiwan, South Korea (non-rubber footwear)			
France		VRA/Taiwan, South Korea: (non-rubber footwear)		
Italy	OMA or VER/Poland, South Korea: (rubber footwear)			
United Kingdom	OMA/Taiwan, South Korea: (non-rubber footwear)			
	Quotas (non-rubber footwear)			
Canada	Quotas (general footwear restraint)/Third World Nations: (leather footwear)			

Consumer electronics products

				April 1988	February 1980
United States	OMA/Taiwan, South Korea: (color TV receivers)				
European Community		QR/Japan: (VTRs, color TV tubes)			
France	Quotas, discretionary licensing/global				
Italy	Quota/Japan: (Radio, TV communications equipment)				
United Kingdom	Quotas/Taiwan, South Korea: (Radio, TV, communications equipment)				

Motorcycles

			April 1988	February 1980
United States		Tariff rate quota		
European Community		VER/Japan		
France	Surveillance/Japan: (cylinder capacity <50cm)			
Italy	Quota/Japan (includes bicycles as well)			

Key:
BPS–Basic Price System
OMA–Orderly Marketing Agreement
QR–Quantitative Restriction
t&q–tariffs and quotas
VTR–Video Tape Recorder
VER–Voluntary Export Restraint
VRA–Voluntary Restraint Agreement

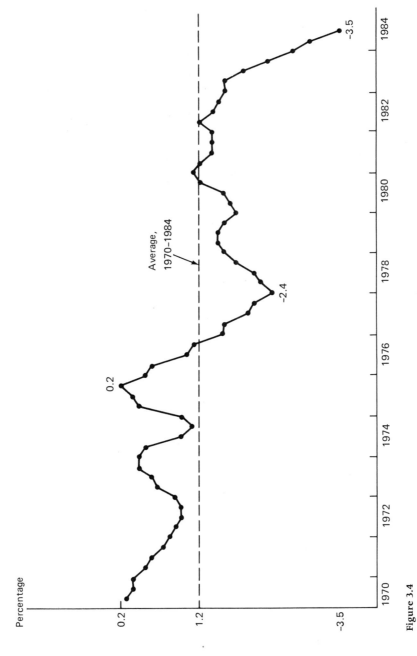

Figure 3.4
U.S. trade deficit as a ratio of GNP (three-quarter centered moving average). Source: Data Resources, Inc., data bank.

production, and competitiveness is measured by the IMF index of the real exchange rate in manufacturing ($RMERM$). In addition the price of oil relative to the U.S. GNP deflator ($ROIL$) is introduced as an explanatory variable. The regression is run with quarterly data for the period 1970, quarter 1, to 1984, quarter 2. The coefficients can be interpreted as semielasticities.[3]

The regression strongly supports the conclusion that relative activity and the real exchange rate are major determinants of the trade balance. Specifically a real depreciation of 13.5 percent will improve (with lags) the trade balance by 1 percent of gross domestic product (GDP). A decline in the relative cyclical position of the United States by 6.6 percent would also bring about a 1 percentage point improvement in the trade balance to gross national product (GNP) ratio.

The evidence in the regression, and indeed all the available evidence in the literature, is so obvious that one is surprised by the claim to the contrary in a recent GATT study by Blackhurst and Tumlir (1980, p. 4):

Empirical evidence calculated for eight major industrialized countries for the 1970's indicates that the response of trade balances to such real exchange rate changes has been hardly significant, manifest if at all only over periods of such length that the relationship is highly tenuous, many other changes having intervened in the meantime. . . . It seems furthermore that the transition to the flexible exchange rate system has weakened the impact of exchange rate changes on trade.

Figures 3.5 and 3.6 show the real exchange rate and the index of relative cyclical positions. They make it clear that the conjunction of competitiveness and the cyclical position help explain the major movements in the trade balance, including in particular the 1982–1984 experience. Net exports clearly respond to these key variables and thus create the potential for a protectionist situation.[4]

Figure 3.7 pursues the cyclical and competitiveness effects. Here we show the volume indexes for U.S. exports and imports in the 1979–1984 period. The striking fact is that exports are far below their previous peak, a reflection of U.S. loss in competitiveness and the weak level of foreign demand, especially in the debtor LDCs.

3.3.2 Imports and Exports in Manufacturing

The broad trend of international influences on the manufacturing sector can also be judged from the data on import penetration and export ratios. Table 3.4 shows these data for 1972 and the most recent period for which they are available, 1981.

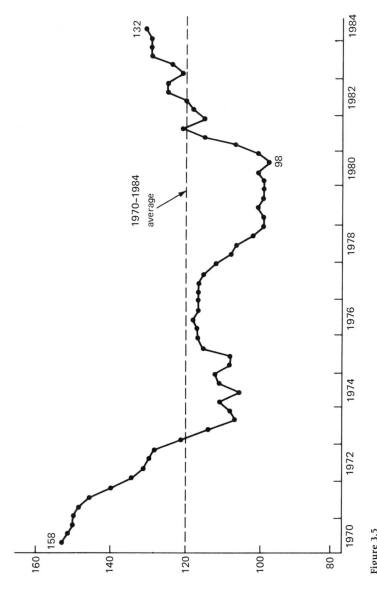

Figure 3.5
U.S. real exchange rate (1980 = 100). Source: Data Resources, Inc., data bank.

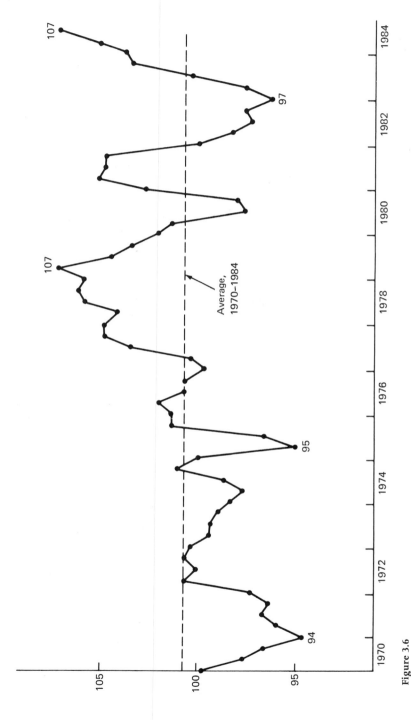

Figure 3.6
Ratio of U.S. to foreign activity (1980 = 100). Source: Data Resources, Inc., data bank.

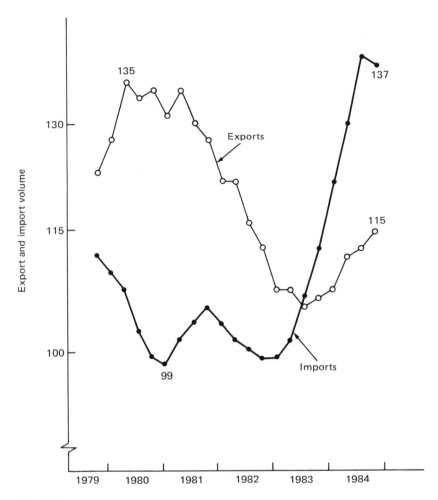

Figure 3.7
U.S. import and export volume (1980 = 100). Source: Data Resources, Inc., data bank.

Table 3.4

Imports and exports relative to domestic manufacturing production

	Imports		Exports	
	1972	1981	1972	1981
Food and kindred products	3.9	4.2	2.9	5.2
Tobacco manufactures	0.6	2.0	5.7	12.7
Textile mill products	5.5	5.9	2.8	5.9
Apparel and related products	6.9	13.7	1.2	3.4
Lumber and wood products except furniture	9.4	8.7	4.3	7.3
Furniture and fixtures	2.6	4.8	0.6	2.6
Paper and allied products	5.7	6.4	4.1	6.2
Printing, publishing, and allied products	0.9	1.0	1.3	1.9
Chemicals and allied products	3.1	4.4	7.7	12.7
Petroleum refining and related products	7.1	6.8	1.9	1.9
Rubber and miscellaneous plastic products	4.7	7.7	3.1	6.3
Leather and leather products	15.9	24.7	1.8	5.4
Stone, clay, glass, and concrete products	3.6	5.1	2.9	5.5
Primary metal products	9.5	14.5	2.9	6.7
Fabricated metal products	2.5	3.9	3.9	6.9
Machinery, except electrical	5.3	8.0	15.0	24.0
Electrical machinery, equipment and supplies	7.7	12.4	6.7	13.5
Transportation equipment	10.1	14.8	9.1	16.8
Instruments (including watches, clocks, photo)	6.9	11.3	12.6	19.0
Miscellaneous manufactured commodities	13.7	23.6	7.6	12.1
Total manufactured commodities	6.1	8.4	5.8	9.9

Source: Bureau of Labor Statistics, unpublished data.
Note: Let M, X, and S be imports, exports, and domestic shipments. The table shows the ratios $M/(M + S)$ and X/S.

Taking manufacturing in the aggregate, the economy has opened on both the import and the export sides. Import penetration as measured by imports as a fraction of apparent consumption rose between 1972 and 1981 from 6.4 to 9.3 percent. Over the same period the fraction of shipments exported rose from 5.8 to 9.9 percent. It is worth noting, in view of the pervasive sense of a loss in external competitiveness, that at least between 1972 and 1981 there had been an increase in the export-to-production ratio for every one of these manufacturing groups. Moreover 1981 is not special; between 1978 and 1981 the export ratio also increased in every industry.

Aggregate data available for more recent years show a significant increase in the import penetration ratio of more than a full percentage point over the period 1981–1983. The question is whether over the same period, unlike in the earlier experience, the share of exports in production declined.

The evolution of the international position of manufacturing has direct implications for employment. About 20.5 percent of U.S. nonagricultural employment is in manufacturing. A large deterioration of manufacturing performance therefore would have a sizable effect on aggregate employment. So far any adverse trade effects have been overshadowed by economy-wide recovery. Aggregate employment today is more than 6 percent above the 1979 level, but that is not true for manufacturing, where employment is 6.4 percent below the 1979 peak level.

Looking back on the evidence of the 1970s, it was possible to argue that foreign trade competition was not a significant source of employment problems. Krueger (1980, p. 145) argued, "Despite the intuitive appeal of the notion that increased imports must have been a significant determinant of the 'impact effect' in layoffs and job losses in the United States, examination of the evidence does not support the case to any substantial degree." It will be interesting to find out, some years from now, whether these conclusions can be sustained for the early 1980s.

From this broad overview of the setting for protection, we now turn to more specific investigation of the macroeconomic determinants of protection.

3.4 Macrocyclical Determinants of Protectionism

What are the determinants of protectionism over time across countries and across industries? The most important economic factors are presumably those that operate on the level of output and employment. The various possible hypotheses can be classified into two broad categories. First are macroeconomic factors, particularly those affecting the aggregate demand for domestic production. They fluctuate with the business cycle and the exchange rate and are often thought to be especially relevant for explaining the overall level of protectionist sentiment economy-wide. Second are microeconomic factors, particularly unit labor costs and other supply variables. They move in long-term structural trends and are often thought to be especially relevant for explaining why some sectors achieve a higher level of protection than others.

As a crude preliminary test, if recent U.S. protectionist pressures were primarily microeconomic in origin, one might expect a trend toward more industry allegations of subsidies and other specific unfair trade practices by foreign competitors as manifest in filing of antidumping (AD), countervailing duty (CVD), and foreign government practices cases. Such allegations are more likely to be sector specific and microeconomic in origin, regardless of whether they are legitimate (identifying foreign subsidies to specific industries or dumping specific products) or imagined (blaming unfavorable structural trends on unfair foreign competition). There are exceptions to the principle that allegations of unfair trade practices tend to be microeconomic and sec-

Table 3.5
Trade actions brought in the United States under the 1974 and 1979 trade acts

	1975–1977	1978–1980	1981–1984
201 escape clause	31	13	10
301 foreign government practicing			
701 Countervailing duty	127	182	391
731 Antidumping			
Total trade actions	158	195	401
Ratio of 201 to all actions	.196	.067	.025

Source: Adapted from Deardorff and Stern, table 2.5.
Note: The section numbers (201, etc.) refer to the 1974 and 1979 Trade Acts.

toral. In the fall of 1983 the textile industry alleged that China's dual exchange rate constituted a subsidy to exports. In the summer of 1984, the copper industry charged that one of the ways in which Chile and other LDC copper producers were unfairly subsidizing exports was by devaluing their currencies; there were similar allegations by the steel industry against Brazil. But allegations related to exchange rates have not gotten far in the AD–CVD process. When the industry has only exchange rate or other macroeconomic factors to point to as a source of its import troubles, it is relatively more likely to turn to the escape clause, section 201(b) of the Trade Act of 1974, by which the industry need not show any sort of unfair trade practice by foreigners.

In the late 1970s one might have expected microeconomic factors to have become more important relative to exchange rate and other macroeconomic factors because many sectors were losing net foreign demand (the trade deficit was rising to record levels) despite substantial gains in competitiveness resulting from the depreciating dollar and rapid growth of domestic demand. Table 3.5 shows that escape clause actions indeed became less common than the other trade actions, declining to 6.7 percent of the total in the period 1978–1980, from 19.6 percent in the preceding three years.

This trend should have reversed in the 1980s if the hypothesis is correct that the recent increases in protectionism are due to the appreciation of the dollar. It should be difficult to allege unfair trade practices credibly if the exchange rate (or other economy-wide macroeconomic factors) is the real problem, and there should be of necessity increased reliance on the escape clause.

There have been 201 cases. In 1982 escape clause relief was extended in two cases (clothespins and porcelain-on-steel cookware) and strengthened in two cases (high-carbon ferro chromium and mushrooms).[5] In 1983 relief was granted in two new major cases, large motorcycles and certain stainless steel and alloy tool steel, and extended in three of the four cases already in effect.[6] During the 1984 presidential campaign, a number of industries filed cases with the International Trade Commission (ITC), timed so that President Reagan would have to make the ultimate determination in the final months of the campaign when political pressures were most intense. The ITC ruled against the footwear industry but in favor of the copper and finished-steel industries. The administration ended up giving no protection to copper but decided to negotiate an extensive system of quotas with steel exporters to reduce import penetration in finished steel to about 18.5 percent of the projected U.S. market over the next several years, as compared to 25.4 percent for the first ten months of 1984.

But there has been a virtual explosion of AD and CVD cases filed since 1980, as table 3.5 shows. The ratio of other trade actions to escape clause actions has risen to 39 : 1, from 14 : 1 in 1978–1980 and 4 : 1 in 1975–1977. The increased number of AD and CVD cases is due in part to the fact that they have become cheaper and easier for an industry to file since the processing was transferred from the Treasury Department to the Commerce Department by the 1979 Trade Act. Some legal expenses that must be incurred when an industry files for 201 relief before the ITC are avoided in the CVD-AD processes. Nevertheless the relatively small number of 201s filed and the very large number of CVDs and AD suggests that economy-wide macroeconomic factors have not been predominant.

3.4.1 Factors Affecting Domestic Demand

The macroeconomic hypotheses can be distinguished according to those that relate to domestic demand and those that relate solely to net foreign demand. Protectionism has long been thought to be countercyclical. Magee and Young (chapter 4) find that the U.S. average tariff rate has depended significantly on the unemployment rate in the twentieth century. Takacs (1981) has shown that when unemployment is high and growth is low, the number of injury cases filed before the ITC goes up. During the 1980–1982 recessionary period in the United States, it seemed to many that protectionist sentiment was on the increase as a reflection of the loss of income and employment economy-wide, in turn generally attributed to the tightening of monetary policy by the Federal Reserve after October 1979 in its fight against inflation.

On several accounts there was no strong reason to identify protectionism with a loss of net demand from foreigners, either as a decrease in U.S. exports or an increase in imports. Although the U.S. trade surplus deteriorated from 1980 to 1982 (by $20.6 billion in net exports of goods and services in 1972 dollars), one could argue that the loss in foreign demand was no worse than the loss in domestic demand. In fact, case-by-case inspection of Standardized Industrial Classification (SIC) categories suggests that most are at least partly traded. Fourteen industries that seem to be the most clearly nontraded initially experienced approximately the same rate of change in employment when the recessions hit as the nonagricultural economy in the aggregate.[8] From July 1981 to the trough of the recession in November 1982, employment in construction fell by 8.5 percent, more than the decline in the total private economy (3.4 percent) and almost as much as the decline in the highly traded manufacturing sector (11.2 percent).[9] This result—that the loss in foreign demand was no worse than the loss in domestic demand—might seem to follow logically from the proposition that the worldwide recession originated with a contraction in U.S. demand. However, such logic would ignore the central role of the exchange rate in creating recent U.S. trade deficits.

After the trough of the recession in late 1982, the relative cyclical position of the United States in relation to its trading partners began to turn around sharply even while real interest rates remained higher in the United States than abroad. The usual explanation given for the strong U.S. recovery and the high real interest rates is the growing structural federal budget deficit. If one judges that protectionist sentiment has continued to increase since 1982, then the monetary-fiscal mix would seem a more promising explanation than the level of overall economic activity. Protectionism, to the extent that it is actually reflected in effective barriers and reduced trade flows, could be thought of as one more channel, in addition to high real interest rates and a high dollar, through which government deficits crowd out other sectors of the economy.

"Not Less Than Any Other Cause" of Injury
An industry suffering from import competition due to general macroeconomic factors was more likely to appeal to the escape clause because it does not require the allegation of any sort of specific foreign subsidy or unfair trade practice. What is required, as the first step for protection to be granted under the escape clause, is that the ITC concludes that each of the following three conditions is met:

1. Imports are increasing, either actually or relative to domestic production.
2. A domestic industry producing an article like or directly competitive with the imported article is being seriously injured or threatened with such injury.
3. The increased imports are a substantial cause of the serious injury or threat thereof to the domestic industry producing a like or directly competitive article.[10]

For an industry to meet criterion 2, a loss in domestic demand is as good as a loss in net foreign demand. (The 1984 Trade Act specifies plant closings as an indication of injury.) But the legal definition of when imports are a "substantial cause of injury" for criterion 3 is a "cause which is important and not less that any other cause."[11]

Thus the law assigns exclusive importance to import competition as a cause of injury justifying protection.

It is difficult to understand how Congress could have meant this definition literally. Why grant protection to an industry suffering from import competition but not to one suffering the same loss from import competition plus worse losses as a result of high interest rates, recession, or other factors? But this is precisely how the ITC has interpreted the law. The most important, and controversial, example was the December 1980 three out of five majority decision denying relief to the automobile industry on the grounds that imports were not a substantial cause of injury. ITC Commissioners Bill Alberger and Michael J. Calhoun judged general recessionary conditions to be a greater cause of serious injury than increased imports.[12]

In the February 1983 decision on motorcycles, although a two out of three majority decided affirmatively, Commissioner Paula Stern again voted to deny relief on the grounds that high unemployment among blue-collar motorcycle consumers was the principal cause of injury.[13]

In a similar dissent on stainless steel plate in May 1983, Stern ruled that "skyhigh interest rates have brought on, deepened and lengthened the current recession" and that they were "a more important cause of injury than imports."[14]

The implication is that an especially large loss of domestic demand, far from being a cause of protectionism of comparable importance with a loss of net foreign demand, reduces an industry's chances for winning protection so far as the escape clause is concerned. Adams and Dirlam (1983, p. 139) portray Commissioner Stern as even finding against substantial cause of injury in the case of stainless steel plate on the grounds that exchange rate fluctuations were a more substantial cause of serious injury than increased imports.[15]

3.4.2 Factors Affecting Net Foreign Demand

There are reasons for expecting a loss of net foreign demand to give rise to protectionist sentiment and to actual protection even aside from the 201 process, to a greater extent than a loss of domestic demand. It is not just that an industry has nothing to gain from protection if it is not currently suffering at the hands of import competition (and if it does not expect to do so in the future).

There is a general belief among the public and among politicians that a firm in difficulty due to import competition is entitled to direct remedies, or at least compensation, in a way that a firm in difficulty due to the vagaries of the domestic marketplace is not—whether the latter's losses are economy wide (recession, oil shock), industry wide (changing tastes or technology), or specific to the firm (mismanagement, labor problems, industrial accidents, and acts of God).[16]

The loss in net foreign demand over the last four years is evident from the $82 billion deterioration of the trade balance. It should be noted that the economy does not in fact divide up neatly into traded goods (those sectors that export or that compete with imports) that have been hurt and nontraded goods that have done well. Over the period May 1981 to May 1984 some traded sectors suffered the greatest losses in employment in the economy—farm machinery and equipment down 30.9 percent—but others grew among the fastest—semiconductors up 20.1 percent. Similarly the nontraded sectors included some with large employment losses—railroads (class 1) down 24.5 percent—and others that benefited—eating and drinking places up 9.2 percent. But on average nontraded industries clearly did better than traded industries. Private employment among the services-producing sector was up 10.2 percent (July 1981–May 1984) and among the goods-producing sectors was down 3.2 percent.[17] Thus the continuation of protectionist pressures during the current recovery supports the idea that net foreign demand is a more important determinant of protectionism than domestic demand.

Macroeconomic factors reducing net foreign demand could be further distinguished according to whether they reduce exports or increase imports.

Exports
If an industry produces goods that are both exported and imported, its success in gaining import protection might be affected by how well it is doing at export sales. As with domestic demand, export sales in one respect could have a counterintuitive positive effect on import protection; an industry is not legally eligible for escape clause protection if reduced export sales (due, for example, to a foreign recession) are judged a greater cause of injury than increased import competition. ITC Commissioner Stern in the 1983 specialty steel cases explicitly considered export losses a competing cause of injury, ruling in the case of stainless steel plate that export losses, together with a decline in domestic demand associated with high interest rates, were more important than imports as causes of injury.[18] But the normal presumption is that industry can expect more sympathy if it is having a tough time all around—

not just with high import competition but also with low export demand, when relevant, as well as low domestic demand.

If proposed reciprocity legislation were passed, this presumption would be formalized. Targets for bilateral balances in specific sectors would imply that a fall in export demand, attributable, for example, to a foreign recession, would be cause for import protection. In the longer run the most important effect of exports on the level of import protection is in creating a political constituency for free trade. In the United States such export sectors as agriculture and capital goods manufacturing have usually been important opponents of protectionism, more visible opponents than consumers. They know that foreigners who cannot earn dollars by selling to the United States will not be able to spend dollars on U.S. exports.

In any case, import competition, to which we now turn, is a more direct determinant of import protection than export sales. The two most important macroeconomic determinants of import competition, as of net foreign demand more generally, are the cyclical position of the domestic country in relation to its trading partners and the exchange rate.

Relative Cyclical Position
We have already mentioned the possible role of foreign recessions and foreign income in affecting protectionism by export sales. On the import side, it is domestic income that matters. We come again to an irony in the determinants of the level of protection. Because imports depend positively on domestic income, an industry may be more successful at winning protection in a boom than in a recession. Even if other factors are working in the direction of strong import competition, a sufficiently severe recession could have a negative enough effect on the level of imports to cancel out the other factors, leaving the industry with no alarming figures of rising imports at which to point. Conversely one could imagine an industry establishing grounds for protection in the midst of a great boom if demand for competing imports rises more rapidly than demand for the industry's products by pointing to rising import penetration ratios. These possibilities run counter to the normal expectation that protectionist pressures are countercyclical.

An Overvalued Currency
Hypotheses concerning the exchange rate may be the most important macroeconomic theories of protection. An overvalued currency clearly makes it difficult for domestic firms to compete with imports.

Many observers have seen the enormous appreciation of the dollar over the first half of the 1980s as the chief cause, by record trade deficits, of increasing

protectionist sentiment. For example, Fox and Cooney (1983–1984, p. 90) of the National Association of Manufacturers write, "Currency misalignments and instability are driving previous staunch defenders of free trade to consider protectionism the only practical alternative."

C. Fred Bergsten has been one of the most visible and articulate proponents of the exchange rate hypothesis. He has argued that it is particularly relevant in U.S.-Japan trade relations. He has identified three recent episodes of economic conflict between the two countries—in 1970–1971, 1977–1978, and 1981–1984—and attributed them primarily to three corresponding upsurges in trade imbalances, particularly in the politically sensitive bilateral trade deficit. He considers in turn the relative cyclical position, Japanese protection-ism, and other possible causes of these three upsurges in the trade imbalance and concludes that only the exchange rate is capable of explaining them. Japan has usually been growing faster than the United States so that the relative cyclical position favors reduced U.S. protectionist pressures. Similarly no one argues that Japanese import barriers, whatever their level in the past, have been rising in recent years, especially not relative to U.S. barriers. The Japanese have accelerated implementation of Tokyo Round tariff reductions and made a variety of concessions regarding NTBs that, even if only the slow result of painstaking U.S. government pressure, are in sharp contrast to the recent U.S. erection of high barriers (chiefly VERs) to Japanese autos, steel, and other goods. Bergsten (1982, p. 1065) concludes,

Of the six possible causal factors, only exchange rate misalignments were present in each of the three periods and go far to explain the difficulties which have arisen on each occasion. In each instance, the yen became substantially undervalued—undermining U.S. competitiveness, both in Japan and else-where. The huge swings in trade and current-account balances which marked each episode, and which triggered the outbreaks of U.S.-Japan hostility, can be traced primarily to these exchange-rate movements.

The timing of swings in the yen-dollar exchange rate is not quite as neatly coincident with the three periods of trade friction as Bergsten would have it. This is particularly true of the second episode. The yen reached an all-time high against the dollar in late 1978. Bergsten must appeal to the much lower value of the yen in 1976, and presumably to lags in the trade response (the J curve) and in the political process, to explain the 1977–1978 episode. As for the third episode, since 1980 the yen has been stronger, not weaker, than during the average of the post-1973 period when exchange rates have been determined by market equilibrium. Only the European currencies have depre-ciated sharply against the dollar.

But if recent exchange rate movements do not support the Bergsten hypothesis as an explanation of problems of U.S. frictions with Japan in particular, they do support it as an explanation of U.S. trade problems more generally.[19] Simple elasticity calculations suggest that the appreciation of the dollar explained roughly 60 percent of the deterioration in the U.S. trade deficit and the relative cyclical position only 40 percent.

It was difficult as of 1982 to distinguish among three competing (though interrelated) macroeconomic explanations of protectionist pressures: the dollar appreciation and trade deficit, a lopsided monetary-fiscal mix manifest in high real interest rates, and the recession. The continued progress of protectionist forces during the very strong eight quarters of the subsequent recovery worked to eliminate the third of the hypotheses from contention. As of mid-1984 the first two hypotheses also had to compete with presidential campaign politics. But since then declining interest rates and the disappointingly enthusiastic administration pursuit of negotiated import quotas on finished steel products have worked to reduce the plausibility of the real interest rate and election campaign hypotheses. Only the continued rise of the dollar remains as the obvious macroeconomic force.

The current vintage of the hypothesis that an overvalued currency exacerbates protectionism is often used by Bergsten and many others as one of the arguments for reforming the system of freely floating exchange rates. But it has an antecedent that fifteen years ago was used in a different, even diametrically opposed, context. During the final decade of the Bretton Woods system, protectionism was cited by the proponents of floating exchange rates as one of the arguments against fixed exchange rates. The argument was that countries facing large balance of payment deficits tended to erect trade barriers, especially if international reserves were running dangerously low and other means of adjustment such as deflation were not practical options. A switch to a freely floating exchange rate would eliminate the balance of payments deficit as a problem: if the central bank does not intervene in the foreign exchange market, then the balance of payments is zero by definition. The switch would therefore eliminate one of the major causes of protectionism.

Dunn (1983, p. 6) is one of several authors who has recently reminded us of the arguments of fifteen years ago:

In addition to gains for macroeconomic policy, flexible exchange rates also promised to eliminate mercantilism as an argument for tariffs and other protectionist devices, thus producing an era of free or at least more liberal trade. Harry Johnson noted that a tariff merely causes an appreciation of the local currency which taxes export and unprotected import competing industries without improving the trade account or increasing aggregate demand. . . . The expectation that protectionism can improve the balance of payments and generate an increase in aggregate demand obviously makes no sense if the exchange rate adjusts to maintain payments equilibrium with most of the payments adjustment to the exchange rate occurring in the current account.

This is not a great exaggeration of the earlier arguments. In his classic paper in support of flexible exchange rates, Harry Johnson indeed wrote (1971, p. 210), "The removal of the balance-of-payments is an important positive contribution that the adoption of flexible exchange rates could make to the achievement of the liberal objective of an integrated international economy."

In the view of the recent authors, things have worked out very differently. Dunn writes (1983, p. 19), "The end of mercantilism and the resulting movement toward free trade, which was another hoped-for result of flexible exchange rates [in addition to macroeconomic independence], has also failed to materialize. Instead there has been a movement toward more protectionism in recent years despite the existence of a flexible exchange rate system which eliminates the mercantilist effects of tariffs."

The 1970 and 1984 views, although obviously in conflict on the desirability of floating exchange rates, are in agreement that an overvalued currency contributes to protectionism through its effect on the trade deficit. The earlier view, which seemed relevant to the dollar in 1970, was that a currency was more likely to become overvalued under a fixed rate system as a result of domestic inflation in excess of foreign inflation together with an unwillingness to devalue. The later view, which seems relevant to the dollar in the 1980s, is that a currency is more likely to become overvalued under a freely floating exchange rate system as a result of large international capital inflows.

To the extent that we are concerned here with the effects of changes in macroeconomic variables rather than the effects of the macroeconomic policy regime, we need not take a position on the issue of fixed versus floating exchange rates. Whether one regards the dollar as being currently overvalued in a normative sense, it is clear that it is overvalued in a purchasing power parity sense—that is, it has appreciated enormously in real terms. The negative implications for the trade balance, already well established in the past, have been amply borne out in the current episode and by regression equation 3.1. If a loss in net foreign demand is considered in general to be a cause of protectionism, then the exchange rate must be considered as important currently as it has ever been. The level of the trade deficit in 1984 and the deterioration over the preceding four years were much worse than was the case in 1972. This is true whether one looks at the trade balance in real terms, on a national income and product accounts basis, or as a percentage of GNP. There would appear to be a strong case against the exchange rate as a suspect in the propagation of protectionism.

Balance of Payments

Although the real appreciation of the dollar and the U.S. trade deficit have been much more extreme in the current episode than in the 1970–1972 period, large capital inflows have meant that the overall balance of payments has looked much better. The United States was losing official reserve assets in 1970 and 1971 as the monetary authorities bought up unwanted dollars. Since 1980 the United States has, to the contrary, been gaining official reserve assets. The magnitude has been small because the Reagan administration has maintained a policy of abjuring foreign exchange intervention except to calm "disorderly markets." But when foreign exchange operations have taken place—for example, intervention in early 1985 (in coordination with larger interventions by European central banks) that may have marked a change in administration attitudes—dollars have been sold rather than bought.[20]

It is interesting to consider the possibility that even if the effects on protectionism of an overvalued currency and the resulting trade deficit are no less damaging now than under the Bretton Woods system, there is still an additional independent effect of the balance of payments that has been eliminated. Clearly the need to defend the stock of reserves or the value of the currency has vanished utterly for the United States. Were balance of payments concerns a source of protectionism in the past, beyond what can be attributed to current account concerns?

In the 1960s the U.S. president responded to rising capital outflows by capital controls rather than by restrictive trade measures. But balance of payments concerns, arising from capital outflows as much as from the trade deficit, were certainly behind President Nixon's imposition of a 10 percent import surcharge in August 1971. Congressional attitudes in at least one piece of protectionist legislation made a balance of payments motive explicit. Section 122 of the Trade Act of 1974, written while still under the influence of the recently ended fixed exchange rate era, provided for a uniform tariff surcharge to be put in place if made necessary by certain future conditions: "to deal with large and serious balance-of-payments deficits" and "to prevent an imminent and significant depreciation of the dollar in foreign exchange markets." Thus balance of payments deficits must be considered one more potential macroeconomic cause of protectionism in addition to trade deficits, one currently absent in the United States.

Although the tariff surcharge provided for in section 122 has never been invoked, the possibility of doing so was raised by a number of congressmen in March 1984 in response to the record U.S. trade deficits. Testimony before the Senate Finance Committee was unanimously in opposition, and the proposal was quickly disavowed by the senators.[21] The major arguments offered against the proposal were the obvious ones: that the growing trade deficit was a symptom of the growing federal budget deficit and could not be suppressed by trade barriers, that a tariff surcharge would lower U.S. economic welfare by raising prices to consumers and industries that use imported inputs, that it would provoke foreign retaliation, and—in one particularly virulent version of the proposal that aims the tariff surcharge only at Japan—that it would violate the U.S. treaty obligation under the GATT to a nondiscriminatory (MFN) trade policy. But the Council of Economic Advisers added in its testimony as a more technical argument against the proposal the point that "section 122 appears not even to apply to the current situation" because it was written to deal with balance of payments and exchange rate problems not relevant in 1984.[22]

Early in 1985 talk resurfaced on Capitol Hill, evidently of a more serious nature than the year before, of imposing a uniform tariff surcharge. Due attention to the balance of payments point should ensure that the proponents of this proposal are not able to appeal to section 122 this time and must instead seek new legislation.

3.4.3 Summary of Macroeconomic Factors

To review the potential macroeconomic determinants of protectionism considered thus far, the most important is probably the exchange rate: an overvalued currency induces a rise in import competition, hypothesized to increase protectionist pressures. Normally one would expect that other factors that hurt output and employment in an industry would raise sympathy for it and strengthen its chance of winning protection; such factors include a loss in export sales and a loss in domestic demand attributable to recession. Indeed one hypothesis is that a loss in domestic demand contributes to protectionist pressure as much as a loss in net foreign demand.

One counterintuitive possibility is that losses in output or employment due to macroeconomic factors other than the exchange rate might actually reduce an industry's chances of winning protection. To win escape clause protection, the industry must convince the ITC that there is no other cause of injury that exceeds import competition in importance. In the case of domestic recession, this counterintuitive result might apply to protectionism even outside the escape clause proceedings. The reason is that the industry is less likely to be able to point to a rising level of imports in time of recession. Furthermore a given numerical import quota will become more binding, and represent a greater rate of protection in tariff-equivalent form, if the level of demand is rising. But the normal presumption is still that protectionism is countercyclical. An industry experiencing rapid growth of output, profits, and employment as a result of a domestic expansion is unlikely to win sympathy merely because domestic residents are increasing their demand for imports as fast as or faster than their demand for the industry's product.

Real interest rates can affect the level of protectionism through a variety of routes. An industry can lose domestic demand, even in the absence of a decline in the level of aggregate GNP, as a result of shifts in the monetary-fiscal mix. Record structural federal budget deficits in the United States in recent years, as a result of tax cuts and rising military expenditure, have driven up real interest rates. Sectors that face demand that is particularly sensitive to the level of real interest rates have been hurt by this factor. These sectors include construction, consumer durables, petroleum and other minerals, agriculture, and forest products. On the other hand, weapons manufacturers and other suppliers to the military have benefited, as have personal computer manu- facturers and other producers of consumer goods able to capitalize on the increase in disposable income resulting from the tax cuts. The effects on domestic demand can then have the same positive or inverse effects on protectionism already discussed.

High real interest rates are also thought to be a major cause of the net capital inflow into the United States in recent years. The effect on protectionist pressures by the appreciation of the dollar and the resulting trade deficit is subsumed in the effect of an overvalued currency.[23] For any given trade deficit, net capital outflow was an additional determinant of the overall balance of payments that was a source of some protectionist pressure under the Bretton Woods system but is absent from the current floating currency regime, at least for the United States.

3.4.4 Evidence on the Competing Hypotheses

One can think of three possible approaches to try to evaluate the empirical plausibility of the macroeconomic hypotheses of protectionism, relative to each other or relative to the alternative set of microeconomic hypotheses considered in the following section. First, one might try to relate the level of protectionism to macroeconomic variables over time, across countries, or across industries. No matter how one approaches it, the difficulty in measuring the level of protection is a serious roadblock to any empirical study. Although the observable level of tariffs has fallen steadily among the industrialized countries, nontariff barriers are increasingly important. One can conclude with some confidence that protectionism was stronger in 1985 than it was at the beginning of the decade. But real interest rates and the real exchange value of the dollar are both higher than they were in 1980 so that this simple observation does not allow us to choose even among the macroeconomic hypotheses.

An examination of the level of protectionism across countries gives slightly more information. A recent study of protectionist actions among the major industrialized countries at the office of the U.S. Trade Representative found that the EC started from a higher level of protection in 1980 than did the United States and that protectionist barriers have since gone up on both sides of the Atlantic, with the United States implementing restrictive actions on manufactured goods of somewhat wider scope that the EC in 1981 and 1982 and of somewhat narrower scope than the EC in 1983. The study also noted that Japan started from a high level of restriction in 1980 but has enacted no further trade restrictive measures since then.

The comparison between the United States and Europe for the period since 1980 offers powerful evidence against the view that the exchange rate is a dominant determinant of protectionist tendencies. If an increase in protectionism results when a real appreciation of the currency deteriorates the trade balance, then one might expect by symmetry that a decrease in protectionism would result when a real depreciation of the currency improves the trade balance. Bergsten and Williamson (1983, p. 111) argue that the restoration of dollar equilibrium by means of the devaluations of 1971 and 1973 corresponded to extensive unilateral U.S. trade liberalization in 1973–1974 and legislation authorizing further liberalization by means of the multilateral trade negotiations and that the 1978–1979 period of dollar weakness helped strengthen congressional support for ratification of the outcome to those negotiations (the Tokyo Round).

But the European currencies have depreciated enormously against the dollar since 1980: 43 percent for the mark, 57 percent for the franc, and 62 percent for the pound (from the 1980 average to February 1, 1985). The trade balance of the EC has improved accordingly, from $3.1 billion to an estimated $14 billion in 1984 and projected $23.5 billion in 1985.[24] Far from undergoing a burst of free trade activity, Europe has experienced a level and rate of change of protectionist barriers that seem to be at least as bad as those in the United States. It is true that other factors exist, and one cannot say what would have happened in the absence of the exchange rate change. Perhaps there has been an exogenous increase in general protectionist sentiment in Europe, arising, for example, from political factors, that has been enough to more than offset favorable effects from currency depreciation. But the depreciation of the

European currencies has been so extreme as to rule out a fully symmetrical argument as to the dominance of the exchange rate as the determinant of protectionism.

Bergsten and Williamson (1983, p. 119) advance a nonsymmetrical version of the exchange argument designed to meet this objection: "Prolonged deviations of exchange rates from fundamental equilibrium can and do generate protectionist pressures, from countries with both overvalued and undervalued currencies. Considerable asymmetries compound the problem and fail to achieve much, if any, in the way of countervailing pressures in the other direction." McCulloch (1983, p. 19) interprets the Bergsten-Williamson hypothesis as a ratchet effect of exchange rate volatility on the average level of protection:[25]

While prolonged overvaluation of the dollar gives rise to new arguments for all manner of sectoral protection, as in 1981 and 1982, any new protection is likely to persist long after the overvaluation has disappeared. Moreover, they [Bergsten-Williamson] argue, even undervaluation might add to protectionist pressures by attracting resources into industries with secularly declining international competitiveness, or at least slowing their exit. When the inappropriately low currency value finally moves upward again, protection will be demanded.

A ratchet argument would attribute current European protectionist barriers to past appreciations of European currencies as in 1977–1978 and to the political difficulty of removing the barriers during the 1980–1984 depreciation of their currencies. It would attribute U.S. barriers to the opposite side of the same exchange rate cycle. This argument could explain a 1985 level of protection that is higher worldwide than in 1977. But it retains the drawback that it is unable to explain an increasing level of European protectionism during the 1980–1984 period; under the ratchet hypothesis one would expect that European barriers would at most have remained at their 1980 levels.

Empirical comparison across industries offers some hope for answering more satisfactorily questions left unanswered by comparisons over time or across countries. It provides a way of getting around the stumbling block of the unmeasurability of the level of protectionist barriers. We know that certain industries have succeeded in attaining import protection and others have not. The story of protectionism in the United States, leaving aside the high barriers benefiting many agricultural products, is overwhelmingly the story of a few key manufacturing sectors—steel, autos, textiles, and footwear—and secondarily the story of a number of much smaller industries. The fact that protection is so much more prevalent in some sectors than others might suggest that sector-specific goals may underlie it more than overall trade balance concerns.[26] But it is possible that the protected sectors are those that are the most sensitive to macroeconomic fluctuations.

What macroeconomic characteristics do these industries have that their less protected sisters lack? Certainly all have suffered losses in income and employment. But to what extent are such losses to be attributed to exchange rate problems, to what extent to the overall level of domestic activity, to what extent to real interest rates, and to what extent to long-run secular trends arising from microeconomic or sectoral factors?

One point is in order even before we attempt to answer these questions systematically. One of the most striking aspects of protectionism among the industrialized countries is the extent to which each of them tends to protect the same set of industries. In the last few years the United States, Belgium, Germany, and then the EC have imposed VERs on autos. France, the EC, and the United States have added barriers to motorcycles. The United States and the EC have increased protection of steel. The most universally protected manufacturing sectors are textiles and footwear (the United States, Europe, Canada and Japan), though most of the barriers went up before 1980.[27]

The fact that barriers in steel, autos, and motorcycles have gone up since 1980 on both sides of the Atlantic is more evidence against the exchange rate hypothesis. If the overvalued dollar were the explanation for U.S. protectionism and an exogenous increase in general protectionist sentiment in Europe the explanation for restrictive measures in Europe despite the depreciation of their currencies, then those sectors that are the most sensitive to the exchange rate and therefore the most protected in the United States should still be among the least protected in Europe.

3.4.5 Econometric Evidence

We now turn to an econometric investigation of the sensitivity to macroeconomic factors of economic activity in autos, steel, textiles and apparel, and metal fasteners (lag bolts, nuts and screws of iron or steel, protected by safeguard from January 1979 to January 1982), as compared to manufacturing in general. The employment results are striking (table 3.6). First, by far the most significant explanatory variable in each case is a simple time trend. Each of these four industries is in secular decline, at rates ranging from 1.64 percent per year for textiles and apparel to 3.60 percent per year for steel, relative to the rest of the economy. Manufacturing in the aggregate is also declining secularly to make room for the services sector but only at 1.08 percent a year relative to the overall economy. All four industries are also highly procyclical, but their sensitivity to the level of GNP is no greater than that for manufacturing in the aggregate.[28]

Table 3.6
Determinants of the (log) employment in protected industries, 1962–1984

	Constant	Log real effective value of dollar (six-quarter lag, sum)	Real interest rate (six-quarter lag, sum)	Log real GNP	Time	$\bar{R}^2$	Standard error of regression	Auto correlation correction
Autos	−13.82 (2.84)	.253 (.168)	−.024** (.009)	2.655** (0.426)	−.0064** (.0012)	.61	.088	.16 (.12)
Steel	−3.95 (3.09)	−.739** (.215)	−.007 (.010)	2.136** (0.428)	−.0090** (.0012)	.96	.044	.77** (.07)
Textiles and apparel	−2.16 (0.88)	.071 (.055)	−.005* (.003)	1.396** (0.127)	−.0041** (.0004)	.96	.016	.59** (.10)
Fasteners	−4.49 (2.47)	−.553** (.192)	.009 (.008)	1.644** (.320)	−.0054** (.0009)	.91	.030	.88** (.05)
Total manufacturing	−8.32 (0.62)	−.004 (.036)	−.000 (.002)	2.121** (0.092)	−.0027** (.0003)	.99	.019	.17 (.11)

Note: Standard errors are reported in parentheses.
*Significant at the 90 percent level.
**Significant at the 95 percent level.

The significant macroeconomic coefficients appear in the protected industry regressions; the exchange rate and real interest rate effects are nil (in terms
of coefficient levels and statistical significance) for overall manufacturing,
though there is presumably less noise in the more highly aggregated variable.
The results for steel support the exchange rate hypothesis strongly; the point
estimate coefficient of $-.74$ would imply that the 60 percent real appreciation
of the dollar against an average of ten trading partners (October 1984 relative
to the 1980 average) has induced a 44 percent contraction of employment in the
steel industry.[29] The overvalued dollar is indeed an explanation for the severe
trade problems in steel and perhaps for the succession of safeguard rulings and
VERs won by the industry in 1982, 1983, and 1984. The exchange rate effect
for metal fasteners is almost as strong. On the other hand the exchange rate
coefficient for autos is neither significant nor of the hypothesized sign,
reflecting the fact that the import—new supply ratio rose during the
1977–1980 period of dollar depreciation (from 9.4 percent to 20.1 percent) and
fell during the 1980–1984 period of dollar appreciation (to an estimated 15.7
percent).[30]

An interesting finding is that the coefficient on the real interest rate is
negative for each of autos (significant at the 99 percent level), steel, and textiles
and apparel (significant at the 90 percent level). The real interest rate has an
independent effect beyond any losses in domestic demand captured by the
GNP variable. To the extent that the rising U.S. structural federal budget
deficit explains the high level of real interest rates that has prevailed since 1980,
losses suffered by the industry can be viewed in part as the result of government crowding out. The shift in demand away from U.S.-produced automobiles may be due less to a shift in consumer demand toward more fuel-efficient
imports than to a shift in government demand toward (fuel-inefficient) tanks.

To the extent that high U.S. real interest rates explain the capital inflow and
the dollar appreciation, the two variables offer complementary explanations as
to why these sectors are the protected ones. But there are two respects in
which the observed negative effect of the real interest rate works to undermine
the exchange rate hypothesis. First, real interest rates have been higher since
1980 in Europe too. The real interest rate effect could explain increased
protection of autos on both sides of the Atlantic in a way that the exchange rate
effect cannot. Second, if the attribution of U.S. protectionism to the dollar
overvaluation is intended as one argument (among others) in favor of government action to reduce the appreciation, through sterilized foreign exchange
intervention or capital controls, then it must contend with the Feldstein
doctrine.[31]

Assume total GNP is exogenously determined by potential GNP or by velocity-shift-adjusted monetary targeting—otherwise known as nominal GNP targeting—on the part of the Fed. Then a reduction in the value of the dollar would succeed in helping those industries that are particularly sensitive to the exchange rate only at the expense of other industries, so that total GNP comes out the same. McCulloch (1983, p. 20) argues that the total level of government distortions (including not only protection but also government procurement, technical assistance, and subsidized credit) is determined by the level of total economic activity: "it is plausible to expect industry-specific intervention to increase when national unemployment is high and to take the specific form of new trade barriers when the dollar is overvalued."

The specific mechanism whereby government action to reduce the value of the dollar would hurt other sectors would be as follows. Whether the capital inflow is shut off by capital controls or the exchange value of the dollar is pushed down by central bank sales of dollar bonds in exchange for foreign bonds, an effect would be to increase domestic interest rates. Those sectors facing demand that is particularly sensitive to real interest rates—construction, capital goods, and autos—would lose. In effect the burden of government crowding out would be redistributed among the other sectors. The auto regression coefficient in table 3.6 is evidence that the auto industry would on net lose by the change, with the possible result of increased protection for Detroit.

To sum up the evidence, the four highly protected sectors are more vulnerable to the level of aggregate demand than the rest of the economy but only to the same extent as the other nonprotected sectors within manufacturing. The steel industry appears to be particularly sensitive to the exchange rate, offering some support for the hypothesis that the overvalued dollar explains recent protectionist actions. But the exchange rate hypothesis is weakened by the observation that the Europeans have also raised barriers to steel in recent years. The auto industry is particularly sensitive to the real interest rate, supporting a hypothesis capable of explaining protectionism on both sides of the Atlantic.

The macroeconomic hypotheses appear to be incomplete explanations of protectionism, however. The most significant explanatory variable in table 3.6 is the simple time trend, suggesting that long-run structural problems, more than macroeconomic factors, may be the root cause of protectionism. It is possible, as McCulloch argues, that the exchange rate and other macroeconomic variables are merely the excuses cited by problem industries in their efforts to obtain government assistance.

3.5 Micro and Structural Reasons for Protection

On the structural and micro side there are four broad reasons for protection: productivity growth abroad, intersectoral misalignments, wage problems, and transfer problems. All of these sources of disturbances have in common that industry loses external competitiveness on the import or export side. They differ, however, in the macroeconomic implications for aggregate employment. For that reason it is worthwhile separating out the microcauses and the macroeffects.

3.5.1 Productivity Shifts

Ricardian models highlight best how trade problems emerge from shifting international productivity differentials. At the competitive margin, unit labor costs are equalized. A gain in foreign productivity, with given wages, causes foreign workers to become cost competitive in a range of industries where previously the United States competed successfully with imports or where it was exporting. The U.S. range of nontraded goods therefore shifts as import-competing firms disappear and export firms lose competitiveness in foreign markets. The effect on employment depends crucially on the flexibility of wages and on the accommodating macroeconomic policies. If wages are sticky downward, some home unemployment must result, and the protection issue will arise.

We can imagine a number of ways in which the productivity growth issue comes up. The simplest is that between advanced and backward countries. The latter benefit from export and harmonization of technology; they catch up. As low-wage countries, they will exploit a common technology or benefit from harmonization, thus expanding the range of goods they produce at the expense of the stagnant country. Their demand for some of the stagnant countries' goods will rise, but that will be insufficient to maintain employment there. Under fixed wages and catch-up productivity growth, the advanced but stagnant country gets caught with unemployment and cumulative lack of competitiveness. In a Keynesian setting this would imply that Japan's dramatic productivity growth of the 1950s and 1960s, and that of the NICs since, work as a cumulative source of unemployment.

Most of the foreign growth may directly reduce the competitiveness of U.S. import-competing firms (textiles, rubber footwear, steel, automobiles) and cost jobs in these sectors. But it is equally possible that the United States loses markets in the growing countries themselves or in third countries. Whichever way the foreign catch-up occurs, the fact is that lack of wage flexibility will mean an inability to offset the foreign gain in competitiveness and an inability to sustain employment. Protection would solve the problems for the particular sector. Protection in the case of import penetration would offset the foreign gain in competitiveness, maintain competitors' tariff-inclusive prices, and hence maintain employment in the affected industry. If the tariff rebates were redistributed, aggregate home employment could even grow.

In case of a loss in export competitiveness, protection cannot help. In fact, if anything, it hurts because it maintains labor demand outside the export sector, thus making it impossible to cut wage costs and sustain export employment. Furthermore import protection will tend to appreciate the currency, making it that much harder for exporters (or any unprotected sectors) to compete. Under fully flexible wages the home wage would decline and thus improve the competitiveness at the import margin and dampen the loss of competitiveness on the export side. Absent flexible wages, only export subsidies (credit subsidies for example) prove effective in maintaining employment.

Among the productivity changes that affect a country's external competitiveness are changes in transport costs. A reduction in international transport costs reduces an import-competing industry's natural protection and thus can serve to provoke protectionism. There are great historical episodes of such reductions. Perhaps the most famous is the Libby process, which allowed Argentina and Australia to become suppliers of meat in Europe and the United States. Years ago the U.S. steel industry had the natural advantage of locating close to supplies of coal and iron ore simultaneously; one reason that it has lost comparative advantage to the Japanese steel industry is that reduced transport costs make Australian coal and South American iron ore internationally accessible. Increased international competition comes in the same way from the growing tendency to assemble rather than produce. A country may lose employment as particular parts of the production process are farmed out to low-wage areas that can compete with a low wage, high skill, and high reliability.

It is worth spelling out in more detail the exact channels through which foreign productivity growth affects domestic employment. This will depend on the market structure. Two main possibilities exist. The first case is one where the home country produces and supplies a competitive world market. A reduction in world price relative to domestic wages brought about by foreign productivity growth will lead profit-maximizing firms to cut output and employment. The second possibility is based on the analysis of Dixit and Stiglitz (1977) in which there is monopolistic competition and the home and foreign country produce imperfect substitutes. In that case demand for domestic output and domestic employment depend on the relative unit labor costs (including transport costs) of domestic and foreign producers. Given wages in each country and given the exchange rate, a rise in foreign productivity or a cut in transport costs will make foreign firms more cost competitive and thus shift demand and employment away from domestic producers. Domestic producers lose customers in both the home market and abroad. The domestic markups over unit labor costs will remain unchanged, and, given wages, so will prices. But that means the relative price of domestic products has risen, and therefore demand and employment must fall.

The reduction in total profits of domestic producers and the decline in employment will lead to a call for protection. Moreover at a time when exchange rates move significantly and where inflation rates and rates of money wage increase differ internationally, it will be hard to resist the claim that an industry's problems are due to the exchange rate rather than adverse relative unit labor costs in a common currency. This is all the more the case because each of the domestic suppliers will have exactly the same experience: their demand curves shift inward as customers shift to foreign suppliers.

3.5.2 Australian Disease

Intersectoral misalignments are a source of protectionist pressure when favorable supply shocks in one industry increase factor costs or cause real exchange appreciation, thus reducing the international competitiveness of other industries. We can separate two main possibilities. One is that a broad sector of the economy not engaged in international trade has growth in productivity and therefore bids up wages relative to the prevailing exchange rate. Profitability in the remaining industries will be squeezed as a result, and this would lead to protectionist pressure, though not necessarily for aggregate employment reasons. The other possibility is that resource discoveries through any of a variety of channels bring about real exchange rate appreciation. The appreciation reduces the competitiveness of manufacturing and as a consequence brings about a call for increased protection as has occurred in the United Kingdom, for example, or in Australia.

It is worth trying to separate out what is macro and micro in these disturbances. Clearly at the level of the affected industry, there is a loss in competitiveness and hence a decline in employment. But there are offsetting effects on employment in other sectors. Specifically the nontraded sector would expand as a result of favorable income effects and might well serve to absorb the labor shed by the unprofitable traded goods sector. Protection then would be primarily the outcome of sectoral adjustment difficulties rather than aggregate unemployment.

3.5.3 Transfer Problem

Shifts in international demand for a country's products or shifts in foreign supply are an important source of sectoral and potentially aggregate adjustment difficulties. A particularly interesting possibility has come up in the form of the debt crisis. Credit rationing in world markets has forced debtor LDCs to reduce absorption while generating net earnings of foreign exchange to service (at least partially) their debts. The turnaround in their trade balances is achieved by restriction of imports and expansion of exports. If these changes are anything but very transitory, they are bound to pose an important adjustment problem in developed countries. Imports from LDCs become more competitive as these countries take real wage cuts. Developed country (DC) exports to these countries are curtailed by reduced competitiveness or outright protection in the debtor countries' markets.

The adjustment difficulty here is the following: LDC absorption is reduced to effect the transfer, and the transfer takes the form of increased import penetration and reduced exports of DCs. But the resources displaced from employment in those sectors are not necessarily absorbed into employment elsewhere. The recipients of the transfer may save rather than spend, or they may spend on foreign goods. There is no assurance that employment creation is automatic or easy. Moreover, that problem will be worse the higher are the transfers being extracted. Receiving interest from abroad is one of the most painful experiences a country can undergo, and this may well be the medium-term aftermath of the debt crisis.

At first sight the receipt of a transfer would appear beneficial. That would be the case if spending propensities of recipients and payers were the same and all goods were traded. But if new money is diverted from LDCs to domestic borrowers, perhaps including the government, spending patterns are very different. Our traded goods sector must lose out to home services and defense; manufacturing hurts while the rest of the economy experiences increased real wages and strong demand.

Here is a particularly difficult issue in adjustment. If the transfer is to be effected, net exports must decline. We can choose to reduce exports or to increase imports but cannot avoid both unless we are willing to pass up the transfer. Protection of the import-competing industry merely means that we are forcing the paying countries to earn their net foreign exchange by cutting down even more on their imports by restriction or depression. A lack of coordination between the financial sector (extracting transfers) and the real sector (seeking protection or foreign market access) betrays the difficulty of

Table 3.7

The transfer problem: 1984 compared to 1982

	Change in exports	Change in imports
Latin America total	7.1%	−14.1%
Latin America/United States	18.6	−15.0

Source: United Nations, *Commodity Trade Statistics.*

Table 3.8

Growth of output and employment (average annual rate)

	1970–1980		1980–1984	
	United States	EC	United States	EC
GDP growth	2.9	2.9	2.0	0.8
Employment growth	2.0	.2	.8	−.6

Source: *European Economy* (November 1984).

having it both ways. Table 3.7 shows some data on the transfer that is underway. We concentrate on Latin America as the main debtor area.

3.5.4 Wages

Wage problems can be a source of protectionist pressure in one of two ways. The first is that economy-wide excessively high wages cause unemployment and hence a motive for protection against imports even if imports are not the cause of unemployment. It is hard to separate the wage problem from the productivity issue. Ultimately employment and trade are determined by relative unit labor costs in a common currency (neglecting other cost elements and policy interventions). Thus wages, exchange rates, and total labor productivity appear on a par. But we concentrate here on wages to make the point that if wages get out of line, given everything else, then unemployment is inevitable and protectionism likely.

The view in Europe is that wage problems account for the dramatic unemployment problem. As noted in table 3.8, over the period 1970–1984, employment in the EC showed no growth, while in the United States employment growth over that period averaged more than 1.4 percent. It is argued that lack of wage adjustments to oil shocks and excessive nonwage increases in costs and restrictions reduced the incentive to use labor in Europe. Slow growth in output and large capital substitution accounted for the lack of employment growth. If we combine this with an increase in import penetration, there is an obvious case on which protectionism can ride.

Protectionism has indeed been high in Europe. In Britain the Cambridge Group, following Keynes's 1931 example, has called for across-the-board protection of manufacturing. In continental Europe protectionist sentiments, particularly in regard to Japan and LDCs, run similarly high. What help could protection bring? The argument would be that with import protection or export subsidies, a beggar-thy-neighbor solution could be brought to the domestic unemployment problem. Even if unemployment results primarily because too high wages make too many goods not produced in the service sector (shoeshines, belly dancing), protection is a solution since the implicit production subsidy will attract skilled labor into manufacturing and thus open up employment to unskilled labor that now is displaced even in the service sector.

But there is the important issue of real wages: import protection would reduce real wages and may therefore lead to offsetting wage demands, thus frustrating the employment effects at least in part.[32] Export subsidies would not have the same effect directly, but they would be a burden on the budget. Combining the two might be thought of as self-financing, but it is also equivalent to a devaluation, thus highlighting the problem of sticky real wages.

The European wage issue is particularly dramatic in view of the obvious overvaluation of the dollar. The dollar appreciation is particularly large relative to Europe. If the dollar is overvalued and European real wages are too high, at whose expense or how can Europe gain competitiveness? If Europe is looking for increased employment through foreign trade, whose exports are to be stopped and who is to import more from Europe?

The combination of dollar overvaluation and European lack of employment might have two answers: yen appreciation or domestic European expansion combined with supply-side policies to promote labor use. The European problem is particularly threatening because the sharp gain in external competitiveness in 1980–1984 surely must account for some of the recent growth. Should the exchange rate protection disappear and domestic macropolicy fail to respond, protectionism may well explode more than it has in the United States. The reason is that Europe today is at an all-time high of unemployment and that unemployment is rising even under the extremely favorable external competitiveness conditions.

The second way in which wage problems arise is sectoral. Particular industries, perhaps because of unionization, achieve a level of wages significantly above the economy-wide average and beyond what is consistent with external competitiveness. In the United States this is the case of the automobile and steel industries. Table 3.9 shows U.S. wages for all manufacturing at large and

Table 3.9
Hourly compensation, 1984 (U.S. dollars)

	Manufacturing	Automobiles	Iron and Steel
United States	$12.82	$19.94	$20.24
Germany	9.57	12.00	10.38
Japan	6.42	8.10	11.12

Source: Bureau of Labor Statistics.

in these two industries. For comparison we also show the wages in Germany and Japan for these sectors.

The misalignment of wages in these key industries is a reflection of strong union power and a long tradition of automatic productivity raises way out of line with actual productivity growth or with economy-wide wage growth. As is well understood, these disequilibrium wages are protected by restrictive trade policies.

There is an interesting difference between the automobile and steel industry on one side and textiles, leather, or rubber footwear on the other. In the latter case there is just as much of a protection problem, but one cannot point to wage problems by the economy-wide standard. Absolute wages are extremely low, but even so the industries are uncompetitive.

3.6 What Is Wrong with Japan?

Japan is the focal point of U.S. protectionism. Protectionism is active for a large number of products, but in no case does it focus on a single country in the way it seizes on Japan. There is some concern about the NICs and a lesser problem with Europe, but the attention focuses on Japan. In 1983 U.S. business sent Secretary of the Treasury Donald Regan to induce the Japanese Ministry of Finance to accept a program of capital market liberalization that was supposed to strengthen the exchange value of the yen against the dollar.[33] U.S. labor would be only too happy to see Japan sink into the sea.

Japan is special in attracting this privileged place of attention. What accounts for the special place? Three common arguments are brought in support of protection against Japan. The first is that exchange rate changes have led to a loss in U.S. competitiveness in relation to Japan and that if the yen cannot be brought up, then tariffs or quotas must do the work. The facts do not support this view.

Clearly the yen today is within a few percent of the average of 1977–1981 and in fact appreciated in 1983–1984 compared to 1982 (table 3.10). Japanese labor compensation, measured in dollars, has increased nearly 20 percent

Table 3.10
Determinants of Japan's competitiveness

	1982	1983	1984
Yen/$	108.7	103.7	103.7
Wages[a]	106.1	114.3	119.6

Note: Index 1977–1981 = 100.
a. Wages measured in U.S. dollars refer to production workers in manufacturing.

above the average of 1977–1981. Of course, in the United States wage inflation has been far higher and productivity growth much lower than in Japan. As a consequence U.S. producers have lost cost competitiveness. If anything one might argue that on purchasing-power-parity grounds, the yen should have appreciated, but certainly it cannot be argued that yen depreciation conveyed gains in competitiveness.

The second argument is that Japan has raised trade barriers that prevent entry into its markets. The argument is incorrect in two ways. First, there has been no increase in barriers. Japan is tradeproof but not because of a new layer of restrictions. The argument is also fallacious to an extent because increased import protection, even if it had taken place, would have reduced export competitiveness. The rise in import barriers would have drawn resources into import substitution, thus raising the costs to exporters and impairing their international competitiveness (for example, by real appreciation of the yen).

A variant of the protection argument focuses on the level rather than the change in Japanese trade barriers. In this perspective Japan is depicted as an economy with a low level of import penetration, and it is concluded that trade restrictions must be the reason. That argument runs into trouble with the identification problem. Low levels of import penetration may be the consequence merely of size, dependence on foreign raw materials rather than foreign manufactures, or geographical remoteness, or they may be due to trade restriction. Overall U.S. import penetration is not much different from that of Japan, and any generalization that applies there could equally apply to the United States.

The third argument concentrates on the bilateral trade balance. One would note the difference (until 1983) between the U.S.-Japan balance and the bilateral balance with, say, Europe. The bilateral balance with Japan is consistently in deficit (figure 3.8). The Council of Economic Advisers, among others, has for some time made the argument that no special significance should be attached to the bilateral balance.[34]

In a multilateral setting Japan buys oil and raw materials from one set of countries and sells manufactures to another set of countries. The United States

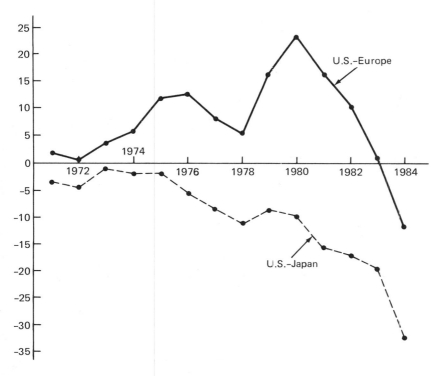

Figure 3.8
Bilateral trade balance (billions of U.S. dollars). Source: Department of Commerce, *Survey of Current Business*, various issues.

happens to be on the receiving side. There is no reason to see in a bilateral imbalance a reason for protection unless one were to accept that any country that runs a bilateral deficit with the United States also has a right to protect itself against the U.S. invasion of its markets.

In the end there is no sound argument for the special place accorded to Japan in U.S. and European protectionist sentiment. One must assume that faced with sheer inimitable Japanese performance, the adversely affected industries seek protection entirely because they do not want the competition. (The remaining logical alternative is racism.)

3.7 Coordination and Consistency

In the 1980–1984 period the world economy was governed by the sharply divergent policy mix in the United States and abroad. U.S. fiscal policy has gone on an expansionary binge, while abroad there has been a sharp contrac-

Table 3.11
General government budget trends (percentage of GDP)

	Actual budget		Cumulated change in adjusted budget, 1980–1985[b]
	1984	1985[a]	
United States	3.2	3.6	4.5
Germany	1.7	0.9	+4.2
Japan	2.2	0.8	+3.2
Non-U.S. OECD	4.0	3.2	+1.7

Source: OECD, *Economic Outlook*, various issues.
a. Forecast.
b. Actual budget cyclically adjusted.

tion. Table 3.11 shows the changes in actual and cyclically and inflation-adjusted budgets.

In addition to divergent fiscal policies, monetary policy has been relatively tight in the United States, producing persistent interest differentials in favor of the United States. The mix of policies has led to a Mundell-Fleming real appreciation of the dollar. The current account deterioration has spread U.S. growth abroad and has partly offset the fiscal stimulus. Crowding out, as predicted by the Mundell-Fleming model, has taken place not in construction but in the international sector. The recovery has been lopsided, largely leaving out trade-oriented manufacturing and agriculture.

As a result of the change in relative activity levels in the United States and abroad and of the real appreciation, the U.S. trade deficit increased over the 1980–1984 period by about 2 percent of GNP. Two-thirds of that deterioration can be attributed to the real exchange rate change and one-third to the relatively stronger U.S. activity.[35] The worsening of the trade deficit was significantly dampened by a large decline in the real price of oil. Looking ahead we can ask where, at the current levels of relative activity, real oil prices, and the real exchange rate, the trade deficit will end up. Assuming that the variables will be sustained at their 1984, quarter 3, levels and using trade equation 3.1, the deficit would rise to 4.2 percent of GNP ($160 billion at current GNP levels). The trade deficit moderated substantially in the last quarter of 1984 and first quarter of 1985, but that can be attributed to the lower cost of imports resulting in the short run from the renewed appreciation of the dollar. Projections show that the trade deficit will again deteriorate rapidly in late 1985 and 1986 as export volumes rise in lagged response to the appreciation (the J-curve). That compares with an average of 3.5 percent in the first three quarters of 1984.

Sensible coordination of policies among industrialized countries must pay attention to the long-run implications of the present imbalance. Ultimately deficits of the current size are unsustainable and will be cut. When that happens, resources will have to be reemployed in the foreign trade sector. But the present loss of competitiveness leads to an erosion of profitability and disappearance of firms as production is shifted abroad. The longer the overvaluation and imbalance persists, the larger will be the ultimate overshooting of real exchange rates required to restore employment and external balance. To restore more balance in the composition of production and aggregate demand, a suitable policy might have the following characteristics:

• In the United States fiscal tightening is accompanied by a monetary expansion that allows real interest rates to decline. The dollar falls in real terms, and growth is maintained slightly above trend.

• In Europe (Germany, the United Kingdom, and France) and Japan, fiscal policy is temporarily eased to sustain growth in the face of real appreciation. Interest rates are allowed to decline, matching the fall in U.S. interest rates. The fiscal expansion can be afforded because the decline in interest rates lowers worldwide public debt service, thus freeing revenue for tax cuts.

• Debtor countries are assured of continued growth in the Organization for Economic Cooperation and Development (OECD) and open markets in the goods they produce (including sensitive sectors as steel, textiles, shoes, copper, meat, and sugar) and have the additional advantages of lower interest rates and, because of dollar depreciation, increased nominal and real commodity prices. Accordingly they gain room to reduce some of their import restrictions and, more important, to expand demand.

The policy package avoids a number of inconsistencies. One is the difficulty of extracting debt service from debtor countries without accepting their goods or suffering losses of export revenue. Under the package less interest will be paid, and part of it will be paid out of LDCs' terms of trade improvements. The other inconsistency avoided by a shift toward restraint concerns the U.S. manufacturing base. Ultimately the United States wants full employment and has to service its newly created external debt. It would be unwise to sacrifice in the interim manufacturing critical to employment and export earnings. It might be argued that the emphasis on manufacturing is entirely misplaced; after all the United States is becoming a service economy, the home of the new information society. The argument is impressive, but it has failed so far to show in the trade figures.

Are there alternatives? The bad dream alternative is a U.S. move to a uniform import surcharge for balance of payments reasons. This might be called the Motorola alternative.[36] Superficially it appears to be the right solution because, with the stroke of the pen, it would kill two birds: increased competitiveness for the import-competing industries in distress and increased fiscal revenue. In fact, it would kill even three birds: under the impact of inevitable foreign contraction and retaliation, U.S. exports would disappear too. Beyond that it is not certain that exchange appreciation might not even offset in good measure the contrived gain in protection.[37] It is extraordinary that good money is being spent on lobbying so idiotic a scheme.

A serious alternative that has been suggested is capital controls.[38] If the strong dollar is due to excessively high yield differentials in favor of the United States, then control of international capital by a real interest equalization tax or a Tobin tax would be an obvious step to reduce the attractiveness of U.S. assets.

It cannot be said that the economist's welfare argument for laissez-faire applies just as strongly to transactions on the international capital account as on the trade account. Much of international capital flows do not take place for the intertemporally optimizing reasons of theoretical models but rather in response to two perennial nonmarket forces: death and taxes. First, large net capital flows are often associated with large government deficits, which in turn are associated with exogenous increases in military spending; in U.S. history the largest net capital outflow (as a share of GNP) was lending to Europe to fight World War I, and the largest net capital inflow is the current borrowing to finance the defense buildup. Second, large gross capital flows are often associated with tax evasion. This and other forms of capital flight are cited as one possible reason for the appreciation of the dollar. The point is that not all capital flows finance productive investment.

On the other hand, even if capital controls could block off the capital currently flowing to the United States and bring the dollar down, there would be high costs in the form of higher interest rates. Semiconductors manufacturers and other exporting and import-competing firms would benefit from the lower dollar, but construction and other interest-rate-sensitive firms would lose. The government crowding out would be merely redistributed among sectors. Simple commercial or capital account policies thus cannot correct the present international misalignment. Corrective action by the United States must go in a more fundamental direction of adjusting its monetary-fiscal mix and relying on the rest of the world, acting in their own interest, to go along.

Notes

1. The document is reprinted in Ratner (1972, pp. 142–144).

2. See Denison (1974).

3. All right-hand-side variables are measured as logs. The real oil price and relative activity levels are entered as the average of the current and past quarter. The real exchange rate is introduced as a third-order, eight-quarters unconstrained Almon lag; t-statistics are shown in parentheses. If the coefficients are divided by the share of exports (or imports) in GNP, approximately 7 percent for the United States, they can be interpreted as elasticities of demand for exports (or imports).

4. We make no attempt to explain the responsiveness of trade flows in more detail. There are obvious steps to take in exploring separately exports and imports, the differential effects of domestic and foreign income or, better yet, spending, disaggregation by commodity group, and experimentation with alternative aggregates of foreign activity.

5. *Annual Report (USTR)* (1981–1982, p. 197). On the other hand, escape clause relief was allowed to expire in four other cases (nuts and bolts, color television receivers, citizen band radios, and footwear) and denied in two cases (tubeless tire values and fishing rods). Clothespins, porcelain cookware, and mushrooms were the three extended.

6. *Annual Report (USTR)* (1983, p. 144).

7. There are fewer affirmative determinations than cases filed: seven AD and eight CVD in 1982, for example. *USTR* (1984, pp. 129, 133).

8. Frankel (1983, table 1 for 1979–1981), from *Supplement to Employment and Earnings*, U.S. Department of Labor, Bureau of Labor Statistics.

9. Employment in services-producing sectors overall, however, which tend to be nontraded, rose 0.4 percent. U.S. Department of Commerce, *1985 U.S. Industrial Outlook* (January 1985), table 3, p. 32, from Bureau of Labor Statistics, seasonally adjusted establishment data.

10. *Annual Report of the President on the Trade Agreements Program (USTR)* (1983, p. 143).

11. Trade Act of 1974, Public Law 93–618, sec. 201, 88 Stat. 2012, as cited by Baldwin (1985) and Adams and Dirlam (1983, p. 132).

12. Adams and Dirlam (1983, p. 132); Stern and Wechsler (1984, pp. 19–20). Commissioner Paula Stern voted with the majority but on the grounds that various microeconomic problems were a greater cause of injury than imports (pp. 20–22). The minority voting affirmatively consisted of Commissioners George M. Moore and Catherine Bedell and argued that the various causes of injury should be broken down into many individual components, none of which was by itself larger than increased imports as a cause of injury (pp. 23–25).

13. Adams and Dirlam (1983, p. 136); Stern and Wechsler (1984, pp. 31–32). Commissioner Veronica A Haggart voted affirmatively, arguing that imports were a far more important cause (of a threat) of serious injury than macroeconomic factors such as high unemployment and high interest rates (p. 31). Only Commissioner Alfred E. Eckes considered explicitly the legal issue of whether, assuming the recession was a more serious cause of injury than imports, Congress had intended that relief be precluded; he decided that it had not, a position opposite to that taken earlier by Bill Alberger and

Michael J. Calhoun in the automobiles case. Stern and Wechsler (1984, pp. 30–31); Adams and Dirlam (1983, pp. 134–135).

14. Adams and Dirlam (1983, pp. 138–140); Stern and Wechsler (1984, pp. 41–42). In a commendable, and rare, attempt to lay out a logically consistent framework for evaluating these issues, Stern and Wechsler (pp. 3, 35–41) propose a middle ground between the two extremes of making it more difficult for more highly procyclical industries to get relief, which would be the consequence of the Alberger-Calhoun opinion on autos, and eliminating recession from the list of competing causes of injury (even while allowing recession-induced effects to help the industry pass the test of whether it has been seriously injured in the first place, condition 2), which would effectively be the consequence of the Moore-Beddell approach. The middle ground proposed by Stern and Wechsler is that only recessionary effects in excess of what is normal for the industry should be considered a competing cause of injury; the normal losses suffered by a procyclical industry in a normal recession would be considered as only an offset to the gains achieved in boom years.

15. Stern obviously recognizes that imports depend on the exchange rate. One could attempt to make sense of such a ruling by distinguishing the exchange rate effects from other import factors for which foreign producers could more easily be held responsible. Grossman (1984, pp. 15–16) makes such an argument and considers the issue unresolved even on a legal level. But such an interpretation would seem to have little basis in the 201 law, which says nothing about the cause of increases in imports needed to qualify for relief.

16. Only difficulties due to predatory pricing and other antitrust violations by rivals entitle one to remedy comparable to import protection. Even here, Finger, Hall, and Nelson (1982, p. 455) suggest that the antidumping and countervailing duty mechanism "imposes constraints on foreign sellers not imposed by equivalent domestic [for example, antitrust] laws." Furthermore in cases such as Japanese auto exports, protection has taken precedence over antitrust considerations in U.S. policymaking; the voluntary export restraints would have violated U.S. antitrust laws if they had been truly voluntary on the part of Japanese auto manufacturers.

17. See tables 4a, 4b, and 3, pp. 30–34, U.S. Department of Commerce, *1985 U.S. Industrial Outlook*. The four individual sector numbers are establishment survey data, seasonally adjusted; the two aggregate numbers are household survey data, seasonally adjusted; from the Bureau of Labor Statistics.

18. Stern and Wechsler (1984, p. 42); Adams and Dirlam (1983, p. 138).

19. Furthermore, although one cannot use past exchange rate movements to explain why U.S. trade frictions with Japan are greater than with Europe, one could still argue with Bergsten that trying to change the exchange rate is a way to alleviate the protectionist pressures that exist.

20. *Wall Street Journal*, January 25, 1985, p. 23. Most of the intervention was undertaken February 28 and March 1, apparently in the neighborhood of $200 million on the part of the U.S. authorities and $4 billion to $5 billion on the part of the Europeans. *Wall Street Journal*, March 4, 11, 1985; Associated Press, March 8, 1985.

21. Those testifying against included Trade Representative William Brock, Council of Economic Advisers chairman Martin Feldstein, Treasury Deputy Secretary Tim McNamar, and C. Fred Bergsten.

22. Feldstein (1984, p. 4).

23. Stern and Wechsler (1984, p. 44) discuss the various channels through which high interest rates have hurt the specialty steel industry in recent years and argue that for the purposes of determining cause of injury, the effects must be separated into the exchange rate–import channel and other channels.

24. OECD, *Economic Outlook* (December 1984): 131.

25. Dunn (1983, p. 13) similarly says, "Exchange-rate volatility is sometimes blamed for increased protectionist pressures when real appreciation imposes injuries on import-competing industries (see McCulloch, 1983, pp. 18–20). The injured firms seek protection from the impacts of the appreciation but are later unwilling to accept the elimination of that protection if the local currency depreciates." It is interesting that everyone seems to attribute this argument to someone else.

26. McCulloch (1983, p. 17) has made this argument.

27. Another transoceanically protected manufacturing sector is radio and television receivers (United States, United Kingdom, Italy, and France). If the machine tool industry in the United States succeeds in its current efforts to obtain protection, it will become another (it is already protected in Italy and the EC). Among agricultural products, the most widely favored are fish (United States, United Kingdom, Italy, and Japan), cheese (United States, EC, Canada, and Japan), mushrooms (United States and EC), and meat (United States, EC, Canada, and Japan). USTR, "Levels of Protection" (1984).

28. If 1.0 is subtracted from the coefficients on the log of real GNP, the dependent variable can be thought of as the level of employment in the affected sectors relative to GNP. This is why the coefficient on the time trend gives the rate of secular decline relative to the rest of the economy.

29. Grossman (1984, p. 22) finds that the dollar appreciation explains the loss of 82,701 jobs in the steel industry, sluggish real income growth explains 33,577 to 44,251 jobs, and technological change and other secular shifts explain 109,600 jobs. The losses are for the August–October 1983 average relative to January 1979.

30. U.S. Department of Commerce, *1985 U.S. Industrial Outlook*, pp. 36–1, 36–12.

31. The argument to follow is made in the Council of Economic Advisers' 1983 and 1984 reports and by Feldstein (1984). The term *Feldstein doctrine* has been used by Williamson (1983, p. 32).

32. In an analysis of the Cambridge Group proposal, Eichengreen (1983) shows that with real wage rigidity, an import tariff will have expansionary effects on employment only in the unlikely case of a Metzler paradox. Otherwise the currency appreciation resulting from the tariff will reduce output and employment, as in the classic Mundell (1968) paper. See also van Wijnbergen (1984).

33. The Japanese agreed to most of the measures demanded of them in the Yen/Dollar Agreement of May 1984. But the apparent effect has been to allow increased capital outflow from Japan and weaken the yen against the dollar, a result that could have been anticipated from elementary economic theory. See Frankel (1984).

34. See *Economic Report of the President* (1983, 1984). See also Frankel (1984).

35. These estimates are derived for the trade equation 3.1.

36. See Mitchell (1984) for more details of the proposed U.S. import surcharge.

37. In addition to the arguments against a section 122 tariff surcharge made in section 3, Frank, Pearson, and Riedel (1979) argue that under flexible rates, there ought to be less of a temptation to resort to uniform tariffs because of the offsetting exchange rate response.

38. See Tobin (1982); Dornbusch (1980).

References

Adams, Walter, and Joel Dirlam. "The Trade Laws and Their Enforcement by the International Trade Commission." In Robert Baldwin, ed., *Recent Issues in International Trade Policy*, NBER Conference Report. Cambridge: NBER, 1983.

Anderson, M. "America's Foreign Trade Crisis." *AFL-CIO American Federationist*, October 13, 1984.

Baldwin, Robert. *The Political Economy of U.S. Import Policy*. Cambridge: MIT Press, 1985.

Bergsten, C. Fred. "What to Do about U.S.-Japan Economic Conflict." *Foreign Affairs* 60 (1982): 1059–1975.

Bergsten, C. Fred, and John Williamson. "Exchange Rates and Trade Policy." In William R. Cline, ed., *Trade Policy in the 1980's*. Cambridge: MIT Press for the Institute for International Economics, 1983.

Blackhurst, Richard, and Jan Tumlir. "Trade Relations under Flexible Exchange Rates." *GATT Studies in International Trade*, no. 8. Geneva: GATT, September 1980.

Czinkota, M., and P. Kollmer. "Foreign Trade and the 98th Congress." Special Publication No. 7. Washington, D.C.: National Center for Export-Import Studies, October 1984.

Denison, E. "Accounting for United States Growth." Washington, D.C.: Brookings, 1974.

Dixit, Avinash K., and Stiglitz, Joseph E. "Monopolistic Competition and Optimum Product Diversity." *American Economic Review* 67 (1977): 297–308.

Dornbusch, R. "Exchange Rate Economics: Where Do We Stand?" *Brookings Papers on Economic Activity* 1 (1980): 143–185.

Dunn, R. "The Many Disappointments of Flexible Exchange Rates." Essays in International Finance, no. 154. Princeton: Princeton University Press, 1983.

Eichengreen, Barry. "Protection, Real Wage Resistance and Employment." *Weltwirtschaftliches Archiv* 119, no. 3 (1983): 429–451.

Feldstein, M. "The Trade Balance: Is a Tariff Surcharge Appropriate?" Testimony before the Senate Finance Committee, March 23, 1984.

Finger, J. Michael, H. K. Hall, and D. R. Nelson. "The Political Economy of Administered Protection." *American Economic Review* 72 (1982): 452–466.

Fox, L., and S. Cooney. "Protectionism Returns." *Foreign Policy*, no. 53 (Winter 1983–1984): 74–90.

Frank, I., C. Pearson, and J. Riedel. "The Implications for Managed Floating Exchange Rates for U.S. Trade Policy." New York University Monograph Series in Finance and Economics, 1979, no. 1.

Frankel, Jeffrey. "The Desirability of a Dollar Appreciation, Given a Contractionary U.S. Monetary Policy." NBER Working Paper, no. 1110. April 1983.

Frankel, Jeffrey. "The Yen/Dollar Aggreement: Liberalizing Japanese Capital Markets." Policy Study 9. Washington, D.C.: Institute for International Economics, 1984.

Grossman, Gene. "Imports as a Cause of Injury: The Case of the U.S. Steel Industry." NBER Working Paper, no. 1494. November 1984.

Hilgerdt, F. *Industrialisation and Foreign Trade*. Geneva: League of Nations, 1945.

Johnson, Harry G. "The Case for Flexible Exchange Rates 1969." In Johnson, *Further Essays on Monetary Economics*. London: Allen and Unwin, 1971.

Krueger, Anne. "Protectionist Pressures, Imports and Employment in the United States." *Scandinavian Journal of Economics* 82 (1980): 133–146.

Kindleberger, Charles P. *The World in Depression*. Berkeley: University of California Press, 1973.

McCulloch, Rachel. "Unexpected Real Consequences of Floating Exchange Rates." Essays in International Finance, no. 153. Princeton: Princeton University Press, 1983.

Maddison, Angus. *Economic Growth in the West: Comparative Experience in Europe and North America*. New York: Twentieth Century Fund, 1964.

Mitchell, J. F. "U.S. Trade Deficits," Testimony before the U.S. Senate Finance Committee. June 28, 1984.

Meltzer, Alan. "Monetary and Other Explanations of the Start of the Great Depression." *Journal of Monetary Economics* 2 (1976): 455–471.

Mundell, R. "Flexible Exchange Rates and Employment Policy." In Mundell, *International Economics*. New York: Macmillan, 1968.

New York Stock Exchange. "U.S. International Competitiveness: Perception and Reality." New York: Office of Economic Research, August 1984.

Pastor, R. A. *Congress and the Politics of U.S. Foreign Economic Policy*. Berkeley: University of California Press, 1980.

Pastor, R. A. "The Cry-and-Sigh Syndrome: Congress and Trade Policy." In A. Schick, ed., *Making Economic Policy in Congress*. Washington, D.C.: American Enterprise Institute, 1983.

Ratner, S. *The Tariff in American History*. New York: Van Nostrand Co., 1972.

Stern, Paula, and A. Wechsler. "Escape Clause Relief and Recessions: An Economic and Legal Look at Section 201." Washington, D.C.: U.S. International Trade Commission, 1984.

Takacs, Wendy. "Pressures for Protection." *Economic Inquiry* 19 (1981): 687–693.

Tobin, J. "A Proposal for International Monetary Reform." In Tobin, *Essays in Economics: Theory and Policy*. Cambridge: MIT Press, 1982.

U.S. Trade Representative. *Annual Report of the President on the Trade Agreements Program*. Washington, D.C., 1983, 1984.

U.S. Trade Representative. "Levels of Protection in Manufacturing Goods: The U.S., the E.C., Canada, and Japan." Mimeo., 1984.

van Wijnbergen, Sveder. "Tariffs, Employment and the Current Account: Real Wage Resistance and the Macroeconomics of Protectionism." Discussion Paper, no. 30. London: Center for Economic Policy Research, October 1984.

Williamson, John. "The Exchange Rate System." Policy Analysis in International Economics, no. 5. Washington D.C.: Institute for International Economics, 1983.

Comment on "Macroeconomics and Protection"

William H. Branson

Dornbusch and Frankel present clearly the links between the macroeconomic events of the 1980s and the rise in protectionism in the United States, which became a congressional groundswell in late 1985. In addition to its clear analytical line, the chapter is full of information—tables, graphs, regression results.

The logical progression that Dornbusch and Frankel lay out runs from macroeconomic events to effects on exchange rates and trade, then to output and employment in manufacturing in the United States, and finally through a political economy link, to the politics of protectionism. Several of the participants in the conference, especially Keohane, Krasner, Magee, and Richardson, know much more about the political economy of protectionism than I do. So in an exercise of comparative advantage, in this comment I focus on the chain from macroevents to manufacturing employment by exchange rates and trade. I conclude with support for a somewhat radical proposal to break the current macropolicy deadlock, an across-the-board tariff on imports.

Macroeconomic Causes of Real Dollar Appreciation

The basic cause of the real appreciation of the dollar since 1980 is the shift of relative full employment fiscal positions in the United States and the rest of the OECD. The shift is highlighted in Dornbusch and Frankel's table 3.2. The adjusted budget deficit of the United States increased by 4.5 percent of GDP from 1980 to 1985; in the rest of the OECD it decreased by 1.7 percent of GDP. The shift in the full employment deficit in the United States was not compensated by a rise in full employment saving, so it reduced national saving. The reduced flow of national saving requires some combination of a reduction in domestic investment or net foreign investment (increase in foreign borrowing) to maintain balance in the national flow of funds. The reduction in domestic investment is achieved through a rise in real interest rates. The

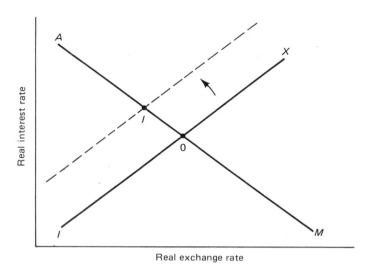

Figure 1
Short-run effects of the fiscal shift.

reduction in net foreign investment, or the current account balance, is achieved by a real appreciation of the dollar. In 1981 when the budget package was announced, the markets could look ahead to these results, so interest rates and the dollar moved then, in anticipation of the coming shift in the full employment deficit.

The argument can be expressed clearly in terms of the national income identity as a constraint on saving investment balances:

$$S + (T - G) = I + (X - IM) = I + NFI.$$

Here S is private saving, $(T - G)$ is the consolidated government surplus, I is domestic investment, $(X - IM)$ is the current account, and NFI is net foreign investment. The budget program of 1981 reduced full employment national saving, $S + (T - G)$, by about 5 percent of GNP. This requires $I + NFI$ to fall by the same amount—hence the rise in interest rates and the dollar.

The mix of investment and current account reduction, or the precise combination of interest rate increase and dollar appreciation, that results from the shift in the fiscal position depends on equilibrium relations in financial markets. The situation is shown in figure 3.1, borrowed from Branson, Fraga, and Johnson (1985). The IX curve shows the trade-off between the real interest rate R and the real exchange rate e that keeps $I + (X - IM)$ equal to a given full employment national saving $S + (T - G)$, in the equation. A reduction in national saving shifts IX up and left, as shown in figure 1. The slope of the asset market (AM) locus shows the trade-off between a rise in U.S. interest rates and fall in the exchange rate (appreciation of the dollar) that maintains financial market equilibrium in the short run, with preexisting supplies of assets. The fiscal shift moves R and e from point 0 to point 1 in the figure, along the short-run AM locus. This is the movement the United States experienced from 1980 to 1984.

Of course, figure 1 shows only the short-run effects of the shift in the budget. As the deficit continues to push dollar-denominated assets into international investors' portfolios, growing resistance to further accumulation means a further rise in U.S. interest rates and a depreciation of the dollar. This would be illustrated by a subsequent upward shift of the AM locus in figure 1. Gradually the burden of financing the budget deficit would be shifted from net foreign borrowing to domestic investment. The full analysis is given in Branson (1985).

Is the Dollar Overvalued?

The appreciation of the dollar is a short-run equilibrium reaction to the shift in the budget position. It is part of a crowding-out mechanism that permits a significant fraction of the deficit to be financed abroad, at least in the short run of a few years. So if the budget deficit is taken as given, some dollar appreciation is expected as part of the equilibrium adjustment of the economy. How large an appreciation would seem reasonable?

By 1985 the shift in the full employment federal deficit was running about $200 billion. This was being financed by a reduction of domestic investment of about $50 billion and a current account deficit of about $150 billion, about 4 percent of GNP. How large a real appreciation is needed to obtain a swing of that size in the current account? Dornbusch and Frankel provide an estimate in their equation, 3.1. A real depreciation of 13.5 percent improves the trade balance by 1 percent of GNP. By linear extrapolation a 54 percent real appreciation would be needed to obtain the 4 percent swing in the trade balance. This is approximately the actual amount of dollar appreciation since 1980. Thus on the Dornbusch-Frankel estimate, the extent of dollar appreciation is not surprising. From the viewpoint of short-run macroeconomic equilibrium, the dollar is not overvalued if we take the budget deficit as given.

In the longer run, the dollar should be expected to come back down as the AM locus in figure 1 shifts up, but this does not imply current overvaluation of the dollar. The dynamics from the short run to the long run give an equilibrium path for the dollar that implies first appreciation and then depreciation, with consistent movement of interest rates. The dollar could be correctly valued all along the path.

Effects on Manufacturing Employment

The argument that the dollar is not overvalued from the perspective of macroeconomic equilibrium must be interpreted with care. It does not mean that there have been small effects on manufacturing employment. In fact, the way the dollar appreciation maintains macroequilibrium is by generating a huge swing toward deficit in the trade balance. This must imply losses in output and employment in the tradable sectors, both agriculture and manufacturing.

In table 3.6 Dornbusch and Frankel provide some fragmentary evidence on the effects of dollar appreciation on manufacturing employment. Table 3.6 gives regressions only for protected industries, but there we see large and significant elasticities of employment with respect to the real exchange rate of -0.7 in steel and -0.6 in fasteners. (A 10 percent dollar appreciation would reduce employment by 7 and 6 percent, respectively.

But there is a puzzle in table 3.6. The elasticity for automobiles is a small and insignificant positive number, and this finding is left unexplained by the authors. They note that the import-to-new supply ratio for automobiles fell during the 1980–1984 period of dollar appreciation, but this is surely due to the VER program, which is not controlled for in the regressions or even mentioned.

More systematic evidence on the effects of dollar appreciation in manufacturing employment, by sector, is being developed in a joint research effort by James Love and me. Preliminary results in Love (1984) show large sensitivities of employment to the exchange rate. For example, in Love's regressions, the elasticities of employment with respect to the real exchange rate by sector are frequently around unity and range up to -2.9 for construction and mining machinery. The elasticity for the nonelectrical machinery aggregate is -0.8. This means that a 60 percent real dollar appreciation may have reduced machinery employment by nearly half, a massive and perhaps irreversible shock to a major source of U.S. export strength.

Through its effects on manufacturing employment and farmers' incomes, the dollar appreciation can have wide political implications. The effect on employment in established manufacturing sectors is creating depression in the rust belt states from New York to Illinois. At the same time the national recovery has expanded activity in the periphery of the country: New England, the sun belt, and California.

Compounding this shift is the probability that when the dollar comes back down, the expanding manufacturing sectors will not be those that contracted when the dollar went up. As the United States temporarily priced itself out of international competition in machine tools, for example, producers abroad got a foothold in the industry and began working down their learning curves. So when the dollar depreciates, the old manufacturing sectors will face formidable new international competition. Some of the effects of the dollar appreciation of the 1980s may be irreversible.

Radical Policy Option

The basic source of the dollar appreciation and the trade problems that are giving rise to protectionism is the shift in the budget position in the United States. The optimal solution would be to reverse this shift with a tax increase and a cut in defense spending, coupled with judiciously easier money. The deadlocks between the administration and Congress, and within Congress itself, suggest that the optimum is not attainable, so we must consider second-best alternatives. One is an across-the-board import tariff, which Dornbusch and Frankel call the Motorola alternative, a proposal they deride: "It is extraordinary that good money is being spent on lobbying so idiotic a scheme." The important aspect of an across-the-board tariff, however, would be that it raises revenue, reducing the budget deficit. Early in their chapter Dornbusch and Frankel discuss the "fiscal effects of a tariff," but these effects seem to have slipped out of mind by the time they came to the conclusions. I think the proposal should be given a more serious hearing. Following the line of argument in Branson and Pearce (1985), if the price elasticity of demand for imports is less than unity in the short run, perhaps -0.5 or so, a tariff will increase tax revenue by more than it reduces imports. This will shift the IX curve in figure 1 down; we are here discussing a revenue tariff. This would bring U.S. interest rates down and depreciate the dollar. These movements would be good for the U.S. economy, and they are widely demanded by policymakers outside the United States.

This proposal meets objections from liberal economists on two grounds. First, they assert that it will cause the dollar to appreciate further. This is based on the implicit assumption in tariff analysis that the revenue is redistributed, so the IX curve would indeed shift up. But the proposal is explicitly not to redistribute the revenue. Second, retaliation may be anticipated. But retaliation would be misguided. The standard objection to retaliation is that if it fails to force a rollback of the original protection, it makes matters worse. And in this case there is a further reason to resist the temptation.

The Europeans, and the DC debtors such as Brazil and Mexico, have rightly been complaining about the effects of the strong dollar and high interest rates on their economies. Given the present political situation in the United States, an import surcharge may offer the best prospect of bringing down interest rates and the dollar. True, it would reduce the volume of exports from these countries to the United States, but so too would the depreciation of the dollar that they have been urging. To quell the public indignation that would erupt at a U.S. import surcharge, these countries would do well to reflect on whether they might gain most by confining their reactions to rhetoric.

A Final Bibliographical Note

Dornbusch and Frankel refer to the Laffer curve effect of import duties on the quantity of imports, and this on tariff revenue. Trade economists recognize the maximum point on the Laffer curve as the optimum tariff point in the absence of retaliation. In that sense the Laffer curve has been known for centuries, since Adam Smith. Jorge de Macedo (1985) has traced the explicit analysis of the optimal tariff, including its formula, back to the Italian philosopher and criminologist Beccaria (1764). He had an intense interest in the effects of tariffs on smuggling and developed the Beccaria curve in pursuit of that line of research.

References

Beccaria, C. "A Tentative Analysis of Smuggling." 1764. Reprinted in *Screttori Classici Italiana de Economia Politica*, vol. 12. Milan, 1804.

Branson, William H. "Causes of the Appreciation and Volatility of the Dollar." Mimeo. Federal Reserve Bank of Kansas City Conference, August 21–23, 1985.

Branson, William H., Arminio Fraga, and Robert Johnson. "Anticipated Fiscal Policy and the Recession of 1982." Mimeo. Princeton, March 1985.

Branson, William H., and J. Pearce. "The Case for an Import Surcharge." Mimeo. Princeton, March 1985.

de Macedo, Jorge B. "Macroeconomic Policy under Currency Inconvertibility." Working Paper, no. 1571. National Bureau of Economic Research, February 1985.

Love, J. P. "Employment Loss due to the Appreciation of the Dollar." Mimeo. Washington, D.C.: Center for the Study of Responsive Law, 1984.

Comment on "Macroeconomics and Protection"

Rachel McCulloch

The traditional U.S. commitment to free trade is becoming frayed around the edges. Calls grow ever louder for new import restrictions, both across the board and directed specifically at U.S. commercial arch-rival, Japan. This crescendo of protectionist sentiment reflects many changes in the nation and abroad, but surely at its heart is the burgeoning U.S. deficit on merchandise trade.

Although dissatisfaction with U.S. trade performance has probably reached an all-time high, the interpretation of recent developments remains ambiguous. The opening quotations in the Dornbusch-Frankel chapter illustrate two vastly different messages the same numbers can convey to interested observers. Many in government, business, and organized labor point to the trade data and proclaim national disaster. Their credibility in promoting this view has been undercut by macroeconomic conditions, however. From 1980 to 1985 the U.S. trade balance looked worse and worse while the economy (at least in the aggregate) looked better and better—a lopsided recovery but a recovery nonetheless.

The juxtaposition of a deteriorating trade balance and an expanding economy should come as no surprise. As Dornbusch and Frankel show in their trade balance regression, trade performance is strongly countercyclical. Moreover the recent U.S. expansion was facilitated by large capital inflows, which in turn raised the value of the dollar and further weakened U.S. trade performance. This role of capital flows offers further opportunity for conflicting interpretation. Although everyone by now recognizes that the high dollar is the consequence of unprecedented capital inflows, there is little agreement about the reasons for the inflows (government deficit? safe haven? LDC debt crises?) and therefore about the likelihood of an abrupt reversal of these flows and of corresponding dollar strength.

To help illuminate issues such as these, Dornbusch and Frankel have prepared a veritable handbook on the broad subject of macroeconomics and

trade. They explore almost every linkage between macroeconomic performance and macroeconomic policies on one hand and trade performance and
trade policies on the other. They begin with the macroeconomic causes and
consequences of the infamous Smoot-Hawley tariff of 1930 and end with the
case for coordination of macroeconomic policies in the OECD in the 1980s.

Since Smoot-Hawley is an international economist's vision of protectionist
hell, Dornbusch and Frankel's soft-landing scenario must correspond to
heaven. Alas, many of us are agnostics or maybe even out-and-out atheists
when it comes to policy coordination among sovereign states. In any case there
is something less than total professional consensus on the merits of U.S.
monetary expansion, one key element of the policy package recommended by
the authors.

Dornbusch and Frankel may have doubts of their own since they go on to
consider the case for a sort of second-best policy: controls on international
capital flows. This might be termed a beggar-your-brother policy. Reducing
U.S. capital inflows would indeed bring the dollar down, thus relieving
pressure on tradables, but it would also mean a squeeze on interest-sensitive
activities. As the authors note, some tradables—perhaps autos and steel—
could be worse off on net, although construction would probably be the
biggest loser.

The macroeconomic roots and implications of the U.S. trade deficit is an
important subject that certainly merits further study. Here, however, my
comments focus on just one set of issues out of the many raised by Dornbusch
and Frankel: the relationships among trade liberalization, protectionism, and
protection and how these are linked to macroeconomic variables.

For the United States trade liberalization has occurred primarily in a multilateral context as one of several activities pursued simultaneously in the
various rounds of GATT negotiations spearheaded by the United States. But as
much as trade liberalization, these rounds have sought to reshape the GATT
rules and to extend their domain. As Richard Cooper and John Jackson
indicate in this book, the underlying motive for the process has not been
entirely or even mainly economic. Rather U.S. trade liberalization is appropriately seen as an integral part of overall foreign policy. Richard Cooper once
described liberal trade as a triumph of pure reason over common sense
(Cooper, 1984, p. 27), but here he suggests that for the United States it is a
triumph of political over economic goals.

Throughout the postwar period the liberalization process has coexisted
with protectionism and increases in protection. The United States was already
asking Japan to exercise self-restraint back in 1957 with regard to textiles, and
the later consequences of this bilateral negotiation became part of the GATT

machinery. In 1985 the Reagan administration pressed for a new multilateral round to deal with services, investment, and high-technology trade, at the same moment that Senators John C. Danforth and John Heinz were bringing forward what the *New York Times* aptly described as "anti-Japan trade bills."

While U.S. trade liberalization has proceeded in a somewhat formal, multilateral fashion, the accompanying increases in U.S. protection have been ad hoc, temporary, and sectoral. And new protection has often affected much the same sectors in other industrialized nations. The single clear instance of new across-the-board protection enacted since 1930 (the 1971 import surcharge) can best be interpreted as a U.S. bargaining ploy. A similar move in the current period would probably have similar basic motivation and brief duration.

Here it becomes important to distinguish protectionism as an activity from protection itself; that is, actual barriers erected. Protection means protection from imports or from foreign competition, a lot of the competitive pressure on U.S. producers now comes from U.S. subsidiaries of foreign-controlled firms, and these obviously share in any benefits from new trade restrictions. But even the most durable protection—in steel and textiles—has been accompanied by a steady decline over time in the protected activity, both in terms of domestic employment and market share. Of course that decline would have been much more rapid without the barriers—or would it?

To some extent the selective barriers erected by the United States may actually have accelerated the evolution of competition from abroad, through the induced shift in the location of production for specific industries from Japan to the Gang of Four and then to other, newer NICs. Also the barred producers have quickly developed alternative as-yet unrestricted markets and product variants, so that the disruptive flows are not so much stopped as deflected. If so, perhaps trade barriers are as much beggar-your-brother as beggar-your-neighbor policies, having their main effect on the form rather than the fact of foreign competition.

This deflection of competitive pressure is related to a point raised by Dornbusch and Frankel. They note that the same industries on both sides of the Atlantic have been the recipients of new import relief. This, they suggest, casts doubt on the exchange rate explanation for protection, since the dollar has been overvalued but the European currencies correspondingly undervalued during the recent period. This ignores the effect of U.S. protection on other markets, however.

Suppose that the overvalued dollar was indeed the last straw for the U.S. auto industry and the proximate cause of the VERs. Those VERs, or even their mere contemplation, had immediate implications for the net supply of autos to other potential importers. Even if there had been no import problem in those markets previously, U.S. trade restrictions would be enough to start one. In an integrated world market, protection is thus a contagious disease, spreading rapidly within a given sector to alternative suppliers, to related products, and to other importing nations.

Coming back to protectionism, it is important to recognize that this is on the whole a rational, gain-seeking activity; thus protectionism is undertaken when the expected return is high. Here is where the link to macroeconomics becomes crucial. While sectoral protection is beneficial to virtually any import-competing industry, one that is already fat and profitable is rather unlikely to benefit from this particular type of intervention. This was illustrated in the U.S. government's 1985 decision to allow automobile restraints to lapse, at least from the U.S. side. Accordingly it is no surprise that protection comes mainly to declining industries and, for those, mainly when secular decline has been augmented by unfavorable macroeconomic developments.

The lobbyists who serve growing and profitable industries will rationally direct their efforts toward other channels of beneficial intervention. Such industries are more likely to get their share of government largess in forms such as defense contracts, export credits, or tax breaks. Many of these alternatives are in fact preferable to import barriers for an industry not in secular decline. Induced entry could quickly erode profits created by protection of a basically healthy industry. (A growing industry ought to seek interventions that limit entry and otherwise favor established firms over new competitors.)

Apart from macroeconomic conditions, what else makes protectionism a more potentially profitable exercise? Econometric studies of the Kennedy Round tariff cuts suggest that short-run labor adjustment costs are an important consideration. At the industry level success in maintaining tariff protection (gaining an exemption from across-the-board cuts) was best where the industry was declining and the labor force relatively old, unskilled, and large (Cheh, 1974; Bale, 1977).

It is easy to understand who wants protection. What is surprising, especially under the current circumstances, is not that there is so much new protection but rather that there is so little. As Dornbusch and Frankel note, it is not consumers who keep things in check, although perhaps in the automobile case consumer resentment helped to undermine the political feasibility of continued protection. Rather the countervailing force is provided largely by the exporting industries. This is partly on the grounds suggested by the authors: that foreigners must be able to earn dollars if they are to buy U.S. goods. More important is the fear of retaliation against the most competitive industries, as well as recognition of the potential bargaining chip value of turning away protectionist pressure or keeping temporary relief temporary.

Another factor is highlighted in Dornbusch and Frankel's table 3.4. Here the authors display striking figures on the increased role of trade in U.S. manufacturing, specifically the growth of imports and exports in every sector. Much of the growth reflects the increasing internationalization of production, both within multinational firms and through various contractual arrangements. This is international division of labor not just for products but for individual manufacturing processes as well. The firms engaged in this activity—from apparel to advanced electronics—are an additional force opposing new sectoral protection and favoring stronger GATT discipline. Still another antiprotectionist voice is that of the retailers who sell imported goods in the United States.

Related to the simultaneous increases in U.S. imports and exports is the effect of heightened foreign competition on domestic labor. Dornbusch and Frankel note that increased supply from abroad means domestic labor must accept lower wages if U.S. producers are to remain competitive; with sticky wages, unemployment results. This, however, refers to the adjustment required to remain competitive in the import-competing activity. An important issue implicit here is the pull of labor and other resources into the sectors of increased comparative advantage. Over the long run U.S. gains from trade depend on the nation's ability to shift labor away from the import-competing activity.

But what if labor resists the pull? A steel or auto worker pulled into electronics will earn less in the short run and maybe even in the long run. Even low-paid textile or shoe workers may find their earnings reduced if forced to accept entry-level employment in the growing services sector. In other words what is good for the nation may not be good for every individual worker.

The 1962 Trade Expansion Act, which authorized the Kennedy Round, initiated the nation's first trade-adjustment assistance program (TAA). That policy innovation was one reason for the belief prevalent in the mid-1960s "that the world was heading fatally toward free trade," in the words of Dornbusch and Frankel. But the TAA approach ignored the potential divergence of social and private returns from adjustment. The failure of TAA to live up to its name is one reason for the belief prevalent in the mid-1980s that the world is heading fatally toward protectionism.

Finally, what about the special love-hate relationship between the United States and Japan? The same U.S. executives who are busily emulating just-in-time inventory systems and quality circles are also sincerely convinced that insidious Japanese trade barriers are the main reason for the huge bilateral trade deficit. But why is it that the United States focused so much attention on Japanese barriers in the first place? After all, the Japanese have been reducing trade barriers while the United States raises its own, and most of the rest of the world does also.

The first reason if Japan's record of sustained growth. Liberal traders are uneasy about the Japanese case. Japan is often cited as an example of success-ful infant industry protection—possibly the only example. Certainly the Japanese did not fail miserably, as has been the typical outcome elsewhere. But did Japan grow because of protected domestic markets or in spite of them? We do not really know the answer to this question, yet a lot of people think they do. Accordingly they worry that the NICs—who have been good customers for U.S. high-technology products and services—will follow the Japanese model and close their markets.

The second reason is the bilateral deficit. For some this is the smoking gun in the case—incontrovertible evidence of Japanese import barriers. But as Dear-dorff and Stern emphasize in their chapter, no particular meaning attaches to bilateral balance or the lack of it within a multilateral trading system. The real significance of the bilateral deficit is the leverage that it gives the United States in negotiations with the Japanese. The Japanese have a great deal to lose from reduced access to U.S. markets. This may be enough to enable U.S. negotiators to pry open the particularly lucrative hunks of the Japanese market that U.S. high-technology firms are salivating over, in the same way that dubious U.S. arguments about the dollar-yen exchange rate provided a key to the Japanese financial services sector—the latter a not-so-improbable outcome of efforts directed by a treasury secretary who arrived in Washington direct from Wall Street.

This brings us back to the relationship between protectionism and protec-tion and my earlier assertion that protectionism should be regarded as a rational, gain-seeking activity. Just as there is a strategic use of protection, there can also be a strategic use of protectionism. The anti-Japan legislation recently introduced in the U.S. Congress may represent the commercial policy equivalent of the MX missile; merely keeping the perceived threat alive can have important deterrent and negotiating value. Adding weapons to the arsenal is not the same as firing them.

To free traders, strategic protectionism sounds like a dangerous game. It may, however, offer an effective strategy for maintaining open international markets in the face of growing protectionist pressures. If the strategy works, the black cloud of the bilateral deficit could reveal a silver lining. As President Reagan has demonstrated in a variety of other policy areas, it is hard to argue with success. And even if worst should come to worst, trade war is surely a less devastating form of policy failure than nuclear war.

Note

This material was prepared while the author was a visiting scholar at the Hoover Institution, Stanford University.

References

Bale, Malcolm D. "United States Concessions in the Kennedy Round and Short-Run Labour Adjustment Costs: Further Evidence." *Journal of International Economics* 7 (1977): 145–148.

Cheh, John H. "United States Concessions in the Kennedy Round and Short-Run Labor Adjustment Costs." *Journal of International Economics* 4 (1974): 323–340.

Cooper, Richard N. "Comment." In Robert E. Baldwin and Anne O. Krueger, eds., *The Structure and Evolution of Recent U.S. Trade Policy*. Chicago: University of Chicago Press, 1984.

4

Endogenous Protection in the United States, 1900–1984

Stephen P. Magee and Leslie Young

4.1 Introduction

Although the welfare effects of protection have been the subject of extensive theoretical and empirical work, the theoretical analysis of the determinants of the level of protection has only recently received attention. This chapter applies some of our work on endogenous tariff theory to an explanation of U.S. protection since 1900. By endogenous protection, we mean that trade restrictions are set by maximizing, self-interested behavior by all of the economic agents, lobbies, political parties, and voters. The empirical work in this chapter is preliminary and should not be viewed as a formal test of the endogenous tariff model since we do not test it against rival models; however, it provides insights and points to several variables that work moderately well in explaining tariff and nontariff protection during this century.

The concept of endogenous policy generates the following paradox: in a highly competitive political system, the equilibrium policies are not under the control of the policymakers. In the case of protectionism, trade restrictions balance the power of narrow interests (lobbies) against that of broad interests (voters). The trade policies are equilibrating variables that clear political markets; they are analogous to prices in product markets, which balance the quantity demanded against the quantity supplied. The policymaker is like an auctioneer in a product market. The policymaker's preferences will matter more in the short run and with more imperfect party competition. But in the long run we believe that even with only two parties, party and lobby competition causes the role of policymakers to be small relative to the underlying power variables. The primary effect of the president on trade policy is through his macroeconomic policy; since that too may be endogenous, even his role is uncertain. It would be unusual for political markets in redistribution between players of unequal strengths to yield outcomes in which the sum of the welfare of all of the players was maximized. In fact the opposite can occur.

Welfare-maximizing economic and political agents (even of equal strength) operating in competitive redistributive markets can end up in (static) equilibria with economic welfare minimized at zero and with infinitesimally small tariffs (Young and Magee, 1984). Thus general equilibrium considerations provide no necessary lower limit to welfare losses in such negative-sum lobbying games. On this question we are less optimistic than, say, Becker (1983). The replacement of tariffs with less efficient nontariff barriers in the last two decades supports a view that special interests can counter Pareto moves by general interests in sophisticated ways.

Empirically long-run protection should be explained by those exogenous variables that drive the behavior of groups (both broad and narrow) that favor and oppose protection (just as prices can be explained by the exogenous determinants of supply and demand). Our empirical work indicates that approximately two-thirds of the changes in U.S. tariffs this century are explained by economic variables suggested by an endogenous tariff model (unemployment, inflation, and the U.S. terms of trade).

4.2 The Literature

The general equilibrium models of endogenous tariffs underlying the work in this chapter are described in Young and Magee (1982, 1983, 1984). They build on earlier work on rent seeking by Tulloch (1967) and Krueger (1974), on partial equilibrium endogenous tariff theory by Brock and Magee (1975, 1978, 1980) and on the general equilibrium specific-factor lobbying model of Findlay and Wellisz (1982). A comprehensive review of the theoretical and empirical literature on trade policy can be found in Baldwin (1984). Magee, Brock, and Young (1983) and Magee (1984) provide a survey of the theoretical literature on endogenous tariff theory. Reviews of the empirical literature on protection appear in Baldwin (1982, 1985) and Frey (1984, chaps. 2, 3).

There are two distinct branches of endogenous tariff theory. The work of Magee, Brock, and Young (1983) describes endogenous special-interest tariffs because they are based on small groups exploiting larger groups through political lobbies. The work of Mayer (1984) describes endogenous median voter tariffs because the equilibrium tariff maximizes the welfare of the median voter. In Mayer's model all voters are fully informed about the effects of tariffs on their welfare; there are no lobbies, and both political parties support the same level of protection. Our model has rationally ignorant voters, protectionist and antiprotectionist lobbies contributing to the political parties, and political parties that differ from each other on protection for strategic reasons. We present evidence here that the parties do differ on the issue of protection. Ratner (1972) has an extensive discussion of the historical role of lobbying in tariff setting.

There are two types of general equilibrium models of a trading country. The choice between them hinges on the time perspective of the analysis. If the time perspective is short, one would prefer a Jones-Neary specific factor model in which capital is immobile between sectors but labor is mobile. If the time frame is longer, then the neoclassical Heckscher-Ohlin-Samuelson pure trade theory model is more appropriate. In it, capital as well as labor have sufficient time to move between sectors. The specific-factors model predicts that capital in import-competing industries will pressure for protection, and capital in exportables will pressure for free trade or export subsidies. The Heckscher-Ohlin-Samuelson model predicts that capital will favor export promotion, and labor will favor import restriction in the United States.

Which approach should be used for the modeling undertaken here? Magee (1980) presented data showing that both capital and labor behaved in an industry-specific fashion when lobbying for the 1974 trade bill. These results appear to dictate a specific-factors approach. It should be noted, however, that tariff legislation since 1934 has required renewal every three to five years. In fact the 1974 Trade Act was replaced by the Trade Act of 1979. Thus the time frame of the lobbyists being monitored by Magee was short, and this biased the results in the direction of factor specificity. Estimation of long-run tariffs (with capital mobile) might better proceed along lines described by the Heckscher-Ohlin-Samuelson political-economic model of Young and Magee (1982, 1983, 1984, 1985). We follow the latter approach here.

Two ironies emerge in a competitive political system. The first is that policymakers do not make policy; the underlying forces of economic and political power combine with party competition to make trade and other redistributive policies endogenous. The second is that intense party competition can result in non-Pareto policy outcomes. We may have tariffs and other obviously inefficient policies because party and lobby competition result in degenerate Prisoners' Dilemma outcomes. Young and Magee (1982) did a grid search across possible parameter values in a Leontief general equilibrium model and found that 40 percent of the equilibria were Prisoners' Dilemma (both the proprotectionist and antiprotectionist lobbies were worse off with lobbying than without). Thus political party competition can result in lower welfare, while a collusive arrangement between parties not to compete on redistributive issues would increase welfare. The latter does not occur because one of the parties almost always loses in the collusive arrangement (its probability of election is lower than in the case of unbridled party competition).

Stephen P. Magee and Leslie Young 148

Since the probabilities of election sum to 1, party competition is a constant-sum game.

The welfare considerations with endogenous protection are thus complicated. When lobbying costs are considered, the range of possible welfare outcomes is vast. Bhagwati (1980) demonstrates that increased lobbying for protection can increase a country's welfare (for example, the welfare loss from wasted lobbying resources might be more than offset by, say, terms of trade gains). At the other extreme Young and Magee (1984) show general equilibrium conditions under which tariff lobbying can generate an economic black hole; that is, all but epsilon of the capital and labor in an economy could be devoted to lobbying. The result was generated by the magnification paradox, with the result that the equilibrium tariff over which the factors were battling was small. The surprise was that decreasing returns to lobbying by both capital and labor were offset by general equilibrium considerations. Thus a general economic-political equilibrium guarantees no downside limit to the welfare losses that can be caused by tariff lobbying.

4.3 The Politics of Protection

The history of tariff legislation for most of this century is well summarized by Ratner (1972) and Baldwin (1985); for a discussion of recent protectionism, see Salvatore (1985). Several generalizations emerge from these studies. First, Democratic presidents in this century have favored freer trade, while Republicans have favored greater protection. Even recent Republican presidents (Eisenhower, Nixon, Reagan) have been somewhat more protectionist than Democratic ones (Kennedy, Johnson, Carter). Second, the House of Representatives is generally more protectionist than the Senate or the president. Third, a major set of changes occurred in the 1930s. Prior to 1934 Congress largely controlled tariff levels; thereafter the executive branch was the dominant force. Fourth, the locus of protectionist pressure in the House of Representatives has switched from the Republican party in 1900 to the Democratic party today. Baldwin (1976) has documented this switch by House Democrats from free trade to protectionism. In the 1970 discussions of the protectionist Burke-Hartke proposal, Democrat Wilbur Mills deviated from his long-standing support of liberal trade policies and sponsored a bill establishing import quotas on textiles and footwear. The House Democrats voted for the protectionist Ways and Means Committee bill 137 for to 83 against, while the Republicans were slightly opposed (78 for and 82 against). These results were reinforced in Baldwin's analysis of the vote on the 1973 trade bill: Democrats in both the House and the Senate were significantly more protec-

Table 4.1
Major trade legislation

Act	Year	Type	Party	President
Dingley	1897	Protectionist	R	McKinley
Payne-Aldrich	1909	Marginally freer trade	R	Taft
Underwood-Simmons	1913	Freer trade	D	Wilson
Fordney-McCumber	1922	Protectionist	R	Harding
Smoot-Hawley	1930	Very protectionist	R	Hoover
Reciprocal Trade Agreements Act (renewed by Congress eleven times between 1934 and 1962)	1934	Freer trade	D	Roosevelt
International trade negotiations: Geneva	1947			
Annecy	1949			
Torquay	1950–1951			
Dillon Round	1956–1961			
Trade Expansion Act (Kennedy Round trade negotiations, 1964–1967)	1962	Freer trade	D	Kennedy
Burke-Hartke bill	1970	Very protectionist	R	Nixon
Trade Act of 1974 (Tokyo Round trade negotiations, 1974–1979)	1974	Freer trade	R	Nixon/Ford
Trade Act of 1979	1979	Freer trade	D	Carter

Sources: Ratner (1972); Baldwin (1981); Pugel and Walter (1985).

tionist than were Republicans, and protectionist labor union contributions were concentrated on representatives who voted against the act.

The chronology of U.S. tariff legislation in this century appears in table 4.1. Although there are exceptions, all of the major early protectionist tariff acts were passed during Republican administrations (McKinley, Taft, Harding, and Hoover); similarly major nontariff barriers such as the oil import quota and VER agreements have been imposed or negotiated by Repubican presidents (Eisenhower, Nixon, and Reagan). Trade liberalizing acts have been the rule under Democratic presidents: Wilson, Roosevelt, Kennedy, and Carter. The information in table 4.1 forms the basis on which we organize our tariff regression data later in the chapter.

This behavior of the two political parties creates a protectionist party paradox: why is it that prolabor Democratic party presidents support freer trade, while procapital Republican party presidents support protection? This occurs in the face of evidence by Baldwin and Hilton (1983) and other scholars indicating that the United States imports unskilled-labor-intensive goods; there is also evidence, though weaker, that the United States exports capital-intensive goods. Thus the behavior of the presidents apparently conflicts with the economic interests of their lobby clienteles. In section 4.6, we offer one explanation for this phenomenon based on our empirical work. The other political surprise is how the presidency, begining with Nixon, has become the locus of protectionist activities through inefficient VER agreements, increased administrative protection, and so forth.

4.4 Political-Economic General Equilibrium Model of Endogenous Tariffs

Many previous studies of protection emphasize industry-specific determinants. Here we focus on the level of protection for the United States as a whole rather than on the structure of protection across U.S. industries. The variable to be explained is the average U.S. ad valorem tariff rate t, calculated as total U.S. tariff revenue divided by the value of all U.S. imports. The average values of t since 1900 are depicted in figure 4.1 for each presidential administration. Notice the general decline from 1900 and the spike in the 1930s following the Smoot-Hawley Act.

In seeking to explain tariffs, factors frequently discussed in the literature include macroeconomic variables such as the unemployment rate and the balance of trade. The paths of these variables, as well as the inflation rate, are depicted in figures 4.2, 4.3, and 4.4. Unemployment, which bears significantly on workers in import-competing industries, obviously creates political pressures for more protection. The influence of a high inflation rate is less clear. Insofar as the U.S. inflation rate is high relative to the rest of the world, imports will rise and pressures for protection from groups harmed by imports will build. Contrariwise, there will be a tendency for consumers and voters to be aroused out of their usual passivity during high inflation periods and to oppose protectionist measures. The effect of the trade balance is also ambiguous; a worsening of the trade balance due to increases in the world supply of importables should increase the demand for U.S. protection, while a worsening due to increased aggregate demand in the United States might result in reduced demand for protection.

In our regressions we found that these macroeconomic variables alone provided an incomplete explanation of the path of U.S. tariffs. We suggest that this is because they do not capture the balance of political forces that enter the tariff-setting process. These forces include the calculations of political parties that must balance the political costs of protection in terms of antagonized voters against the political support that protection will attract from special-interest groups. Since the primary elements in these calculations (such as,

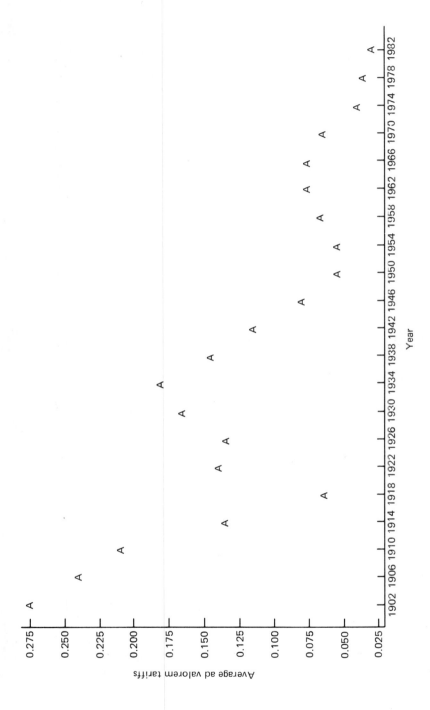

Figure 4.1
Average ad valorem tariff rates in the United States, 1900–1978.

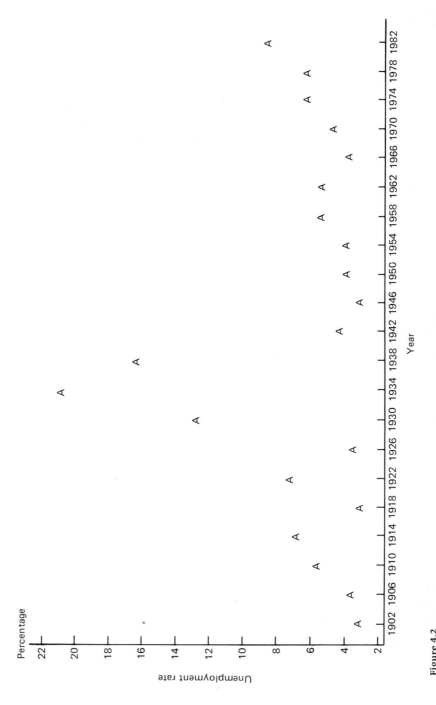

Figure 4.2
U.S. unemployment rates, 1902–1978.

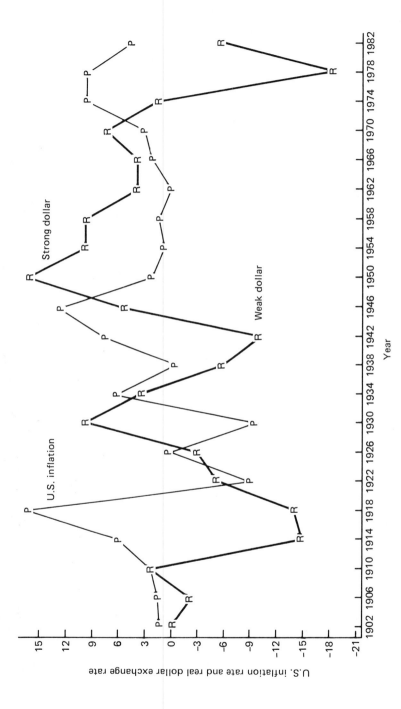

Figure 4.3
U.S. inflation rate (P) and real dollar exchange rate (R), 1902–1982. Note: R is the percentage excess of U.S. prices over U.K. prices in dollars.

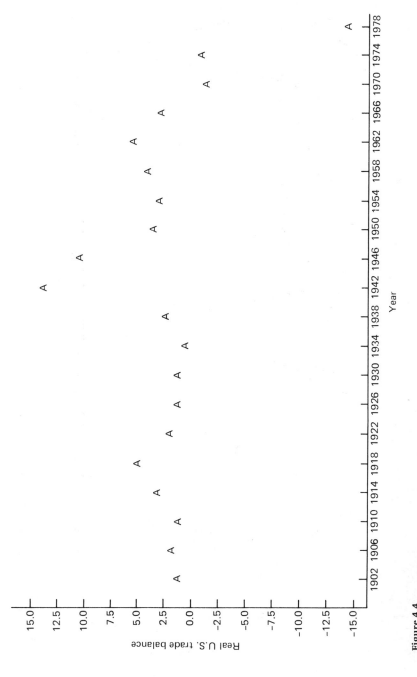

Figure 4.4
Real U.S. trade balance, 1902–1978 (billions of 1972 dollars).

funding from protectionist lobbying and voter hostility to protection) are difficult to observe, it is useful to refer to theoretical models of tariff setting as the equilibrium of rational political calculations. If the equilibrium level of tariffs can be linked theoretically to observable parameters, then this will suggest variables to focus on in explaining the path of tariffs.

The model that we use is based on the $2 \times 2 \times 2 \times 2$ political-economic general equilibrium model developed by Magee and Brock (1983), containing two goods, two factors, two lobbies, and two political parties and with all of the actors maximizing their self-interest. The specific theoretical results invoked here were developed in Young and Magee (1982, 1983, 1984). The model adds lobbies, parties, and voters to the standard neoclassical Heckscher-Ohlin-Samuelson open economy. Here we give a more intuitive presentation of the results, necessarily obtained under restrictive assumptions. The starting point of the model is the assumption that because of information costs and rational free riding, the general voter is incompletely informed about the consequences of trade legislation. The voter has some perception that trade legislation benefits special-interest groups but at a cost to the general welfare. Their incomplete information on this and other issues means that each party can improve its electoral odds by using campaign contributions to fund its message. To attract these resources, it offers legislation favoring special-interest groups, trading off the benefits of the electioneering resources that this attracts against the hostility that it arouses from the general voter. Special-interest lobbies also calculate rationally, comparing the returns of the resources that they own in their direct economic use with the returns that they obtain from the campaign contributions. Tariff setting is modeled as the equilibrium of this game between the two lobbies, the two political parties, and the voters. The battle is centered on the domestic product price ratio. (Although we use the word *tariff* throughout the discussion of the policy variable, the arguments presented here would apply to trade restrictions generally and perhaps to other redistributive policies. Also, although we label the protectionist party Democratic and the proexport party Republican in discussing our model, this is done to facilitate the exposition and not to assert our understanding of the U.S. political process.)

In the U.S. context we suppose that labor is used relatively intensively in import-competing industries and benefits in the long term from tariffs, while capital (both physical and human) is used relatively intensively in export industries and benefits from negative tariffs (export subsidies). (On this point, see Baldwin and Hilton, 1983, and Stern and Maskus, 1981. Evidence from Baldwin (1976) indicates that the House Democrats favor protection, while House Republicans favor freer trade. In our modeling we assume that the

Democratic party supports a tariff, while the Republicans support a negative tariff (an export subsidy). Given the lobbying resource flows, each sets its policy to maximize its probability of election. Since tariff levels are determined as the equilibrium of the political game, tariffs can be explained by variables that affect the protectionist lobby, the proexport lobby, and voters. Another point to stress is that protectionism is not a two-player game between protectionists and voters; rather it is a three-player game among protectionists, proexport interests, and voters (with the parties acting as intermediaries). For this reason we model both protectionist and proexport special interests.

A diagrammatic presentation of the political equilibrium appears in figure 4.5, which summarizes the basic reasoning by the political parties and the lobbies in all of the Brock, Magee, and Young papers. The diagram describes only the behavior of the protectionist labor lobby and the protariff (Democratic) party; we hold constant the behavior of the Republicans and their lobby (their behavior is modeled similarly). The Democrats will set their tariff to maximize their anticipated votes in the next election (we use votes in the figures rather than probabilities of election for expositional reasons). Consider part A of figure 4.5. Any tariff set by the Democrats will generate a direct loss of votes because of the unpopularity of tariffs, distortion effects, and so forth, reflected in the voter loss function OL. The tariff also generates a gain in votes derived from the value of the protectionist lobby contributions, reflected in the vote gain curve OG. The equilibrium tariff set by the Democrats (Te) will be the one that maximizes the difference between the vote gain and the vote loss (the distance RS). At this equilibrium tariff, the slopes of the vote gain and the vote loss curves are equal.

The level of protectionist contributions to the Democrats will be driven by the protectionist lobby's self-interest. Consider part B of figure 4.5. The horizontal axis is the dollar value of protectionist lobby contributions. Ignoring organization costs, the cost of lobbying is just the campaign contributions themselves (the 45 degree line OC); this cost line is independent of the tariff rate (with lobby organizational costs, OC would be steeper than 45 degrees). The benefits of contributing to the Democrats, however, depend on the level of the Democrats' tariff. A high tariff such as T_2 generates a high benefit curve while a low tariff such as T_1 generates a low benefit curve. Consider an intermediate tariff level such as T_e. Although the tariff set by the Democrats is fixed at T_e for all points along the curve, the benefit curve OB increases for the protectionist lobby because their contributions increase the expected votes for the Democrats. If the Democrats support a 20 percent tariff while the Republicans support a negative 20 percent tariff (an export subsidy), it is rational for the protectionist lobby to follow a campaign-contribution-specialization

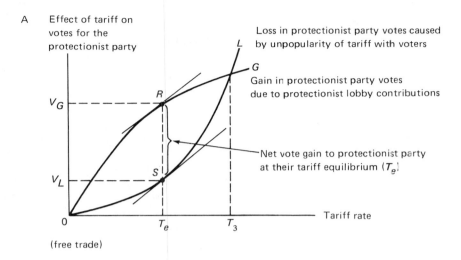

A Effect of tariff on
   votes for the
   protectionist party

L Loss in protectionist party votes caused
     by unpopularity of tariff with voters

G
Gain in protectionist party votes
due to protectionist lobby contributions

V_G R

Net vote gain to protectionist party
at their tariff equilibrium (T_e)

V_L S

0   T_e T_3 Tariff rate

(free trade)

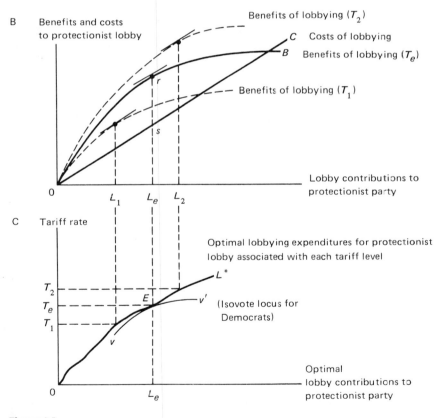

B Benefits and costs
   to protectionist lobby

Benefits of lobbying (T_2)

C Costs of lobbying

B Benefits of lobbying (T_e)

r

Benefits of lobbying (T_1)

s

0   L_1 L_e L_2 Lobby contributions to
                                    protectionist party

C Tariff rate

Optimal lobbying expenditures for protectionist
lobby associated with each tariff level

L^*

T_2 E v' (Isovote locus for
T_e Democrats)
T_1

v

Optimal
lobby contributions to
0   L_e protectionist party

Figure 4.5
Diagrammatic presentation of the Brock and Magee (1975, 1978, 1980) endogenous tariff and
lobbying equilibrium.

theorem and contribute only to the Democrats. At the optimal level of lobbying contributions L_e, the vertical distance (rs) between the benefit curve OB and the cost curve OC is at a maximum. The slope of the OB curve at r is 1; the slope at all contributions levels below L_e is greater than 1, implying that the marginal lobbying benefits below L_e per dollar contributed are greater than their cost.

The information in part B of figure 4.5 can be used to derive the optimal level of protectionist lobbying expenditures, L^*, associated with each possible tariff. We show this relationship in part C of figure 4.5. The strategy of the Democrats is to search along the curve OL^* for the tariff rate that maximizes their net votes. The only two variables affecting voter decisions are shown in part C: the tariff rate and the campaign resources of the Democrats (the export subsidy of the Republicans and their lobbying resources provided by the proexport lobby are held constant by the Democrats). Assume that the tariff maximizing the Democrats' votes is T_e, denoted by point E on OL^*. At E there will be an isovote locus vv' just tangent to OL^*. The isovote loci will have higher net votes for the Democrats southeast of E (because campaign contributions to the party are greater at each tariff rate) and lower votes northwest of E. Parts A and C of figure 4.5 are just different ways of showing the Democratic party's tariff equilibrium. For example, the number of net votes that the equilibrium tariff T_e yields to the Democrats along vv' in part C will equal the difference between V_G and V_L (distance RS) in part A. Also, the curve OG in part A incorporates the electoral value to the Democrats of the protectionist lobby contributions along OL^* in part C.

The mathematics behind the tariff and lobbying equilibria are:

Protectionist lobby's objective:

$$\text{Max}_{L} \; B(V(L, T)) - L \tag{4.1}$$

yielding $(dB/dV)(dV/dL) = 1$ (4.2)

i.e., $L^* = L^*(T)$ (4.3)

Protectionist party's objective:

$$\text{Max}_{T} \; V(L^*(T), T) \tag{4.4}$$

yielding $(dV/dL^*)(dL^*/dT) = -(dV/dT)$ (4.5)

where B is the dollar value of the benefits from contributing to the protectionist party, L is the dollar value of the contributions from the protectionist lobby to the protectionist party, and V is the number of votes received by the protectionist part.

The left-hand side of 4.2 is the slope of the OB curve in part B of figure 4.5, and the right-hand side is the slope of OC; equation 4.3 is the curve OL^* in part C of figure 4.5; and the left-hand side of equation 4.5 is the slope of OG in part A of figure 4.5 while the right-hand side is the slope of OL.

What are the major determinants of tariff changes in this model? Theoretical analysis and simulation of special cases of the formal model suggest that four effects have important bearing on the tariff and lobbying equilibria in the model.

1. The endowment effect. A decline in the relative strength of one lobby moves the political equilibrium against it. Thus if labor becomes relatively less important in the U.S. factor endowment, we expect tariff levels to decline. The readiest measure of the relative strength of labor is the ratio of labor to capital for the United States as a whole. Figure 4.6 is a plot of the U.S. endowment of the number of workers per $100,000 of real U.S. capital (in 1972 dollars) since 1900. The only rise came in the period of the Great Depression and early World War II. The decline flattened in the 1950s and the 1970s. There is casual empirical support from other countries that national tariff levels should vary with national factor endowment ratios. The capital deepening that occurred in the advanced countries from World War II to the early 1970s was accompanied by decreases in tariffs on labor-intensive imports and increases in export subsidies, as the model and intuition suggest they should. Capital accumulation slowed in the 1970s and protectionism increased. The Leontief paradox notwithstanding, the endowment effect is supported by Ray's (1981) cross-section evidence that U.S. tariffs are significantly lower in industries with higher capital-labor ratios and Finger, Hall, and Nelson's (1982, p. 460) result that nontariff protection is significantly lower in industries with high capital-labor ratios. The survey evidence by Pugel and Walter (1984) indicates that U.S. firms favoring free trade tend to be large, a result consistent with Ferguson's (1984) thesis that capital-intensive U.S. multinationals have been a powerful political force for free trade in the United States in the last fifty years.

2. The magnification paradox. Protectionist lobbying increases but tariffs decrease with increased magnification (with increased responsiveness of factor prices to product prices). Consider an increase in magnification caused by a decrease in the share of capital income in the production of U.S. exportables. This increases the elasticity of wages with respect to product prices. With increased magnification, labor becomes more interested in manipulating its wages through the political system. Consequently it increases the proportion of its resources that are channeled to the Democratic party. Increased magnifi-

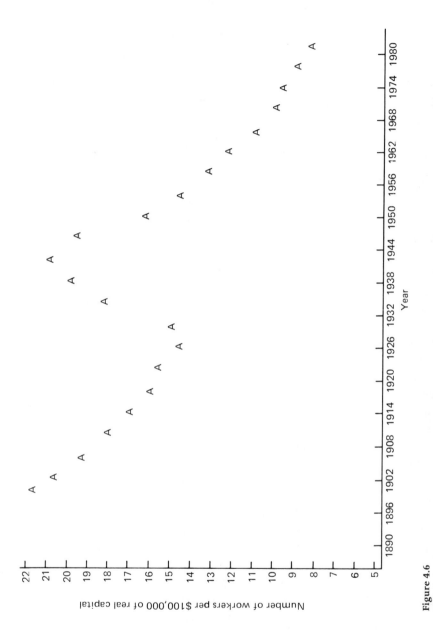

Figure 4.6
Number of workers per $100,000 of real capital in the United States 1900–1980 (1972 dollars).

cation also means an increase in the elasticity of capital returns with respect to product prices. For similar reasons capital increases its political effort for the Republicans.

Paradoxically both parties ultimately find it optimal to offer less extreme policies in order to attract resources from their lobbies so that both the tariff rate and export subsidies decrease in the general political-economic equilibrium. In effect the party gets the luxury of more resources from the protectionist lobby without incurring the cost of greater voter hostility from having to sponsor a higher tariff. The magnification paradox suggests that observers of protectionism must be careful not to confuse increased demands for protection with the actual supply of protection. For example, the demand for protection increased dramatically in the 1970s while the supply increased marginally, if at all (witness the trade bill of 1979). The magnification effect predicts that the tariff should move directly (while the level of protectionist lobbying should move inversely) with the share of capital income in U.S. production.

We were unable to devise a long series for the shares of capital and labor in exportable and importable production (which would be proxies for factor intensities, assuming Cobb-Douglas production). The closest we could come was to calculate the capital share of all of U.S. national income since 1900. This variable is plotted in figure 4.7. Notice the secular decline during this century and the generally procyclical movement of the series. Under some reasonable assumptions these movements would be consistent with increased magnification of factor returns with respect to relative product prices; an increased proportion of U.S. GNP expended on lobbying for and against protection; and the paradoxical decline in protection just described.

3. The compensation effect. When any factor's economic fortunes decline, it transfers effort out of economic activity and into lobbying and political activity. When applied to tariffs, this principle applies to all variables affecting the economic fortunes of protectionists. For example, increased unemployment, a rise in the terms of trade, and a strengthening of the real dollar exchange rate cause protectionist forces to devote more resources to lobbying for protection. The result is an increase in the equilibrium tariff level.

Let us apply the compensation effect to an increase in the U.S. terms of trade caused by the relative decline abroad in the price of U.S. importables (for example, the Japanese automobile phenomenon). Assume that the Democrats are the focus of protectionist contributions while the Republicans are the reverse. Since importables are labor intensive, the initial effect of the terms of trade increase is for U.S. blue-collar wages to fall. This, in turn, lowers the opportunity cost of lobbying for labor. Labor substitutes out of economic

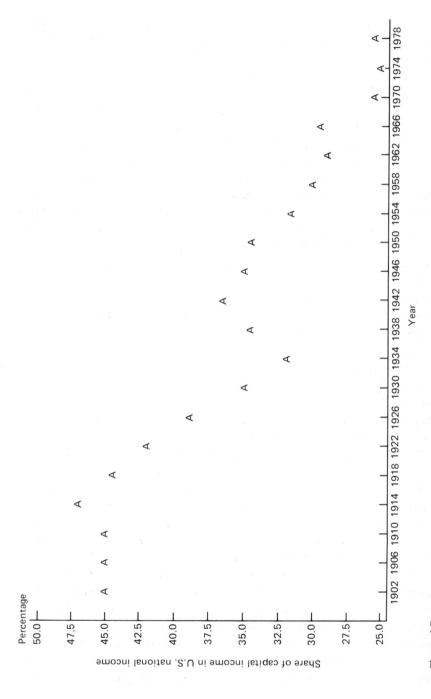

Figure 4.7
Share of capital income in U.S. national income, 1902–1978.

activity and into political activity (increases its protectionist lobbying pressure and its campaign contributions to the Democrats), with the result that U.S. tariffs increase. Even with the higher tariff, wages of labor still fall (the tariff provides only a partial offset to the increase in the terms of trade). In the new equilibrium the Republicans offer a smaller export subsidy than before, and this gains them general-interest votes. The Republicans also receive fewer campaign contributions from capital, however. The net effect of both of these changes is to raise the electoral cost to the Democrats of their higher special-interest tariff. It turns out that this increased cost to the Democrats dominates the benefits of greater contributions from labor so the Democratic party is worse off (its electoral chances fall). In sum, the welfare of labor and the Democrats' electoral fortunes move together in response to an increase in the terms of trade: labor's income falls, and the Democrats lose votes. These results were generated in a model with Leontief production (Young and Magee, 1982). For the Cobb-Douglas model reported in Young and Magee (1984), the equilibrium lobbying ratios, tariffs, and probabilities of electoral outcomes are independent of a country's terms of trade. Thus the result is dependent on the functional form of the model. A final point relating to estimation is that this terms of trade effect on tariffs is in the same direction as the traditional tariff effect on a large country's terms of trade. If the latter effect is at work, simultaneous equation bias may cause the significance of the terms of trade effect on tariffs to be overstated.

Figure 4.8 reports the U.S. terms of trade for manufacturing over the past eighty years. The improvement in the terms of trade in the 1930s may have been assisted by the Smoot-Hawley tariff's being more beggar-thy-neighbor than those of U.S. trading partners. Notice, however, that the U.S. terms of trade increased from 1926 to 1930 and rose steadily from 1950 until 1970, which may have contributed to the Burke-Hartke protectionism of 1970. Notice too the rise from Ford through Reagan, which contributes to current protectionist pressure. Given the industrialization of the Third World over the next few decades, we expect further relative declines in the prices of labor-intensive goods on world markets and hence continued increases in the U.S. terms of trade. If this occurs, the model predicts an increase in protectionism in the advanced countries as pressure on wages causes labor to substitute toward protectionist lobbying.

4. Voter behavior. We assume that individual voters act in their own interest and remain rationally ignorant about many economic issues, including protection. It should be obvious that a single voter will have no effect on the outcome of most elections; thus the expected gain from collecting information about tariffs and other issues is minimal. We assume that voters generally

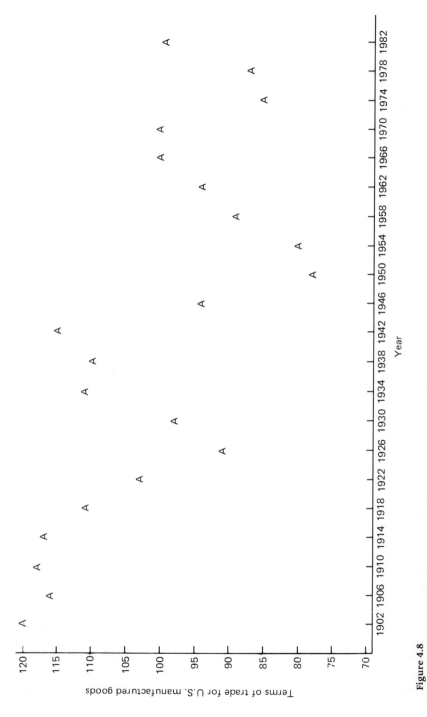

Figure 4.8
Terms of trade for U.S. manufactured goods, 1902–1978 (price of exports/price of imports).

oppose protection but are insufficiently informed for it to go away. Hence they are malleable through advertising financed by lobby contributions. Apparently one situation that rouses voters is a period of high inflation, when they, as consumers, are more hostile to protectionist policy and are more politically vocal. This lowers the equilibrium level of protection. According to this argument, the high inflation period of the 1970s generated pressure for import liberalization, while the low inflation period of the 1980s encourages greater protection. Notice that our argument is the reverse of older macroeconomic arguments about the effect of inflation on protection. According to these, higher U.S. inflation would increase U.S. imports, and this pressure on the importable sector would cause it to lobby for greater protection. The inflation rate for U.S. producer prices (P) is shown in figure 4.3.

There is a second mechanism by which higher inflation reduces protectionist pressures. Periods of high inflation are correlated with declines in the real exchange rate (by currency depreciation during floating periods or by negative deviations from purchasing power parity during fixed rate periods). The rise in the dollar prices of U.S. importables reduces compensation pressures for protection through lobbying. The variable R in figure 4.3 is the real dollar exchange rate between the United States and the United Kingdom. It equals the percentage excess of the U.S. price level in dollars over the price level (of wholesale prices) in the United Kingdom, also expressed in dollars. R was constructed by assuming that its average value between 1901 and 1984 was zero. Notice the negative correlation between U.S. inflation and the real value of the dollar: the simple correlation between P and R is -.38, significant at the .10 level. That is, periods of low U.S. inflation are associated with a strong dollar (high U.S. price levels relative to foreign prices) and hence compensating behavior by U.S. special interests toward greater protectionist pressure.

The other macroeconomic variable that appears to affect voter sentiment toward protection is the unemployment rate shown in figure 4.2. Increased unemployment should render voters less hostile to the protection of jobs and hence should increase the supply of protection even while it increases the demand for protection (by compensation behavior by labor).

Let us illustrate what a change in the U.S. terms of trade does to the OG and the OL curves and the tariff equilibrium in part A of figure 4.5. Increased market pressure on U.S. importable industries causes greater labor contributions to flow to the Democrats by means of the compensation effect. This shifts the OL^* curve to the right in part C of figure 4.5 and hence shifts up the Democrats' gain curve OG in part A. After all of the general equilibrium adjustments, however, the Republicans reduce their special-interest stand by reducing their export subsidy. This increases the electoral cost to the Democrats of their tariff, so that the Democrats' *OL* curve also shifts up. With Leontief production, the maximum distance between the two curves is smaller than before and occurs to the right of the former equilibrium. Thus, the equilibrium tariff rises (to a level above T_e) while the net votes obtained by the Democrats from their tariff falls below the original level *RS*.

4.5 Empirical Results for U.S. Tariffs, 1900–1984

When economic and political agents act rationally in the setting of redistributive policies, they do so indirectly through lobbying, campaign contributions, and logrolling, and they must operate through multiple branches of government. Because of this, we felt that it would be difficult empirically to relate tariff movements to their underlying determinants. Two theoretical considerations made our empirical job easier, however. First, explicit solution of our model permitted elimination of difficult endogenous variables from the tariff equation (such as campaign contributions and probabilities of electoral success of the political parties). In effect we estimate a reduced-form equation for tariffs. Second, solution of the model permits us to predict the effect that changes in each variable will have on tariffs in the reduced-form equation. The intuition for each effect has been discussed.

A long time series is required to capture the political consequences of the long-run neoclassical determinants of protection such as factor endowments, factor intensities, and terms of trade effects. The information in table 4.1 suggests a way to organize the data for an empirical estimation of the determinants of U.S. tariff levels in this century. Only four observations were taken on tariffs before Franklin Roosevelt, corresponding to the presidential administrations of the major tariff acts: Payne-Aldrich, Underwood-Simmons, Fordney-McCumber, and Smoot-Hawley (the results are not altered if all eight terms before 1932 are included). After 1934 (inclusive) the tariff level of each of the twelve administrations from Franklin Roosevelt through Carter is included because of the continuous renewal of the trade acts and their nonspecific nature. For these sixteen administrations we regressed the average tariff level in the presidential administration of the act on exogenous variables in that or the previous administration (depending on whether the exogenous variable is lagged).

Our statistical modeling was constrained by the following consideration. We wanted observations longer than one year because of the long-run nature of the political process that determines tariffs. Four years seemed appropriate for observation length because it coincides with the length of presidential administrations, and there has typically been about a four-year lag between renewals of trade acts since 1932. But four-year observation intervals generate only sixteen observations, limiting the number of exogenous variables that could be successfully included in a given regression equation. Fortunately there is considerable variation in most of the variables because these series extended over a long period.

Table 4.2 lists the variables used in the regressions and their sources, and tables 4.3 through 4.8 report the tariff regressions using ordinary least squares over the sixteen administrations in the period 1905–1980. The raw data are presented in the chapter appendix (table 4A.1). In each equation the log of $(1 + t)$ is regressed on the exogenous variables, where t ($LMTARTOT$) is equal to tariff duty revenue collected by the United States divided by the value of all U.S. imports for each observation. Unfortunately t does not include non-tariff barriers. We consider antidumping barriers in a subsequent section.

Table 4.3 reports the regression of t on a set of macrovariables that our intuition initially suggested might be important in explaining protection: the unemployment rate ($MUNEMP$), the value of the real U.S. trade balance ($MRTB$), and the inflation rate ($MINFLATE$). No lags are present, meaning that the average tariff rate for a given four-year period is being explained by the macrovariables for the same period. The fit is not good, with an adjusted R square of only .35; there was serious positive serial correlation in the residuals; and only unemployment was significant. When the same variables were lagged one administration, the fit was much worse, with an adjusted R square that was actually negative.

We next added two variables suggested by our work on endogenous tariffs: the U.S. labor-capital factor ratio ($LAGLPERK$) to capture the endowment or political clout effect and the U.S. terms of manufacturing trade ($LAGTMT$) to pick up possible compensation effects. Both variables were lagged one administration because they are expected to have longer-run effects. The real trade balance became insignificant and was dropped. The terms of trade effect was positive and significant, while the endowment effect had the right sign but was not significant at the .10 level. These results are shown in table 4.4. The equation appears to be a significant improvement over the simple macromodel in table 4.3. Table 4.4 indicates that U.S. tariffs fall (though insignificantly) with decreased importance of labor in the U.S. factor endowment; they increase with the U.S. terms of manufacturing trade; and they decrease with the higher inflation (greater voter hostility to protection and a weaker dollar).

A modeling as well as conceptual issue arises at this point. If one accepts the hypothesis that a country's factor endowment influences very long-run movements in protection (say, with a lag of several decades), then it might be acceptable to relate levels of tariffs to the level of the U.S. labor-capital ratio. It

Table 4.2
Variables in the regressions

Variable/source	Definition

Tariff regressions
(each observation is one four-year presidential administration)

LMTARTOT	dependent variable = 1 plus the average ad valorem tariff rate = tariffs duties collected/value of total U.S. imports
LMTARLAG	dependent variable lagged one period
LAGLPERK	lagged number of U.S. employees per $100,000 of real capital (1972 dollars)
LAGTMT	lagged value of U.S. terms of manufacturing trade = price of U.S. manufactured exports/price of U.S. manufactured imports
MREPUB	Republican dummy = 1 if the administration contained a Republican president
LAGREPUB	Republican dummy lagged one administration
DREPUB	change to a Republican administration from a Democratic administration (=1); otherwise, $DREPUB = 0$
LR1	=1 if the previous observation was a Republican president, 1900–1932
LR2	=1 if the previous observation was a Republican president, 1933–1984
MINFLATE	average inflation rate in current administration
MUNEMP	average unemployment rate for current administration
LAGUNEMP	U.S. unemployment rate lagged one period
MRTB	real U.S. trade balance
NOTAX	=1 in the period 1900–1920 (no income tax period)

Antidumping regression
(annual data, 1954–1981)

S2	= share of antidumping cases with proprotectionist outcomes; =1 minus the proportion of cases that found that there were no sales at less than fair value
LAG2TMT	lagged terms of manufacturing trade
LAG2IN	lagged U.S. inflation rate in producer prices
LAG2RTB	lagged real trade balance
LAG2UN	lagged U.S. unemployment rate
LAG2UKUS	lagged real exchange rate between the United States and the United Kingdom
LOGTAR	log of $(1 + t)$, where t is defined above

Table 4.2 (continued)

1 *Economic Report of the President,* February 1985
2 *Highlights of U.S. Export and Import Trade*
3 *Statistical Abstracts of the U.S.,* 1975, 1979, 1984
4 *Historical Statistics of the U.S.,* 1976 and 1957
5 *Economic Indicators,* 1985
6 *National Income and Product Accounts of the U.S.,* 1929–1965
7 *Survey of Current Business articles by John Musgrave,* April 1976, August 1984
8 Lee, *Purchasing Power Parity* (New York: Marcel Dekker)
9 IMF, *International Financial Statistics*
10 B. Brown (1985)

U.S. export and import unit value indexes for finished manufactures (terms of trade)	1900–1970	4, 892, 893	U226
	1971–1982	3	
	1983–1984	2	
U.S. wholesale price indexes/producer price indexes (inflation)	1900–1947	4, 116	E13 (WPI)
	1948–1984	1, 297	(PPI)
U.S. unemployment	1900–1957	4, 73	D47
	1958–1983	1, 259	
	1984	5	
Compensation of employees as percentage of national income (capital share)	1905–1930	4, F55	141 (every 5 years + interpolated)
	1929–1965	6, 14–15	
	1966–1984	1, 256	
Federal government receipts	1900–1928	4, 712	Y259
	1929–1984	1, 318	
Exports, imports (free and dutiable) for trade balance and tariff revenue	1900–1957	4, 539	U16–18
	1958–1970	4, 888	U208–210
	1971–1981	3	
U.S. civilian labor force	1900–1946	4, 126–127	
	1947–1984	1, 266	
Net stock of fixed nonresidential private capital (total equipment and structures)	1900–1929	4, 256 F450(structures) & F455(equip) + interpolation	
	1925–1975	7, 49 1976	
	1976–1983	7, 54 1984	
U.S. wholesale prices and U.K. foreign exchange rate	1900–1970	8	
	1971–1984	9	
Antidumping cases		10	

Table 4.3
Regression results for a simple macromodel of U.S. tariffs

Variable	Parameter estimate	Standard error	T for HO: parameter = 0	PROB > |T|
INTERCEP	0.053630	0.021124	2.539	0.0260
MUNEMP	0.005778797	0.002129179	2.714	0.0188*
MINFLATE	−0.00189553	0.001715859	−1.105	0.2909
MRTB	0.002385622	0.001746151	1.366	0.1969

Durbin-Watson D, 0.528.
First-order autocorrelation, 0.414.
F value, 3.741.
Prob. > F, 0.0416.
R-square, 0.4833.
Adjusted R-square, 0.3541.
*Significant.

Table 4.4
Regression results of endogenous tariff model 1

Variable	Parameter estimate	Standard error	T for HO: parameter = 0	PROB > |T|
INTERCEP	−0.801442	0.260863	−3.072	0.0106
LAGLPERK	0.050229	0.033345	1.506	0.1601
LAGTMT	0.160052	0.064713	2.473	0.0309*
MINFLATE	−0.00244376	0.001267532	−1.928	0.0800*
MUNEMP	0.004580705	0.001498741	3.056	0.0109*

Durbin-Watson D, 1.561.
First-order autocorrelation, −0.035.
F value, 8.719.
Prob. > F, 0.0020.
R-square, 0.7602.
Adjusted R-square, 0.6730.
*Significant.

Table 4.5
Regression results of first differences

Variable	Parameter estimate	Standard error	T for HO: parameter = 0	PROB > |T|
INTERCEP	−0.00344418	0.004687149	−0.735	0.4778
DTMT	0.115204	0.047225	2.439	0.0329*
DUNEMP	0.002400746	0.000981096	2.447	0.0324*
DINFLATE	−0.0016073	0.0005207374	−3.087	0.0103*
NOTAX	−0.040637	0.013275	−3.061	0.0108*

Durbin-Watson D, 3.196.
First-order autocorrelation, −0.648.
F value, 8.647.
Prob. > F, 0.0021.
R-square, 0.7587.
Adjusted R-square, 0.6710.
* Significant.

Table 4.6
Rise in the unemployment rate associated with Republican administrations

Variable	Parameter estimate	Standard error	T for HO: parameter = 0	PROB > |T|
INTERCEP	−1.038889	1.492014	−0.696	0.4976
MREPUB	3.792460	2.255714	1.681	0.1149

Durbin-Watson D, 1.476.
First-order autocorrelation, 0.260.
F value, 2.827.
Prob. > F, 0.1149.
R-square, 0.1680.
Adjusted R-square, 0.1086.

Table 4.7
Decline in inflation associated with a new Republican administration

Variable	Parameter estimate	Standard error	T for HO: parameter = 0	PROB > |T|
INTERCEP	−1.081240	2.114921	−0.511	0.6171
DREPUB	−6.261957	3.197460	−1.958	0.0704

Durbin-Watson D, 2.038.
First-order autocorrelation, −0.036.
F value, 3.835.
Prob. > F, 0.0704.
R-square, 0.2150.
Adjusted R-square, 0.1590.

Table 4.8
Log of the tariff level increase with a Republican in office in the previous term

Variable	Parameter estimate	Standard error	T for HO: parameter = 0	PROB > |T|
INTERCEP	−1.019510	0.270378	−3.771	0.0031
LAGLPERK	0.069087	0.035506	1.946	0.0777
LAGTMT	0.199702	0.065663	3.041	0.0112
LAGREPUB	0.043639	0.015188	2.873	0.0152
MINFLATE	−0.00365909	0.001261186	−2.901	0.0144

Durbin-Watson D, 1.841.
First-order autocorrelation, 0.045.
F value, 8.107.
Prob. $> F$, 0.0027.
R-square, 0.7467.
Adjusted R-square, 0.6546.

is possible that the long-run downward trend in tariffs is caused by the endowment effect, so that the trend effect should be allocated to the factor endowment variable. If the endowment effects have very long lags, even our eighty-year time series may be too short. If the long-run tariff and the endowment trends are unrelated to each other, however, then allocating the trend in tariffs to factor endowments is inappropriate.

Our next experiment is to first difference all of the variables, using the values reported in the appendix in table 4A.2. The labor-capital ratio remains insignificant and is dropped; apparently there are no short-run (four to eight year) endowment effects. All of the remaining variables remain significant, however, and have the right signs: the terms of trade, unemployment, and inflation. Surprisingly the real dollar foreign exchange rate between the United States and the United Kingdom was never significant in either levels or first differences. This was true both with and without the inflation variable present. A dummy variable for the period before the adoption of the income tax in 1917 (NOTAX) becomes significant and is included. The share of tariff revenue in U.S. federal government revenue shown in figure 4.9 could not be included on the right-hand side directly because it contains the dependent variable. Also, in most formulations, we found that the capital share variable (acting as a proxy for the magnification effect) was statistically insignificant or had the wrong sign. The first difference equation for tariffs is shown in table 4.5. It has an acceptable R square of .67, although it displays negatively autocorrelated errors. Also, the trend effect (we would have anticipated in a significantly negative constant) is not apparent.

When a party dummy was included in the equation in table 4.5, it was insignificant. This does not mean, however, that the party of the president

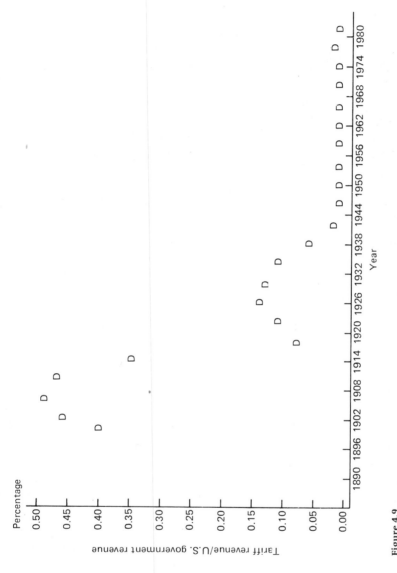

Figure 4.9
Tariff revenue as a proportion of U.S. government revenue, 1898–1982.

does not affect the level of protection, because both the unemployment rate and the inflation rate are affected by a president's macropolicy. We tested the effect of presidential administrations on macropolicy by regressing the unemployment rate as well as the inflation rate on the presidential dummy ($MREPUB = 1$ when Republicans occupy the White House and $=0$ with Democrats). Table 4.6 indicates that the unemployment rate increases by 3.8 percentage points with Republican presidents, although the relationship is significant only at the .11 level. Since we included the Franklin Roosevelt administrations in these regressions, the party unemployment effect is probably swamped by the Great Depression. In some subsequent data summaries by administrations, we omit the three Franklin Roosevelt administrations and get the expected result that Democratic presidents have lower unemployment rates (we omitted Roosevelt's third term so as not to let World War II bias the unemployment rate in our favor). With regard to inflation, table 4.7 reports that in periods of transition from a Democratic to a Republican administration, the rate drops by 6.3 percentage points (significant at the .07 level). We also investigated the effect of the party of the president using equations for the level of tariffs and their first differences. The best such equation using levels is reported in table 4.8. Notice in this equation that both the lagged labor-capital endowment ratio ($LAGLPERK$) and a Republican in office in the previous administration ($LAGREPUB$) are statistically significant, and both have positive effects on U.S. tariffs. When we break the Republican dummy into two subperiods, we find that its coefficient is stable and significant pre-1932 and post-1932. The results for both levels and first differences show that Republican administrations generate significantly more protection than Democratic ones. This raises the protectionist party paradox.

Actual and predicted values of the changes in tariffs using the regression equation in table 4.5 are shown in figure 4.10. The equation predicts heavy pressure for increased protection in the 1920s and the early 1930s; in the late 1950s (in 1958 the oil import quota was imposed); and in 1982 (recall that the first Reagan administration is after the period of estimation for the equation). Notice the absence of tariff protectionist pressure in the Ford administration (1974).

The equation is of interest because the first Reagan term reveals the highest increase in protariff pressure since Fordney-McCumber in 1922 under Harding and Smoot-Hawley in 1930 under Hoover. Notice in the appendix data table 4A.1 that all three of the major indicators of protection increased from the Carter to the Reagan administration: the unemployment rate rose from 6.4 to 8.4 percent, the terms of trade for manufactures rose from 87 to 100, and the inflation rate dropped from 10 percent per year to 4 percent. We predict that

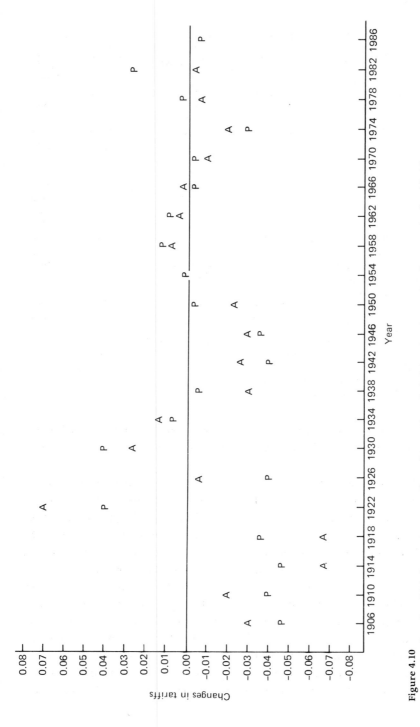

Figure 4.10
Actual (A) and predicted (P) changes in U.S. tariff rates by presidential administration. Source: Based on equation in table 4.5.

Table 4.9
Administrations ranked by actual changes in their tariff levels

Rank	President[a]	DTARTOT	PDTAR	ACTMACRO	X Year
1	Harding	0.069829	0.038796	72.11	1922
2	Hoover	0.026069	0.041224	140.46	1930
3	Reagan1[b]	0.025886	0.025886	52.90	1982
4	F. Roosevelt1	0.014641	0.006383	−34.29	1934
5	Ike2	0.011299	0.010834	18.39	1958
6	Kennedy	0.006044	0.005007	48.02	1962
7	Johnson	0.001611	−0.003512	−476.11	1966
8	Ike1	−0.001031	0.001094	−165.34	1954
9	Coolidge	−0.005405	−0.040125	412.59	1926
10	Carter	−0.005481	−0.000313	0.13	1978
11	Nixon	−0.010686	−0.002819	−7.21	1970
12	Ford	−0.020320	−0.028938	32.01	1974
13	Taft	−0.021114	−0.038920	−14.91	1910
14	Truman2	−0.023847	−0.004645	−79.59	1950
15	F. Roosevelt3	−0.026274	−0.039165	156.57	1942
16	Truman1	−0.031113	−0.038158	35.92	1946
17	F. Roosevelt2	−0.031269	−0.005790	2.51	1938
18	T. Roosevelt2	−0.031556	−0.047106	−4.24	1906
19	Wilson1	−0.065208	−0.048013	4.25	1914

Notes: DTARTOT, actual change in the tariff; PDTAR, predicted change in the tariff using table 4.5; ACTMACRO, percentage of the actual change explained by macrovariables inflation and unemployment.
a. Number after the name refers to number of term in office.
b. Predicted rather than actual change used.

protectionist pressures will drop during the second Reagan term, assuming no change in the terms of trade, that unemployment will fall, and that inflation will rise.

The seriousness of the increased protectionist pressure in Reagan's first term is illustrated in table 4.9. This lists the actual increases in U.S. tariffs by administration from 1901 through 1980 and includes the predicted increase under Reagan's first term (using the equation in table 4.5). Notice the sizable lead that Harding has over the others in terms of tariff increases (over .06) and how close Reagan comes to beating out Hoover for the second largest increase of the century (both around .025). (In fairness to Reagan, the Hoover administration includes a year or so before Smoot-Hawley.) The minidepression of the first Reagan term resulting in increased unemployment and reduced inflation accounts for only 52.9 percent of the predicted tariff increase. The rest is explained by the increase in the U.S. terms of trade in manufacturing caused by falling import prices (for example, the Japanese trade phenomenon). The variable ACTMACRO gives the percentage of the actual tariff change

Table 4.10
Administrations ranked by actual tariff levels

Rank	President[a]	LMTARTOT	DTARTOT	PDTAR	X Year
1	Roosevelt2	0.213347	−0.031556	−0.047106	1906
2	Taft	0.192233	−0.021114	−0.038920	1910
3	F. Roosevelt1	0.166695	0.014641	0.006383	1934
4	Hoover	0.152054	0.026069	0.0041224	1930
5	F. Roosevelt2	0.135426	−0.031269	−0.005790	1938
6	Harding	0.131390	0.069829	0.038796	1922
7	Wilson1	0.127025	−0.065208	−0.048013	1914
8	Coolidge	0.125985	−0.005405	−0.040125	1926
9	F. Roosevelt3	0.109152	−0.026274	−0.039165	1942
10	Truman1	0.078040	−0.031113	−0.038158	1946
11	Johnson	0.072116	0.001611	−0.003512	1966
12	Kennedy	0.070505	0.006044	0.005007	1962
13	Ike2	0.064461	0.011299	0.010834	1958
14	Reagan1[b]	0.061886	−0.001870	0.025886	1982
15	Wilson2	0.061561	−0.065464	−0.035097	1918
16	Nixon	0.061430	−0.010686	−0.002819	1970
17	Truman2	0.054193	−0.023847	−0.004645	1950
18	Ike1	0.053162	−0.001031	0.001094	1954
19	Ford	0.04110	−0.020320	−0.028938	1974
20	Carter	0.035628	−0.005481	−0.000313	1978

Note: LMTARTOT, actual tariff level (except Reagan1); PDTAR, predicted change in the tariff using table 4.5; DTARTOT, actual change in the tariff.
a. Number after the name refers to number of term in office.
b. Predicted rather than actual change used.

attributable to the macrovariables (inflation and unemployment). Notice that 72 percent of the tariff change under Harding was macrodriven, while the macrovariables overpredict the Smoot-Hawley change under Hoover (see table 4A.3 for more details). The increased pressure for protection under Reagan must be kept in perspective, however. When we add the .025 predicted increase in protection during Reagan's first term to the actual tariff level under Carter, we get only the .062 tariff level shown in table 4.10 (for a ranking of fourteenth in the century). This analysis ignores nontariff protection.

4.6 Resolution of the Presidential Party Paradox: The Isoprotection Curve

The paradox is that prolabor Democratic presidential administrations generate freer trade (which should hurt labor) while Republican administrations do the reverse. One explanation is provided by Ferguson (1984), who argues that Democratic presidents since Franklin Roosevelt have favored freer trade because they have obtained substantial campaign financing from U.S. multi-nationals. According to his argument the multinationals do not care about the prolabor stance of the Democrats because they have low wage bills, specializing instead in physical and human-capital-intensive activities that benefit from free world trade. Ferguson's argument is ingenious but incomplete; it does not explain why Democratic presidents would support free trade when this works counter to the interests of blue-collar and much union labor.

Our explanation is that the amount of protectionist pressure generated by each administration is largely derived from its macroeconomic policies and that these generate pressures for protection whose redistributive effects are opposite to that of the macropolicies. Consider the macroeconomic policies of the two parties. Democratic presidents favor macroeconomic policies that benefit labor: low unemployment and high inflation. The loose monetary policy that generated the higher inflation causes the dollar to weaken. Republicans do the reverse, favoring high unemployment and low inflation, resulting in a strong dollar. These macroeconomic policies benefit the economic clienteles of the parties in the expected way: the Republican macropolicies favor capital, creditors, financial intermediaries, and so on, and the Democratic macropolicies favor labor, debtors, and so on. The first Reagan administration fits this historical pattern: it experienced the worst minidepression since the Great Depression, and it favored Volcker's Federal Reserve policy of monetary stringency and a strong dollar. The reduced inflation has reduced consumer pressure on Congress against protection, and the stronger dollar increased pressure on Congress from labor and the U.S. importable sector because of the cheaper imports. Notice that the protectionist party paradox does not reverse the party-lobby alignment so long as the redistributive effect of the trade policy is smaller than that of the macropolicy. For example, labor is still better off economically under the Democratic administrations because the Democratic freer trade effects will generally be dominated by Democratic prolabor macropolicy effects.

This solution to the protectionist party paradox can be shown using Magee's (1982) isoprotection curve (for a published discussion of the curve, see Frey, 1984, pp. 56–58). Each curve depicts combinations of unemployment and inflation yielding the same level of equilibrium protection. Notice in figure 4.11 that the typical Democratic president has favored macroeconomic policies at the northwest corner of the diagram (point A), which generate freer trade sentiments, while the typical Republican president has favored macroeconomic policies at the southeast corner (point B), which generates protectionism. Empirical estimates of the isoprotection curves are shown in figure 4.12 (see the data in table 4.11, which excludes the three terms of Franklin Roosevelt because of the depression effects). Notice that inflation

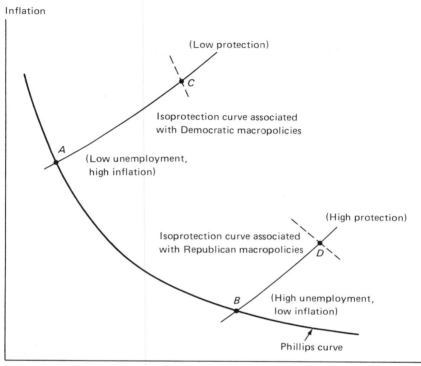

Figure 4.11
Resolution of protectionist party paradox using isoprotection curves.

rates are higher under the Democrats, while unemployment rates are lower. Isoprotection curves can be drawn through each of these points. The one associated with the Democrats will have lower protection ($t = .071$), and the one through the Republican point will have higher protection ($t = .107$).

The equations in table 4.4 and 4.5 provide an estimate of the isoprotection curves in figure 4.12. The slope of the curve equals $-a/b$ where a and b are the coefficients on unemployment and inflation in table 4.4 (equal to $-46/(-24) = 1.9$ according to our estimate). The implicit slope in table 4.5 is a bit lower at 1.5. For simplicity we assume that the slope of the isoprotection curves is 2. This means that every 1 percentage point rise in the unemployment rate requires a 2 percentage point rise in the inflation rate to keep the equilibrium level of protection constant.

The Republican isoprotection curve in figure 4.12 is drawn through the mean values of unemployment and inflation for Republican administrations (in table 4.11), while the Democratic curve goes through the Democratic mean (recall that it excludes Franklin Roosevelt). The first Reagan administration

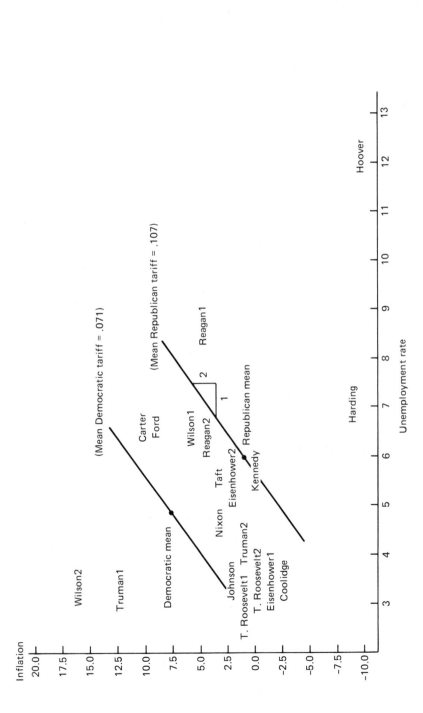

Figure 4.12
Isoprotection curves drawn through mean inflation and unemployment rates for the two parties, 1901–1988. Note: The analysis excludes Franklin Roosevelt. The numbers after presidents' names refer to term.

Table 4.11
Means and standard deviations of variables

Variable	N	Mean	Standard deviation
Democrats (excluding Franklin Roosevelt)			
LMTARTOT	7	0.07129544	0.02831945
MUNEMP	7	4.69642857	1.52946264
MINFLATE	7	6.98963920	6.11684210
MTMT	7	97.28618972	13.34449246
DCAPSH	7	−0.35714286	1.31384568
DKL	7	0.08962716	0.04608992
DTARTOT	7	−0.02620823	0.02981977
DUNEMP	7	−0.65357143	1.67987032
DINFLATE	7	1.28230906	6.50869131
DTMT	7	−0.04296943	0.10820611
DRTB	7	−2.91056042	5.76959494
Republicans			
LMTARTOT	10	0.10689300	0.06502135
MUNEMP	10	6.17500000	2.82299585
MINFLATE	10	0.48967825	5.83368943
MTMT	10	97.98644628	12.21339832
DCAPSH	10	−1.95833333	1.70477271
DKL	10	0.05786013	0.04286642
DTARTOT	10	0.00152139	0.02917908
DUNEMP	10	1.83000000	3.22468345
DINFLATE	10	−2.31114688	9.65727161
DTMT	10	−0.00432344	0.09696018
DRTB	10	−0.84553661	1.64042978
Total			
LMTARTOT	17	0.09223518	0.05481774
MUNEMP	17	5.56617647	2.43363381
MINFLATE	17	3.16613276	6.63678401
MTMT	17	97.69810534	12.28051273
DCAPSH	17	−1.29901961	1.71519426
DKL	17	0.07094067	0.04571567
DTARTOT	17	−0.00989669	0.03178470
DUNEMP	17	0.80735294	2.91458837
DINFLATE	17	−0.83148855	8.46579626
DTMT	17	−0.02023650	0.10031595
DRTB	17	−1.69584053	3.88512727

displays more protectionist pressure than the mean Republican isoprotectionist curve; however, the Republican mean is heavily influenced by the
deflationary Harding and Hoover administrations. Only Truman and Wilson
had greater macroeconomic pressures for free trade than the mean Democratic
isoprotection curve. The forecasts of unemployment and inflation by the
Reagan administration for its second term place it in a much less protectionist
position (to the left of the mean Republican isoprotection curve).

The issue of protection and stagflation can be illustrated using figure 4.11. If
the Phillips curve shifts out with no change in the party in power, no change in
protection need occur. For example, start from point A during a Democratic
administration and let the Phillips curve shift outward. If the reasons for the
Phillips curve shift do not affect the demand and supply of protection (apart
from the inflation and unemployment effects), the new domestic equilibrium
will be at point C, and the U.S. level of protection is unchanged.

The evolution of U.S. macroeconomic policy, trade policy, and the political
fortunes of the two parties also has an interpretation in figure 4.11. The
following suggestions are speculative and are advanced without hard
evidence. Since a majority of the U.S. populace is a net debtor, the median
voter is also a debtor. The ascendancy of general interests (see Olson, 1982) and
the rise in the power of the presidency over the past few decades would bias
both parties toward inflation. This will work as a redistributive mechanism
only if the inflation is unanticipated and hence for a limited time. During the
period it is unanticipated, however, the process transfers wealth from creditors and owners of financial intermediaries to debtors, constituting a majority
of the voters. Eventually the losers from these transfers replace fixed-rate
lending with variable-rate loans, as they have done. Early in this process both
parties favor higher inflation rates, and the Phillips curve shifts out (for
example, from B to D in figure 4.11). The level of protection need not change.
This scenario is consistent with (though by no means the only explanation of)
the stagflationary rise in unemployment and inflation in the 1960s and the
early 1970s.

Is there an explanation to the rise in protectionism? Paralleling stagflation,
the factor endowment of the United States has been moving away from blue-
collar labor and toward more human and physical capital. This, coupled with
the decline in union participation, means declining success for the prolabor
Democratic party, which has had only one president in the last five terms. This
phenomenon shifts the political equilibrium in a southeasterly direction in
figure 4.11 (in the direction of D). While the move toward lower inflation and
higher unemployment has been particularly dramatic in the first Reagan
administration, we view this as a long-term trend. Most important, the long-

term shift toward D is also accompanied by higher protection (because unemployment is up and inflation is down). Higher protection came in the 1970s (with VER agreements, rising nontariff barriers, and greater pressure for antidumping decisions). Congress appears ready to advance it again in the mid 1980s.

4.7 Nontariff (Antidumping) Protection

Are the determinants of nontariff protection the same as those for tariff protection? Our answer is a qualified yes. We present evidence in this section indicating that the special-interest determinants of tariff protection (unemployment, the real dollar exchange rate, and the terms of trade) also hold for nontariff (antidumping) protection. The general-interest determinant (the inflation rate) has the wrong sign, however. Since antidumping protection is an administrative matter, the result is consistent with antidumping protection being more vulnerable to special-interest pressures than to general-interest pressures. The result supports the finding of Finger, Hall, and Nelson (1982) that antidumping protection is less visible to the public and hence biased in favor of narrow protectionist interests over general freer trade interests (in their language, antidumping protection is "lower track"). The business cycle effects we find (such as the unemployment effect on dumping) are consistent with the Takacs (1981) study of escape clause protection.

Our measure of nontariff protection is the proportion of antidumping cases ($S2$) in which the U.S. government finds in favor of the protectionist petitioner. Annual data for this variable were available from 1954 through 1981. We estimate a reduced-form equation, attempting to explain $S2$ using the determinants from both the demand and the supply of protection. We include most of the variables used in the tariff analysis, including the real exchange rate between the United States and the United Kingdom. All of the exogenous variables are lagged one year.

The regression results are shown in table 4.12. Notice that all of the exogenous variables are significant except the real trade balance; the adjusted R square is .87; and the first-order autocorrelation of the residuals is acceptable. All of the compensation effects have the correct sign, except for the inflation rate. When the Republican dummy was added, it was insignificant. We also included the tariff rate in the equation to see if antidumping protection is substituting for tariff protection. The results indicate significant substitution: each .01 decline in tariff protection measured by the log of $(1 + t)$ is associated with a .01 increase in the proportion of proprotectionist findings in antidumping cases. The significance of this result is that the welfare gain from

Table 4.12
Equation explaining the proportion of proprotectionist antidumping decisions, annual data, 1954–1981

Variable	Parameter estimate	Standard error	T for HO: parameter = 0	PROB > $|T|$
INTERCEP	−11.118865	1.657593	−6.708	0.0001
LAG2TMT	2.846051	0.406516	7.001	0.0001*
LAG2IN	0.024934	0.011535	2.161	0.0430*
LAG2UN	0.041455	0.023112	1.794	0.0880
LAG2RTB	−0.0085439	0.006165926	−1.386	0.1811
LAG2UKUS	−1.136623	0.318439	−3.569	0.0019*
LOGTAR	−0.933581	0.243056	−3.841	0.0010*

Durbin-Watson D, 2.383.
First-order autocorrelation, −0.208.
F value, 29.134.
Prob. > F, 0.0001.
R-square, 0.8973.
Adjusted R-square, 0.8665.
*Significant.

an exogenous reduction in U.S. tariffs may be offset by increases in nontariff (antidumping) protection.

The results also indicate that both long-run tariff and short-run nontariff protection have some common determinants: the terms of manufacturing trade and the unemployment rate. The major new compensation effect not present in the tariff equation is the real exchange rate (LAG2UKUS). This is the U.K. price level expressed in dollars divided by the U.S. price level. When this variable is low, U.S. antidumping protection is high. This will be the case when the real dollar is strong because a strong dollar reduces the dollar cost of foreign goods relative to U.S. goods. This price pressure leads the U.S. importable sector to demand greater protection.

Figure 4.13 shows the actual (A) and predicted (P) proportion of proprotectionist decisions in the antidumping cases using the equation in table 4.12. There appears to be an upward shift in the proportion of proprotectionist case findings around 1970. A test for an upward shift in the constant of the estimating equation for S2, however, revealed no significant change apart from the forces already reflected in the exogenous variables. The data for both the tariff and the antidumping regressions are shown in table 4A.3.

4.8 Summary

1. The endogenous policy paradox. The equilibrium trade policies are largely outside the control of the policymakers in a competitive political system.

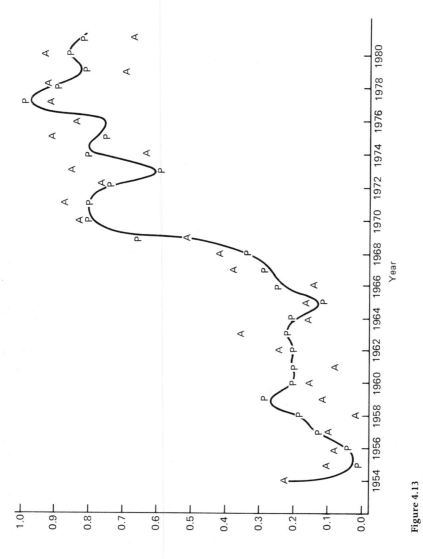

Figure 4.13
Proportion of proprotectionist antidumping decisions: actual versus predicted. Source: Based on the equation in table 4.12.

Protectionism equilibrates redistributive markets, just as prices equilibrate product markets. Policymakers intermediate between groups with narrow interests (proprotectionist and antiprotectionist lobbies) and those with broad interests (voters). Empirically protection will be explained by those exogenous variables that drive the behavior of these interests (both broad and narrow) that favor and oppose protection (just as prices can be explained by the exogenous determinants of supply and demand).

The determinants of protection can be separated into those that motivate special interests to demand protection and trade intervention (import taxes and export subsidies) and those that motivate general interests to oppose intervention. Special-interest lobbying pressure for trade intervention is driven by pure trade theory variables (the factor endowment, magnification, and terms of trade effects) and cyclical variables (the U.S. unemployment rate and the real exchange rate). General-interest voter pressure against trade intervention is most heavily influenced by the U.S. inflation rate. Increases in inflation mobilize voter and consumer opposition to trade restrictions, while decreases in inflation do the reverse.

2. The endowment effect. Changes in a country's factor endowment alter the political clout of special-interest lobbies representing the factors of production. For example, as labor has become a less important factor of production in the United States in this century, its political influence has waned and tariff protection has declined. The number of workers per unit of capital today in the United States is less than half that at the turn of the century. The prolabor party is also suffering at the polls: the Democratic party has controlled the White House for only one of the last five terms.

3. The public furor over protectionism in the 1970s might be an example of the magnification paradox. An increased magnification effect of product prices on factor prices causes both protectionist and proexport forces to devote more economic resources to politics but to come away with a lower equilibrium level of protection. Thus the political noise level and the protection level can move in opposite directions. Magnification increases occur when the factor intensities of production in exportables and importables become more similar.

4. An important principle in endogenous tariff theory is the compensation effect. When a special-interest group's return from economic activity declines because of any adverse shock, the group compensates by investing more resources in lobbying and politics. Its political party responds with an increase in the policy variable that benefits it. For example, increases in the unemployment rate lead protectionists to greater pressure for protection, and the U.S. political system generally responds with greater protection. A second important example is the effect of the terms of trade on the equilibrium level of

protection. Advances by the Japanese in automobile production and the industrialization of the Third World have reduced the relative prices of U.S. importables and increased the U.S. terms of trade. U.S. factors of production in importables, following the compensation principle, have increased their lobbying and received more protection. In this argument the direction of causation is the reverse of that in the usual theoretical argument that an increase in U.S. protection will improve the U.S. terms of trade.

5. The macroeconomic by-product effect. Protection is a by-product of each administration's macropolicy. Two of the most important determinants of protection are unemployment and the inflation rate. The level of protection generated by most U.S. presidential administrations in this century has been driven by the macroeconomic policies it chooses and the macroeconomic shocks it experiences. The unemployment effect has been recognized for years, but the inflation effect is new.

6. We estimate Magee's (1982) isoprotection curve. It can be drawn on the familiar Phillip's curve diagram and shows combinations of unemployment and inflation that generate equal equilibrium levels of protection. Along these curves we found that a 1 percentage point increase in the U.S. unemployment rate requires a 2 percentage point increase in the U.S. inflation rate to keep the equilibrium level of protection constant.

7. The protectionist-party paradox. Republican presidential administrations generate more protection, while prolabor Democratic administrations generate freer trade. Our explanation is that Republican macropolicies increase protectionist pressure, while Democratic macropolicies increase antiprotectionist pressure. Republican presidents (such as Reagan) generate antilabor macroeconomic policies that locate them on isoprotection curves with high unemployment and low inflation, both of which increase protectionist pressures in Congress. The Congress occasionally responds with protectionist legislation. This pattern has also held for other Republican presidents (Harding, Hoover, Eisenhower, and Nixon). The reverse pattern was generated by Democratic presidents (Franklin Roosevelt, Johnson, and Carter), whose macroeconomic preferences locate them on freer trade isoprotectionist curves, characterized by lower unemployment and higher inflation.

8. Unanticipated inflations may increase the welfare of median voters (because they are net debtors). Stagflation's effect on protectionism can be neutral; increasing unemployment raises the equilibrium level of protection, while increasing inflation reduces it. The net effect of stagflation on protection depends on the strengths of these two opposing forces. The increase in pressure for protection (caused by the rise in unemployment) should not be confused with an increase in protection itself, since the higher inflation effect may dominate.

9. According to our regressions, the three presidential administrations in this century with the largest increases in protection have been Harding (with the Fordney-McCumber tariff, the largest increase of the century), Hoover (with Smoot-Hawley), and Reagan (who faces considerable protectionist pressure following his first term). The actual Smoot-Hawley tariff increase was smaller than our endogenous tariff model predicted, meaning that protectionist pressure was considerable during the Hoover administration and that the tariff passed was less protectionist than it could have been.

Reagan's first term had the third highest predicted increase in protection this century because of an increase in the U.S. terms of trade index from 87 to 100, a rise in the U.S. unemployment rate from 6.4 percent to 8.5 percent, and a drop in the U.S. inflation rate for producer prices from 9.7 percent per annum to 4.2 percent (all compared to the Carter administration). We predict a decline in protectionist pressure for the second Reagan term as unemployment falls and inflation rises.

10. When compared with the rest of the century, the 1970s was a period of low long-run protection. We speculate that this is true even if the ad valorem equivalent of all nontariff barriers were measured along with tariff rates. The reason is that three out of four factors point to lower protection: the continued decline of labor in the U.S. factor endowment, the low level of the U.S. terms of manufacturing trade, and the high level of U.S. inflation (which mobilized consumers against protection and contributed to the weak dollar).

11. Increasing Republican presidential electoral success is increasing protectionism in the United States because of Republican macropolicy preferences for high unemployment, low inflation, and a strong dollar.

12. Historically the Congress has been more protectionist than the executive branch. In the last two decades, however, the executive branch has become increasingly protectionist in its negotiation of VER agreements with the Far East and in its administrative protection (antidumping, for example). The Congress now appears to be battling the White House to regain control of protectionist policy. In addition to the current high demand for protection, the Congress may wish to recapture both protectionist and proexport lobbying resources, which have been focused on the White House.

13. Nontariff protection. The same principles explaining tariff protection apply to nontariff protection provided by the U.S. antidumping statutes; however, because antidumping protection is less visible to the public, the general-interest variable (the inflation rate) does not even have the correct sign, while the special-interest variables (the unemployment rate, the terms of trade, and the real exchange rate) are statistically significant and have the right signs. Because of its shorter-run nature, the antidumping restriction is consist-

ent with an insurance model of protection (see Anderson, 1978; Eaton and Grossman, 1985; Baldwin 1982, p. 272; and the conservative social welfare function of Corden, 1974). That is, protection can be viewed as sectoral insurance against macroeconomic or sector-specific shocks. These models are theoretical alternatives to the views presented here. The equilibrium level of antidumping protection has been rising steadily over the past three decades.

Note

We are especially indebted to Tom Ferguson, Ed Leamer, and Peter Neary for helpful comments and suggestions on earlier drafts of this chapter. We have also benefited from discussions of these issues with Robert Baldwin, William A. Brock, and Ed Ray. We wish to thank Liming Han and Cheng Kuo for research assistance in the preparation of the chapter.

Data Appendix

Table 4A.1
Tariff and related data

OBS	Year	Administration	President	LMTARTOT	MUNEMP	MINFLATE	MTMT	LPERK	MCAPSH	NOTAX
1	1906	2	T. Roosevelt	0.213347	3.550	1.4044	115.503	19.3241	45.0000	1
2	1910	3	Taft	0.192233	5.625	2.5486	117.868	17.9822	45.2500	1
3	1914	4	Wilson	0.127025	6.725	5.9312	117.010	17.1101	46.7500	1
4	1918	5	Wilson	0.061561	3.125	16.5287	110.964	15.9792	44.5000	0
5	1922	6	Harding	0.131390	7.050	-9.0538	103.367	15.6964	42.0000	0
6	1926	7	Coolidge	0.125985	3.600	-0.2907	91.182	14.7540	39.2500	0
7	1930	8	Hoover	0.152054	12.800	-9.3758	97.758	15.1522	34.7500	0
8	1934	9	F. Roosevelt	0.166695	20.825	5.7992	111.187	18.2505	32.0000	0
9	1938	10	F. Roosevelt	0.135426	16.275	-0.5358	109.645	19.9731	34.7500	0
10	1942	11	F. Roosevelt	0.109152	4.425	7.3989	114.887	20.9141	36.5000	0
11	1946	12	Truman	0.078040	3.125	12.4346	93.587	19.6057	34.7500	0
12	1950	13	Truman	0.054193	4.050	1.9603	78.495	16.4636	34.7500	0
13	1954	14	Eisenhower	0.053162	3.825	0.5575	80.422	14.5607	31.5000	0
14	1958	15	Eisenhower	0.064461	5.400	1.6209	89.388	13.2322	29.7500	0
15	1962	16	Kennedy	0.070505	5.600	0.1070	93.771	12.4046	29.0000	0
16	1966	17	Johnson	0.072116	3.825	2.2385	100.140	10.8563	29.2500	0
17	1970	18	Nixon	0.061430	4.875	3.3320	99.976	9.8956	25.2500	0
18	1974	19	Ford	0.041110	6.550	9.9100	84.726	9.5834	25.0000	0
19	1978	20	Carter	0.035628	6.425	9.7271	87.036	8.9166	25.5000	0
20	1982	21	Reagan	0.033758	8.475	4.2435	99.675	8.4769	24.6667	0
21	1986	22	Reagan	.	6.700	4.1000	99.670	.	.	0

Table 4A.2
First differences of tariff and related data

OBS	Year	President	DTARTOT	DUNEMP	DINFLATE	NOTAX	DTMT	DCAPSH	DKL
1	1906	T. Roosevelt	-0.031556	0.425	-0.200	1	-0.03518	0.0000	0.05971
2	1910	Taft	-0.021114	2.075	1.144	1	0.02027	0.2500	0.07197
3	1914	Wilson	-0.065208	1.100	3.383	1	-0.00731	1.5000	0.04971
4	1918	Wilson	-0.065464	-3.600	10.598	0	-0.05305	-2.2500	0.06838
5	1922	Harding	0.069829	3.925	-25.582	0	-0.07092	-2.5000	0.01786
6	1926	Coolidge	-0.005405	-3.450	8.763	0	-0.12542	-2.7500	0.06192
7	1930	Hoover	0.026069	9.200	-9.085	0	0.06963	-4.5000	-0.02664
8	1934	F. Roosevelt	0.014641	8.025	15.175	0	0.12872	-2.7500	-0.18604
9	1938	F. Roosevelt	-0.031269	-4.550	-6.335	0	-0.01397	2.7500	-0.09019
10	1942	F. Roosevelt	-0.026274	-11.850	7.935	0	0.04670	1.7500	-0.04604
11	1946	Truman	-0.031113	-1.300	5.036	0	-0.20505	-1.7500	0.06460
12	1950	Truman	-0.026847	0.925	-10.474	0	-0.17586	-0.0000	0.17467
13	1954	Eisenhower	-0.001031	-0.225	-1.403	0	0.02425	-3.2500	0.12283
14	1958	Eisenhower	0.011299	1.575	1.063	0	0.10570	-1.7500	0.09567
15	1962	Kennedy	0.006044	0.200	-1.514	0	0.04786	-0.7500	0.06459
16	1966	Johnson	0.001611	-1.775	2.132	0	0.06572	0.2500	0.13332
17	1970	Nixon	-0.010686	1.050	1.094	0	-0.00165	-4.0000	0.09265
18	1974	Ford	-0.020320	1.675	6.578	0	-0.16551	-0.2500	0.03207
19	1978	Carter	-0.005481	-0.125	-0.183	0	0.02691	0.5000	0.07212
20	1982	Reagan	-0.001870	2.050	-5.484	0	0.13559	-0.8333	0.05057
21	1986	Reagan	.	-1.775	-0.143	0	-0.00005	.	.

Table 4A.3
Administrations ranked by predicted changed in their tariff levels

	President[a]	PDTAR	PCTMACRO	XMACRO	XTMT	XUNEMP	XINFLATE	XOTHER	XERROR	DTARTOT	YEAR
1	Hoover	0.041224	88.82	0.036616	0.008007	0.02208	0.014536	-0.0034	0.015155	0.026069	1930
2	Harding	0.038796	129.79	0.050352	-0.008156	0.00942	0.040932	-0.0034	-0.031033	0.069829	1922
3	Reagan1	0.025886	52.90	0.013694	0.015593	0.00492	0.008774	-0.0034	0.027757	-0.001870	1982
4	Ike2	0.010834	19.18	0.002078	0.012156	0.00378	-0.001702	-0.0034	-0.000465	0.011299	1958
5	F. Roosevelt1	0.006383	-78.64	-0.005020	0.014803	0.01926	-0.024280	-0.0034	-0.008257	0.014641	1934
6	Kennedy	0.005007	57.97	0.002902	0.005504	0.00048	0.002422	-0.0034	-0.001037	0.006044	1962
7	Ike1	0.001094	155.85	0.001704	0.002789	-0.00054	0.002244	-0.0034	0.002125	-0.001031	1954
8	Carter	-0.000313	2.34	-0.000007	0.003094	-0.00030	0.000293	-0.0034	0.005168	-0.005481	1978
9	Nixon	-0.002819	-27.33	0.000770	-0.000189	0.00252	-0.001750	-0.0034	0.007867	-0.010686	1970
10	Johnson	-0.003512	218.38	-0.007671	0.007558	-0.00426	-0.003411	-0.0034	-0.005124	0.001611	1966
11	Truman2	-0.004645	-408.58	0.018979	-0.020224	0.00222	0.016759	-0.0034	0.019202	-0.023847	1950
12	F. Roosevelt2	-0.005790	13.54	-0.000784	-0.001606	-0.01092	0.010136	-0.0034	0.025478	-0.031269	1938
13	Ford	-0.028938	22.48	-0.006505	-0.019033	0.00402	-0.010525	-0.0034	-0.008618	-0.020320	1974
14	Wilson2	-0.035097	72.93	-0.025596	-0.006101	-0.00864	-0.016956	-0.0034	0.030367	-0.065464	1918
15	Truman1	-0.038158	29.29	-0.011177	-0.023581	-0.00312	-0.008057	-0.0034	-0.007046	-0.031113	1946
16	Taft	-0.038920	-8.09	0.003149	0.002331	0.00498	-0.001831	-0.0444	-0.017805	-0.021114	1910
17	F. Roosevelt3	-0.039165	105.03	-0.041136	0.005371	-0.02844	-0.012696	-0.0034	-0.012891	-0.026274	1942
18	Coolidge	-0.040125	55.58	-0.022301	-0.014424	-0.00828	-0.014021	-0.0034	-0.034720	-0.005405	1926
19	F. Roosevelt2	-0.047106	-2.84	0.001340	-0.004046	0.00102	0.000320	-0.0444	-0.015550	-0.031556	1906
20	Wilson1	-0.048013	5.77	-0.002772	-0.000841	0.00264	-0.005412	-0.0444	0.017195	-0.065208	1914

Note: PDTAR, predicted change in the tariff using table 4.5; PCTMACRO, percentage of predicted tariff change due to macrofactors; DTARTOT, actual change in tariffs during the administration; XTMT, unemployment and inflation; XUNEMP, unemployment; XINFLATE, inflation; XOTHER, other (trend plus notax dummy for 1905–1916); and XERROR, error term in the regression equation.

a. Number after the name refers to number of term in office.

Table 4A.4
Antidumping data

OBS	Year	DUMP	NSLFV	S2	TMT	UNEMP	RTB	UKUS	TARTOT
1	1954	31	24	0.225806	78.511	5.0	2.931	0.88175	0.0516602
2	1955	20	18	0.100000	80.973	4.0	3.275	0.89931	0.0558349
3	1956	28	26	0.071429	82.715	3.8	5.347	0.89848	0.0567274
4	1957	30	27	0.100000	86.340	4.3	6.806	0.89082	0.0577355
5	1958	35	34	0.028571	89.183	6.6	3.648	0.88585	0.0644427
6	1959	31	27	0.129032	91.083	5.3	1.183	0.88775	0.0701661
7	1960	40	34	0.150000	90.947	5.4	5.123	0.89874	0.0739932
8	1961	24	22	0.083333	92.252	6.5	5.870	0.91310	0.0721108
9	1962	29	22	0.241379	94.099	5.4	4.787	0.93979	0.0751139
10	1963	30	19	0.366667	93.789	5.5	5.550	0.94822	0.0729369
11	1964	33	28	0.151515	94.942	5.0	7.226	0.96695	0.0720391
12	1965	12	10	0.166667	98.109	4.4	5.120	0.98858	0.0772014
13	1966	15	13	0.133333	98.465	3.7	3.846	0.97903	0.0757098
14	1967	16	10	0.375000	100.000	3.7	3.800	0.96958	0.0754124
15	1968	17	10	0.411765	103.988	3.5	0.584	0.84702	0.0707978
16	1969	21	10	0.523810	105.304	3.4	0.563	0.84976	0.0711338
17	1970	17	3	0.823529	103.030	4.8	2.357	0.88223	0.0649965
18	1971	34	4	0.882353	98.510	5.8	−1.935	0.93947	0.0607918
19	1972	32	8	0.750000	93.059	5.5	−5.461	0.99023	0.0565021
20	1973	21	3	0.857143	86.221	4.8	0.704	0.95511	0.0524455
21	1974	11	4	0.636364	80.226	5.5	−3.729	0.97009	0.0376573
22	1975	23	2	0.913043	83.444	8.3	5.447	1.01563	0.0391645
23	1976	13	2	0.846154	89.013	7.6	−5.510	0.93032	0.0385978
24	1977	37	3	0.918919	88.591	6.9	−17.061	1.01156	0.0372939
25	1978	36	3	0.916667	85.051	6.0	−17.305	1.12316	0.0414103
26	1979	27	8	0.703704	85.954	5.8	−12.632	1.25210	0.0349742
27	1980	46	3	0.934783	88.549	7.0	−10.324	1.41034	0.0314033
28	1981	16	5	0.687500	96.051	7.5	−10.378	1.22683	0.0343343

References

Baldwin, Robert E. "U.S. Tariff Policy: Formation and Effects." Discussion paper. U.S. Department of Labor, 1976.

Baldwin, Robert E. "The Political Economy of Protection." In J. Bhagwati, ed., *Import Competition and Response*. Chicago: University of Chicago Press, 1982.

Baldwin, Robert E. *The Political Economy of U.S. Import Policy*. Cambridge: MIT Press, 1985.

Baldwin, Robert E. "Trade Policies in Developed Countries." In R. W. Jones and P. B. Kenen, eds., *Handbook of International Economics*. Amsterdam: North-Holland, 1984.

Baldwin, Robert E., and R. Spencer Hilton. "A Technique for Indicating Comparative Costs and Predicting Changes in Trade Ratios." *Review of Economics and Statistics* 30 (1983): 411–420.

Bale, Malcom D. "United States Concessions in the Kennedy Round and Short-Run Labor Adjustment Costs." *Journal of International Economics* 7 (1977): 145–148.

Becker, Gary S. "A Theory of Competition among Pressure Groups for Political Influence." *Quarterly Journal of Economics* 98 (1983): 371–400.

Bernholz, P. "Dominant Interest Groups and Powerless Parties." *Kyklos* 30 (1977): 411–420.

Bhagwati, Jagdish N. "Lobbying and Welfare." *Journal of Public Economics* 14 (1980): 355–363.

Brock, William A., and Stephen P. Magee. "The Economics of Pork-Barrel Politics." Report 7511. University of Chicago, School of Business Administration, 1975.

Brock, William A., and Stephen P. Magee. "The Economics of Special Interest Politics: The Case of the Tariff." *American Economic Review* 68 (1978): 246–250.

Brock, William A., and Stephen P. Magee. "Tariff Formation in a Democracy." In John Black and Brian Hindley, eds., *Current Issues in Commercial Policy and Diplomacy*. New York: St. Martin's Press, 1980.

Brock, William A., and Stephen P. Magee. "The Invisible Foot and the Waste of Nations: Redistribution and Economic Growth." In D. C. Colander, ed., *Neoclassical Political Economy*. Cambridge, Mass.: Ballinger Press, 1984.

Brown, B. "Protectionist Pressure in the Eighties." Professional report, University of Texas at Austin, 1985.

Conybeare, J. A. C. "Tariff Protection in Developed and Developing Countries: A Cross-Sectional and Longitudinal Analysis." *International Organization* 37 (1983): 441–467.

Corden, W. M. *Trade Policy and Economic Welfare*. Oxford: Clarendon, 1974.

Curzon, Gerard, and Victoria Price. "Is Protection Inevitable?" Discussion paper, no. 8401. Geneva: Graduate Institute of International Studies, 1984.

Eaton, Jonathan, and Gene Grossman. "Tariffs as Insurance: Optimal Commercial Policy When Domestic Markets Are Incomplete." *Canadian Journal of Economics* 18 (1985): 258–272.

Ferguson, Tom. "From Normalcy to New Deal: Industrial Structure, Party Competition, and American Public Policy in the Great Depression." *International Organization* 38 (1984): 41–94.

Frey, Bruno. *International Political Economics*. Oxford: Basil Blackwell, 1984.

Findlay, Ronald, and Stanislaw Wellisz. "Endogenous Tariffs, the Political Economy of Trade Restrictions and Welfare." In J. N. Bhagwati, ed., *Import Competition and Response*. Chicago: University of Chicago Press, 1982.

Finger, J. M., H. K. Hall, and D. R. Nelson. "The Political Economy of Administered Protection." *American Economic Review* 72 (1982): 452–466.

Krueger, A. O. "The Political Economy of the Rent-Seeking Society." *American Economic Review* 64 (1974): 291–303.

Magee, Stephen P. "Three Simple Tests of the Stolper-Samuelson Theorem." In P. Oppenheimer, ed., *Issues in International Economics*. London: Oriel Press, 1980.

Magee, Stephen P. "Protection in the United States." Manuscript. University of Texas at Austin, 1982.

Magee Stephen P. "Endogenous Tariff Theory: A Survey." In D. Colander, ed., *Neoclasical Political Economy*. Cambridge, Mass.: Ballinger, 1984.

Magee, Stephen P., William A. Brock, and Leslie Young. "Endogenous Tariff Theory: Endogenous Redistribution, Black Hole Tariffs, Politics and Lobbying in General Equilibrium." Manuscript. University of Texas at Austin, 1983.

Mayer, W. "Endogenous Tariff Formation." *American Economic Review* 74 (1984): 970–985.

Olson, M. *The Logic of Collective Action*. Cambridge: Harvard University Press, 1965.

Olson, M. *The Rise and Decline of Nations*. New Haven: Yale University Press, 1982.

Pugel, T. A., and I. Walter. "U.S. Corporate Interests and the Political Economy of Trade Policy." *Review of Economics and Statistics* 67 (1985): 465–473.

Ratner, S. *The Tariff in American History*. New York: Van Nostrand, 1972.

Ray, Edward J. "The Determinants of Tariff and Nontariff Trade Restrictions in the United States." *Journal of Political Economy* 89 (1981): 105–121.

Salvatore, Dominick. "'The New Protectionism and the Threat to World Welfare: Editor's Introduction." *Journal of Policy Modelling* 7 (1985): 1–22.

Stern, Robert M., and Keith E. Maskus. "Determinants of the Structure of U.S. Foreign Trade, 1958–1976." *Journal of International Economics* 11 (1981): 207–224.

Takacs, W. "Pressures for Protectionism: An Empirical Analysis." *Economic Inquiry* 19 (1981): 687–693.

Tulloch, G. "The Welfare Cost of Tariffs, Monopolies and Theft." *Western Economic Journal* 5 (1967): 224–232.

Young, Leslie, and Stephen P. Magee. "A Prisoners' Dilemma Theory of Endogenous Tariffs." Econometric Society Meetings, December 1982.

Young, Leslie, and Stephen P. Magee. "Factor Returns and Resource Allocation in the Political Economy of Protection." Mimeo. University of Texas at Austin, 1983.

Young, Leslie, and Stephen P. Magee. "A Black Hole in the Political Economy of Protection." Working Paper. Department of Finance, University of Texas at Austin, 1984.

Young, Leslie and Stephen P. Magee. "The $2 \times 2 \times 2 \times 2$ Endogenous Tariff Model: Theory and Evidence." Mimeo. University of Texas at Austin, 1985.

Comment on "Endogenous Protection in the United States, 1900–1984"

Edward E. Leamer

Magee and Young are to be complimented for the boldness with which they attack the problem of explaining the history of tariffs in the United States during the twentieth century. The tariff averages that they illustrate in figure 4.1 decline dramatically from 1900 to 1918, then begin to increase to a peak in 1933, and thereafter generally decline. What accounts for this pattern, especially the pronounced secular decline? I can think of several hypotheses. Possibly it is the growing role of the United States as a leader of the international community. Foreign policy goals such as the reconstruction of Western Europe and the containment of Soviet expansionism would not be well served by the closing of U.S. markets to allies. Another hypothesis is that the growing dependence of the United States on foreign trade has increased the exchange losses from trade restrictions, thereby deterring the use of tariffs as tools for income redistribution. A third hypothesis, related to the second, has to do with the institutionalization of reciprocity and MFN status. Reciprocity has been a cornerstone of all the tariff reduction negotiations since the 1934 Reciprocal Trade Agreements Act. Reciprocity makes tariff reductions more likely by directly engaging the interests of U.S. export industries. A fourth hypothesis is that institutional changes have provided more efficient ways of achieving the same goals toward which tariffs are aimed. If revenue of the federal government is the goal, the income tax comes to mind, though the Reagan administration seems to think differently. If income redistribution is the goal, there is the safety net of the social security system, unemployment benefits, food stamps and others.

These are just four hypotheses. I am confident there are others. Indeed Dornbusch and Frankel in chapter 3 have offered several having to do with cyclical pressures for tariff protection. It is not my intent to provide a complete list of alternative hypotheses but only to suggest the rich diversity of possibilities that come easily to mind. Magee and Young have offered several of their own. Their hypotheses are derived from a formal two-good, two-factor general equilibrium model, onto which is tacked two lobbies and two political parties. The Stolper-Samuelson result that the scarce factor gains from tariff protection implies that labor favors tariffs and supports the Democrats and capital favors export subsidies and supports the Republicans. The probabilistic electoral outcome is influenced by efforts made by laborers and owners of capital in discussing the variables to be included in their model, Magee and Young offer the following interpretations:

1. The effect of the secular increase of the capital per person has been to lower the average level of tariffs. This is because capital earnings are used to purchase tariff reductions through the electoral process, and capital earnings increase relative to labor earnings as the level of capital increases relative to labor.

2. The effect of the secular decline in the capital share of GNP has been to lower the average level of tariffs. This is not because of increases in capital earnings. Rather the Stolper-Samuelson sensitivities of capital earnings vary inversely with the capital share if the production function is Cobb-Douglas. This, according to Magee and Young, leads to lower average tariffs.

3. Unemployment, and other adverse events affecting the import substitute sector, lead to higher tariffs. This is not because the rest of us feel more charitable in such times, but because workers increase their political activity.

4. Inflation lowers the average level of tariffs because it rouses voters out of their normal stupor. (This strikes me as very informal theory.)

In my view, Magee and Young's model has a large number of questionable elements:

1. The model has only two goods and two factors. In a multifactor, multigood world, the Stolper-Samuelson linking of goods to factors is highly complex, and it is impossible even for an econometrician to say with confidence which goods are associated with which factors. It is consequently very much in doubt whether the particular average tariff Magee and Young use increases the return to labor in the long run.

2. The model has no dynamics in the tariff-setting process. I have the impression that in fact tariffs are not set; rather they are raised or lowered. If the model is taken literally, each time there is a change in political party in office, the levels of tariffs and export subsidies are dramatically altered.

3. There are no adjustment costs in the model. Magee and Young argue incorrectly that interest in long-term trends dictates the use of a theory that has no short-run effects. Possibly the long-term movement of the average level of tariffs is the result of an accumulation of policies, each aimed at the short

run. It is difficult for me to imagine that the current debate over trade restrictions for automobiles, iron and steel, and textiles, to name a few industries, would be so intense if workers and capital in those industries could costlessly move to other industries. I have the impression that recent trade intervention in the United States is used like federal disaster assistance as a publicly provided insurance scheme to supplement other forms of public insurance such as unemployment compensation. Tariffs and other forms of trade restrictions can be expected to occur when these other forms of insurance are inadequate.

4. The platforms of the parties are one-dimensional. Do these simple results hold up when competition for votes occurs in many dimensions with a heterogeneous constituency?

5. The only instrument for income redistribution is the tariff. I think that more effective instruments are generally available, and tariffs are used only in those special circumstances when they are most efficient. This, by the way, is a serious criticism of most studies of tariff formation. Regressions of tariff levels on various characteristics of industries are usually interpreted in terms of the costs and benefits of income redistribution. These regressions might instead be revealing when tariffs are the most efficient means of income redistribution.

6. Capital is assumed to be immobile internationally. There is, of course, considerable international mobility of capital, and this tends to alter substantially the long-run interests of capital labor as well. For example, tariffs on imported steel may force users of steel to locate elsewhere, in which case cheap foreign steel may continue to be imported though packaged in finished products.

7. Capital in the model seems not to be owned by humans. If capital represents both physical and human capital, aren't there skilled workers who oppose the tariff?

8. There are no incumbency effects. The units of time are not spelled out in the model, but in the empirical work the unit is a presidential term.

9. There is no foreign retaliation, no reciprocity.

All this reminds me of Milton Friedman's (1953) advice in his essay "The Methodology of Positive Economics": "Truly important and significant hypotheses will be found to have 'assumptions' that are wildly inaccurate descriptive representations of reality, and, in general, the more significant the theory, the more unrealistic the assumptions (in this sense)." But this quotation is not to be interpreted as a call for the construction of bizarre theories for their own sake. The proper test of a theory is not the validity of its assumptions but rather the accuracy of its predictions. The surprise in this chapter is that Magee and Young in fact offer some empirical evidence in support of their theory. The criticisms that follow should not detract from the enthusiasm that properly greets work that combines theory with empirical evidence. The majority of papers written in international trade stop with the theory, and we are left on our own to guess their practical relevance. The comments that follow would do a great disservice if they dissuaded even one theorist from examining a data set. Let us have more of this kind of work, not less.

The basic problem with doing empirical work in this area is that the space of alternative hypotheses is extraordinarily diverse, and the quasi-experiment that nature has provided is very, very weak. There are certain things that data will not be able to tell us. We cannot tell from cross-state data whether capital punishment deters murder. We cannot tell from cross-city data whether air pollution causes heart disease. And we cannot tell much about the determinants of tariffs from a study of the average level of U.S. tariffs in each of the sixteen presidential terms during the twentieth century. This time series probably embodies only three or four separate quasi-experiments in which the course of the average tariff level was fundamentally changed. The effective sample size of three or four can hardly support by itself the high dimensional model required to encompass the rich space of hypotheses. It is therefore essential that some additional information be used, either through a formal Bayesian analysis or through a specification search, such as the one that Magee and Young have reported.

Magee and Young use eight explanatory variables: capital per person, terms of trade, Republican dummy, administration change dummy, inflation rate, unemployment rate, trade balance, and income tax dummy. This leaves the degrees of freedom equal to seven, which is less than one per parameter. And, as I have argued, this list could easily be supplemented with many more variables. Even within the confines of the model with eight variables, the scarcity of observations does not allow much attention to serial correlation or any attention to nonlinearities or to simultaneity.

My prior is that the level of unemployment has an important effect on the changes in the tariff level. I suppose that the trade balance could also have an effect. The other variables seem to me to be very doubtful. Magee and Young do not allow the change in the tariff to respond to the levels of the explanatory variables, so the evidence that they present is not directly relevant to me. The regressions that Magee and Young report do not dissuade me from my original opinions.

Finally I wonder about the series for the share of capital income. The theory calls for the shares at the industry level, not the aggregate share that can change because of changes in the composition of output. More important, I wonder where these data come from. Recall that Solow's (1957) conclusion that a Cobb-Douglas function is adequate to describe the aggregate production function is a consequence of the long-run constancy of the shares of labor and capital. Solow's data have the share of property income hovering between 33 and 36 percent from 1909 to 1949. How does this square with the decline in capital share from 45 to 24 percent in Magee and Young's data?

In conclusion, I repeat my opening sentence. Magee and Young are to be complimented for the boldness with which they attack the problem of explaining the history of tariffs in the United States during the twentieth century, but much remains to be done to convince me.

References

Friedman, Milton. *Essays in Positive Economics*. Chicago: University of Chicago Press, 1953.

Solow, Robert. "Technical Change and the Aggregate Production Function." *Review of Economics and Statistics* 39 (1957): 312–320.

Comment on "Endogenous Protection in the United States, 1900–1984"

J. Peter Neary

This is a nice paper; it is also an ambitious one. Its starting point is a fairly complete model of the economy on which is superimposed a detailed specification of the political process. This framework is then used as a basis for an empirical study of the determinants of the levels of tariff rates and antidumping legislation in the United States since 1900. In my comments, I follow the version of the paper that was presented at the March 1985 conference and concentrate on the underlying theoretical model, leaving Leamer to discuss the empirical results.

In trying to understand how the Magee-Young model works, I found it helpful to compare its structure with two other models: that of Findlay and Wellisz (1982), the first fully-specified general equilibrium model of endogenous trade policy formation; and a general model of my own devising, which encompasses both the Findlay-Wellisz and Magee-Young models as special cases. The general model is neither analytically tractable nor empirically estimable, but it provides a useful framework for discussing some of the issues raised by the work of Magee and Young and others. All three models are compared in table 1.

Production, Structure: Inside the Economic Black Box

The starting point of each model is a specification of the economy's production technology. In the general model, I follow recent presentations of international trade theory (see, for example, that of Dixit and Norman (1980)), which allow for any number (M) of factors and any number (N) of goods. Rather than specifying the structure of the economy in detail, I summarize it in the form of a "black box" or national product function, which expresses the value of GNP as a function of domestic commodity prices (represented by a vector p) and domestic factor endowments (represented by a vector v). This formulation is consistent with many different assumptions about the degree of internal

Table 1
Models of lobbying and endogenous protection

	General model	Magee and Young	Findlay and Wellisz
Factors, goods, lobbies, parties	$m \times n \times k \times 2$	$2 \times 2 \times 2 \times 2$	$3 \times 2 \times 2 \times 0$
Production technology	$g(p, v)$	Heckscher-Ohlin	Specific-factors
Lobbying technology	$I_i = w'v_i - w'\tilde{v}_i$	$I_K = r(K - \tilde{K})$	$I_K = rK - wL_K$, etc.
Policy technology			$t = t(L_K, L_T)$
Election technology	$P = P[\{\tilde{v}_i\},$ $\{u_h(p, I_h)\}]$	$P = P\left[\dfrac{K}{L}\left(\dfrac{1 + t}{1 + s}\right)^q\right]$	
Party behavior	Republicans: Max P Democrats: Min P	as in general model	
Lobby objective function	$PU_i(p_R, I_i^R)$ $+ (1 - P)U_i(p_D, I_i^D)$	as in general model	$I_K = rK - wL_K$

I_i^D, I_i^R = Income of lobby i or household h under Democrat and Republican administrations
L_K = Amount of labor hired for lobbying by capital-owners (in Findlay-Wellisz)
L_T = Amount of labor used in lobbying by land-owners (in Findlay-Wellisz)
p_D, p_R = Domestic relative price of imports under Democrat and Republican administrations
P = Probability of Republicans being elected
s = Rate of export subsidy
t = Tariff rate
$\tilde{v}_i$ = Amount of factor i used in lobbying
w_i = Return of factor i

mobility of factors of production. By contrast, Magee and Young adopt the standard Heckscher-Ohlin assumption of two factors, each perfectly mobile between two sectors: and Findlay and Wellisz use the so-called "specific-factors" framework: each of two sectors uses an immobile factor specific to it and also draws on an economy-wide pool of mobile labor.

Both the Heckscher-Ohlin and specific-factors models have been widely applied in the field of international trade theory (see Jones and Neary (1984) for a recent survey), and each has its uses. In the context of endogenous trade policy formation, however, the choice between them is crucial, since in all these models to date political lobbies are indistinguishable from factors of production. It might be mentioned in passing that this identification is not necessarily plausible since it is inconsistent with diversified factor ownership (for example, the large capital holdings of workers' pension funds). But taking this aspect at face value, the question that immediately arises is whether lobbies are best viewed as being sector-specific or not.

In my view the answer is yes for at least two reasons. The first is theoretical. The work of Olson (1965) suggests that the costs of coalition formation are likely to be greater and the benefits less tangible the more dispersed is the group in question. Members of an economy-wide group such as unskilled labor may share a common interest in policies that raise the wage rate, but they are likely to disagree on many other issues. The second reason is empirical and derives from the work of Magee himself, in particular his 1980 paper that provides strong evidence in favor of the sector specificity of lobbying activity by both capital and labor. On both these grounds, therefore, I am doubtful if the Heckscher-Ohlin assumption of economy-wide factors of production (and so economy-wide lobbies) is appropriate in the context of endogenous trade policy formation.

Lobbying, Parties, and Elections: Inside the Political Black Box

The next component of each model is what I call its assumptions about the lobbying technology: the manner in which resources are diverted from the productive process to the political process of lobbying for policy changes. In general, we might expect the income of factor i, I_i, to equal its income from production (given by its factor reward, w_i, times its employment level, v_i), less the cost of the vector of factors that it hires to carry out its lobbying activity, $\tilde{v}_i$. Both of the particular models make more restrictive assumptions: Findlay and Wellisz assume that lobbying is carried out by the two sector-specific factors, but that it requires the services of labor; Magee and Young assume that lobbying by each factor requires only the services of the lobbying factor itself. While both specifications can be criticized, I find that of Magee and Young more persuasive in this case. In particular, it draws attention to the fact that the direct resource costs of lobbying derive not so much from the increased demand for, say, public relations consultants; rather, they derive from a diversion of managerial resources from thinking up ways of outcompeting the Japanese toward thinking up ways of persuading legislators to exclude Japanese goods from U.S. markets. Of course, once again, the plausibility of this specification in the context of an economy-wide factor such as labor may be questioned.

Devoting resources to lobbying is only the first step in the political process in these models. It is also necessary to consider how these resources yield a payoff. Findlay and Wellisz take a shortcut here and assume simply a black box in the form of a "policy technology" function relating the tariff rate to the amounts of resources devoted to the political process by the two lobbies. Magee and Young are more ambitious and attempt to specify a political structure which resembles that actually prevailing in the United States. They assume an "election technology," whereby the probability of a Republican victory depends positively on the resources devoted to lobbying by capital and negatively on the resources devoted to lobbying by labor; and also (because of adverse demonstration effects) depends positively on the ratio of the average tariff level to the average export subsidy. Each party is then assumed to focus on this probability, with the Republicans aiming to maximize and the Democrats to minimize it.

All this is reasonably plausible, although it is open to the criticism that it both underestimates the complexity of the political process and overestimates the information available to political parties. As the first column outlines, the probability of a Republican victory depends in general on the amounts of all resources devoted to lobbying by all lobbyists; and also on the utility of each individual household under both incumbent and alternative administrations. Once this general specification is adopted, it becomes increasingly difficult to accept that the form of the P function is known by both parties.

Finally, both models specify an objective function that each lobby is assumed to maximize. Findlay and Wellisz assume simply that this equals each lobby's income (net of lobbying costs); but, as Young (1982) pointed out, this specification is not invariant to the choice of numéraire. A problem with the alternative specification adopted by Magee and Young, however, is that it assumes that each lobby looks after the consumer as well as the producer interests of its own members; in other words, that the lobby acts like a monopsonist, taking account of the general equilibrium effects of its actions on factor prices. This is surely going too far: Magee and Young are right to deflate each factor's returns by an appropriate price index, but they are surely wrong (or, at best, implausible) to assume that the lobby takes account of the effects of its own actions on that index. Not even General Motors or the UAW can reasonably be assumed to have that degree of sophistication (not to mention that degree of knowledge of the structure of the economy) in planning their actions.

The Empirical Specification

So much for the underlying model of Magee and Young. While I have pointed to a number of its inadequacies relative to my hypothetical "general" model, it could still be defended as a reasonable theoretical simplification and a useful starting point for empirical work. Unfortunately, when Magee and Young come to estimate their model, they work with a relatively crude reduced form that bears only a tenuous relationship to their elaborate theoretical framework. Of the various exogenous variables included in their regressions, only one—the aggregate capital-labor ratio—is reasonably consistent with their model; and, as argued above, it is very model-dependent, since it assumes that lobbying is carried out by two large and diffuse groups of factor owners. Another exogenous variable—the share of capital in aggregate output—is claimed to be consistent with the theoretical specification in that it captures the "magnification effect" of Heckscher-Ohlin theory. But in fact that effect should properly be tested by including sectoral capital shares, which even with Cobb-Douglas production functions in both sectors need bear no simple relationship to the aggregate share. In any case, this variable is not significant in any of the estimated equations reported.

None of the other exogenous variables whose influence is tested by Magee and Young are in any way related to their theoretical model. Apart from some dummy variables for the political party in power in the current or previous presidential term, the remaining variables consist of "a set of macrovariables which our intuition initially suggested might be important in explaining protection." They include the terms of trade, unemployment, and inflation, and they prove reasonably successful in econometric terms; although, as the authors admit, considerable experimentation with alternative specifications was carried out. Since the estimates are based on extremely small samples and do not have any sound theoretical basis, it is hard to have great confidence in them, and their likely robustness to the inclusion of additional observations must remain in doubt. The results may be of interest as an empirical quantification of the relationship between tariff levels and an assortment of macroeconomic variables. They cannot claim, however, to provide a successful test of the theory of endogenous protection.

Conclusion: Whither Endogenous Protection Theory?

My overall impression of the literature to which Magee and Young are contributing is that models of lobbying and endogenous tariff formation are unlikely to be successful in explaining the *average* level of protection. At best, they may be able to explain the sectoral *pattern* of protection. Even in this connection, they are vulnerable to a different criticism recently made by Mayer and Riezman (1985): that lobbying theory cannot provide a rational explanation for the use of tariffs as opposed to other forms of trade protection. The underlying reasoning is analogous to the standard welfare theoretic argument that distortions provide a second-best justification not for tariffs but rather for targeted subsidies. In the same way, a rational lobby should always recognize that a given degree of protection can be obtained at a lower cost (whether measured in terms of standard utility criteria or in terms of voter alienation) by subsidies than by tariffs.

Finally, if endogenous tariff theory is unlikely to provide a satisfactory route, how can the average level of tariff protection be explained? My own view is that a satisfactory theoretical and empirical approach must be rather different from that of the present paper, which provides an explanation for the most part in terms of purely domestic considerations. This is ironic for a paper presented to a conference on international trade policies. In particular, it makes no reference to considerations of international political economy; for example, to multilateral tariff reductions as a cooperative solution to the prisoners' dilemma posed by tariff wars. This suggests to me that it will be necessary to bring a country's trading partners explicitly into the picture before we can hope to provide a satisfactory theory of endogenous trade policy formation.

References

Dixit, A. K., and V. Norman. *Theory of International Trade: A Dual, General Equilibrium Approach.* Welwyn: James Nisbet and Cambridge University, 1980.

Findlay, R., and S. Wellisz. "Endogenous Tariffs, the Political Economy of Trade Restrictions, and Welfare." In J. N. Bhagwati, ed., *Import Competition and Response.* Chicago: Chicago University Press, 1982.

Jones, R. W., and J. P. Neary. "The Positive Theory of International Trade." In R. W. Jones and P. B. Kenen, eds., *Handbook of International Economics, Volume 1.* Amsterdam: North-Holland, 1984.

Magee, S. P. "Three Simple Tests of the Stolper-Samuelson Theorem." In P. Oppenheimer, ed., *Issues in International Economics.* London: Oriel Press, 1980.

Mayer, W., and R. Riezman. "Endogenous Choice of Trade Policy Instruments." Working Paper No. 85–8. College of Business Administration, University of Iowa, 1985.

Olson, M. *The Logic of Collective Action.* Cambridge, Mass.: Harvard University Press, 1965.

Young, L. "Comment" on R. Findlay and S. Wellisz, "Endogenous Tariffs, the Political Economy of Trade Restrictions, and Welfare." In J. N. Bhagwati, ed., *Import Competition and Response.* Chicago: University of Chicago Press, 1982.

5 Strategic Sectors and International Competition

Paul Krugman

5.1 Introduction

Economic debate arguments for activist government policies in the United States must contend with both a strong ideological commitment to free markets and a deep distrust of government. As a result it is usually not politically viable to argue for an expanded government role in the economy on the basis of expected gains from this role. Instead advocates of activism must appeal for government action to prevent losses. For those who advocate an industrial policy—which I will take to mean a deliberate attempt to influence the industrial composition of U.S. output—it is necessary to argue not just that such a policy can strengthen the economy but that without such a policy the economy will deteriorate.

In the mid-1980s the natural focus of such arguments is on the problem of U.S. international competitiveness. The strong dollar and the uneven world economic recovery have created a situation where the U.S. competitive position appears weaker across the board. Hardly a week goes by without a major news story about a once-preeminent U.S. industry losing market share, going into net trade deficit, or shifting its operations abroad. Although the economics profession is virtually unanimous in regarding the deteriorating trade position of the United States as a macroeconomic problem, the pervasive sense of lost competitiveness helps create an atmosphere favorable to microeconomic activism.

Some of the cruder advocates of U.S. industrial policy argue that the absence of such a policy is causing the United States to lose ground in all markets, its industry at the mercy of foreign governments that protect everything and subsidize everything. More sophisticated advocates, such as Ira Magaziner, Robert Reich, and Lester Thurow, put the issue more sensibly as a competition over the composition of output rather than over its level. Their argument is that in the absence of an industrial policy, the United States will have the wrong industrial mix, devoting too little labor and capital to sectors essential to its economic performance. The issue is not one of overall competitiveness but of competition over those sectors that are of special value to an economy. I will refer to these sectors as strategic sectors; this chapter is concerned with their existence and importance.

The question of whether there are identifiable strategic sectors that constitute valuable stakes in international competition can be viewed as a sort of litmus test for distinguishing between trained economists and lay commentators. To noneconomists (and a few defrocked economists) it seems obvious that some sectors are more desirable than others. High-value-added sectors, linkage sectors, sunrise industries, and catalytic industries have been identified as areas that need special promotion or protection. The basic models in which economists are schooled, however, tell us that there are no strategic sectors. Starting from a competitive equilibrium, there is no reason to favor particular sectors over other sectors. In conventional economic models, private returns to factors of production are equalized across sectors by competition, so there is no direct gain to be had from redistributing sources from one part of the economy to another. At the same time market prices are also social returns, so there is no indirect gain either. Few applied economists regard the competitive general equilibrium model as a perfect description of the world or the conclusions derived from that model as exactly true; but to an economist schooled in general equilibrium analysis, any attempt to designate particular sectors of the economy as being especially strategic raises immediate skepticism.

Most challenges to this laissez-faire view do not arise out of a perception of the weaknesses of neoclassical economics and an addition of new insights that go beyond conventional analysis. Instead they typically reflect a failure to understand even the conventional arguments. Nonetheless the conventional economist's wisdom is open to challenge, for it is based on insecure foundations. In particular the assumptions that competition is perfect, on one side, and that private and social returns are equal, on the other, are clearly untrue. Although neither imperfect competition nor divergence between private and social returns figures much in popular discussions of international competition, it is on the basis of these concepts that we are most likely to discover which sectors, if any, are strategic and deserving of special concern.

This chapter, then, is addressed to two questions. First, do strategic sectors exist? Second, how important is international competition over those sectors that can be identified as strategic? Ultimately, of course, we want an answer to the question of whether international competition over strategic sectors constitutes a justification for explicit government action to protect or promote these sectors.

In form the chapter is neither a fully worked-out theoretical treatment nor an empirical study. It is in part a literature survey, but for the most part it should be viewed as an exploratory essay. Through a combination of literature survey and illustrative examples, it attempts to raise the main issues in the discussion of strategic sectors; some casual empiricism is used to suggest preliminary judgments on the issues raised, but no claims are made to have finished the job. The chapter is in two main parts. The first part examines the possibility that strategic sectors, and the scope for strategic trade policy, may exist because of imperfect competition. The second part examines the alternative possibility of justifying a concern with strategic sectors by an appeal of the role of external economies. A final brief section draws the implications together.

5.2 Imperfect Competition and International Rent Seeking

One of the most popular concepts in recent discussions of industrial policy is the idea that policy ought to target sectors that yield high value-added (sectors in which output per worker is high). This theme has been emphasized in particular by Magaziner and Reich (1982) and by Reich (1983). At first the idea seems reasonable. If sectors differ in their value-added per worker, as they certainly do, then shifting an economy's labor force toward higher value-added sectors surely ought to raise the average. It also seems natural to imagine this as the basis of an international competitive strategy: try to get your country into high-value production while getting other countries to supply you with lower-value-added products. This is, in fact, precisely the trade strategy Reich and others advocate.

To economists who believe in a competitive economy, however, the high-value-added concept seems foolish. Reasonably competitive markets will equalize the earnings of equivalent factors in different sectors; if value-added per worker is different across industries, it is because inputs per worker are different. Sectors with high value-added per worker are, in theory and in fact, typically capital or skill intensive. Since capital and skill are scarce resources, the high value does not come free. As I and others have argued, a policy of targeting capital- or skill-intensive industries is likely to raise unemployment in the short run and lower real wages in the longer run.[1]

Yet the conventional economist's critique of the idea of targeting high-value sectors, although vital as a check on naive views, may go too far. In a perfectly competitive world, wages and the return on capital would be equalized across sectors, and thus no sector would be preferred at the margin to any other. But in the real world many sectors are far from perfectly competitive. The question is whether this changes our view. Are there not sectors in which excess returns are earned by some factors and in which, due to some form of entry barrier, these excess returns are not competed away? Surely the answer is yes (within limits).

Sectors in which substantial excess returns or rent are earned are in a sense characterized by high-value-added—not per unit of labor but per unit of input, where the input is measured at its market value. But the high-value label is probably misleading since it is conceivable that excess returns might be earned in a labor-intensive industry in which value-added per worker is low. Thus it might be better to refer to these as high-rent sectors.

It is clear that, other things equal, the more a country produces of high-rent goods, the higher will be its national income. But should the promotion of these sectors be a goal of national policy? This is a more problematic question, which has been the subject of considerable recent research. The purpose of this section is to examine this research.

5.2.1 Restricted Entry and International Competition: The Brander-Spencer Model

The recent literature on trade policy under imperfect competition has as its starting point an ingenious analysis by Brander and Spencer (1985). The Brander-Spencer work is stimulating—and also probably misleading; for both reasons it is worth reviewing.

In their basic model Brander and Spencer envisage an industry in which the competitive aspects of trade policy are emphasized to the exclusion of everything else. Two countries both sell a product to a third country; neither exporter consumes the product itself, so that there are no domestic consumer interests to consider. Furthermore each country's industry consists of only a single firm. The effect of these assumptions is to make trade policy for this industry essentially a problem of promoting the interests of a national champion in international competition—something that is often the way governments see the issue but usually at best incomplete as a description of national interest.

How do the firms compete? In the simplest Brander-Spencer analysis, they are assumed to behave in a Cournot fashion. Each firm chooses its output level (equivalent in this setup to choosing its level of deliveries to the export market), taking the other firm's level of output as given. Given appropriate technical assumptions, this means that each firm's behavior may be described by a downward-sloping reaction function relating its output to the other firm's output. These reaction functions are illustrated in figure 5.1. Also illustrated in

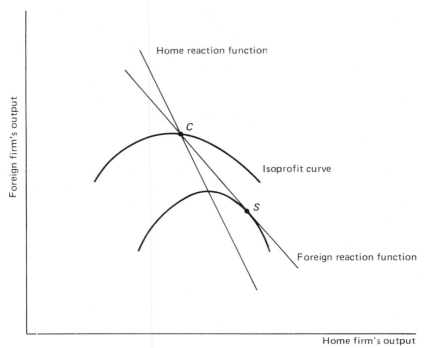

Figure 5.1
Brander-Spencer model of firm behavior.

the figure are iso-profit curves for the domestic firm. Because each firm maximizes profit, taking the other firm's output as given, the reaction function of each firm passes through the top of each of its own iso-profit curves; in effect that is how the reaction functions are defined.

In the absence of any government intervention, the market outcome would be the levels of output indicated in the figure by the Cournot equilibrium C. It is a familiar point from duopoly theory, however, that each firm would like to do better. In particular, if the home firm (say) could commit itself to produce more than the Cournot output, it could push its competitor down its reaction function, increasing its profits at its rival's expense. Ideally it would drive its rival to point S, assuming the role of a Stackelberg leader.

The problem is that firms may not have the ability to make such a commitment. Even if a firm were to announce its intention to produce off its reaction function, ex post it would still have the incentive to return to that function— and its rival knows this. Thus the Cournot outcome remains plausible.

What Brander and Spencer have pointed out—and it is one of those insights that seem simple after they are offered but are no less profound for that—is that government action may be able to provide the ability to commit that private firms lack. Suppose that the home government institutes an export subsidy. This subsidy will push the home firm's reaction function to the right, changing the equilibrium outcome and, because it leads the foreign firm to reduce its output, raising the home firm's profits by more than the amount of the subsidy. The optimum subsidy is one that shifts the reaction function out just enough to shift the outcome from C to S. In other words the optimum subsidy is one that in effect substitutes for the strategic commitment that firms are unable to make themselves.

In spite of its obvious abstraction and unrealism, the simplest Brander-Spencer model is important and unsettling. Analysis of trade policy based on competitive models offers little support for trade policy activism of any sort and none at all for export subsidies, which generally seem likely not only to distort allocation but also to worsen the subsidizer's terms of trade. Here we have the simplest possible model of imperfect competition, that of Cournot duopoly, and it seems to turn all our conventional wisdom on its head. Strategic trade policy, designed to shift the terms of competition in imperfect markets to domestic firms' advantage, abruptly becomes desirable. Export subsidies appear to be, if not necessarily the best strategic policies, at least reasonable policy instruments.

But are the conclusions of standard trade policy analysis really this fragile? A numer of criticisms can be and have been advanced against the Brander-Spencer analysis. I will focus on four. First, the effects of the specific policy of export subsidy depend crucially on implausible assumptions about competition. Second, conclusions from partial equilibrium analysis are misleading when the general equilibrium consequences are taken into account. Third, when we go beyond duopoly to more realistic oligopolistic models, the interests of firms and nations diverge. Finally, the scope for raising national income through strategic trade policies is negligible.

The first point has been made forcefully by Eaton and Grossman (1983). They point out that the case for export subsidies depends crucially on the assumption that firms compete in quantities—that is, that each firm takes the other's output as given. As they point out, if each firm takes the other's price as given (which is at least as plausible if not more so), an export subsidy, instead of reducing competition through its deterrent effect, will in effect intensify the price war and thus raise an exporter's profits by less than the amount of subsidy. Indeed an export tax is the indicated policy.

As a criticism of the case for export subsidy, this argument is well taken. It is less clear whether it is a fatal blow to the case for the broader range of strategic policies. Spencer (1986) has made this point effectively. She suggests that we think of interfirm competition as a process involving several stages: a first stage in which firms invest in R&D, a second stage in which they invest in productive capacity, and a third stage in which they compete in the marketplace. It is only to this last stage that the issue of prices versus quantities applies. It is much more plausible to suppose that firms, say, take each others' R&D or capital expenditures as given (there is no marketplace in which to have price-type competition). It follows that subsidies to R&D or capital formation can have the desired deterrent effect on foreign investment, which will then be reflected in a change in the subsequent market outcome.[2] Thus Spencer suggests that strategic trade policies should not target trade flows directly but instead should target the earlier stages in the competitive process. At the risk of using words loosely, this amounts to saying that competitive policy should be industrial policy rather than trade policy.

The second objection to the case for activist policy has been put forward by Dixit and Grossman (1984). They point out that even in a world where strategic trade policies are possible, it is still not possible to subsidize everything. It is therefore not possible to give every domestic firm a strategic advantage against its foreign competitors. In subsidizing one activity a government raises the cost of inputs to other activities, and thus in deterring foreign competitors in one sector it encourages such competitors elsewhere. The problem of conducting successful strategic policies thus becomes one of selecting the right sectors. What gives this argument special force is Dixit and Grossman's suggestion, which they embody in a simple illustrative model, that likely candidates for targeting are also likely to be competing for the same inputs. For example, suppose that R&D-intensive sectors seem most suitable for promotion and that R&D subsidy is the preferred policy. If there are typical inputs used in a variety of types of R&D—scientists, graph paper—and if these inputs are in inelastic supply, then any attempt to promote some R&D-intensive sectors will crowd out others. Choosing the right sectors, as Dixit and Grossman show, requires a good deal of hard-to-acquire information, and it is difficult to believe that government policies could be much better than random.

But this argument, although useful as a check on excessive enthusiasm for schemes of industry promotion, is not quite as compelling as we might like. The key point to note is that Dixit and Grossman emphasize specific factors in inelastic supply rather than the overall economy-wide resource constraint. One reason for this is that on an economy-wide basis, it does not seem implausible to imagine that we could identify broad sectors with the potential for successful strategic promotion (for example, oligopolistic manufacturing sectors appear to be better prospects than agriculture). The force of Dixit and Grossman's point derives from their assertion that promotion of such broad sectors is not possible; it is necessary to make a much finer division among sectors. The crucial assumption is the inelastic supply of factors specific to oligopolistic sectors. The problem is that this inelasticity is not plausible given sufficient time for adjustment. Scientists, engineers, graph paper, and other inputs can be created over time and do not have the same claim to be regarded as primary factors as broader aggregates such as labor and capital. But allowing the oligopolistic sector as a whole to expand substantially weakens the information requirement for a successful strategic industrial policy.

The third objection to strategic trade policy has been emphasized by Dixit (1986). The key to the strategic argument is that the problem of domestic firms is their inability to be credibly aggressive; they cannot convince foreign rivals that they will produce enough to deter as much as they would like. But as soon as we introduce competition between domestic firms as well as between domestic and foreign firms, it becomes unclear whether insufficient aggressiveness is necessarily the problem. On the contrary, domestic firms may easily be too aggressive, producing more than would be in their joint self-interest.

This point may be illustrated by referring back to figure 5.1. There the domestic reaction function is shown as passing through the top of the iso-profit curves. If we think of a multifirm domestic industry, however, we should interpret these as iso-profit curves for the domestic industry as a whole. If there were only one domestic firm, the firm would maximize industry profit (which is simply its own profit), and the domestic reaction function would pass through the tops of the iso-profit curves, as shown. Suppose, however, that there are two or more domestic firms. Then unless they collude perfectly, they will produce more than the joint profit-maximizing output. This will mean that the domestic reaction function will be shifted out, and thus the outcome will be somewhere to the southeast of C.

It is immediately apparent that this creates an ambiguity about the desirability of any strategic policy. If the outcome is to the left of S, it will still be the case that the domestic industry could gain by committing itself to larger output, and an export subsidy would raise national income. But if competition among domestic firms is sufficiently intense, so that the outcome is to the right of S, the firms will already be exporting too much. That is, it would raise their joint profits if they restricted their exports, even if foreign firms knew they were going to do so. There is room for an activist policy to raise national income in this case, but it is one of reducing exports by an export tax or VER. Indeed this situation is not at all unrealistic. It seems quite possible, for example, that the restraints imposed on Japanese automobile exporters have in fact raised their joint profits. The strength of this criticism thus depends on the intensity of competition between domestic firms currently in the industry.

The final argument, advanced forcefully by Dixit (1984), rests on potential competition through entry. Dixit points out that the national gain from strategic policies in the Brander-Spencer analysis comes from a redistribution of economic rents toward the activist country. Dixit's challenge then becomes the question, Where's the rent? An industry in which firms earn above-normal profits will be attractive to new entrants. This potential competition may, in several ways, tend to eliminate the above-normal profits. If markets are contestable, in the manner of Baumol, Panzar, and Willig (1982), incumbent firms will be forced to keep prices low to avoid entry. If entry actually takes place, increased competition will drive economic profits toward zero. Or in Dixit's favorite example, firms may be forced to undertake competitive investment in risky projects, where the winners earn large profits ex post, but the ex ante return on investment is only normal.

This final criticism is much more fundamental than the others. The initial criticisms I offered are critiques of the particular policy suggested by the Brander-Spencer analysis; they are not necessarily critiques of activism in general. In each case the possibility remains open that a better-formulated policy can overcome the critique, as illustrated by Spencer's suggestion that, given uncertainty about the process of competition in the goods market, strategic policies focus on earlier stages of competition. If Dixit is right, however, there is no way in which strategic policy can yield a benefit because there are no excess returns to capture.

To evaluate this criticism, it will be helpful to change the focus and adopt a perspective somewhat different from most of the other literature to date on trade policy in the presence of imperfect competition. The concern of most of this literature has been with the effects of specific trade policies when there are excess returns to be distributed. What has received less attention is the prior question of what characterizes sectors with excess returns and the limits on how much a nation can gain by enlarging these sectors.

5.2.2 Entry and the World Distribution of Income

Potential competition from new entrants need not eliminate above-normal returns even if there are no legal or institutional constraints on entry (that is, even if in some sense there is free entry). Industrial organization theorists have pointed to a number of not entirely distinct reasons why excess returns can persist, including the following:

• Integer constraints: If economies of scale are large relative to industry size, the requirement that the number of firms be an integer may allow high profits without providing an incentive for entry. Suppose that two firms can make above-normal returns but that adding a third would lead all three to make losses; then the outcome would presumably be a highly profitable, two-firm industry.

• Advantages to early arrivals: If firms that get an early start are able to move more quickly down a learning curve, they may be able to establish a permanent cost advantage over later entrants. Or, with much the same effect, firms that arrive early may have enduring marketing-consumer loyalty advantages. In either case above-normal profits need not be competed away.

• Strategic deterrence: Incumbent firms may be able to eliminate any expected economic profits for potential entrants without eliminating their own profits by such strategic policies as investing in excess capacity undertaking too much R&D.

The categories in this list are neither mutually exclusive nor jointly inclusive. They make the point, however, that industrial organization theory does not support the view that excess returns (alias rent) are something necessarily competed away.

The next question is how excess returns manifest themselves in the pattern of international trade. Until recently this question has been left largely unanswered. In perfectly competitive models of trade, there is no rent to worry about. In monopolistically competitive models of the type that became popular a few years ago, it was assumed that profits were driven to zero. In the Brander-Spencer model, as well as in most of the critical literature generated by that model, the number and location of firms are taken as exogenous. We want to be able to allow for industries with nonzero economic profits in our trade model without prejudging the question of who gets the rent.

A general analysis is not easy to come by, but a good deal can be learned by considering two simple examples. In each example there is assumed to be an industry in which a single firm will be able to establish itself as a profitable monopolist. The question is what stake countries have in the location of the firm.

For the first example, suppose that there is only one factor of production and two countries. Each country is capable of producing either the monopolized good, X, or a competitive good Y. Technologies of production are assumed to be the same, and demand for X is assumed to be small enough that both countries always produce at least some Y, which implies that wages are equalized.

The implications of these assumptions are shown in figure 5.2. The line OO^* represents the world endowment of labor, which is divided between a home

Figure 5.2
Location of production with a monopolized and competitive good.

country endowment OE and a foreign endowment EO^*. The labor devoted to producing the monopolized good X is indicated by $OQ = Q'O^*$; the labor devoted to producing Y is indicated by $QO^* = OQ'$.

It is clear that X could be produced in either country. If it is produced in the home country, the home country will devote only an amount of labor QE to producing Y, while the foreign country produces only Y. If X is produced in the foreign country, the home country will produce only Y while the foreign country devotes only EQ' of its labor force to Y. In either case wages will be equalized, and thus the price, output, and profits of the monopolized sector will also be the same.

Where the location of the monopolized firm does matter is for the distribution of income between countries. The distribution of wage income is the same as the distribution of labor; the home country's share is OE/OO^*. But factor income is not all of income. Part of world income shows up as profits in the X sector, and thus the home country share in world income will exceed its share of world employment if it manages to arrange to be the home of the profitable firm.

One way to look at this is to note that X is in fact a high-value-added sector, where the value of output per worker is higher than in the competitive sector. So in this example a country can in fact raise its national income by shifting its production to high-value-added products. The example is, however, somewhat misleading in that labor is the only factor of production. This means that there is a one-to-one correspondence between excess returns and high value-added per worker. This is by no means generally true, as the second example makes clear.

Again suppose that there is a monopolized sector that earns some excess returns. Suppose now, however, that there are two factors of production, capital and labor, and also that there are at least two nonmonopolized sectors. Under certain conditions—loosely, if the size of the imperfectly competitive firm is not too large and if countries have sufficiently similar factor endowments—factor prices will be equalized. (For a detailed formal analysis, see Helpman and Krugman, 1985.) Let us assume that this is true.

In this case, as in the simpler example, the distribution of factor income depends only on the distribution of factors but factor income will not be all of income. Whichever country gets the monopolized industry will have a larger share of world income than would be predicted from its factor endowments alone. In effect the monopolized industry in the country that gets it will increase its relative national income.

The important point here, however, is that the sector is desirable because it has high value-added per unit of input, alias excess returns, and that this need not correspond to high value-added per unit of labor. There is no reason why a labor-intensive sector might not have characteristics that allow firms in that industry to earn monopoly rents; such a sector will be strategic though it may well have low value-added per worker.

The analysis so far has suggested that if we drop the assumption of perfect competition, there may be sectors whose prices more than cover the earnings their inputs could earn in alternative uses. And it has also suggested that there may be some arbitrariness in the location of such sectors. The question then becomes one of practical implications: should the pursuit of such sectors be an objective of policy? Or, more modestly, should the government be concerned about efforts of other countries to ensure that they get the rent-generating sectors?

Although one cannot reject the argument for concern over who gets the rent on principle, there are two reasons for doubting its importance in practice: the stakes are probably not that large, and such benefits as there are from rent shifting policies may not accrue to the right people in any case.

In raising the first doubt, we have in effect returned to Dixit's question, "Where's the rent?" It is certainly not the case that there is no rent; there is enough excess return to make the creation and protection of this excess return a central preoccupation of the theory and practice of competitive strategy at the level of the firm. But nations are not firms writ large, and variations in value-added per unit of input that can be decisive for firms can be of minor importance to nations.

How can this be? First, firms are interested in the rate of return on equity, while countries are interested in the income of all factors of production. This means that firms are highly leveraged with respect to the effects of monopoly power (or anything else). In 1984 profits of nonfinancial corporations were less than 10 percent of the national product generated in that sector, so if a typical firm could manage to earn an excess return of 10 percent of value-added, it would double its profit rate—something presumably quite rare. By contrast a nation that managed to capture rents equal to 10 percent of the value of production would raise its national income by only 10 percent.

Second, large countries such as the United States sell most of their output to themselves. The possibility of raising national income through capture of rent-generating sectors arises only when the sectors can substitute either for low-rent alternative exports or high-rent imports. For the United States, where imports plus exports are less than a quarter of GNP, this considerably limits the scope for rent to matter for good or evil.

Finally, for firms, the stakes are higher than for countries because firms are highly open to factor movements. A firm that can generate above-normal value-added per unit of input can attract capital and labor, leading to sustained growth. A country is not in the same position. Although there is significant mobility of financial capital, by and large factors of production are fairly immobile internationally. This means that any gains realized through a shift to high value-added sectors are once-and-for-all gains, not the basis for continuing growth.

The combined effect of these three differences between nations and firms is to make it questionable whether even a highly successful program of rent snatching could have more than a minor effect on the national income of either the snatcher or the snatchee. Suppose that Japanese industrial targeting were to induce the United States to shift resources amounting to 10 percent of GNP from high-rent to low-rent sectors, which would be an enormously successful piece of predation. Suppose also that the typical high-rent sector had excess returns equal to 10 percent of value-added—a very high number—while low-rent sectors are no-rent sectors. Even given these implausible magnitudes, the total loss to the United States would be only 1 percent of GNP, and this would be a once-and-for-all loss, not a reduction in the U.S. growth rate. Such hypothetical numerical exercises are not a substitute for detailed empirical research, but this kind of back-of-the envelope calculation makes it hard to believe that international rent seeking can be more than a minor issue for large countries.

To this should be added another question, Who gets the rent? So far we have taken it as our goal to maximize national income, where this includes the profits of domestic firms. But a policy that raises profits of exporters at taxpayers' expense may not be very desirable even if it does raise profits by more than the subsidy. One could try to tax away the profit gains; this is not paradoxical if the tax subsidy package fiddles with incentives and inframarginal burdens cleverly enough, but this begins to look too complex to be workable.

Furthermore in an age when both the operations and the ownership of corporations are multinational, what does it mean to refer to national firms? Is Vauxhall a British firm? For that matter, is GM a U.S. firm? In each case the answer is "only partly." This is not a judgment on the character or behavior of the firms but simply a recognition that the benefits of strategic policies accrue to stockholders who are not all domestic residents and to taxers of corporate profits that may appear in a variety of jurisdictions.

5.2.3 Summary and Evaluation

One of the main criticisms of the economist's case for free trade and laissez-faire industrial policy has always been that it is based on the clearly untrue assumption of perfect competition. To this the reply of economists has generally been that the clarity gained by assuming perfect competition outweighs the loss of realism—that allowing for imperfect competition would not change the conclusions much.

This argument is not necessarily right. The Brander-Spencer model shows that conventional views about trade and industrial policy may not be at all robust to assumptions about the nature of competition. More generally we can see that the existence of economic rents makes invalid the economist's usual dismissal of the idea that there are strategic sectors whose promotion will raise national income.

The question therefore becomes one of magnitudes. How far are we from the competitive model? At the level of the firm or the industry, perfect competition is clearly a terrible assumption. To make international competition over strategic sectors a major concern of economic policy, however, deviations from perfect competition must be very large. The reason is that the importance of excess returns undergoes a double gearing down as we go from the level of the firm to that of the nation. Firms are concerned about profit and nations about value-added; this by itself reduces the proportional importance of excess returns by a factor of perhaps 10. Furthermore international competition for rents can occur only if rent-yielding goods are traded, adding a further considerable limitation on the extent of potential gains or losses. My calculations suggest that international rent seeking cannot be very important. Others may disagree. If we accept this judgment, however, it means that the search for strategic sectors must go elsewhere. Thus we now turn to an alternative approach.

5.3 Externalities and Linkage

In the first part of this chapter we examined the possibility that some sectors may be strategic because of the high returns they offer to the factors of production they employ. The result of that investigation was the conclusion that there probably are sectors in which significant amounts of rent are earned and that countries could in principle raise their national incomes by promoting these high-rent sectors. The magnitude of the potential redistribution of world income looks modest at best, however, even if policies are conducted optimally. The information requirements for effective policy are high; and it is doubtful whether the general public would reap the benefits even if policy is successful. This suggests that a better place to look for strategic sectors is not in the returns directly received by factors in an industry but in the benefits generated indirectly by the industry's activities. That is, the best bet for finding strategic sectors may be to focus on external benefits.

The role of positive externalities as a justification for special promotion of particular sectors has been known for a long time and was a central theme of the postwar literature on economic development. (Indeed much of the debate over industrial policy is a replay of the development literature of the 1950s and 1960s.)[3] There are, however, still some new things to be said about the externality argument for strategic sectors.

One reason to reconsider the externality argument is that it has become more plausible with changes in the structure of the economy. The rise of high-technology industries is good news for believers in the importance of externalities. The generation of knowledge is an activity unlikely to be rewarded at its marginal social productivity. Although it is possible to develop models in which excessive R&D results from the strategic moves of firms, most economists still believe that the fact that firms can learn from each other creates a presumption of underinvestment in knowledge creation. The economic geography of high-technology industry in the United States can also be seen as evidence for powerful externalities.

A second reason for going over ground that may have seemed familiar is that the traditional analysis of policy toward externalities has not been oriented toward issues of international competition. The early development literature was essentially aimed at closed economies; the later trade and development literature, while acknowledging a trade role, tended to focus on the problems of countries small in world markets. In the context of the U.S. industrial policy debate, we are talking about an economy that is open but is also a large part of the world. Some of the analytical tools we need to analyze the implications of externalities under these circumstances have become available—and different results may emerge as compared to the traditional analysis.

The discussion will therefore proceed in two stages. First is a review of some new thinking about the nature of externalities and, second, a consideration of the implications of externalities in a trading world.

5.3.1 Thinking about Externalities

Traditionally economists distinguish between technological externalities, in which one firm's decisions affect another firm's production function, and pecuniary externalities, in which the interfirm effects run only through prices of inputs and outputs. In competitive models only technological externalities provide a case for government intervention. With imperfect competition, the distinction is less clear-cut. It is reasonable, however, to begin with a discussion of pure technological externalities.

While bees-and-orchards examples may be imagined, the most plausible source of pure technological externalities is the incomplete appropriability of knowledge. What one firm learns through experience or explicit R&D cannot always (or usually) be kept entirely hidden from other firms, or patent protection, by all accounts, is useful only for a limited range of innovation; most economically useful knowledge either cannot be specified in a patentable form or can be used in ways that circumvent the patent. There is a clear problem of appropriability.

One might be tempted to conclude that there is an automatic case for deeming knowledge-intensive sectors as strategic and for concern that the United States maintain a preeminent position in as many such sectors as possible. But this is too quick a judgment. As I have emphasized elsewhere (Krugman, 1984), the case for concern over foreign competition in high-technology sectors depends on the geographic diffusion of knowledge. It is useful to think in terms of an idealized three-part scheme: knowledge that can be internalized within the firm, knowledge that spreads beyond the firm but not beyond national boundaries, and knowledge that once generated is available internationally. An example of the first type of knowledge might be highly specific production knowledge. At the other extreme, features of innovations embodied in products can often be imitated by anyone with the appropriate skills, anywhere in the world. In between is a gray area of knowledge that diffuses by movement of people or word of mouth, and thus it tends to be limited in geographic spread.

The electronics industry offers examples of all three types of knowledge. At one end there is a well-documented learning curve in the production of semiconductor chips, in which reliability increases sharply over the production run. The knowledge involved in this learning curve is so specific that it does not generalize across different plants owned by a single firm, let alone across firms. On the other hand, reverse engineering of product design is common and clearly does not stop at national boundaries. Finally, the middle ground of geographically limited diffusion of knowledge is provided by the movement of personnel and informal communications within the high-tech clusters of Silicon Valley and Route 128.

Special concern about maintaining a domestic presence in knowledge-generating industries hinges essentially on the existence of the middle ground, knowledge that diffuses only locally. If knowledge can be internalized, then the resulting dynamic increasing returns will lead to imperfect competition and possibly to an issue of international distribution of rents, but that issue will not be fundamentally different for high-technology industries from what it is for any other high-rent industry. If the externality is international in scope, it will not matter how the industry is distributed between domestic and foreign producers. Only in the middle ground does a special problem of international competition for externalities arise.

Restricting the range of externalities that matter in this way does not eliminate the issue. Quantitative estimates are not available, but several kinds of evidence point to significant localized externalities. The economic geography of the U.S. electronics industry is surely evidence of significant local spillovers. The presence of Stanford University and MIT may have started the process but cannot be viewed as the current explanation of the Silicon Valley or the Route 128 industrial localizations. Case study evidence also points to national or regional externalities. Collis (1985), for example, has documented how links between firms and the university system help perpetuate the strength of the German machine tool industry.

We have here a bona-fide criterion for identifying a strategic sector: look for a sector that appears to generate knowledge that cannot be appropriated by the firm but is restricted in its geographic spread. One wonders, however, whether this is the only way in which special national advantages can be created. The pattern of industrial localization within countries suggests that there are forces at work that look like localized externalities but cannot be attributed simply to incomplete appropriation of knowledge. The advantages of technological spillovers may explain Silicon Valley, but can they explain, say, the concentration of musical instrument makers in Elkhart, Indiana?

We are on somewhat speculative ground here, but some recent theoretical analysis suggests a variety of ways in which effects that resemble those of externalities can arise even if true technological externalities are absent. This means that the domain of externality-type arguments may be considerably larger than the technological spillover case would suggest.

The traditional view teaches that only technological externalities provide a divergence between private and social cost; interdependence between firms that proceeds by prices does not create such a divergence. The reasoning on which this view is based, however, assumes constant or decreasing returns at the level of the firm and perfect competition. If this is not true, pecuniary externalities may sometimes represent real social externalities.

The case that has been most explored is that where intermediate goods are produced with economies of scale internal to firms. In the international trade context this case has been emphasized in particular by Ethier (1979, 1982b).

Ethier's argument runs as follows. Suppose that an industry uses a variety of specialized inputs produced by monopolistically competitive firms operating with increasing returns to scale. If the industry grows, it will typically be able to support a greater variety of inputs produced at larger scale; because of greater specificity and lower prices of these inputs, the costs of the industry will fall. Ethier points out that for all practical purposes this fall in costs might as well have come from a technological externality. The decline in costs does not reflect a loss to anyone but rather a real saving in resources; the fact that costs decline with output causes a true divergence between private and social marginal cost.

There does not seem to be any established name for this phenomenon, where private increasing returns at one stage of the production process give rise to social increasing returns at the final stage. It is not a technological externality, yet unlike a conventional pecuniary externality it does give rise to divergence between market prices and social cost. For current purposes I will refer to the phenomenon as a linkage externality.

Linkage externalities, once recognized, can seem pervasive. The case of intermediate goods produced with increasing returns is the simplest but not the only one. To explain industrial localization within the United States, other stories may be more relevent. For example, suppose that several firms have in common their use of some specialized factor such as a particular kind of skilled labor. Suppose also firm-specific uncertainty about markets or technology, which makes each firm's demand for the common factor random ex ante. Then it is mutually advantageous for the firms and the workers if the industry is sufficiently concentrated geographically so that workers can easily shift from one firm to another. This allows workers to move away from firms with a bad draw and thus low demand for labor, while at the same time allowing firms with good draws and high demand for labor to expand their work forces without substantially increasing wages.[4]

In this last example the linkage externality appears to be geographically restricted in extent. In the discussion of technological externalities, the geographical extent of the externality assumed a crucial role. The same is true for linkage externalities. In this case, however, it is much easier to ascertain the forces that determine the geographic extent. The question is simply one of the tradability of the inputs to which the linkage applies. Ethier, emphasizing linkage externalities in intermediate goods, argued that these goods can be traded and that the relevant variable for increasing returns is therefore the scale of world industry rather than that of the national industry. This is certainly the case for many inputs, such as machine tools. On the other hand, not all inputs are freely tradable; where the linkage externality involves inputs difficult to trade because of natural or artificial barriers, the linkage externality is only national in scope. Creation of flexible labor markets for specialized skills would be a case in point.

Linkage externalities are a national competitive concern only if some aspect of nontradability makes them so. In the past such industries as steel, petrochemicals, and capital goods have been portrayed as vital linkage industries; more recently the semiconductor and machine tool industries have been described in the same way. In each case the linkage argument is clearly subject to abuse. LDCs are free to buy steel and capital goods from more advanced countries (and vice-versa); European countries can make use of Japanese semiconductors and numerically controlled (NC) machine tools. Only where nontradability is significant does a national linkage externality arise.

Despite this caveat the addition of linkage externalities to strict technological externalities does seem to widen the scope for designating certain sectors as strategic. Once we introduce international trade, however, we will need to narrow the scope again, for even if the external economy, technological or linkage, is national in scope, the benefits of that externality may end up being shared internationally.

5.3.2 Externalities and International Competition

It is widely believed that countries will find it in their interests to promote domestic production of goods that yield positive externalities and that there is an issue of international competition over who gets to be the producer of the externality-generating goods. Surprisingly this is not necessarily the case. Even more surprisingly the fact that this is not necessarily the case can be seen in the simplest and most familiar example of the role of externalities in trade.

Consider the most basic model of trade under increasing returns. We assume that there are two goods: X, which is produced with country-specific external economies, and Y, which is produced at constant returns. There are two countries and only one factor of production. This is the classic externalities model in trade, carefully reanalyzed by Ethier (1982a)

This model has a variety of possible types of equilibria. We can narrow the range of outcomes by supposing that the demand for the increasing-returns good is not too large and that neither of the countries is too small. In that case there will be two equilibria: one with all Y produced in the home country and the other with all X produced in the foreign country. In either case both countries will continue to produce some Y, and as a result wages will be equalized. We can illustrate the situation using figure 5.2, which we used to illustrate the role of monopoly earlier.

As before, OO^* is the world endowment of labor, divided into a home endowment OE and a foreign endowment EO^*. If the home country produces X, it devotes OQ to X and QE to Y. If the foreign country produces X, it devotes $Q'O^* = OQ$ to X and EQ' to Y.

Two outcomes are possible. First, how is the world distribution of income affected by who gets the increasing returns sector? The surprising answer is that as long as both countries produce some Y, it makes no difference. Because X is priced at average cost, the benefits from concentrating the industry are passed on to consumers in a lower price regardless of where the consumers are located. (One way of looking at this issue, suggested in Helpman and Krugman, 1985, is to note that in this example "trade reproduces the integrated economy": the outcome in terms of prices and welfare is exactly the same as would have happened if all factors of production were concentrated in the same location.)

To press the point home even further, let us ask what the optimal trade policy of the X-importing country would be in this case. A little reflection will reveal that the optimal policy is not to protect local X production, which would fragment the industry and make everyone worse off; it is to subsidize consumption of X. This will enlarge world production—never mind that the production is in the other country—and thus lower the price.

The example shows that even when significant country-specific externalities arise from an activity, it is not necessarily in the national interest to make special efforts to ensure existence of a domestic presence in that industry. One might wonder how general this point is. This issue is examined at some length in Helpman and Krugman (1985), who show that the range of situations in which the location of externality-generating sectors does not matter is much broader than the simple example given here. The necessary conditions are that demand for any individual increasing-returns sector not be too large, that countries not be too dissimilar in their factor endowments, and that there be enough demand for a range of goods produced with constant returns. Given these conditions, one can take a benign view of the role of external economies in trade. According to this view, the production of each good yielding external economies will be concentrated in a single country. The actual location of production will be somewhat arbitrary but will make no welfare difference. Whatever the precise pattern of specialization, it is in everyone's interest that industries be concentrated so as to reap the gains from local external economies; that is, it is important that the industries be concentrated, not where these are concentrated.

Suppose there are strong local external economies in the production of NC machine tools, the creation of business applications software, and the provision of international financial services. At the moment it seems likely that the first of these would end up concentrated in Japan and the others concentrated in the United States. The point of the view we have been describing is, first, that it is to both countries' advantage that the industries be so concentrated— we get better, cheaper machine tools because of the positive spillovers between Japanese manufacturers—and, second, that it would not especially raise U.S. real income if it had somehow managed to establish an advantage in all three.

This benign view may not be too good to be true, but it is too good to be universally true. Clearly the location of industry can make a difference in some cases. We may distinguish three such cases, in increasing order of likely importance.

First is the possibility of specialization. If a country manages to specialize in the production of goods subject to external economies, factors of production in that country could end up receiving higher payments than their counterparts in other countries, even if other countries have the same initial capacities. This point may be illustrated in terms of the simple example with which we began. In figure 5.2, it is assumed that the increasing returns sector is not too large— specifically that the labor devoted to production of X, OQ, is less than the labor force of either country, OE or EO^*. Suppose, however, that OQ were greater than OE. Then by specializing in production of X, the home country could end up with a higher wage than the foreign.

Although this possibility has received a good deal of attention in the theoretical literature on trade under increasing returns, it is hard to believe that it is very important in practice. First, in the real world there are not just two sectors but a vast number, none very large relative to any individual economy. More to the point, the major industrial countries all appear, to casual observation at least, to be producing a number of goods unlikely to be characterized by strong externalities. The fact that these goods are produced in common is evidence against the kind of extreme specialization needed for one country to capture the benefits of industry concentration.

A second, more plausible way in which the location of external-economy sectors can matter is through its effect on the returns to specific factors. Suppose that there are factors of production that are either immobile or highly specific to an activity that ends up being concentrated. These factors may end up receiving much higher returns in the country that gets the sector.

If one tries to make this idea concrete, one ends up with the suggestion that the gains to the United States from the existence of Silicon Valley have essentially been capitalized in the value of northern California real estate. (If all of the gain in value could actually be attributed to this cause, it would be far from trivial.) One might also argue that the line between specific and general factors is not sharp. Given some sluggishness in the movement of factors, a nation's success in gaining advantage in external economies may be reflected in a temporary windfall in higher wages and returns on capital. This suggests, however, that in order to capture the benefits of strategic sectors, one should slow rather than accelerate the movement of resources into those sectors, which should be recognized as in effect a sort of optimum tariff argument.

The most persuasive case for considering sectors that generate external economies to be strategic is the argument that the externalities are not confined to the industry itself but also yield interindustry spillover. Return to our example again, but now suppose that it is not only productivity in the X sector that is increasing in X production but productivity in the Y sector as well. Now it will make a difference who produces X; the country that does will gain a productivity advantage in both sectors.

What is the nature of interindustry spillovers? It is easy to imagine that several different industries might use similar kinds of knowledge and thus be able to learn from each others' R&D or gain from each others' experience. Alternatively there could be linkage externalities among a number of industries: forward linkages, where a group of inputs produced with economies of scale is used by several downstream industries; backward linkage, where several types of input are used by a single downstream consumer; or combinations of the two that link together a whole group of upstream and downstream industries. (For a formal treatment of these linkages, see Helpman and Krugman, 1985.) But such relatively narrow interindustry effects need not lead to special national advantage. Instead what will be concentrated will not be individual industries but industrial complexes of sectors related by technological spillovers or linkage externalities. Provided that these complexes are not too large, the same arguments I made about industry-specific externalities will apply: there are benefits to the geographical concentration of industrial complexes, but these benefits do not especially accrue to the country in which the complex is located.

To make a strong case for a special national advantage from possession of externality-generating sectors, one must argue that the interindustry spillovers are not restricted to a narrow group of related sectors but broadly spread through the economy. The question is what kinds of sectors would yield this type of broad spillover.

One area in which broad interindustry spillovers seem plausible is in infrastructure. Transportation and communication enter into production throughout the economy; they are characterized by significant economies of scale; and at least in the telecommunications sector there are probably substantial technological externalities (although these may be international in scope). In terms of international competition, however, the argument is least forceful in the area to which it has been most applied in recent debate: that of telecommunications equipment, which is tradable. So we are left with an argument for some deliberate national policy for infrastructure development, which is not much of a departure from conventional wisdom.

Much more controversial is a different possibility that may be at the heart of concern over U.S. competitiveness in high-technology sectors. This is that countries are better able to apply new technology if the technology is developed at home. The argument is sometimes made that awareness of new developments in semiconductor technology will come more quickly if there is close contact between producers and consumers and also that the technology will be better tailored to what domestic producers require. (There are obvious parallels with LDC arguments for the necessity of a domestic capital goods industry providing appropriate technology.) In its alarmist form, the argument runs that if you do not produce semiconductors, you will lag in the application of technology in computers, robots, and control systems, and that if you do not produce information-processing equipment you will lag in technology generally. If this sort of spillover is in fact important, many arguments become possible. An example is the argument, put forward by a participant in a panel on high technology, that the Japanese export success in consumer electronics will eventually lead to the collapse of the United States as a world power. The argument, though not put in these terms, was that there is a linkage externality between consumer electronics and semiconductors and that semiconductor technology is both pervasive and impossible to apply effectively if a country does not develop the technology itself. As a theoretical argument, this is not at all unsustainable.

Such evidence as is available, however, does not support the idea that the application of technology depends on domestic production of high-technology products. The anecdotal evidence suggests the opposite. Japanese success in consumer electronics was initially based on imported chips; later, success in semiconductors was achieved with U.S.-made capital equipment. Sweden is a world leader in installation of robots, made in Japan; the United Kingdom, despite considerable success in generating a Route 128–style high-technology area around Oxford, has lagged in the actual application of microprocessors to manufacturing. The U.S. textile industry experienced something of a high-tech revival in the 1970s, based on European capital goods. No doubt examples can be found where dependence on foreign technology means a lag in application, but such examples seem more likely to be exceptions than the rule.

5.4 Summary and Conclusions

Are there identifiable strategic sectors in the economy, which are more valuable to the economy at the margin than other sectors? Does the United States, by lacking an explicit policy toward such sectors, run the risk of being displaced from strategic sectors by foreign competition? These questions go to the heart of the intellectual debate over industrial policy.

I have suggested two ways in which some sectors can be strategic to the economy. The first is that some sectors may directly yield higher value per unit of input. In a perfectly competitive economy this could not be the case, but with imperfect competition sustained by economies of scale and entry barriers, some industries may be able to generate persistent excess returns. The second possibility is that some sectors indirectly yield high returns per unit of input because they generate external economies.

Much of the recent drift in the academic analysis of international trade has been toward an increased appreciation of the importance of imperfect competition and externalities. On one side there has been widespread acceptance of the proposition that economies of scale internal to firms play a major role in explaining trade in manufactures among the industrial countries. On the other side the rise of high-technology industry has made technological spillover a more salient concern than in the past. Thus one might expect that the innovations in academic analysis would provide increased support for policy arguments in favor of special concern for strategic sectors.

To a limited extent this is true. Once we abandon the certainties of the traditional competitive model, suggestions that particular sectors need to be protected or promoted cannot be dismissed a priori, as they might have been before this new work. When we look in detail at the justifications for regarding some sectors as strategic, however, the support from theory begins to look highly qualified.

The qualifications I have suggested may be summarized briefly. First, policies intended to capture the excess returns of oligopolistic sectors are difficult to devise because the nature of the appropriate policy depends crucially on the process of imperfect competition. Since this is not well understood, it is hard to know which assumptions are most reasonable.

Second, even if markets can be understood well enough or if policies that are robust to our uncertainties can be devised, the stakes in international competition for excess returns are probably not large. Actual or potential entry limits excess returns, and remaining levels of excess returns, although possibly large relative to the profits of firms, are probably not large enough to make their capture or defense a major national priority.

Third, externalities are arguably quite important. This is especially true because to pure technological externalities we must add linkage externalities resulting from economies of scale in multistage production. To be an object of international competition, however, external economies must be country specific—and in many cases they are not. Knowledge diffuses across international boundaries; intermediate goods can be traded. Whenever the external economies are international in scope, special concern about sustaining sectors in international competition is misplaced.

Finally, even when the external economies from a sector are country specific, the benefits will often be shared internationally through lower prices. A special national advantage from an externality-generating sector is likely to arise only if, in addition to sector-specific external economies, the sector generates broad spillover to the rest of the economy—and these are country specific.

None of these qualifications makes a watertight case against a special concern for competition in strategic sectors. Instead they justify a healthy skepticism about the designation of any particular sector as strategic—even glamor sectors such as microelectronics. Before we accept a sector as worthy of special protection or promotion, many difficult questions should be asked. Since we live in neither a perfectly competitive world nor one where market prices and social products always coincide, some sectors will pass the inquisition. But this is not a blanket endorsement of protectionism. Indeed I would be surprised if a rigorous attempt to apply the principle of optimal intervention would not actually lead to considerably freer trade than we now have.

Notes

1. See Krugman (1983). The point was emphasized in Charles Schultze's (1983) influential *Brookings Review* critique of industrial policy.

2. We should also note that the effects of policies toward final stage competition depend on their effects on earlier stages. An unexpected export subsidy will induce competitive price cuts by foreign competitors and thus lower profits; but if the subsidy is anticipated, the foreign firms will have invested less, and the result may still be to raise profits.

3. An entertaining account of this literature, which is sobering in its revelation of what sensible economists have believed, is contained in Little (1982).

4. What one can show is that a simultaneous increase in the number of firms and workers that leaves expected wages unchanged will raise expected profits.

References

Baumol, William, John Panzar, and Robert Willig. *Contestable Markets and the Theory of Industry Structure*. New York: Harcourt Brace Jovanovich, 1982.

Brander, James A., and Spencer, Barbara L. "Export Subsidies and International Market Share Rivalry." *Journal of International Economics* 18 (1985): 83–100.

Collis, David. "Industrial Policy and Competition in the Machine Tool Industry." Presented at Conference on International Competition, Fort Lauderdale, March 9–11, 1985.

Dixit, Avinash. "International Trade Policy for Oligopolistic Industries." *Economic Journal* 94 (1984): 1–16.

Dixit Avinash. "Trade Policy: An Agenda for Research" in Paul Krugman, ed., *Strategic Trade Policy and the New International Economics*. Cambridge: MIT Press, 1986.

Dixit, Avinash, and Gene M. Grossman. "Targeted Industrial Policy with Several Oligopolistic Industries." Working paper. Princeton University, 1984.

Eaton, Jonathan, and Gene M. Grossman. "Optimal Trade and Industrial Policy under Oligopoly." Discussion Paper in Economics, no. 59. Princeton University, Woodrow Wilson School, 1983.

Ethier, Wilfred. "Internationally Decreasing Costs and World Trade." *Journal of International Economics* 9 (1979): 1–24.

Ethier, Wilfred. "Decreasing Costs in International Trade and Frank Graham's Argument for Protection." *Econometrica* 50 (1982a): 1243–1268.

Ethier, Wilfred. "National and International Returns to Scale in the Modern Theory of International Trade." *American Economic Review* 72 (1982b): 389–405.

Helpman, Elhanan, and Krugman, Paul R. *Market Structure and Foreign Trade: Increasing Returns, Imperfect Competition, and the International Economy*. Cambridge: MIT Press, 1985.

Krugman, Paul R. "Targeted Industrial Policies: Theory and Evidence." In Federal Reserve Bank of Kansas City, *Industrial Change and Public Policy*. Kansas City: Federal Reserve Bank of Kansas City, 1983.

Krugman, Paul R. "The U.S. Response to Foreign Industrial Targeting." *Brookings Papers on Economic Activity* (1984): 77–121.

Little, I. M. D. *Economic Development: Theory, Policy, and International Relations*. New York: Basic Books, 1982.

Magaziner, Ira, and Reich, Robert B. *Minding America's Business*. New York: Random House, 1982.

Reich, Robert B. "Beyond Free Trade." *Foreign Affairs* (Fall 1983).

Schultze, Charles. "Industrial Policy: A Dissent." *Brookings Review* 2 (1983).

Spencer, Barbara. "What Should Trade Policy Target?" In Paul Krugman, ed., *Strategic Trade Policy and the New International Economics*. Cambridge: MIT Press, 1986.

Comment on "Strategic Sectors and International Competition"

Marina v.N. Whitman

Krugman's sophisticated and comprehensive review addresses the issue of whether arguments supporting government intervention as a means to promote or protect so-called strategic sectors are theoretically sound. In addition he examines the empirical relevance of the arguments; that is, he considers whether such measures are likely to provide significant national welfare benefits. In his review and analysis of recent work, he identifies two conditions under which intervention may be theoretically justifiable: imperfect competition, where excess returns exist, and the existence of externalities that create a divergence between private and social returns to a particular activity.

Krugman's work takes full account of recent developments in trade theory, assessing the role of imperfect competition, scale economies, and product innovation as the basis for noncomparative advantage trade or, more accurately, trade based on patterns of comparative advantage that are endogenously rather than exogenously determined and rapidly changing rather than semipermanent. At the same time his analysis ties back to traditional arguments for intervention: the optimum tariff and infant industry cases. In addition to showing that the necessary theoretical conditions are very restrictive, he also indicates why government intervention may be inappropriate even when strategic sectors can in principle be identified: the optimal policy action is often ambiguous, the welfare impact is usually small and not widely distributed, and the governmental process is a poor substitute for the marketplace in evaluating and selecting the sectors worthy of assistance.

I basically agree with Krugman's analysis; therefore I will try here to broaden the discussion by presenting a business view of a particular intervention issue of current interest: whether the voluntary restraint agreement (VRA) on Japanese automobile exports should have been extended beyond the March 1985 deadline. I will start by discussing why theoretical and environmental considerations might lead one to expect traditional industries to seek help, then review the typical response of most firms and unions, and finally explain why General Motors developed a different position. In effect GM's support for open trade is based on a dynamic view of business management in a world of imperfect but rigorous competition. Finally, I will discuss the disturbing microeconomic or structural effects of the major macroeconomic problems confronting the United States today: the growing twin deficits in the federal budget and the trade balance.

Most basic industries claim to have strategic value, derived from imperfect competition, linkages, externalities, or national defense essentiality, when they seek protection. These claims are increasingly pervasive because, as suggested by Staffan Burenstam Linder a number of years ago, exports of manufactures are an outgrowth of home production and market characteristics, implying that trade will increase rather than decrease as countries grow more similar in industrial structures and levels of per capita income. Hence such market characteristics of mature economies as innovation, product differentiation, increasing returns to scale, and imperfect competition give rise to extensive intraindustry trade flows that have two effects. First, the case for open trade on national welfare grounds seems less compellingly obvious to the mythical man (or woman) in the street than in the case of goods one cannot produce at home or only at exorbitant cost. Second, the traditional comparative advantage arguments based on relative factor endowments become more ambiguous and fragile when comparative advantage is perceived to be made rather than born because the factors that underlie existing trade configurations are dynamic and often endogenous rather than static and exogenous. Specifically the role of government policies, including trade or trade-related policies, in determining the pattern of comparative advantage becomes something more than a curiosum with the growing importance of intraindustry trade and the increasingly complex interplay among government policies, country factor endowments, and characteristics of firms and their products in determining international patterns of production, trade, and investment.

Although the characteristics of intraindustry trade have in some cases obscured the perceived benefits of the economists' case for open trade, environmental developments confronting a number of large so-called traditional industries (including automobiles) have dramatized the costs of adjustment:

1. The effects of a surge in intraindustry international competition in recent years have been compounded by rapid shifts in product demand and the overvalued dollar.

2. Firms that have experienced either a secular decline in demand (such as steel) or a decline in their growth rate (such as automobiles) have been unable to rely on strong industry-specific growth to lubricate change and ease dislocations.

3. The huge investments of capital and the large labor forces associated with economies of scale in these industries are relatively immobile, creating high frictional costs when resources must be reallocated.

4. Numerous regulations (such as environmental, safety, and fuel economy standards) and shifting trade policies (for example, so-called performance requirements) have increased costs.

Under these circumstances the challenge to public policy is to encourage a business environment conducive to the long-run national goal of efficient and globally competitive industries while holding down the inevitable costs of transition borne by specific sectors to socially and politically tolerable levels and distributing the burdens of adjustment in a manner widely perceived as equitable.

From the business perspective the frame of reference as well as the very terminology in which trade issues are discussed are quite different from the long-run cosmopolitan perspective of academic economists. The fundamental aim of a firm, like that of any other institution, is viability and growth. Institutional suicide is not an option. In this context the first allegiance of senior management is to the panoply of stakeholders who are directly affected by their decisions—including stockholders, employees, and communities— rather than to the more amorphous and indirectly affected public weal. Consequently although there is generally a sincere belief in and commitment to congruity between the two, firms and unions in traditional industries have typically taken a relatively narrow view in recent years when they have come under severe pressure from external market and competitive developments. They have tended to argue that industries such as steel and autos are important because they are basic to an advanced industrial society, with linkages to many other, including high-technology, sectors. The automobile industry, for example, has been a major factor in the development of robots and factory environment technology, as well as in the application of electronics, new materials, and coating developments. Such basic industries, it is argued, are a major engine of productivity growth, as well as a major source of high-wage employment.

Affected firms and unions frequently also contend that such basic industries are required as part of an economic base for purposes of national security. The predatory practices of others, if allowed to destroy such industries, could imperil national security or force the United States to pay monopoly rents to foreign countries in the future. Against this backdrop they conclude that such industries must be protected from foreign competition until they can compete. Ford, Chrysler, and the United Auto Workers have strongly pursued this line, arguing in addition that different national tax systems (particularly Japan's) and the overvalued dollar create an unfair handicap for domestic producers.

While agreeing on the importance of such industries' survival and health to national economic well-being, General Motors has a different view of how best to maximize the likelihood of a favorable outcome. That is that the re-emergence and maintenance of a dynamic motor vehicle sector in the United States in the face of pressure from Japan's emergence as the world's low-cost producer—what Altshuler et al. (1984, p. 11) have termed the third transfor-mation of the automobile industry—requires an aggressive response under open competition. The forces that will drive the diffusion of best practices (that is, competitive design, production, and marketing processes) throughout the automobile industry under open trade are the high political and econo-mic costs associated with the only two alternatives: the erosion of domestic automobile production and employment by increased foreign penetration, with its attendant economic, social, and political disruptions, or the survival of domestic firms as high-cost, relatively inefficient producers dependent on permanent protection, an alternative likely to be ultimately self-defeating. As costs to consumers increase, the political will to maintain the barriers would be likely to weaken. The eventual removal of protection under this scenario would expose an even weaker industry to foreign competition.

Global competitiveness is the only durable guarantor of profitability for firms and job security for workers. Open competition is essential to preserve market pressures on management, workers, and suppliers to make the often painful adaptations required to achieve global competitiveness. Protection offers no place to hide; if we close our doors, they will (and have) come in the windows by establishing production facilities in the United States. The United States will continue as the favored market for many foreign producers; hence the market shares of domestic producers will be under constant pressure. Given this situation, and the obvious fact that the United States (and Europe as well) is a mature, limited-growth market for many traditional industries, the United States must participate in the faster-growing markets of Asia and the rest of the developing world if it is to remain dynamic and competitive. Operating behind barriers, voluntary or otherwise, will not encourage the adjustments essential to achieve such a goal.

To the skeptics who may believe that GM's position is rooted in its desire to bring in vehicles produced by Japanese affiliates, I would note that such plans would encompass less than 3 percent of total car sales in the U.S. market and a small fraction as well of GM's current and projected domestic capacity to produce subcompact cars. The fact that Chrysler and Ford have similar arrangements has not prevented them from maintaining a significantly more protectionist stance.

At GM we have reviewed the effects of the VRAs over the past four years and conducted a number of competitive analyses. The results suggest four important conclusions. First, the VRA did give domestic makers time to begin the process of adaptation to a substantial Japanese cost advantage—which will require more than one product and labor negotiation cycle to complete—without serious financial repercussions. The restraints contributed to, though they were not a major cause of, the recovery of profits in the automobile industry. Second, as Krugman and Dixit suggest, the VRA appears also to have assisted the larger Japanese manufacturers by restraining competition and permitting capture of the resulting rents. Because per-car rents were substantially greater for the larger Japanese firms than for U.S. manufacturers, the additions to resources that could be committed to future product and process development were proportionately greater as well. Moreover, although Japanese capacity in product segments other than subcompact lines is still limited, the existence of the restraints has accelerated their upscale push into the Detroit heartland of larger, higher-profit vehicles. Third, the VRA also helped induce Japanese investment in the United States, by Honda, Nissan, and Mazda in particular. This capacity provides them with production not subject to restraints and sustains pressure on the market shares of U.S.-based producers. The Japanese producers' ability so far to retain most of their quality and cost advantages when production is transferred from Japan to the United States (although it remains to be seen whether some part of this phenomenon will turn out to be a temporary Hawthorne effect, which erodes as the novelty fades) underscores the importance of domestic firms' efforts to become competitive. Finally, our studies at GM suggest that the Japanese cost advantage is due primarily to differences in input costs and factor productivity rather than to differences in tax rates, which are negligible, or deviations from equilibrium exchange rates based on purchasing power parity calculations, which are substantial but not dominant. In sum, the net effect of the VRA over a four-year period suggests that continuation of the program would not be in the long-run interest of either the nation or the domestic producers.

Finally, I agree with Krugman and, indeed, most other economists that the United States' large and growing budget and trade deficits are fundamentally macroeconomic problems requiring macroeconomic solutions. But to stop there is to ignore their significant structural effects. For if, as many of us believe, the federal budget deficit is a primary determinant of the dollar's overvaluation and the resulting trade deficit, then it is crowding out export- and import-competing industries rather than domestic consumption or investment as it would in a closed economy. These are several reasons why such structural pressures may be a cause for concern.

First, the sheer magnitude of the adjustment process, particularly in the light of existing labor market rigidities, is somewhat daunting, and the possibility of labor market congestion may increase the costs of adjustment. In addition, if the overvaluation of the dollar continues for an extended period but is not ultimately sustainable (and few believe that it is), then the incurring of transition or adjustment costs in both directions could involve a significant welfare loss. Second, because the measured level of productivity and its growth rate are both higher in the aggregate in manufacturing than in nonfarm business as a whole, there is widespread concern about the loss of a significant source of productivity growth if the decline of tradable-goods sectors continues. Finally, the constituencies supporting open trade are being significantly eroded. Export industries, in both manufacturing and agriculture, that were once strong advocates of open competition are shifting position under the impact of the strong dollar. At the same time the nontradable sectors that benefit from the current environment are by definition less directly concerned with the maintenance of open trade.

Against this backdrop the continuation of current imbalances may eventually create uncontrollable pressures on government for microeconomic tinkering, despite ideological convictions that mitigate against it. And business itself stands to be a substantial loser if government increases its intervention in market-determined resource allocation and decision making.

The implications of this situation for business, academia, and government are clear. First, measures to restore currency relationships to more sustainable levels, including deficit reduction in the United States and some fiscal relaxation and structural measures on the part of some more important trading partners to reduce their excessive dependence on export-led growth, are essential and urgently overdue. Second, it is important for government to recognize the interaction between trade policy and other regulatory policies and apply its nonintervention principles to other issues confronting the automobile industry. For example, the negative impact of the ending of Japanese restraints on U.S. producers' sales, earnings, and jobs that occurs indirectly by a deterioration in their ability to meet corporate average fuel economy requirements as competition increases at the smaller end of the product spectrum could well swamp the direct effects of increased Japanese penetration. The theory of the second best is alive and well; by eliminating some distortions, we may well worsen others.

Reference

Altshuler, Alan, et al. *The Future of the Automobile: The Report of MIT's International Automobile Program.* Cambridge: MIT Press, 1984.

Comment on "Strategic Sectors and International Competition"

Gary R. Saxonhouse

More than any other individual, Krugman has taught economists, noneconomists, and policy makers how to think clearly on the relationship between industrial policy and trade policy. He has written a pellucid account of the relationship between the so-called strategic sector issue and the way economists conventionally think about international competition. Krugman asks in what sense it is possible to identify sectors that are strategic to an economy. He finds two ways: (1) a sector may yield high returns for resources committed because of the existence of imperfect competition; and (2) a sector may yield a high return indirectly because of the external economies generated.

Krugman rightly points out that the argument for strategic sectors that stresses the role of externalities is really a replaying of the debates of development economists from the 1950s and 1960s.[1] I would go further and argue that even Krugman's first conception of a strategic sector that stresses the high returns obtained from resources committed to a sector imperfectly competitive finds its precursor in the debates of development economics in the 1980s. Such an outlook is a close cousin of the once-famous Prebisch (1959) thesis.

On examining each of these two concepts of strategic sectors in some detail, Krugman concludes that any particular policy result that stresses a role for the government in promoting rent-collecting strategic sectors rests on special behavioral assumptions. It is difficult to know whether these assumptions are in any sense reasonable. The case for a government role in promoting an externality-generating strategic sector is somewhat more promising. This is especially true when in addition to pure technological externalities, consideration is given to what Krugman calls the linkage externalities arising from economies of scale in multistage production. Like so many other elements in this discussion, the idea of linkage externalities is not at all new. Although Krugman attributes the concept to Ethier (1982), it actually goes back to the genesis of externalities in Alfred Marshall's *Principles*, where in chapters 10 and 11 of book 4, Marshall takes up the matter of industrial location using externalities as an explanatory variable in much the same fashion as Ethier and Krugman. Krugman notes that although such externalities may be an important part of the production environment, to be the object of international competition, their benefits must be country specific. As Marshall himself notes in a section that anticipates Krugman's analysis, this is often not the case. Externalities can be embodied in goods and trained individuals that are internationally traded or otherwise migrate. Even where externalities do remain largely country specific, benefits may be shared through lower international prices. Krugman concludes that special national advantage from having an externality-generating strategic sector really arises only if it creates technological spillovers that are broadly beneficial to the rest of the economy and that are somehow country specific in character.

Krugman's analysis leaves me nodding with him and with the observations in the Deardorff-Stern and Dixit chapters that the information costs of even a limited venture into industry policy are very large. I would go further than Krugman and argue that the substance of these matters is even less well understood than he suggests. For example, has there been much high-quality evidence generated to date that suggests that either such mundane stylized facts as scale economies or learning curve effects are important determinants of the pattern of international trade and specialization? Reviewing modern work on the determinants of international trade through the early 1980s, Deardorff (1984, p. 511) concludes, "Empirical work on the importance of scale economies for the pattern of international trade has had mixed results." Still more recent work by Leamer (1984, p. 154) comes to a similar conclusion: "The anticipated non-linearities of the trade equation [which would give some indication of the presence of scale economies] generally failed to emerge."

Evidence for the importance of learning economies is still more limited. The learning curve was first popularized by the Boston Consulting Group (1972). It quickly entered the curricula of most business schools (Porter, 1980), and it is now commonplace amid the parlance of practical people. Unhappily one looks in vain for detailed empirical evidence that might justify the widespread use of this concept. At the time the Boston Consulting Group popularized this concept, it released a number of sectoral studies purporting to demonstrate the existence of a systematic linear logarithmic relationship between accumulated firm production and the average cost of production and Japanese firms' making explicit use of this relationship in their competitive strategies.[2]

Close analysis of the Boston Consulting Group data reveals that the strong linear relationship found between the logarithm of cumulated sales and the logarithm of cost is an artifact of the inappropriate deflation of Japanese costs by the GNP deflator. As Balassa (1964) established, given the much slower rates of productivity growth in nontraded goods and services, rapid growth in the productivity of traded goods will result in rapid increases in the price of nontradables.[3] The GNP deflator, by definition, contains price relatives for nontradables, as well as for tradable goods and services. Comparing the movement of the costs of any particular product in the fast-growing Japanese economy with the slower-growing U.S. economy where the data have been deflated using the respective GNP deflators will give the illusion of an overly sharp drop in Japanese costs relative to the accumulation of productive experience. Absent the evidence from these Boston Consulting Group studies, the documentation for the learning curve, for all its discussion in the semiconductor industry, rests primarily on Rapping's (1965) almost ancient experience of U.S. shipyards during World War II.

In one of the most interesting sections of his chapter, Krugman makes a wonderful back-of-the-envelope calculation by showing how capturing a strategic sector and its attendant economic rents may be very important for firm equity holders without being of much significance for the economy as a whole. Although such analyses are useful in puncturing the hyperbole served up by industrial policy enthusiasts, it is certainly possible to question whether Krugman is correct to assess the benefits of a strategic sector policy by the standard of whether it makes a significant contribution to the raising of national income. A more reasonable standard would seem to be the opportunity costs of the resources committed to the policy. For example, if the size of the government's economic policymaking establishment is taken as given and if macroeconomic policy impotence is taken seriously, perhaps there is little for government officials to do but think about strategic sector policy.

Considering the various issues that Krugman raises, it is probably incumbent on me to say something about how Japanese experience bears on these matters. If a strategic sector policy is so difficult to implement, what has Japan been doing all these years? Much of Japan's economic development experience during the past forty years is not directly relevant to the issues Krugman has been discussing. For most of this period, Japan was not on the technological frontier; it was catching up to more advanced economies. As Saxonhouse (1983a) noted, strategic sector policy meant ensuring that the actors in Japan's heavily concentrated financial system did not use their market power to frustrate the dictates of a changing Japanese comparative advantage.

Some more recent examples of Japanese strategic sector policy do bear closer scrutiny. In particular it seems intriguingly possible that Japan may have developed the ultimate in efficient industrial policy. On the one hand, as shown in Saxonhouse (1983b), by comparison with Western Europe and the United States, the Japanese government appears to spend very little furthering the interests of its high-technology sectors. At the same time, many Japanese industries are not shy about proclaiming the close and beneficial relationship they have with the Japanese government.[4] So successful is such advertising by Japanese industries that it is quite common for U.S. businessmen to state flatly that although they can compete with the Japanese private sector, they cannot compete with Japan, Inc. Is it possible that in the face of considerable ignorance by foreigners, Japanese firms are trying to scoop up all the benefits of a credible government commitment without actually imposing any real cost on the government?[5]

Notes

1. See, for example, Scitovsky (1954).

2. See Abegglen and Rapp (1972); Dresser, Hout, and Rapp (1972); and Hout and Rapp (1972).

3. Balassa identifies a positive linear relationship between the ratio of the GNP deflator and the wholesale price index of manufactures and the rate of increase of productivity in manufacturing.

4. See *Scientific American* (October 1982): J1–J20.

5. See Saxonhouse (1985).

References

Abegglen, James, and William V. Rapp. "The Competitive Impact of Japanese Growth." In Jerome B. Cohen, ed., *Pacific Partnership: United States–Japan Trade.* Lexington, Mass.: Lexington Books, 1972.

Balassa, Bela. "The Purchasing Power Parity Doctrine: A Reappraisal." *Journal of Political Economy* 72 (1964): 584–596.

Boston Consulting Group. *Perspectives on Experience.* Boston: BCG, 1972.

Deardorff, Alan V. "Testing Trade Theories." In Ronald W. Jones and Peter B. Kenen, eds., *Handbook of International Economics*, vol. 1. Amsterdam: North-Holland, 1984.

Dresser, James Van B., Thomas Hout, and William Rapp. "Competitive Development of the Japanese Steel Industry." In Jerome B. Cohen, ed., *Pacific Partnership: United States–Japan Trade.* Lexington, Mass.: Lexington Books, 1972.

Hout, Thomas M., and William V. Rapp. "Competitive Development of the Japanese Automobile Industry." In Jerome B. Cohen, ed., *Pacific Partnership: United States–Japan Trade.* Lexington, Mass.: Lexington Books, 1972.

Leamer, Edward W. *Sources of International Comparative Advantage.* Cambridge: MIT Press, 1984.

Marshall, Alfred. *Principles of Economics.* 8th ed. London: Macmillan, 1966.

Porter, Michael E. *Competitive Strategy*. New York: Free Press, 1980.

Prebisch, Raoul. "The Role of Commercial Policies in Underdeveloped Countries." *American Economic Review*, Papers and Proceedings (1959).

Rapping, Leonard. "Learning and World War II Production Functions." *Review of Economics and Statistics* 47 (1965): 81–86.

Saxonhouse, Gary R. "The Micro- and Macroeconomics of Foreign Sales to Japan." In William R. Cline, ed., *Trade Policy for the 1980s*. Cambridge: MIT Press for the Institute for International Economics, 1983a.

Saxonhouse, Gary R. "What's All This about Industrial Targeting in Japan?" *World Economy* 6 (1983b): 253–273.

Saxonhouse, Gary R. "Industrial Policy and Factor Markets: Biotechnology in Japan and the United States." *Prometheus* 3 (1985): 277–314.

Scientific American. "Advertising Supplement of the Electronic Industries Association of Japan." October 1982.

Scitovsky, Tibor. "Two Concepts of External Economies." *Journal of Political Economy* 62 (1954): 143–151.

6

How Should the United States Respond to Other Countries' Trade Policies?

Avinash Dixit

6.1 Perception of the Problem

In the first thirty years following World War II, international trade in manufactures was gradually liberalized. The main instrument behind this change
was the MFN-based GATT code. Successive rounds of multilateral negotiations, conducted under the auspices of GATT, led to substantial reductions in
tariffs and formal quotas on trade in manufactured goods among industrial
countries. After the conclusion of the Tokyo Round, such obstacles to trade
could be said to have quite minor importance. The United States played a
leading role in all these developments and can claim a significant amount of the
credit for the outcome.

The new arrangements were far from perfect. The almost total exclusion of
agriculture on the one hand, and services on the other, from the coverage of
GATT limited its scope considerably. Even in the area of manufacturing, some
sensitive industries were not covered. The Multi-Fiber Arrangement (MFA) is
the most prominent such deviation, and it has achieved a labyrinthine complexity that departs ever further from the spirit of GATT. The articles also
contained several loopholes and escape clauses that could be misused, and
duly were. The enforcement powers were often too weak to deter the determined transgressor countries. Most ominous of all was the emergence of
bilateral or multilateral arrangements that restricted trade, whose supposedly
voluntary nature kept them outside GATT's purview. Such schemes are
emerging in many important industries, of which steel threatens to be the
latest. Finally, countries are devising imaginative new policy instruments to
replace ones proscribed by GATT: informal and bureacratic barriers instead of
tariffs or quotas and various kinds of industrial targeting instead of export
subsidies. These developments are gradually eroding the GATT framework,
and the more liberal trading order is at risk.

The United States has not been innocent in these slides toward a new protectionism. Its role in the MFA and its imposition of voluntary restraints in autos, steel, and other sectors must not be overlooked. But the widespread belief in the United States is that others, especially Japan and the EC, are the real culprits and that the United States has suffered as a result. Added to the perceived economic injury is the insult of other countries' ingratitude for years of U.S. leadership in working toward a liberal trading order. The corollary drawn by the advocates of this view is that the United States should recognize the ideal of free trade as a mirage, and instead seek fair trade. They ask for protection or subsidies that will overcome the disadvantage of U.S. industries stemming from foreign countries' trade policies and ensure a level playing field. Some also believe that the United States should employ policies of aggressive reciprocity, consisting of threats to compel other countries to abandon their measures of import restriction and export promotion.

Documentation of these views is hardly necessary; a recent representative sample can be found in some congressional hearings (U.S. Congress, 1983a, 1983b), held in connection with a mass of legislation intended to give practical effect to various active and reactive kinds of trade and industrial policies. The beliefs are very widely held by businesspersons, labor unionists, politicians, and government officials—in fact by almost everyone except academic economists.

The writings of economists on the subject are far less categorical, and their policy prescriptions are far more cautions. The first note of doubt concerns the view of foreign governments as aggressive and successful makers of trade and industrial policies. Cline (1982, pp. 9–15) argues that other countries' trade restrictions are not generally more severe than those of the United States Krugman (1984) finds that "the industrial policies of foreign governments have not been a serious problem for the United States." The second point pertains to the costs and benefits of aggressive action on the part of the United States. Krugman recognizes that policies of other governments could in principle damage the United States and call for a response, but his factual findings make the question moot for him. Cline makes a similar point and emphasizes the prospect that aggressive U.S. policies will invite retaliation, leading to great mutual harm. Economists are also more aware than others of the gains to consumers from foreign export subsidies and the costs to them of U.S. import restrictions. To quote Krugman again, these considerations can govern "whether the U.S. should retaliate or send a note of thanks" when others sell subsidized or dumped goods in our markets. Richardson (1986) points out some other realities of the situation. The United States is a far less dominant presence in world trade and is itself far more sensitive to international events than formerly. Successful pursuit of aggressive reciprocity needs political and administrative institutions that are lacking in the United States. Finally, the informational requirements of such policies are onerous. The overall conclusion of academic economists is that the case for an active or responsive U.S. trade policy, although conceivable in theory under some circumstances, is weak in theory and practice.

This wealth of material leaves me with a difficult task of saying anything new on the subject. I shall aim to clarify the debate in some respects and to answer some unresolved questions. My focus will be on the strategic interactions that exist among various governments, firms, and consumers in the process of making and implementing trade policies.

6.2 Formulation of the Questions

Philosophers tell us that to achieve clarity of thought, a good starting point is to clarify the meaning of the words we use. Ramsey (1931, p. 267) described the method: "Simply to think out with myself: 'What do I mean by that?' 'What are the separate notions involved in this term?' 'Does this really follow from that?' etc." My assigned title is ideal for such an exercise. There are some key words that, under such scrutiny, will reveal the sources of the differences of opinion that exist on this subject.

The first key word is *should*. This has a normative connotation, and I shall take it seriously. I shall first examine the appropriate social criteria for economic policy and then look for the optimal policies to suit the criteria. Of course, I must pay attention to the constraints placed on our freedom to choose policies, and such constraints arise from the realities of the political process, as well as from resource or technology limitations. But I shall not go all the way to the view of the positive theory of economic policy, which argues that the political process leaves no freedom to pursue normative goals at all, and we can only describe the equilibrium outcome of the process.

This is not to say that normative goals are clear or unique. On the contrary argument over them is perhaps the area of the greatest disagreements, which give rise to heated debate or, worse, total lack of communication. Economists usually assign a central place to efficiency in the allocation of resources. They are also concerned with equity or distributive justice but to different degrees. There is also an important distinction of kind. Equity in this context can mean equality of opportunity or equality of outcomes. The former commands wider support; the latter provides insurance to those who are unlucky in their economic endeavors but can destroy incentives to exercise effort or care. Therefore the extent of equality of economic outcomes a society should seek is a subject of hot debate.

Other contributors to the argument have other ideas about the society's goals, ranging over such matters as national security, implications for the world order, claims of various special interest groups, and political necessity. Sorting these out is made more complicated by the fact that the stated reason sometimes conceals a true motive that is quite different.

Finally, many of these criteria involve further considerations of trade-offs between the short run and the long run. For example, niceness that is costly in the short run may provide a basis for beneficial ongoing cooperation. In other circumstances aggression that is costly now may establish a reputation for toughness that helps in the long run.

In the next section I shall consider some of these objectives and see how they are affected by some trade policies of other countries. That will set the stage for the second key word, *respond*. Here it is essential to distinguish three notions. One is the reaction we would find desirable given other countries' policies as fait accompli. Such responses might include the introduction of some totally new policy measure but will more typically consist of changes in the levels of some policy variable we were already using. For example, our best tariff rate would be different depending on other countries' rates. Discretionary reactive policies, such as the provisions of section 301 of the Trade Act of 1979, fall in this first category. The second notion is that of policies we should pursue now in readiness for policies that we know, or believe, are likely to be followed by other countries in the future. Thus we might respond to the prospect of a future embargo by building a stockpile now. This notion of a reaction that precedes the action may seem strange at first glance but is very natural when policymakers employ strategically rational foresight. The third notion of response is a policy rule, which precommits the United States to react in a specified way if other countries act, or fail to act, in certain specified ways. The aim is to alter their expectations of the consequences of their actions and thereby to deter or compel them in ways that will suit our interest. Typical policy rules of this kind are the nondiscretionary provisions for countervailing and antidumping duties. This is also the essence of reciprocity, whether the old kind that works toward a more liberal trading order on the basis of mutual promises or the new aggressive kind that employs threats to further our own interests.

The importance of distinguishing among these three categories is twofold. First, there are circumstances where one kind of response is appropriate but another kind is not. Such differences must be properly understood if the correct policy is to be followed. Second, the three kinds have very different procedural requirements for their successful use. Clear knowledge of what needs to be done in each context is very important. Such questions will be taken up in section 6.4, when the desirability and the efficacy of various commonly suggested U.S. responses to other countries's trade policies will be examined.

The third key word is *how*. This presupposes a range of policies from which the United States is to choose. Popular discussion is often focused on responses that directly match or oppose other countries' actions: countervailing duties against subsidized sales to U.S. markets, matching export credits when U.S. firms compete against theirs in third markets, reciprocal denial of market access in each industry, and attempts to achieve bilaterally balanced trade, for example. Such a direct connection between action and reaction is not required by the logic of strategy. Some examples will make the point. First, much of the success of the GATT rounds involved trading concessions in one industry against those in another. Second, the best U.S. response to some international events is one of adjustment in the domestic economy rather than protected resistance to the change. Third, when it comes to threats or promises, they need not even be confined to economic policy measures. Thus foreign policy might be used as an instrument of trade policy, and vice-versa. Of course, there may be ethical or practical constraints on such a linking of different policy arenas. All of these considerations must be kept in mind when exploring the possible responses.

The final key words are *trade policies*. There are numerous channels of interconnection among different activities in any economy, and most policies have some bearing on trade. In a sense, therefore, all economic policies (and some others too) are trade policies; the only difference is the degree of directness. Import tariffs or quotas, and export taxes or subsidies, are the most direct. At one remove, consumption taxes on an imported good have some features of a tariff, while production subsidies for an exported good are partly like export subsidies. Various policies of industrial targeting, and promotion of R&D, are often undertaken at least in part for their trade effects. The question is, Which of these policies are appropriate objects for a U.S. response and which are not?

The GATT takes a narrow view. Its articles allow a country to countervail foreign direct export subsidies if they cause material injury to its economy. There have been attempts to achieve agreed reductions in export credit subsidies. In fact, most countries' laws and practices provide for responses under much broader circumstances. There are pressures for further broadening. The argument that border tax adjustments under a value-added tax constitute an export subsidy is well known from the Zenith case, although it did not prevail at that time. There are some who go so far as to claim that Japan's use of the Japanese language constitutes a nontariff barrier. I have in mind a relatively broad notion of the scope of trade policies but not one as broad as that.

6.3 Judging the Effects of Other Countries' Policies

In this section I shall examine the criteria commonly used for evaluating economic outcomes and consider how various trade policies of foreign countries yield costs or benefits to the United States according to these yardsticks. Krugman (1984) conducts a similar analysis with respect to targeting policies; I shall look at a broader range of trade policies. My discussion of the criteria has also benefited from Krugman (1983) but is somewhat differently organized. I shall begin with primary economic objectives and then go on to noneconomic ones and some popular aims that are best understood as indirect proxies for the primary economic goals. I shall attempt to preserve a conceptual distinction between national interests and various sectional or special interests.

6.3.1 Economic Efficiency

This is the objective that most economists regard as the most important. It is served by maximizing real national income—that is, the real value of all the goods and services at the disposal of the nation as a whole. So far as international trade is concerned, there are two prominent ways in which other countries' policies can change U.S. real national income: by changing U.S. terms of trade and by changing the net pure profit the United States gets from the rest of the world.

Terms of Trade
U.S. terms of trade are measured by an index of the prices of its exports relative to the prices of its imports. An improvement in the terms of trade (that is, an increase in this price index) means that each unit of goods and services the United States exports (gives up to the foreigners) yields more units of imports available to the U.S. economy.

U.S. terms of trade can change because of shifts in other countries' demand for U.S. exports or their supply of U.S. imports. Such changes can arise from changes in the underlying economic conditions of technologies, preferences or resource endowments in those countries, or from the tax, subsidy, or targeting policies of their governments. Similarly, and to the extent that the United States is large in world trade, changes in U.S. economic conditions or policies can also alter its terms of trade. This is in fact the basis for the standard optimum tariff argument. If the United States has market power in world trade but individual buyers and sellers are too small to recognize this and act upon it, then the government can employ trade restrictions to secure this benefit for the nation.

I shall review and classify these effects on U.S. terms of trade to provide the basis for my discussion of the U.S. response. (Readers who are familiar with the elementary economic arguments can glance briefly at the points being made and pass on to the discussion of excess profits.)

Textbook expositions usually assume that there is one aggregate exportable good and another aggregate importable good. This has the merit of emphasizing that only relative prices matter and that monopoly power over aggregate exports and monopsony power over aggregate imports are two sides of the same coin. A tariff that restricts imports to drive up their price will, by the same token, drive down the price of U.S. exports and so discourage their production. Once this general point is understood, however, it is useful to allow more disaggregation, with several exported and imported goods, and think in terms of the supply and demand curves for each, the prices being expressed relative to an aggregate of all goods. This has the advantage of recognizing that U.S. market power in trade is not uniform across commodities but is strong in some and nonexistent in others.

Figure 6.1 shows the case of a good imported to the United States. The rest of

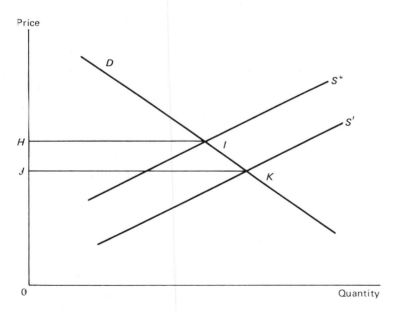

Figure 6.1
Effect of foreign export subsidies on domestic welfare.

the world's supply curve is S^*. The U.S. demand curve for imports is D, and the market price under free trade is OH. Suppose foreign subsidies or targeting policies lower the supply curve to S' and the price to OJ. Then the U.S. real income will increase by the amount of the area $HIKJ$. Since D is the U.S. demand curve for imports, it shows U.S. consumption minus production. Correspondingly this area of gain conceals some loss of producer surplus and a larger gain in consumer surplus. This may give rise to a distributive conflict that needs to be considered separately, but for the moment I shall concentrate on the issue of aggregate economic efficiency.

It is in this sense that foreign export subsidies are economically beneficial to the United States. The above argument assumed a policy of free trade in the United States, but the result has much wider validity. In the general setting of competitive markets, the aggregate economic welfare of the United States could be lowered by foreign export promotion only if the United States were heavily subsidizing imports. In that case their policies would further increase the volume of U.S. imports, and they would collect more of the generous subsidies the United States was offering. It is clear that such a case can safely be assumed to be outside the realm of practical policy.

If the rest of the world includes a large exporting country and if it is motivated by the same criterion of aggregate economic efficiency, then it will not promote exports at all. On the contrary it will exercise its monopoly power by restricting the quantity exported and thereby driving up the price. The rest of the world acting together could best exploit the United States in this way by finding the marginal curve M to U.S. demand curve D and seeing where it meets their net supply curve S^*. Figure 6.2 shows the outcome. The United States pays the price OP and suffers a loss of real income equal to the area $PUIH$. The price in the rest of the world is OQ, and the difference PQ is the export tax that implements the restrictive policy. The revenue from this tax is the area $PUVQ$.

By the same argument if the United States is a large importer (it faces a rising supply curve S^*) then U.S. national interest is best served by exercising monopsony power. Readers can easily construct the formal demonstration by analogy with figure 6.2 and find the optimum tariff. It is important to note that an equally restrictive quota or VER would not achieve the same result since some or all of the amount corresponding to the tariff revenue would be captured by the foreigners.

If the United States is importing a good and some other large importer restricts the access to its own market, then the rest of the world's supply to the U.S. market will shift outward and result in a lower price, thus improving the terms of trade for the United States. This may be of some significance in the

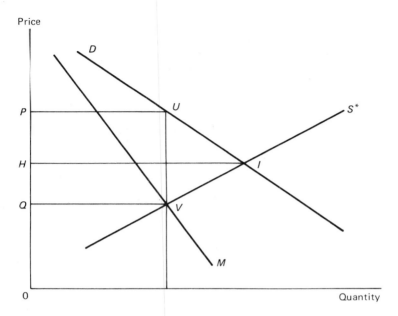

Figure 6.2
Effect of foreign monopoly power on domestic welfare.

case of international capital flows. As the United States becomes a net debtor, it helps if other debtor countries restrict their capital inflows, thereby leaving more capital available to the United States on better terms.

Next consider a good exported by the United States. An importing country's restrictive policies, or a competing exporter's subsidy or targeting policies, will lower the price fetched by U.S. exports (worsen U.S. terms of trade). Lawrence, in his discussion of Krugman (1984), points to this as a possible justification for some recent complaints about foreign targeting heard from U.S. exporters. Of course, to have an appreciable effect, the country pursuing the targeting policy has to be large in the world market for this good.

If the United States is a large exporter, the terms of trade argument holds to restrict exports by means of an optimum export tax. This is just the case of figure 6.2 with the roles of the two countries reversed. The idea that it is desirable to restrict exports runs against the mercantilist arguments for export promotion often heard in public debate. If such arguments have any validity, they must be based on considerations other than monopolistic improvement of the terms of trade. If foreign countries are pursuing policies of export promotion, their actions must be similarly explained by other arguments.

Finally, consider the case where the United States exports a good and faces a large importer, whose optimum tariff turns the terms of trade against the

United States. A small exporter can do nothing on its own. But if it has counter-vailing market power, then it pays to use it. Of course we gain something by using our power whether or not the other country uses its, and there is no general argument that a more vigorous pursuit of monopsony against us calls for a more vigorous pursuit of our own monopoly. The optimum tariff, like any monopolist's optimum restriction, depends on the elasticity of demand, not on its level. The foreigners' import restrictions may increase or decrease this elasticity, depending on the exact shape of their demand curve.

In either case there is a risk that such a bilateral monopoly will lead to mutually harmful trade restrictions on both sides. Governments following such restrictive trade policies against each other will typically find themselves in a Prisoners' Dilemma. This brings the issue of the time horizon of policy into sharp focus. The long-run real national income of both parties will be better served if each can forgo the temptation of making short-term gains at the expense of the other. The question is how to make the parties trust each other and so establish a viable regime of free trade. I shall return to this question in section 6.4.

To sum up the examination of the terms of trade criterion, other countries' trade policies may affect the U.S. real national income favorably or adversely, depending on the circumstances. These include considerations of whether the United States imports or exports the goods in question, whether the other country competes with the United States or is on the other side of the market, and whether its policy restricts or promotes its trade activities. I have developed a scheme of reasoning that enables us to calculate the effects in each specific case but have found no general presumption of harm. The empirical research of Krugman (1984) supports this theoretical argument. He finds that there has not been a significant adverse shift in the U.S. terms of trade over the recent decades. Some adverse shift should be expected in the natural course of evolution of comparative advantage because the differences of capital-labor ratios between the United States and its major trading partners have narrowed during this period. Since the total adverse shift is seen to be small, any effect attributable to foreign countries' trade policies is, a fortiori, smaller still.

In this connection it is important to point out that the economic effects on the United States are the same, irrespective of the causes, whether natural economic changes in the other countries or any deliberate policies of their governments that artificially alter or create comparative advantage. All that matters is what happens to the demand or supply curves, and not why. Lobbyists who ask for protection or matching export promotion often say that they can compete with foreign firms but not with foreign governments, thus maintaining a distinction between the two causes, but this is irrelevant from

the point of view of the United States as a whole as long as the country judges
the outcomes by the criterion of aggregate real national income.

Excess Profits
The pure or excess or economic profit in an industry is the revenue in excess of
all costs, including materials, wages, and the normal return (including any risk
premium) required to attract capital to this industry. Such excess profits can
exist only if there are barriers to entry. They are therefore important in
industries with large sunk costs, significant scale economies, or a high degree
of product differentiation. In international trade industries such as commercial
jet aircraft and large mainframe computers are clearly imperfectly competitive
in this way and allow excess profits. Many others, such as automobiles, steel,
and some consumer electronics, have varying degrees of imperfect competition. Still others such as pharmaceuticals exhibit great monopoly power and
excess profits for new drugs but keen competition at the stage of the research
that leads to these discoveries and inventions.

Until recently international trade theory assumed that all markets were
perfectly competitive. Therefore the theory was unable to deal with some
important features of today's trading environment and policies. Some recent
work, notably Brander and Spencer (1984, 1985) and Eaton and Grossman
(1983), has remedied this deficiency to a great extent. A technical survey with
some extensions was in Dixit (1984) and a less technical one in Grossman and
Richardson (1985). My discussion relies on these, especially the last.

When there are pure profits, a country's real national income increases if its
residents, or firms owned by them, acquire more of these profits, usually at the
expense of other countries' residents. The firms in such industries are strategic
profit maximizers, aware of their market power and the rivalry with other
firms. They are working to capture the profits for their own sakes. Therefore
the mere existence of imperfect competition with pure profits does not justify
an activist trade policy. Such intervention can further the national economic
interest only to the extent that the government can employ better strategies to
capture the profits than those available to the firms.

The simplest such action is to avoid rivalry among firms. When they
compete with each other, they do not exercise their market power in relation
to foreign firms most effectively. The government might help by relaxing the
antitrust laws so far as international trade activity is concerned, but that runs
the risk of encouraging parallel tacit monopolization of the domestic market.
Alternatively firms might be induced to avoid excessive price cutting, or,
equivalently, to restrain their sales, through export taxes or restrictions. This
is similar to the optimum export tax argument. There the idea is to get small,

perfectly competitive firms to restrict exports and act like monopolists in international markets. Now the same is to be done for larger, imperfectly competitive firms. Once again, notice that the idea of restricting exports is contrary to the popular mercantilist position.

Sometimes the other country's trade policies, motivated by quite different considerations, will facilitate some monopolization of U.S. export activity. If they restrict their imports using VERs, then the administration of these quotas falls to the U.S. government or a producers' organization. That allows the United States to act as a cartel and allocate quantities. Each firm can then follow a more monopolistic pricing policy, secure in the knowledge that rivals from its own country will not have anything to gain from undercutting it.

We would not want too restrictive a quota; the ideal would be just our monopoly amount. There are also distributive conflicts in the allocation of the quota to firms, but there are good prospects for overall gain in real national income. It is believed that the U.S. restraints on automobile imports helped Japan in this way (see Crandall, 1984). It was also suspected that Japan would attempt to continue some restraint on its exports of automobiles to the United States even after the United States lifted the VERs, and this has duly happened.[1] Also VERs can facilitate the collusion of all producers in both countries, leaving the consumers in the importing countries as the only losers (Krishna, 1984).

Having seen the problem of coordination of each country's producers, let us continue the analysis in a somewhat simpler setting of a duopoly, with just one firm from each country. The question is how trade policy can alter the strategic rivalry and the division of the profits between them. As Eaton and Grossman (1983) have shown, the answer depends crucially on the way in which the rivalry is conducted. It is most instructive to contrast two cases. One is known as Cournot competition. Here each firm fixes the quantities it will produce and offer for sale, and the prices adjust to clear the markets. The other is Bertrand competition, where the firms fix their prices and then produce enough to meet the demand that comes their way.

In Cournot competition one firm can gain at the expense of the other if it can make a credible commitment to produce a larger output, up to a point. The other firm, faced with such a fait accompli, will cut back its own output. The problem is that once the second firm has responded in this way, the first has an incentive to renege on its commitment and produce less, driving up the price. The second firm, suspecting this, will not believe the first firm's output announcement unless it is accompanied by visible and irreversible deeds ensuring that the stated action will occur. There are some policies that the firms themselves can employ in this way; a well-known example is that of installing product-specific capacity sufficient to produce the asserted output. But in equilibrium all such strategies and counterstrategies must have been exhausted. Can the first country's government do any more? If it can make a credible commitment to subsidize its firm's sales in the markets where it competes with its foreign rival, then its firm will have a lower cost and a greater incentive to expand such sales. The other firm will recognize this fact and therefore regard the first's output expansion as credible. This is the Brander-Spencer argument for export subsidies. For once, we see export promotion being justified by consideration of real national income.

In Bertrand competition both firms will gain if they can agree to raise prices. If one firm credibly commits itself to charging a higher price, the other will raise its price under the first's umbrella. The second firm will be a clear gainer; so will the first within some limit on its price commitment. Once again the credibility of the promise is questionable. Having lulled the second firm into raising its price in response, the first would want to renege and undercut it. A government can lend credibility to a higher price for its firm if it levies a tax on its sales in markets where it competes with its foreign rival. The motive is the same as in Cournot competition—increasing the profits accruing to our country's firm—but the strategic policy implied is just the opposite—an export tax rather than an export subsidy.

Eaton and Grossman (1983) construct a more general model that encompasses Cournot and Bertrand as special cases. Each firm's conjecture about the rival's output reaction is treated as a parameter. The larger are these parameters, the higher are the price-cost margins in equilibrium; that is, the more collusive is the outcome. They find that the proper policy is an export subsidy if the duopolists' conduct is more collusive than a critical level and a tax if it is more competitive. The borderline case is one where each firm has a conjecture consistent with its rival's actual reaction. This is as if each has correctly calculated the other's response, so no further profit shifting is possible, and free trade is optimal.

This analysis assumes that the government's objective in this industry is the same as that of the firm: profit maximization. If the industry has nonnegligible sales in our own country, then our real national income should include our consumers' surplus. A more collusive duopoly will mean prices further above marginal costs, and this will hurt us. The conclusions are then modified in the direction of less taxation or more subsidies. However, the policy of subsidizing a monopolist to induce it to price closer to the true marginal cost has severe adverse incentive effects. Firms will redouble their efforts to monopolize industries and then will exaggerate their costs. Therefore we do not normally solve the problem of monopoly in this way.

Now we can ask how another government's trade policies will affect us in such an industry. If the competition is Cournot, their export subsidies will shift profit from us to them and will usually lower total industry profit. This clearly hurts us. If the competition is Bertrand and if they are motivated by the criterion of real national income just as we are, then they will be taxing their firm's sales. Our firm can securely raise its price and reap the higher profits that come to a price follower. This is beneficial, unless the market is our own, when the loss of consumer surplus will more than offset the profit gain and cause us harm.

If the trading relationship is ongoing, longer-term considerations will appear. In Cournot competition, for example, both governments will have incentives to subsidize their firms, and the result of the subsidy competition between the governments will lead to lower profits for firms. Unless the offsetting gain in consumers' surpluses dominates, the governments will want to establish mutual promises to avoid subsidies. The problem is a Prisoners' Dilemma similar to the tariff war mentioned in the discussion of the terms of trade.

Finally, a word of warning about the scope of validity of the profit-shifting argument. It would seem that R&D-intensive industries, where a winner emerges to become a monopolist for a while, would be ideal candidates for such policies. But we must not forget the competition at the prior stage of the race to win. If our subsidies make the prize more attractive to our firms, then there will be more U.S. entrants to the race. The probability of the winner's being one of our firms will be increased, but there will be more U.S. losers too. The resources they expend in the race will have to count as a negative contribution to real U.S. national income. If the firms are risk neutral—for example, because the risks are diversifiable—then the whole process of R&D followed by production will be one with zero expected pure profits, and the arguments of this section will not apply.

6.3.2 Distributional Conflicts

The discussion of the real national income criterion showed that the net figures could conceal large gains and losses of consumer or producer surpluses. Although firms should not be direct objects of economic concern, their gains or losses pass on to the workers or the owners of other factors specific to the industry. This change in their real income is a relevant consideration. If a foreign exporter subsidizes a good we import, for example, then the owners of factors specific to the import-competing industry will lose, even after their ability to buy imports more cheaply is taken into account. They will therefore oppose the note of thanks for the subsidy that the rest of the nation would wish to send.

Such distributional conflicts are ubiquitous in the arena of trade policy. When other countries' actions affect different groups or individuals in the United States differently, the question of what it can, or should, do in response becomes that much more difficult.

When there are aggregate economic gains, the response most favored by economists is to use domestic redistributive policies that will compensate the losers and still leave the gainers with positive benefits. This should ensure unanimous acceptance of the overall change. The policies usually suggested for this purpose—lump sum transfers—are quite impractical; however, recent work by Dixit and Norman (1984), Diewert, Turunen, and Woodland (1984), and Dixit (1985a) has shown that, in a wide variety of situations encountered in practice, appropriately calculated indirect taxes and subsidies on goods and factors can achieve the same results. This makes the compensation response a much more practicable option.

The next question is whether the United States should act in this way. Policy may be made with an explicit or implicit social welfare function that adds up individuals' gains or losses, with different weights reflecting the social valuations of the different dollar amounts. If such a measure of social welfare increases in the comparison being made, then the losers might be made to bear their losses for the society's sake, without compensation.[2]

In reality policy is rarely made in this way. There is some reason to think that in the United States, potential losers have an effective veto over any economic change. Then some kind of compensation is a practical necessity. Refusal to offer compensation might lead to the emergence of a worse policy, such as protection or regulation that thwarts the change altogether. An acceptance of a change that is beneficial in the aggregate, with accompanying redistributive measures, would be better for all. Compensation that is desirable in the context of an event that occurs only once and without forewarning, however, may have harmful effects if offered as an ongoing policy rule in an economy that is always likely to meet changes in its trading environment. Such a society should make the best preparation it can for the risks it faces. It should use the best available information about the likelihood of the changes and adapt the investments or resource commitments to be flexible across the spectrum.

Short-run specificity of factors usually arises because of investments made in the past, in the form of resources sunk in particular industries or training acquired that has no other use. The guaranteed availability of compensation against future losses will destroy the individuals' incentives to exercise caution when they make these investment decisions. If the terms of the compensation are better for some risks than for others, then there will be excessive investment in the well-insured ventures. A long-term view of redistributive policies should take these incentive effects into account.

On the other side of the argument, there is genuine and legitimate social concern to prevent economic distress. It is not possible to reconcile the twin objectives of insurance and incentives. This relates to the wider conflict between the equality of outcomes and the equality of opportunities. It seems to me that a good compromise is the negative income tax. This would provide a backstop against economic distress from whatever cause but would not favor the losers from one kind of economic change over those from another. Such a mechanism has to be put in place at the time when the constitution governing economic policy is being drawn up and before the precise identities of the winners and the losers in any particular context are known. Then the constitution has to decree that such swings and roundabouts of economic life will not justify any other special relief. Friedman (1962) gives an eloquent and detailed argument for a negative income tax.

6.3.3 Other Economic Criteria

Real national income and its distribution are the primary economic criteria for judging outcomes. Popular discussions, however, often focus on others such as job creation or loss or market shares. These have some role as secondary or proxy criteria. If the primary effects are difficult to compute and some secondary measure is known to be strongly correlated with the underlying objectives, then there is much to be said for using such a proxy. I shall discuss these alternative criteria from this viewpoint.

Comparisons of market shares, or measures of bilateral cross-penetration of imports in particular industries, are often cited as evidence by those who complain about other countries' trade practices. For example, Japan has about 18 percent of the U.S. automobile market, while the United States has very little market share in theirs. Although import restrictions or informal bureaucratic obstacles in Japan may be responsible for such a result, the argument does not establish the link. A counterexample is the wheat and barley market, where the United States has 39 percent of the Japanese market, while Japan has almost no sales in the United States.[3] This does not prove that the U.S. trade policy in agriculture is unfair. In fact the disparity of market shares would be even greater but for Japanese import restrictions. It is also worth remembering that the pursuit of bilateral and industry-specific parity of market penetration is a road that leads to total autarky.

To be fair, I should admit that trade in wheat differs from that in automobiles. Absent policy intervention, wheat trade would be perfectly competitive. Trade restriction to improve the terms of trade would be the only primary economic justification for an active policy. In the automobile market there is some imperfect competition although less than is commonly thought (see Dixit, 1985b). Correspondingly there is some possible case for protection or export promotion policies to capture excess profits. But my general point is that market share comparisons do not bear any systematic relation to these primary criteria; they are a poor proxy.

Another popular criterion is high value-added per worker. This was advocated by Magaziner and Reich (1982) and has been picked up by many others. Krugman (1983) has examined it at length. He argued that high value-added per worker goes hand in hand with low value-added per unit of capital and a low labor requirement per unit of capital. Therefore such a criterion for investment allocation will yield low output with little job creation. The proper economic criterion is the marginal productivity of the investment. If the capital market works well and if there are no externalities or problems of appropriability of the returns to the investment, then private profit incentives will cause the investment to flow in the socially desirable direction, and no policy intervention will be necessary.

In most people's minds, however, industries with high value-added per worker are those on the cutting edge of technology and production. This is where external economies or spillover benefits are likely to be most important. Thus the criterion of value-added per worker might serve as a proxy for the underlying considerations of market failure that justify an active policy to redirect investment. To test this hypothesis, I have calculated the figures for value-added per worker in three-digit U.S. manufacturing industries for 1981. Table 6.1 shows some with especially high value-added per worker, and some mainstream or high-technology industries for comparison. The former have no systematic link with technology, spillover benefits, or market failures in general. If anything they seem to support Krugman's view that high capital intensity is the primary determinant of high value-added per worker. Of course, the three-digit level may not be the appropriate one for this calculation, but it does show that the proxy is likely to be misleading and subject to misuse. It would be better to try to identify market failures and remedy them directly.

Employment is the last criterion of this kind I shall discuss. The popular perception is that exports create jobs and imports destroy them. There are factual as well as conceptual problems with this. First, we have to find the actual effects of import competition on employment. Since employment in any

Table 6.1
Value-added per worker in selected three-digit U.S. manufacturing industries, 1981

SIC number	Industry	Thousands per worker
Examples of industries with high value-added per worker		
204	Grain mill products	$ 90.4
208	Beverages	74.6
211	Cigarettes	134.8
213	Chewing and smoking tobacco	101.8
261	Pulp mills	76.4
284	Soap, cleaners, and toilet goods	113.8
291	Petroleum refining	221.5
Comparison figures from basic and high-tech industries		
331	Blast furnance and basic steel products	51.7
353	Construction machinery	57.5
357	Office and computing machines	54.6
371	Motor vehicles	50.1
372	Aircraft and parts	48.4
381	Engineering and scientific instruments	44.2
382	Measuring and control devices	40.4

Source: *Statistical Abstract of the United States* (1981).

industry changes for a variety of reasons, we must control for these other causes in order to isolate the effects of import competition. Grossman (1983) has done this for a number of industries. He finds that the effect has been much smaller and of significance in a much smaller number of industries than popular arguments would have us believe.

Turning to conceptual matters, the popular perception is at best an incomplete picture. It looks at the demand for labor and not at its supply. We must ask where a worker who joins an export industry comes from and where one who leaves an import-competing industry goes. In the textbook world of a labor market in competitive equilibrium, the answer in each case is employment somewhere else in the economy at the going wage. Thus there should be no aggregate effects on employment. Actual labor markets differ from this picture, but that does not automatically establish the legitimacy of the common anti-import or proexport arguments. We must ask just how the differences arise and what implications they have.

First, there will be redistributive effects even in an economy with full employment. Workers who lose jobs in one industry may find others only at substantially lower wages. This may be because their skills are specific to the old jobs; perhaps they had made investments in human capital whose asset value has been reduced or destroyed by the change. We may think that this is a legitimate case for compensation, although we should be aware of the trade-off between equity of outcomes and incentives for investment. The other possibility is that union monopoly wage premia in the old industry do not obtain in the new one. Our attitude toward such losses will depend on the view we take of the role of unions. In this case there is also the loss of real national income pointed out by Krugman (1984). The union monopoly keeps the level of activity in that industry at a suboptimally low level; any further reduction increases the social cost of the distortion. But again import restriction is not the optimal policy.

Second, there will be general effects on wages because of the standard link between the prices of traded goods and the returns to factors, as in the Stolper-Samuelson theorem for the two-good, two-factor case. While there may be legitimate social concern about such distributive effects, it calls for appropriate compensation policy and not a refusal to accept the change.

Third, there may be wage or price stickiness in the economy that gives rise to involuntary unemployment. Once again the appropriate policy is one that addresses the problem of employment as a whole by means of fiscal and monetary policies and not one of creating or preserving jobs in particular sectors. To the extent that U.S. exports are especially skill or technology intensive, export promotion will be a poor employment policy. But protection may have a role if all better policies are unavailable.

Finally, we must be aware of important side effects of policies. If we create jobs in the export sector by promotional policies, the exchange rate will appreciate, and this will hurt import-competing sectors. Protection will similarly hurt the exporting industries; there will also be a negative effect through an increase in the prices of any protected imported goods they use. Studies show that when all such repercussions are taken into account, the net employment effects of trade policies are quite small. Studies of the effects of the GATT Tokyo Round tariff cuts show this clearly (Deardorff and Stern, 1983).

My conclusion is that employment is also a poor secondary or proxy criterion. In view of these findings, I shall conduct the economic evaluation of U.S. policy responses in terms of the primary criteria of aggregate real income and its distribution.

6.3.4 Noneconomic Criteria

Trade policies of other countries are asserted to harm many noneconomic interests of the United States, and national security is clearly the predominant one. I shall therefore confine my discussion to it. The problem is to understand what it comprises and how foreign governments' trade policies affect it.

Broadly, people seem to mean by national economic security the ability to sustain the production of materials of defense or offense in a situation of war and the consumption of essential goods in a civilian or military emergency. This calls for enough productive capacity in place, the ability to install it quickly, or sufficient inventories. This is best achieved by subsidies that maintain output levels above the requirements of normal times or encourage the use of more flexible techniques of production or stockpiling.

How do other countries' trade policies affect U.S. national security? The common perception is that import dependence is harmful to security. Therefore foreign export subsidies that encourage such dependence are bad. They may tempt with low prices for a while, but the nation will have cause to regret such indulgence when an emergency arises.

Our assessment of this view must consider several other points. First, we must ask if the prospect of such an embargo is real. Next, we must assess the cost if an embargo is attempted. Conventional economic wisdom holds that economic sanctions rarely succeed. The incentives of other suppliers to step in, the possibility of adjustments in the affected economy, and the use of stockpiles serve to reduce the effect of the embargo to a minimal, or at least tolerable, level. Recent reexaminations by Hufbauer and Schott (1985) and Cooper in chapter 7 force us to revise this judgment to some extent, but even then the verdict is at best mixed. Third, we must keep in mind the possibility of using the subsidized imports that are available now to build up a stockpile against possible future sanctions.

There is also the problem that the advocates of the national security argument in each instance are usually those whose own interests are clearly tied to the success of that industry. One is therefore suspicious that the real aim of the proponents is their self-interest and that national security is being invoked to hide this fact. The well-known English mathematician G. H. Hardy suggested a test that applies to this situation: "If the Archbishop of Canterbury says he believes in God, that's all in the way of business, but if he says he doesn't, one can take it he means what he says." [4] Most instances of the national security argument in practice fail this test. Thus when the president of the National Machine Tool Builders' Association asserts that "America is the defender of the industrial West and machine tools are the foundation of our industrial defense preparedness," one is entitled to a suspicion that the claim is all in the way of business, [5] I shall consider possible effects of other countries' policies and of U.S. responses on U.S. national security but with some caution.

This has been a lengthy discussion, but I hope it is justified by the complexity of the subject and the depth of common misperceptions of it. Other countries' trade policies affect the United States in different ways, the important considerations being whether the policies restrict or promote trade, whether the United States imports or exports the good in question, and whether the industry in question is perfectly or imperfectly competitive. Our judgment of the desirability or otherwise of the effect depends on our concerns for the real national income, its distribution, and other aspects such as national security. Our responses can be ones of retaliatory or accommodating trade policies, other domestic policies such as compensation of losers, or even a passive acceptance of the change. These possibilities must be kept in mind as we turn to an examination of the principles governing response.

6.4 Nature and Efficacy of U.S. Response

The conventional sense of response is that of reaction after others' policy actions have taken place. I argued that a broader interpretation is necessary to encompass precautionary actions undertaken in anticipation of others' policies and strategic moves like threats and promises intended to alter their future choices. In this section I shall examine the requirements and the characteristics of such policies, but it seems natural to begin with a brief review of conventional responses.

6.4.1 Reactive Policies

Many of these were already mentioned in the discussion of criteria, and it remains only to look at them from a different angle. In most instances a change in another country's trade policy changes the optimum values of our own policy instruments. We can therefore construct a policy reaction function, linking our policy to theirs. In a given context such a function will differ according to our objectives.

First consider foreigners' export promotion to the U.S. market in a perfectly competitive industry. If we are concerned only with U.S. aggregate real income, then we should respond by thanking them and inviting even larger subsidies. If our primary concern is to avoid losses in U.S. import-competing industries, then the trade response depends on the available domestic instruments of redistribution. In the complete absence of such tools, the United States will have no option but to countervail the subsidy fully. If it can use transfers or indirect taxes, it can compensate the losers while continuing to enjoy the benefits of the improvement in its terms of trade.

If the industry is imperfectly competitive and foreign export subsidies are shifting profit to them, then the U.S. concern for aggregate real national income will dictate some countervailing response to balance the loss of profit and the gain in consumer surplus. If the demand curve is linear and the competition is Cournot, then exactly half of the subsidy should be offset by a countervailing duty (Dixit, 1984). I have subsequently calculated that the offset fraction is smaller for isoelastic demand and with more competitive conduct.

Once again the economic effects on the United States are the same whether the foreign firms are being subsidized by their governments or have a genuine cost advantage. U.S. firms express special concern about foreign subsidies but only because they hope to cash in on the public's perception of fairness, not because of any difference to them or to the rest of our economy. If they thought the public was receptive to complaints about genuine foreign cost advantage, they would be bringing such complaints too. To some extent the escape clause (section 201) does just that, but a stricter standard of damage is required to qualify for relief.

Similar policy interactions will arise if U.S. exports compete with foreign exports in a third market. But it is not possible to say in general whether the U.S. subsidy should increase if that of the foreigners does. That depends on the market conduct and the degree of substitutability between the two countries' products.

If two countries are engaged in such a war of mutual subsidies, they will find themselves in a Prisoners' Dilemma and will have a common incentive to get out of it. The same situation will arise if their trading relation is one of bilateral monopoly, and each one seeking improved terms of trade means that both restrict trade. The possibility of successful resolution of such conflicts is considered later.

There are some other policies that are commonly seen as harming the United States but may actually call for a passive response. One is an import quota against the United States, which may help it by facilitating its exercise of monopoly power. Another example is the promotion of some kinds of R&D in foreign countries. The common fear is that it is immensely harmful to the United States to fall behind the frontier of technology in any field. If the R&D has international spillovers, however, then U.S. aggregate interest may be best served by being free riders on the others' efforts. They have benefited in the past from U.S. research in just this way. But such a policy may hurt particular sectors of the U.S. economy, and the question becomes one of U.S. distributive criteria and policies.

6.4.2 Precautionary Policies

It may be neither necessary nor desirable to wait for another country to act before responding. We can often make a rational forecast of what they are likely to do and take appropriate measures in advance. In this part I shall consider some such anticipatory policies.

Disruptions of trade are the commonest foreign country policies calling for such a response. Restrictions on goods the United States exports or embargoes on goods it imports can cause it economic harm. The cost is greater if it in the meantime has made sunk investments based on an assumption that the trade relationship would continue. Such commitments make the economy inflexible. The resources sunk into the export sector have lower value in use elsewhere. The consumers or downstream producers who come to rely on the imports find it very costly to do without them. The appropriate response of an economy faced with such a prospect is to remain more flexible: use furnaces that can switch from oil to gas or vice-versa, cultivate a more diverse clientele for exports, maintain other sources of supply (including stockpiles), and so forth. Whether this response requires policy measures is a separate question.

The private sector has some of the same motives for maintaining flexibility and can forecast the same prospects to some extent. They can take many of the necessary actions through the usual market channels. Consumers will pay more for dual-fuel furnaces, traders will see profit in stockpiling, and so on. Policy measures are needed to further this process only to the extent that the private sector's expectations are overly sanguine and there are costs to the nation not already included in those borne by the private sector. Although both possibilities exist, we should be cautious about relying on the superior judgment of the policymakers about trade disruption risks and on the frequent assertions of special dangers to national security. Both can be masks for private interests.

There is also the problem of judging other countries' motives when we try to forecast their policies. Should we assume that they will do only what is in their rational interest, or should we expect the worst? There are difficulties with both approaches. We may not know what the foreigners' rational interest is; figuring out our own is hard enough. Their attitudes or governments may change. On the other hand, preparing for the worst entails a great deal of expenditure that will most likely prove unnecessary. We must balance these possibilities and their costs when designing the best precautionary policy.

Some assumptions about other countries' policies are particularly questionable. Consider an example analyzed by Bhagwati and Srinivasan (1976). If the probability P of a future embargo increases with the level of U.S. current imports M, then the marginal unit of imports carries a cost over and above the price the United States pays for it. This cost equals $R \cdot dP/dM$, where R is the present value of the loss of real national income the United States suffers in the event of an embargo, and dP/dM is the increase in the probability of its occurrence. If the private sector does not internalize this cost in their decision to import, then a tariff of this amount will increase their private cost to the true social level. The problem is that it is not at all clear why P should depend on M in this way. The foreigners' decision to impose an embargo will be made in the light of its costs and benefits to them. U.S. imports are their exports, so a greater quantity may mean a greater cost of the disruption to them. The benefits consist of some concessions they hope to extract, and the prospect of success depends on U.S. vulnerability. But that is not necessarily or systematically linked to U.S. imports. It may be an increasing function of U.S. consumption or a decreasing function of U.S. production. In such cases a consumption tax or a production subsidy is the appropriate policy to reduce vulnerability. If the product in question is an exhaustible natural resource, then current imports may make the United States less vulnerable by allowing it to leave more of its own stocks in the ground against future contingencies. The overall conclusion is that self-sufficiency is not necessarily the best route to flexibility and trade restrictions are not always the right policy when we face the possibility of trade disruption.

This last discussion has introduced a new consideration: the effect U.S. anticipatory policies can have on other countries' future actions. U.S. systematic use of such leverage constitutes strategic use of its policy, in the sense of the term in the theory of games of strategy.

6.4.3 Strategic Policies

The seminal and insightful work of Schelling (1960, 1965) has given a good working definition of strategic behavior: "concerned with influencing the choices that another party will make, and doing it by influencing his expectations of how we will behave [in response]" (Schelling 1960, p. 13). The United States is clearly important enough in world trade to have scope for such actions, and there are many calls for it to do so: demands for aggressive reciprocity from home and for leadership to preserve the liberal trading order internationally. I shall begin by reviewing some general principles governing the use of such strategies and then consider U.S. trade policy from this angle. In addition to Schelling's work, I shall rely on the study of negotiations by Raiffa (1982) and that of cooperation by Axelrod (1983). I have also benefited from Richardson's (1985) analysis of such tactics in U.S. trade policy.

Schelling identifies three basic kinds of strategic moves: commitments, threats, and promises. A commitment is an unconditional, irreversible prior policy choice. A free trade clause in the Constitution would be an example; so

would an undertaking to provide interest-free export credits. Once we have
made such a choice, the foreigners' policies must be made in the light of ours,
but they do not have to take into account any further repercussions on our
actions. By contrast, threats and promises are prior choices of contingent
policy rules. The rules themselves are irreversible, but the actual actions they
dictate depend on what other countries do in the meantime. A countervailing
duty (CVD) code, or an aggressive reciprocity law, are examples of threats; a
formula for reciprocal tariff cutting is an example of a promise. Threats are
further divided into deterrent and compellent ones. The CVD is of the former
kind; its purpose is not to collect revenue but to prevent foreigners from
subsidizing their exports. Aggressive reciprocity is for compellence; we
threaten damaging actions unless others open their markets. With both threats
and promises, but especially with the latter, there is a further difference
between unilateral and mutual use. Sometimes it suffices for just one country
to use the policy; at other times, such as Prisoners' Dilemma situations, both or
all countries must participate to sustain the desired outcome.

If the action we commit ourselves to, or threaten, or promise were the
optimal response to the other country's action after the fact, there would be no
need for us to do anything in advance. At the most and just to be sure, we
might remind the others of the coming response.[6] Only when such is not the
case do we have to adopt the action or the policy rule in advance. Two
questions arise. First, why might it be advantageous to take a prior action that
is not optimal after the fact? Second, how can it be taken in such a way that the
others believe us?

The answer to the first is that if we can take the action demonstrably and
credibly, it alters the others' expectations and therefore their actions. The
"fact" in "after the fact" itself changes, and this can be beneficial to us. For
example, a deterrent threat, such as retaliation leading to a trade war, may be
too costly to carry out if the occasion arises, but if others see that we are
committed to do so regardless of the cost, they will not take the first steps that
lead to the crisis. The occasion for the trade war will not arise, and the whole
situation will have changed to our benefit. As another example, the promise of
reciprocal tariff concessions may be costly for us to fulfill once their concession has been received. But it would not have been forthcoming had our
promise not been credible, and the whole package of concessions may be
better for us than the status quo.

The second question is trickier. The others would need assurance that we
would not renege on our promises. Nor would they fear our threats if they
know that we had the freedom to back down if the matter were put to the test.

They would not consider our commitments binding if they believed we had avenues of retreat from them. The problem of achieving credibility is subtle in both theory and practice.

Schelling (1960, chaps. 2, 3, 5; 1965, chaps. 2, 3) considers several devices by which credibility can be maintained and several loopholes through which it can be lost. First, there is the primary importance of moving first to establish the commitment, threat, or promise. If the others can act or have to act while we are still prevaricating, we cannot alter their expectations in the desired way.

Second, embodying the commitment, threat, or promise in a legal form that is hard to reverse, such as a constitutional provision rather than a simple act of Congress, gives it more credibility. Of course, this is a matter of degree.

Third, the use of mandated agents, whose instructions cannot be changed during the process of negotiation, gives irreversibility and therefore credibility to our position. So does an automatic procedure for enforcement, such as the CVD code in current U.S. trade law. By contrast a discretionary procedure such as section 301, or a partly discretionary one like the escape clause, will have less credibility as strategic policies.

Fourth, our commitments, threats, or promises will be more credible if we have a clear motive to maintain a reputation for fulfilling them. That can arise because we will be involved in such interactions repeatedly with the same party or because there are similar relationships with others who would know of our actions in this one. Tit-for-tat strategies are ways of sustaining the former kind of reputation; the MFN principle is an example of the latter.

Fifth, with threats and promises, it is very important to be precise about the actions by others that would constitute a breach or a fulfillment of our stipulations, calling for our response. Otherwise our deterrent threats will be whittled away by small encroachments on the zone of ambiguity; Schelling calls these salami tactics. Similarly compellence will be forthcoming only in minimal amounts, and we will be asked to deliver on our promises in return for minimal performance by others. The problem is that we often find it desirable to leave some ambiguity to deal with genuinely unforeseen circumstances. This must be traded off against the others' exploitation of such vagueness.

Sixth, there is another kind of vagueness that may be actually desirable. This leaves some uncertainty in our response, even when the circumstances in which some response will be forthcoming are precise. This must not be confused with genuine ex post freedom of action. We must be committed in advance, but we can be committed to letting things get somewhat out of control, so that not even we know how harmful the response will be. Schelling calls this brinkmanship. It can be helpful when an extremely damaging response is too severe to be credible. Leaving it to chance is one way of scaling down its size and thereby making it more credible.

Finally, if it is not in our rational ex post interest to carry out the threat or the promise, we can achieve credibility if we can get the other party to believe that our response will be irrational. The adversary knows this, and our assertions of our own irrationality will not be readily believed. We could achieve a similar end by handing over the power of fulfillment of the response to someone whose interests are genuinely inclined that way, but then there is the problem of ensuring that he does not take the action on his own initiative when it is uncalled for.

Armed with these ideas, we can examine some strategic polices the United States could pursue as an advance response to other countries' trade policies. I shall follow Schelling's classification.

Deterrent Threats

The kinds of actions by others that the United States would want to deter depend on its objective. If this is to maximize real national income and the industry is perfectly competitive, then it would want to deter actions that worsen its terms of trade: closing of their markets when they import a good and the United States exports it, as in the case of Japan and computers; exercise of monopoly power over a good they export and the United States imports, as with OPEC and crude petroleum; and subsidizing their exports when they compete with those of the United States in a third market, as in the case of the EEC and surpluses of agricultural products. As usual, in all of these cases, the United States is not concerned with why they might be doing any of these things, only with how the actions would affect U.S. real national income.

If the industry is imperfectly competitive and allows pure profit, then the United States wants them to refrain from policies that would shift some profit from it to them. This might include subsidizing the variable costs of a Cournot competitor; automobiles might be a plausible instance. The United States would also want to deter their promotion of the entry of a new firm or product into such an industry. The attitude of the United States to the emergence of Airbus is a case in point, and this was the example that suggested the theory developed in Dixit and Kyle (1985).

If U.S. concern is with national security, it would want to deter other countries from imposing any embargoes on it. The basic strategy for deterrence is the threat. In principle, this can be anything that would hurt the other party so much that they find it better to accede to the U.S. demand. The threatened action does not have to be confined to trade policy or even to economic policy. Thus a U.S. threat of abandoning its defense commitment to

Europe or Japan might achieve economic aims. In practice ethics and credibility demand a closer link between the threat and the action to be deterred. In fact it is largely the perceived impropriety of an unrelated response that makes the adversary think that it will never be used and so removes its credibility.

Thus practical threats involve responses such as a reciprocal denial of market access or the implementation of matching subsidies. We now have two problems: How do we ensure that the threats are strong enough to achieve the deterrent effect? and Will the other countries regard them as credible?

We know that the response has to be sufficiently harmful to the other country. In the case of reciprocal denial of market access, for example, the other country has to be sufficiently dependent on that component of trade to be seriously hurt by its cessation. If the United States wants to ensure that the Japanese do not close their market to U.S. computers, it has to threaten the closure of the U.S. market to Japanese cars, VCRs, or enough of these products together to cause Japan more harm than the benefit they expect from their restrictive policy on computers.

This is a tricky calculation. The United States has to know the objectives of Japanese trade policy, and in this case it might mean knowing the relative political strengths of the automobile and VCR exporters on the one hand, and the budding computer firms on the other, guessing the importance the Japanese government attaches to its vision of future industrial development and similar strategies. If the United States gets the calculation wrong, it will fail to achieve deterrence and will have the bad choice between backing down and losing its reputation or going through with the response and suffering the economic damage to consumers in the form of the higher prices of the restricted goods.

There is also a trade-off. A stong threat that hurts them a lot typically hurts the United States a lot too. It is true that a successful threat never has to be carried out, so the hurt to the United States should not be a relevant consideration. But unforeseen circumstances or errors can occur, and the threat can go off when it should not. Because of this, the United States will be cautious in committing itself to extreme threats. The adversaries know this. Therefore threats that are large enough to be sure deterrents are also likely to be less credible.

The question of credibility is of central importance in the use of threats. Therefore we must examine how the United States fares in this regard. That is most easily done by going down the earlier list of the desiderata for credibility. The picture that emerges is not encouraging. In most respects, the United States is poorly situated for the successful strategic use of threats.

1. Speed. The legislative and administrative machinery in the United States moves very slowly compared to that in many trading partners. To give an extreme example, in the United Kingdom the annual budget is presented to the Parliament and passed in a single afternoon; in the United States the process goes on for months. Proposed legislation undergoes lengthy scrutiny in congressional committees, with hearings at which numerous affected parties are represented. The administrative procedures of trade policy are similarly lengthy and take months to resolve. An explanation for this can be found in the great importance attached to due process in a generalized sense. There is much to be said for such openness and safeguards in decision making, but they hinder the conduct of strategic policy where it is of the essence to be the first to stake out a position. An exception occurs in the U.S. practice whereby the Congress mandates the administration to participate in multilateral trade negotiations under strictly defined limits. Properly used, this device can secure us a first mover's advantage in the negotiations.

2. Irreversibility. The recent history of U.S. conduct of trade policy, and of economic policy more generally, is one of frequent amendments of laws and of administrative reorganization. There were major changes in trade laws and their administration in 1974 and 1979; another change has been mooted in recent years. Tax laws have reversed themselves from one year to the next. It is difficult to detect any underlying principle or common purpose in most such changes. Rather each new policy departure is a response to the problem of the moment, whether it is inflation, job losses, or oil price rises. It is possible to argue in favor of such flexibility or pragmatism on other grounds, but in the area of strategic behavior, it is essential to make irreversible commitments to influence others' expectations. The general U.S. record makes it difficult for the country to convince others that its actions are indeed irreversible in the instance at issue.

3. Automaticity. Here too the record shows too much ex post discretion. The United States does provide for automatic responses in many circumstances. But when the event actually arrives, it frequently bypasses the stipulated procedure. The provisions of the escape clause have been circumvented in this way and discretionary VERs negotiated instead, notwithstanding an unfavorable decision on automobiles in 1981 and a favorable one on steel in 1984. Firms have increasingly resorted to the fully discretionary section 301, and although there are very few instances of direct action under this heading, some of these petitions have led to indirect, agreed-upon protection. On the other side of the coin the antidumping and countervailing duty provisions of the Trade Act of 1979 have reduced the exercise of discretion in these areas. (For more detailed discussion of these issues, see Baldwin, 1984.)

4. Reputation. The most important requisite for the development and maintenance of a reputation is a long time horizon. The U.S. political process seems to produce just the opposite. The Congress, and even the executive, are often subjected to immediate political pressures and are therefore ruled by very short-run considerations. This is not a problem unique to the United States; it is endemic to most other democracies too. Its most extreme manifestation was the dictum of former British Prime Minister Harold Wilson: "A week is a long time in politics."

5. Precision. Trade policy is only a part of economic policy, which in turn is only a part of domestic and foreign policies as a whole. Each issue of trade policy involves considerations of these other angles, which introduce conflicting objectives. Therefore it becomes difficult to maintain precise standards of transgression that will trigger threats. An example from a related area is the Hickenlooper amendment, which provides for a cutoff of U.S. aid to any country that expropriates U.S. investments. For humanitarian reasons as well as the requirements of foreign policy, this provision is more honored in the breach than the observance (see Dunn, 1983, p. 154; Wong, 1985, pp. 49, 57). Similar indecision and conflict will arise in any circumstance that calls for economic reprisals against political allies, and any of U.S. trade rivals are geopolitical allies. Once again good arguments can be deployed in the defense of such multidimensionality of policy, but once again, it makes the conduct of strategic trade policy difficult. We cannot communicate the precise limits of our tolerance to other countries, and they can take advantage of this vagueness.

6. Brinkmanship and irrationality. Here at last we have two respects in which the United States is well placed to achieve credibility. In its threats the executive branch can practice brinkmanship, or argue irrationality, by saying, "If we do not succeed reasonably well, then the initiative will pass to the Congress. There is no telling what they will do, but it is sure to be a lot worse for you." Such tactics are used in practice, but the skill with which they are executed is a matter for doubt. According to Schelling, brinkmanship is the use of controlled risk. The device suggested above can introduce risk; it is not clear that we can control it within effective and tolerable limits.

To sum up, it appears that on balance the United States will not be able to use deterrent threats very effectively. Richardson (1986) has also noted many similar problems in the U.S. trade policy institutions.

One further aspect of deterrent threats is worth pointing out. The desirability and the efficacy of such threats to the United States depends not only on the outcome that another country is trying to achieve and the United States is trying to deter but also on the policies at their disposal. This is illustrated in

Dixit and Kyle's (1985) stylized model of the game where the EEC tries to promote the entry of Airbus into the medium-range commercial jet aircraft market, and the United States tries to deter it. Consider a case where the entry cost is so large that Airbus cannot be profitable unless it has a protected home market and access to the U.S. market. Suppose the EEC is contemplating closing its market to Boeing in its attempt to promote Airbus's entry. The United States can deter this by threatening to close its market to Airbus should it enter the industry. With access to the U.S. market no longer available, it is pointless for the EEC to provide protection alone. The United States can gain from this strategy because Boeing then makes monopoly profit in the European market. Now suppose the EEC has available the additional instrument of subsidizing Airbus's entry cost. It no longer has to rely on access to the U.S. market, and the U.S. threat is ineffective. Dixit and Kyle find that threats of retaliatory protection are generally less powerful against foreigners' subsidies than against protection.

Compellent Threats

The kinds of actions we want to compel from others are to a large extent the opposites of those we want to deter them from taking. From the perspective of U.S. real national income, for example, we want potential customers for U.S. exports to open up their markets if they are now closed. The case of Japanese restrictions on beef and citrus fruit is a good example. From a national security angle, the United States would want other countries to comply with any embargoes it imposes. The Soviet pipeline issue of 1982 is a case in point.

Threats that aim to compel others are even harder to implement than deterrent ones. Schelling (1965, pp. 69–91) examines the conditions for successful compellence. The basic difference is one of initiative. A deterrent threat is passive. We legislate our countervailing duty or matching subsidy or reciprocal market closure provision, and wait. The next move is up to the other country; it decides whether to challenge or to accede. If compellence is to mean anything, we must set a time limit by which it must be forthcoming. If it does not, we have to set our costly punishment in motion. Even more typically compellence has to be achieved by starting to punish the other party and then relaxing if they do what we want. Thus we might try to compel Japan to open up their beef and citrus fruit markets by the end of the year, the threat being that U.S. automobile or VCR market will be closed to them if they do not. More typically we will have to close our market and offer to open it if they open theirs. This is in fact the essence of the policy of aggressive reciprocity that is being proposed.

The greater initiative we have with compellence works against us. Domestic differences of opinion about whether to try to achieve the outcome we seek and the ways in which we do so get a clearer opportunity to arise afresh each time we have to take some action. The compromises struck in these respects make our goal somewhat less precisely defined. All of these things detract from the credibility of our compellent threat and give the adversary more opportunity to exploit its imprecision.

It is possible to view a compellent threat as a change of the status quo followed by a promise. "Give me your money or I'll cut your throat" is not too different from "Here is a knife at your throat; I promise to remove it if you give me your money." In this sense, the credibility of a compellent threat is the credibility of its attendant promise. If we close our market to Japanese automobiles and promise to open it if they let in our beef, they will not readily believe us. The issue is what our automobile industry and the labor unions will do when the time comes to deliver. Will they get used to a protected market and then successfully claim relief under the escape clause? Such doubts will detract from U.S. credibility and make the compellent threat less effective.

The theoretical prediction that compellence is harder to achieve is borne out in practice. The United States has not been very successful in inducing the others to open their markets to its exports. The difficulties it met in negotiations with the Europeans on the Soviet pipeline issue are also contributory evidence.

Promises

Unilateral promises have a place in strategic trade policy. An example occurs in the model of entry promotion and deterrence analyzed by Dixit and Kyle (1985). Suppose the size of the entry cost is such that Airbus will be profitable if it has either a protected European market or access to the U.S. market. Suppose the ex post U.S. interest would be best served by closing its market. Now the EEC has an incentive to close its own market to induce profitable entry. If the United States can credibly promise to keep its market open, the EEC does not need to close its. When entry occurs with both markets open, each firm gets duopoly profits from both markets, and each country's consumers enjoy lower prices and higher surpluses. This effect can be large enough to make both countries prefer this outcome to that where both market are closed. The U.S. promise has dissuaded the EEC from pursuing a mutually harmful policy of protectionist entry promotion.

A much more common situation is that where credible promises must be made by both sides if a mutually beneficial cooperation is to be sustained. In fact it is possible to view the GATT as an institution collecting such promises on a multilateral basis. The recent decline of the authority of GATT can be seen as a gradual loss of credibility of these promises or a circumvention of them to exploit the loopholes and ambiguities in their terms.

In most such cases the underlying strategic interaction is of the Prisoners' Dilemma type. All participants are better off when they all adhere to the agreement than when none do. But for each separately, cheating is the preferred strategy, no matter what the others do. If others adhere to the agreement, I gain by cheating; if they do not, I would be a fool to stay honest. Problems of this kind arise in tariff negotiations where adherence consists of free trade, and cheating means using trade restrictions to exploit one's own monopoly power or protect one's powerful special interests. Cheating usually takes the form of circumventing the agreement by using forms of protection not explicitly covered by it—for example, using nontariff barriers, VERs, or bureaucratic procedures to get around tariff agreements. Similar problems arise in subsidy wars where countries promote exports to shift profits in imperfectly competitive industries or to satisfy mercantilist sentiments or domestic exporting interests. Again the method of cheating is to use indirect subsidies, tax breaks, and similar means not explicitly ruled out by the agreement.

It has long been known that cooperation can be sustained in such an interaction if it occurs on an ongoing basis and if the parties do not discount future returns too heavily relative to the present ones (Luce and Raiffa, 1957, p. 102). The general idea is that once a cooperative arrangement gets going, each party will test whether the short-run profits from cheating are worth the long-run losses from the collapse of mutual trust. Further advances in game theory have made this idea rigorous. In an infinitely repeated Prisoners' Dilemma with a sufficiently low discount rate, tacit coordination can be sustained as a noncoordinated (Nash) equilibrium. If each party follows the strategy "adhere to the agreement so long as the other does, but if the other cheats, then revert to cheating thereafter," then the pair of strategies is in mutual equilibrium. Here we have a combination of a threat and a promise. If, by some mistake, an episode of cheating were to occur, then the fulfillment of the threats implicit in the strategies constitutes an equilibrium from that point on. Therefore the threats are credible. The promises are credible because, given the threats, an attempt at cheating creates sufficient future losses to be not worthwhile. The equilibrium of the whole repeated game is said to be perfect.

The theory has some hidden difficulties, however. The perfect equilibrium is far from unique in two senses. First, several other outcomes, all less cooperative, can also arise as perfect equilibria with different strategy pairs.

Second, each outcome can be supported by different strategies (that is, embodying different threats). Therefore the mutual understanding that keeps the process going might have quite weak foundations.

In view of these problems there is much to be said for a simple rule of thumb that could be common knowledge to the parties, or be a "focal point" in Schelling's terminology. Therefore Axelrod's (1983) finding that the simple strategy of tit for tat, which returns what the other party did in the previous round, has very good cooperative properties is an extremely interesting one. In fact, tit for tat is not free from difficulties. Although it is an equilibrium of an infinitely repeated Prisoners' Dilemma with a sufficiently low discount rate if both players follow tit for tat, its perfection is questionable, however, the simplicity and uniqueness of tit for tat constitute powerful opposing arguments.

It is also important to note that Axelrod attaches significance to the underlying properties of tit for tat rather than to the specifics of one round of retaliation for one round of cheating. These properties are niceness (not being the first to cheat), forgiveness (not holding a grudge about the other's cheating for too long), clarity (precision and simplicity of circumstances under which retaliation would be forthcoming), and provocability (certainty of retaliation). These make eminent good sense and are likely to remain as attributes of any strategy conducive to sustained cooperation.

Let us examine the problem of avoiding tariff wars or subsidy wars from this point of view. GATT attempts to ensure the former, and recent agreements by exporting countries to reduce the subsidy element in their credit provisions is a case in point for the latter. How does the United States fare in its ability to follow a cooperative strategy? It seems that it has traditionally scored very well in the niceness category, but recent actions like the VERs on Japanese automobiles in 1981 and on various other countries' steel in 1984–1985 should count as black marks. The United States has done fairly well in the forgiveness category for reasons that often have to do with more general issues of foreign policy. The record on provocability is mixed and that on clarity abysmal. The problem once again is that of the mixture of pressures and interests that enter into policymaking at each stage. There is a lot of doubt as to which one will prevail at any one point. U.S. threats and promises accordingly lack clarity and certainty and therefore credibility.

My judgment, however, is that the best prospects for improvement in the conduct of U.S. trade policy are to be found in this sphere of making credible promises to avoid Prisoners' Dilemmas. The United States already scores well on two of the necessary properties. Better provocability should be easy to achieve in the climate of opinion that prevails now. Only clarity is problematic; this is where the efforts of policy design should be concentrated.

This review of strategic behavior and its role in the context of trade policy has shown several places where the United States could beneficially use such strategic advance responses to alter other countries' trade policies. However, the requirements for successful deployment of these strategies led me to argue that the United States would not be able to do so in practice. If the United States is to change this situation, it has to change its conduct of trade policy, and perhaps of economic policy more generally, in quite substantial ways. Policy mechanisms should be based on firmer and clearer rules and allow less discretion after the fact. There should be less scope for continuous political input or pressure from affected interests. And, if possible, there should be greater unity of purpose and better agreed objectives. Some of these may be impossible to achieve. Others may be undesirable to undertake for other reasons. But without them, strategic responses in U.S. trade policy must remain matters for theoretical speculation.

7.5 Concluding Remarks

I was asked to address the question, How should the United States respond to other countries' trade policies? As might be expected from an economist, I have produced a catalog of alternatives instead of a clear answer. A few items from that list are worth reiteration here.

We saw that many of the policies that produce complaints—promotion of exports to U.S. markets—are actually beneficial to the U.S. economy as a whole, although they hurt those whose incomes depend on import-competing production. The proper response, if any, is compensation for the losers. The rest of us should be particularly wary of the advocacy of self-interest under the guise of national security in this context.

There are instances when other countries' policies harm the United States. Promotion of exports when they compete with our own exports, especially in imperfectly competitive industries, and closing of their markets to our exports, are prominent examples. The United States can respond to such practices by appropriate strategic actions like deterrent or compellent threats. But policy institutions are ill equipped for the successful exercise of such power.

The United States has a somewhat better record of success in cooperating with other countries to maintain a broadly liberal trading order, but this record is becoming increasingly tarnished, and the order is under increasing pressure. These are unfortunate developments for the long-run interests of all countries. We should strive to restore effective cooperation.

Notes

I am grateful to Peter Kenen for his thorough and valuable comments on an earlier draft and to Robert Axelrod and Richard Cooper for useful comments and discussions.

1. *Wall Street Journal*, February 12, 1985; *Business Week*, February 18, 1985.

2. A suitable (maybe partial) compensation may give an even higher value of social welfare and so be desirable anyway.

3. Japanese output and exchange rate figures from the *Japan Statistical Yearbook* (1983), and trade figures from the *U.N. Yearbook of International Trade Statistics* (1981).

4. Quoted in Snow (1962, p. 69).

5. *Economic Handbood of the NMTBA*, August 1983, quoted in Collis (1985, p. 2).

6. But if they do not know our value system or criteria, there can be severe difficulties in communicating the information truthfully and convincingly. See Schelling (1960, pp. 115–116).

References

Axelrod, Robert. *The Evolution of Cooperation*. New YorK: Basic Books, 1983.

Baldwin, Robert E., ed. *Recent Issues and Initiatives in U.S. Trade Policy*. Cambridge: National Bureau of Economic Research, 1984.

Bhagwati, Jagdish, and T. N. Srinivasan. "Optimal Trade Policy and Compensation under Endogenous Uncertainty: The Phenomenon of Market Disruption." *Journal of International Economics* 6 (1976): 317–336.

Brander, James A., and Barbara J. Spencer. "Tariff Protection and Imperfect Competition." In Henryk Kierzkowski, ed., *Monopolistic Competition and International Trade*. New York: Oxford University press, 1984.

Brander, James A., and Barbara J. Spencer. "Export Subsidies and International Market Share Rivalry." *Journal of International Economics* 18 (1985): 83–100.

Cline, William R. *"Reciprocity": A New Approach to World Trade Policy?* Washington, D.C.: Institute for International Economics, 1982.

Collis, David. "The Machine Tool Industry and the Impact of Industrial Policy." Paper presented at a conference on International Competition, Harvard University, Kennedy School of Government. March 7–9, 1985.

Crandall, Robert W. "Import Quotas and the Automobile Industry: The Costs of Protectionism." *Brookings Review* (Summer (1984): 8–16).

Deardorff, Alan V., and Robert M. Stern. "Economic Effects of the Tokyo Round." *Southern Economic Journal* 49 (1983): 605–624.

Diewert, W. Erwin, A. H. Turunen, and Alan D. Woodland. "Productivity and Pareto Improving Changes in Taxes and Tariffs." Dicussion Paper 84–06. University of British Columbia, 1984.

Dixit, Avinash. "International Trade Policy for Oligopolistic Industries." *Economic Journal*, supplement 94 (1984): 1–16.

Dixit, Avinash. "On Pareto-Beneficial Redistributions of Aggregate Economic Gains." Working paper, 1985a.

Dixit, Avinash. "Trade Policy: An Agenda for Research." In *Strategic Trade Policy and the New International Economics*, ed. Paul Krugman. Cambridge: MIT Press, 1986.

Dixit, Avinash, and Albert Kyle. "The Use of Protection and Subsidies for Entry Promotion and Deterrence." *American Economic Review* 75 (1985): 139–152.

Dixit, Avinash, and Victor Norman. "Trade Gains without Lump-Sum Compensation." Discussion Paper, no. 75. Woodrow Wilson School, Princeton University, 1984.

Dunn, John. "Country Risk: Social and Cultural Aspects." In Richard J. Herring, ed., *Managing International Risk*. New York: Cambridge University Press, 1983.

Eaton, Jonathan and Gene M. Grossman. "Optimal Trade and Industrial Policy under Oligopoly." Discussion Paper, no. 59. Woodrow wilson School, Princeton University, 1983.

Friedman, Milton. *Capitalism and Freedom*. Chicago: University of Chicago Press, 1962.

Grossman, Gene M. "The Employment and Wage Effects of Import Competition in the United States." Working Paper, no. 1041. National Bureau of Economic Research, 1983.

Grossman, Gene M., and J. David Richardson. "Strategic U.S. Trade Policy: A Survey of Issues and Early Analysis." Princeton University, International Finance Section, Special Paper, no. 15. Princeton: Princeton University Press, 1985.

Hufbauer, Gary C., and Jeffrey J. Schott. *Economic Sanctions Reconsidered: History and Current Policy*. Cambridge: MIT Press, 1985.

Krishna, Kala. "Trade Restrictions as Facilitating Practices." Discussion Paper, no. 1119. Harvard Institute of Economic Research, 1984.

Krugman, Paul R. "Targeted Industrial Policies: Theory and Evidence." In *Industrial Change and Public Policy*. Kansas City: Federal Reserve Bank of Kansas City, 1983.

Krugman, Paul R. "The U.S. Response to Foreign Industrial Targeting." *Brookings Papers on Economic Activity* 2 (1984): 77–121.

Luce, R, Duncan, and Howard Raiffa. *Games and Decisions*. New York: John Wiley and Sons, 1957.

Magaziner, Ira C., and Robert B. Reich. *Minding America's Business*. New York: Random House, 1982.

Raiffa, Howard. *The Art and Science of Negotiation*. Cambridge: Harvard University Press, 1982.

Ramsey, Frank. *Foundations of Mathematics*. London: Routledge and Kegan Paul, 1931.

Richardson, J. David. "The New Political Economy of Trade Policy." In *Strategic Trade Policy and the New International Economics*, ed. Paul Krugman. Cambridge: MIT Press, 1986.

Schelling, Thomas C. *The Strategy of Conflict*. Cambridge: Harvard University Press, 1960.

Schelling, Thomas C. *Arms and Influence*. New Haven: Yale University Press, 1965.

Snow, C. P. *The Affair*. London: Penguin, 1962.

U.S. Congress. House of Representatives. Committee on Ways and Means. *Hearings on Reciprocal Trade and Market Access Legislation*. Committee Serial, no. 97–77. Washington, D.C.: Government Printing Office, 1983a.

U.S. Congress. House of Representatives. Committee on Energy and Commerce. *Hearings on General Trade Policy*. Committee Serial, no. 98–55. Washington, D.C.: Government Printing Office, 1983b.

Wong, Clarence. "Extra-Legal Protection Strategies against Expropriation of Multinational Corporations' Investments in the Third World." Senior thesis, Princeton University, 1985.

Comment on "How Should the United States Respond to Other Countries' Trade Policies?"

Robert Axelrod

Dixit provides an excellent introduction to the issues of how the United States should respond to the trade policies of other countries. He starts with a discussion of how the main issues should be formulated and then gives a fine analysis of how to judge the effects of other countries' policies. He considers not only efficiency effects but also distributional conflicts within the U.S. economy, as well as noneconomic criteria including national security. Finally, he provides much useful advice on the nature and efficacy of alternative U.S. responses.

Dixit deals with both the economic and political factors that have to be considered in trade policy. But since his analysis of economic factors is more thorough than his analysis of political factors, I would like to develop some of the political themes more fully in these comments.

Consider the relationship among four roles played by a typical individual. The person might be an employee in some industry that may or may not be strongly affected by international trade; the person might be a stockholder in a firm engaged in international trade; the person is almost certainly a consumer of many products, some of which are commonly imported or exported; and the person is probably a citizen who often votes with due respect for the antici-pated economic consequences of public policy. Thus the typical person can, in principle at least, have an impact on public policy through a reasoned vote that takes into account his or her interests as both producer and consumer.

Public policy can be affected by the perceived interests of both producers and consumers, and everything should work out well. There are, however, two major problems: the political system is biased in the way it aggregates perceived political interests, and much of the public misperceives its own economic interests. Let us consider these problems.

That bias in the political system exists is clearly recognized by Dixit. He points out that there is some reason to think that in the United States the potential losers may have an effective veto over any policy change. Beyond this it is not hard to see that concentrated interests are typically more effectively organized than diffuse interests, and for this reason the interests of producers are given disproportionate weight compared to the interests of consumers.

The other bias is that much of the public misperceives its own economic interests. Dixit points out four erroneous beliefs about the effects of trade policy that are widely held.

1. "It never pays to restrict our exports." In fact, if the United States is a large exporter, the terms of trade argument says that it can gain by using an optimum export tax. Also if it has large, imperfectly competitive firms, restricting exports can help.

2. "In recent years we have been badly hurt by the ever more harmful trade policies of others." Actually the empirical work of Krugman (1984) finds no significant adverse shift in U.S. terms of trade over the recent decades.

3. "Exports create jobs, and imports destroy them." This is an incomplete picture because it looks only at demand for labor and not at the supply of labor.

4. "Import dependence is harmful to our security." Historical evidence suggests that economic embargoes have not been very successful and that in the case of nonrenewable resources (such as oil), the United States might actually be better off importing in peacetime so as to preserve its own limited resources for an emergency.

Since the public plays an important part in determining national policy through its influence on Congress and the president, we need to take seriously these commonly held errors. It seems that there are two complementary explanations for the errors. The obvious one is that the eighteenth-century mercantilist ideas about the virtue of exports and the evil of imports still hold great power. The zero-sum view of the world that these mercantilist ideas represent is easy to grasp and compelling in its simplicity. As Keynes said, practical people are usually the slaves of some defunct economist.

The complementary explanation is that export-oriented themes are fostered by specific sectors of the economy with disproportionate power because of their relative concentration in specific industries. Also anti-import themes are fostered because of the effective concentration of industries that compete with imports. Conversely the diffuse benefits of imports to consumers make less of an impact on the political debate because of the greater difficulty of organizing consumers compared to producers. It is no coincidence that the mass media refer to a "flood of cheap imports" rather than a "cornucopia of cheap imports."

Whatever the reasons for the persistence of mercantilist ideas, the partisans in any political debate find it easier to appeal to widely held beliefs than to fight such beliefs. This tends to reinforce these beliefs by lending them the authority of the respected leaders.

What can be done about the bias in the political system? First, college faculty members should take seriously their own role as public educators so that voters have a clearer perception of their true interests, not only as stockholders and employees but also as consumers. This educational effort should not only be aimed at college students but also at writers of high school textbooks, journalists, and potential candidates for public office. Second, in doing quantitative analysis of the effects of specific trade policies, we should not only organize the results by industry but also present the results by states and by congressional districts. These are the units that the political system naturally takes into account. By presenting data in this way, the political process can more readily take account of the interests of consumers as well as producers.

Now let me turn to the discussion of strategic actions in international trade policy. Dixit's theme here is that the United States can respond to others' policies with appropriate strategic actions like deterrent or compellent threats but that policy institutions are ill equipped for the successful exercise of such power. I am pleased that he finds my work on the evolution of cooperation to be useful and that he agrees that any strategy conducive to sustained cooperation should be nice (not the first to defect), provocable, forgiving, and clear.

Applying these ideas to international trade policy, he finds that the United States has done fairly well on forgiveness but has had a mixed record on provocability and an abysmal performance on clarity. In short, the United States is hard to predict. This means that its threats and promises lack credibility, making it difficult for others effectively to adapt their actions in ways that the United States would prefer. I share most of his pessimism about improvements in the political system that would allow policy mechanisms to be based on firmer and clearer rules, with less discretion after the fact. The reason is that there will always be great scope for political input from affected groups and that the United States will always have trouble achieving a unity of purpose and better fully agreed objectives.

To promote clarity, I suggest that the United States pay greater attention to the updating of bilateral and multilateral international arrangements that would effectively precommit it to those contingent strategies that it wants to pursue anyway. GATT has been a substantial help in this regard, especially by virtue of its provisions for permitting constrained retaliation against violations of its agreements on tariffs. The United States needs to go further in developing the international institutions and norms that would allow comparable constrained self-help enforcement mechanisms for agreed-upon reductions in nontariff barriers (see Axelrod and Keohane, 1985).

Note

For their support, I thank the National Science Foundation and the Harry Frank Guggenheim Foundation.

References

Axelrod, Robert, and Robert Keohane. "Achieving Cooperation Under Anarchy: Strategies and Institutions." *World Politics* 38 (1985): 226–254.

Krugman, Paul R. "The U.S. Response to Foreign Industrial Targeting." *Brookings Papers on Economic Activity* 2 (1984): 77–121.

Comment on "How Should the United States Respond to Other Countries' Trade Policies?"

J. David Richardson

Dixit's chapter suggests to me two fruitful directions for future research, two practical conclusions about the political economy of U.S. trade policy, and one important perspective on conflicting rationales for reactive trade policy.

One direction for research is to refine the concept of equilibrium in strategic environments (those with small numbers of self-consciously interdependent agents). Refinements might include the identification of short and long runs, temporary and indefinite equilibria, and natural and artificial barriers to entry. Dixit suspects, for example, that the case for trade policy as a profit-shifting device may vanish when one takes account of a prenatal phase for a product that ultimately earns supernormal profits. In the prenatal phase many firms compete with each other in research and development to be one of the few ultimate producers. The winning firms earn supernormal profits over the whole life of the product, but the losers earn subnormal profits, and the industry profit rate thus turns out to be roughly normal. Naive trade policies that aim to preserve or increase the supernormal profits of the winning firms may also increase the losses of the losers by diverting resources into the prenatal R&D competition, having no profit-shifting payoff in the aggregate over firms and phases. Future research should examine Dixit's suspicions more carefully and perhaps identify optimal phase-contingent trade policies for strategic environments.

Along the same lines, future research might usefully identify more than two phases in a product's life cycle. For example, one might define a third phase called senility in which subnormal profits are earned (variable costs perhaps being covered but not fixed costs). Trade policies aimed at optimal profit shifting would seem at first to include import subsidies, or at least the rejection of any added protection from imports. Yet these products are those most likely in reality to pass material injury tests in U.S. trade legislation and hence most likely to receive additional import protection. So there may be a unique profit-shifting loss to many of the most significant U.S. trade barriers that is not captured in traditional calculations of their social cost.

A second direction for future research is to examine trade policy in a setting where there are more than two self-consciously interdependent rivals. Most research on reactive or strategic trade policy has assumed only two active agents—either two imperfectly competitive firms or two governments. Expanding the focus to three agents would have more than abstract interest if many of the undesirable side effects of reactive trade policy could be traced to third-party agents' taking advantage of the two primary agents. For example, Dixit's doubts about strategic discretion in U.S. trade policy would be deepened by third-party predation—any tendency for strategic discretion to encourage resource diversion into lobbying for discretionary favors. In this case seemingly advantageous bargains between two governments might have a costly side effect; third parties might be tempted to pour resources into creating and politically capturing the rents implicit in discretionary strategic trade policy. Advantageous policies in a "spy-versus-spy" world may not always be advantageous in a spy-versus-spy-versus-spy world. As a first step toward accounting for this, researchers might begin conditioning evaluations of U.S. responses to trade policy abroad by structural characteristics of U.S. industry. Ideal U.S. responses to policy thrusts abroad might depend, for example, on whether a U.S. industry is monopolistic, oligopolistic, or competitive and on whether markets for its most essential factors are monopolistic, oligopolistic, or competitive.

One of Dixit's most important practical conclusions for U.S. trade policy in strategic environments is that "mechanisms should be based on firmer and clearer rules and allow less discretion." His principal reason for this conclusion is that it makes U.S. policy responses very clear; it deters the kind of beggar-the-U.S. trade policy abroad encouraged by inscrutable, apparently random U.S. responses. Inscrutable trade policy discretion is thus to be shunned for the same reason as passive U.S. trade policy. Neither provides any clear incentive for foreigners to seek mutually cooperative outcomes with the United States in trade policy initiatives. Foreigners are instead encouraged to do what is best for them alone, taking U.S. response as given, either because it is random (passivity) or because it appears to be so (discretionary inscrutability).

I agree with Dixit's preference for rules-based reactiveness in U.S. trade policy and distrust of discretionary reactiveness. Clarity is not the only reason. Cumbersomeness is another. Discretionary reactiveness fits the structure of U.S. government poorly, especially its checks and balances. This means that the resource cost of implementing effective strategic discretion in U.S. trade policy would be very high. Side effects might also be unfortunate, such as precedents for other U.S. policy administration to become more managerial and less accountable. Strategic discretion would furthermore be subject to third-party predation. In this context one might point with concern to the influential role that the U.S. steel industry itself played in the recently negotiated VRAs and wonder whether predictable enforcement of U.S. trade law on subsidies and dumping would have yielded a better outcome.

Dixit draws a second practical conclusion: a generally cooperative posture for U.S. trade policy is not inconsistent with rules-based reactiveness in strategic environments. Others have expressed the related view that the United States still has too much leadership potential in trade policy to become solely reactive. Yet cooperative initiative certainly becomes more difficult to maintain in the face of the "perceived economic injury ... [and] insult of other countries' ingratitude" that Dixit identifies in the United States.

This suggests to me that cooperative initiative in U.S. trade policy must become more subtle in style and scope than it has traditionally been. With respect to style, there may be merits in a three-phase initiative that we might call seductive responsiveness. Its basic posture is inviting: it invites (cooperative) initiative from a trading partner; it promises in return a warm (cooperative) response. The implied suggestion for U.S. policy is to search out some seductive signals that invite cooperative trade policy initiatives from abroad. (These signals need not concern trade directly; they might instead concern exchange rates, investment, tax treaties, migration, or defense sharing.) Because of the perceptual and political changes Dixit described, the United States today is much more likely to be able to respond cooperatively to cooperative initiatives abroad than to initiate them. Seductive responsiveness as a strategy takes seriously the well-accepted decline in U.S. influence and hegemony. It abandons the postwar tradition that the United States itself should initiate cooperation in trade policy in favor of more subtle (seductive) means toward the same end.

With respect to scope, there may be merits in cooperative initiatives that are minilateral (neither bilateral nor fully multilateral but somewhere in between). The idea is to form mutually advantageous trade policy coalitions with small numbers of like-minded participants—for example, Pacific rim countries. Restricting agreements to small numbers of like-minded participants keeps bargaining costs low, reduces the chance of deadlock or protracted negotiation, and eases the monitoring of adherence to or defection from the agreement. Later, if more combative countries want to join the coalition, let them sue for peace and membership. Minilateral cooperative innovations in trade policy have more than just abstract appeal. They are the historical norm, illustrated in the early history of both the GATT and its codes governing nontariff measures.

A word of perspective is finally in order. Dixit primarily describes optimal trade policy reactions in strategic environments, whose limit in the extreme, as the number of rivals increases, is the familiar perfectly competitive environment. Only in section 6.3.2 on income distribution and compensation does he devote much attention to another environment in which reactive trade policy has a very natural place. That is the uncertain environment—more precisely the environment of missing insurance markets. Trade policies aimed at alleviating injury from imports can be defended as a kind of insurance against policy initiatives abroad that domestic workers and firms cannot understand or forecast very accurately. Import relief is the natural payout of insurance policy benefits to domestic residents in response to adverse policy developments abroad. From this perspective many questions remain unanswered about reactive trade policy. Should import relief be available only against policy shocks abroad—not against policy shocks at home or against any sort of market shock? If private insurance markets are missing because of moral hazard problems, how can trade policy as insurance alleviate moral hazard? By conditional import relief (such as adjustment plans)? If moral hazard cannot be alleviated should trade policy rush in where markets fear to tread? Is funding of trade policy as insurance out of general revenues really the best way? Should there be analogs in import relief policy to deductibles, copayments, and so forth?

Finally it is interesting to note the inherent conflict between insurance and strategic rationales for reactive trade policy. Trade policy as insurance creates perverse profit-shifting effects. By protecting the value of specialized skills and investments in declining industries, it slows the exit of resources from activities with subnormal profits, deterring them from entering activities with normal or above normal profits.

7 Trade Policy as Foreign Policy

Richard N. Cooper

7.1 Introduction

A perusal of the memoirs of those foreign policy decision makers who had considerable knowledge and background in economic afairs, such as Dean Acheson and George Ball, not to mention those who had little economic background, such as George Kennan, Henry Kissinger, and Zbigniew Brzezinski, suggests how little attention has been given by key foreign policy decision makers to economic issues in general, and even less to trade issues. A casual reading of these works leaves the impression that trade issues have had little importance for or influence on the major foreign policy questions of the day. But this would be a quite wrong impression. The economic background, and especially the trade flows that link the diverse national economies, play a key role in setting the stage on which other, often more exciting, actions take place. A smoothly running world economy is a necessary condition to permit other issues to occupy the attention of foreign policymakers. The moment economic issues go badly awry, they push other issues to the side or come to dominate the evolution of apparently noneconomic events. One only has to think of the two major oil shocks of the 1970s or the Latin American debt crisis of the early 1980s as illustrations of this point. A test of effective foreign policy leadership is how aware it is of the importance of underlying economic events to the day-to-day and month-to-month management of foreign policy issues.

The most disastrous single mistake any U.S. president has made in international relations was Herbert Hoover's signing of the Smoot-Hawley Tariff Act into law in June 1930. The sharp increase in U.S. tariffs, the apparent indifference of the U.S. authorities to the implications of their actions for foreigners, and the foreign retaliation that quickly followed, as threatened, helped convert what would have been otherwise a normal economic downturn into a major world depression (Temin, 1976). The sharp decline in foreign trade and economic activity in turn undermined the position of the moderates with respect to the nationalists in Japanese politics and paved the way for the electoral victory of the Nazis in Germany in 1932. Japan promptly invaded China in 1931, and the basis for World War II was laid.

Valuable lessons were learned from the Smoot-Hawley tariff experience by the foreign policy community: the threat of tariff retaliation is not always merely a bluff; tariffs do influence trade flows negatively; a decline in trade can depress national economies; economic depresssion provides fertile ground for politically radical nostrums; and political radicals often seek foreign (military) adventures to distract domestic attention away from their domestic economic failures. The seeds of World War II, in both the Far East and in Europe, were sowed by Hoover's signing of the Smoot-Hawley tariff. Commercial policy and foreign policy do interact, although often not in the ways intended.

We have conventionally associated trade policy with the tariff, or more recently, with nontariff barriers (NTBs) that have a similar motivation: to protect a particular sector of the national economy or even a particular firm from import competition. In this regard trade policy was largely a matter of domestic politics, not of foreign policy, until the last fifty years and the reactions to the Smoot-Hawley tariff. But on reflection trade policy is much broader than tariff policy, and on the broad construction trade policy has been intimately related to foreign policy since before the United States came into being as a state. Indeed trade policy played an important role in bringing the United States into existence, for it was a dispute mainly over tariffs that induced the American colonies to revolt against British rule. There has been a long history of interaction between U.S. trade policy and U.S. foreign policy, but the nature and the thrust of that interaction has altered over time. We can broadly divide U.S. history into three phases: 1765–1820, 1820–1934, and 1934–1985, it being understood that the boundary lines between these periods are somewhat arbitrary, that important changes took place within each period, and that occasional exceptions to the general characterization of each period can be found within each period. Trade policy was an instrument of foreign policy in the first period, aimed at other objectives and in particular at establishing nationhood. In the second period trade policy and in particular the sale of U.S. products abroad was a principal objective of foreign policy, during many decades the leading objective of foreign policy. In the third period commercial policy came to be directed at fostering an economic environment of full employment and growth, conducive to nonturbulent political developments within countries and harmony among countries, although during this period some aspects of trade policy also reverted to its instrumental character, notable in the first period, toward achieving other foreign policy objectives.

7.2 Commercial Policy in the New Nation, 1765–1820

Before independence the American colonists were concerned mainly about their security and about the symbols, status, and dignity of a free people. After independence the new nation was concerned with achieving full recognition and the status of a sovereign nation without suffering indignities at the instigation of others. During this period what we would now call commercial policy was frequently used as an instrument to achieve these objectives. This instrumental use of commercial policy started when the colonists boycotted British goods in 1765 to protest Parliament's passage of the Stamp Act, which levied a small tax on all paper transactions. The Stamp Act was repealed. But the boycott was reintroduced in 1768 to protest the Townshend Acts of 1767, which among other things imposed customs duties on goods entering the colonies. The Massachusetts Bay Colony acted first, with the colonists agreeing not to import any goods from Britain during 1769 other than "salt, coals, fishhooks and lines, hemp, and duck bar lead and shot, wool cards and card wire" (Commager, 1958, p. 68). This boycott was soon followed by other New England towns and New York but not by Philadelphia—the leading city in North America—until late 1769. The effect of the boycott was to reduce British exports to the colonies by over one-half between 1768 and 1769. The Townshend Acts were largely repealed.

Then Britain gave a monopoly on the sale of tea in the colonies to the East India Tea Company and imposed a small duty on tea. The colonists objected in a variety of ways, the most dramatic and colorful of which was the Boston Tea Party of December 1773, when a number of Bostonians dressed as Indians boarded an East India ship and dumped the boxes of tea into Boston harbor. Britain responded to this destructive act by closing that port of Boston and by enacting other "intolerable acts." Emerging solidarity among the colonies led them to protest the closing of the port of Boston and the other acts. Virginia was the first to adopt a nonimportation agreement in August 1774 (adopted the following month by the Continental Congress), which resolved not to import any British goods, including, importantly, goods from the British West Indies, directly or indirectly, except for medicines, after November 1, 1774, and not to export tobacco or any other article after August 1775, unless the grievances were redressed (Commager, 1958, p. 80). The resolutions also stipulated that merchants who did not respect the boycott should be boycotted. As a result British exports to the colonies dropped from about 2.5 million pounds sterling in 1774 to about one-tenth of that in 1775. This political unrest in the colonies also raised doubts about whether the English would be repaid their large financial claims on American planters, put in excess of 2 million pounds.

Recounting the sharp reductions in British exports in 1766 and 1769, London merchants petitioned the British government in January 1775 to back off and remove the grievances. The North administration and King George III had a contrary view, shooting ensued at Lexington and Concord in April 1775, and the colonies sought and won their independence over an issue of trade policy and more particularly over who should determine it.

Trade policy continued to be used for broader political objectives after independence. In 1793 Secretary of State Thomas Jefferson advocated restricting imports of manufactures, overwhelmingly from Britain, as a way of supporting postrevolutionary France in its struggle with England. In fact no action was taken, and the moderate (5 to 15 percent duties) Tariff Act of 1789 was retained (Taussig, 1931, p. 14). Restrictive import policy was used later during the Napoleonic Wars, however. In reaction to British seizures of U.S. ships, including notably the naval vessel *Essex*, and impressment of U.S. seamen, the Congress in response to President Jefferson authorized an embargo on British goods in 1806. The blockade system was extended throughout Europe. Britain's navy blockaded the Continent, and through the Berlin decrees Napoleon declared a blockade of Britain, though he had no navy worthy of enforcing his paper blockade. In December 1807 the United States introduced an embargo on all imported goods. President Jefferson thought this would induce the Europeans to lift their blockades against neutral ships. It was not sustained, however, and in March 1809 the Non-intercourse Act embargoed only British and French goods but permitted removal of the embargo if Britain and France ceased violating the rights of U.S. ships and seamen through their seizures and impressment. The restrictions were removed against France in 1810 and expired at the the end of the year with respect to Britain, but a new act aimed at Britain was passed in March 1811. Britain finally complied by amending its Orders in Council the following June, but by then the War of 1812 had already erupted. British response was delayed by assassination of British Prime Minister Perceval (Commager, 1958, P. 198) and by the five weeks required to transmit information across the Atlantic in square-rigged sailing ships. Commercial policy as an instrument of foreign policy would have succeeded in its aims had it not been for the delays in reacting and getting the reaction known.

7.3 Export Promotion as an Aim of Foreign Policy, 1820–1934

After the end of the European wars and the economic depression that followed, U.S. tariffs were put up to protect the nascent manufacturing industry that had thrived during the nearly two decades that European exports had been disrupted or diverted. For the next century the U.S. tariff was all but exclusively within the domain of domestic politics, with little or no reference to foreign affairs. The main orientation of foreign policy, after the boundary settlements with Spain, France, Britain, and Mexico and the efforts surrounding the Civil War, gradually became increasingly commercial, preoccupied with maintaining and enlarging markets for U.S. exports. This effort or orientation was reinforced by the gradual settlement of the American continent—hence reduction of new internal trading opportunities, combined with what was seen as the European tendency to divide East Asia and Africa into colonial empires that were actually or potentially exclusive trading zones. Thus the early effort to open up Japan in the 1850s, the embracement of the open door policy in China later in the century, and even the Spanish-American War arguably were all motivated by a desire to expand markets for U.S. exports.

In this context it was recognized that a reduction of tariffs on foreign products into the United States could be helpful in inducing foreign countries to reduce their barriers to U.S. exports, and a series of reciprocity agreements were negotiated in the 1880s and 1890s with the aim of reducing selected U.S. and foreign duties to encourage trade between the two countries. Altogether eleven reciprocity treaties were negotiated between the 1883 treaty with Mexico and the Kasson Treaties of the 1890s. None was ratified, however, either because the Senate was unwilling to accept the reductions in duties or because the administration withdrew them consequent upon unacceptable conditions being imposed by the Senate. In addition eighteen executive agreements—therefore subject to change whenever Congress changed the underlying legislation—reduced duties on a selected line of products (Bemis, 1955, pp. 730–734).

The most remarkable effort along these lines was the attempt by Secretary of State James Blaine in 1889 to form a Pan American customs union. Blaine observed that the United States had a substantial trade deficit with Latin America and that most of the Latin American goods coming into the United States were on the duty-free list. For a combination of political and economic reasons, Blaine thought that it would be generally beneficial, and particularly beneficial to the exports of the United States, to create a customs union in the Americas. For the same reasons, however, a number of Latin American countries thought that the idea was not such a good one, and the project failed in its main purpose, although it did represent the early beginnings of what later became the Pan American Union and subsequently the Organization of American States.

This period was not immune from more strictly foreign policy uses of tariff policy. Canada, still a British colony, was economically distressed during the

1850s, and there were strong sentiments on both sides of the border for Canada to join the United States. Such a move would have upset the delicate balance between free and slave states within the United States, and hence was not desired either by the U.S. South or by those concerned with preserving the Union. As a result a treaty was installed between Canada and the United States in 1854 to provide for reciprocal duty-free treatment for all "articles produced or grown" in either of the two countries (that is, excluding manufactured goods). It was designed to head off the absorption of Canada by undercutting the Canadian proponents of annexation by removing some of the economic rationale that annexation contained. The treaty lasted for ten years with a two-year grace period. It was allowed to expire in 1866.

There was also agitation for annexation of Hawaii in the 1850s, but this too was unpopular in the United States and especially in the Congress. The result was a later compromise: a reciprocity treaty with Hawaii in 1876 that permitted duty-free entry of Hawaiian products, especially sugar, into the United States. This arrangement was motivated in part by a general feeling that Hawaii was crucial to the national security of the United States. It was thought to control the approaches from the mid-Pacific not only to the west coast of the United States but also to the newly acquired Alaska and to an isthmusian canal across Central America, which had become a gleam in the eye of many Americans. The canal in turn was motivated partly by national security concerns and partly by commercial concerns. Hawaii was considered to be strategically dangerous if controlled by a foreign power.

Although the motivation for the treaty was mainly strategic, the economic effect, especially on the Hawaiian sugar industry, was dramatic. Sugar production increased from barely 20 million tons before the treaty to around 300 million tons in the 1890s. The McKinley tariff of 1890 made sugar from all sources duty free and compensated U.S. producers with a bounty of 2 cents a pound. Hawaii lost the duty protection and did not gain the bounty. This loss contributed to the revolution of 1892 and appeal for annexation, which was finally accomplished in 1898 after the term of President Cleveland, who opposed annexation. So the 1876 treaty at least indirectly led to annexation (Taussig, 1915, pp. 58–63).

After the Spanish-American War special trade provisions were made for both the newly independent Cuba and the semiautonomous Philippine Islands. In 1903 the United States entered a reciprocity treaty with Cuba that called for a 20 percent reduction in U.S. duties on products coming from Cuba and a 20 to 40 percent reduction on U.S. products imported by Cuba. This discriminatory arrangement, with political and commercial motivation, laid the basis for Cuban sugar prosperity in the decade that followed.

Finally there was the reciprocity treaty of 1911 with Canada. The tariff increases of the Payne-Aldridge tariff of 1909 created serious problems in Canada, now an independent British dominion, and to alleviate them the Taft administration negotiated a reciprocity treaty that put many goods from Canada on the free list and lowered U.S. duties on others. The treaty was ratified in the United States—unlike the many reciprocity treaties of the preceding two decades—but failed ratification in Canada because it became linked in public debate with annexation, following the precedent of Hawaii in 1898, after U.S. Speaker of the House Clark unwisely announced his support of the treaty because "I hope to see the day when the American flag will float over every square foot of British North American possessions clear to the North Pole" (quoted in Bemis, 1955, p. 735).

On the whole, however, the tariff remained a matter of domestic politics. It is true that in his last speech (in September 1901), President McKinley, who as chairman of the Ways and Means Committee had been the sponsor of the McKinley tariff of 1890, recognized the link between trade and good foreign relations. He advocated negotiating reciprocal reductions in tariffs in order not only to provide a vent for growing U.S. surpluses but also because "commercial wars are unprofitable. A policy of good will and friendly trade relations will prevent reprisals" (Commager, 1958, p. 199). Nonetheless, President Woodrow Wilson, in a speech to the special session of Congress he called immediately after his 1912 election in order to deal with tariff reform, did not mention foreign policy at all as a reason for reducing tariffs. Rather he focused on improvements in efficiency and on combating monopoly. It is also noteworthy that in his celebrated "peace without victory" speech of January 1917 on the nature of the postwar world system, Wilson laid great emphasis on freedom of the seas (against the background of German submarine warfare) but none on freedom of commerce (Commager, 1958, pp. 305–308). But in his even more celebrated fourteen points speech a year later, Wilson addressed commerce in his third point: "The removal, so far as possible, of all economic barriers and the establishment of an equality of trade conditions among all nations consenting to the peace and associating themselves for its maintenance" (Commager, 1958, p. 318). In explanatory notes to the fourteen points prepared by Colonel House for the Versailles Peace Conference, it is said that this point means MFN treatment for all members of the League of Nations. House added that "this clause naturally contemplates fair and equitable understanding as to the distribution of raw materials." whatever that means. The Allies accepted the fourteen points as a basis for negotiations with Germany in November 1918. They reserved on the second clause, regarding freedom of the seas, but not on the clause dealing with commerce. The Senate's rejection of U.S. membership in the League of Nations and the "return to normalcy" of the Harding administration restored to oblivion these beginnings of wisdom, and the nineteenth-century pattern of treating the tariff exclusively as a matter of domestic policy continued, culminating in the Smoot-Hawley tariff of 1930. In petitioning President Hoover to veto the Smoot-Hawley Tariff Act, the 1,028 American economists, led by Paul Douglas of Chicago, Irving Fisher of Yale, Frank Graham of Princeton, and Frank Taussig of Harvard, focused mainly on the domestic disadvantages of the act but added at the end, "The higher duties proposed in our pending legislation violate the spirit of this agreement and plainly invite other nations to compete with us in raising further barriers to trade. A tariff wall does not furnish good soil for the growth of world peace" (cited by Ratner, 1972, p. 144).

Henry Stimson was Hoover's secretary of state and later Roosevelt's secretary of war. He favored low tariffs and had voted for Grover Cleveland on the tariff issue. His biographer reports the following with respect to Smoot-Hawley:

There were two major foreign issues before the American govrnment in 1929 . . . one was the tariff and to Stimson's great relief this subject did not fall within the jurisdiction of the State Department. He had seen in 1909 what happens when Republicans revise the tariff and he had shuddered in 1928 when he found that Mr. Hoover as a candidate had promised tariff revision. But it was a settled decision; when he reached Washington [in March 1929, from the Philippines] a special session of Congress had already been called. He kept out of it. (Stimson and Bundy, 1947, p. 162)

The second major question was naval limitation, leading to the London Naval Agreement of 1930, to which Stimson devoted much attention.

Even in retrospect, Herbert Hoover denied the crucial role played by tariffs in generating the Great Depression. He remained an avowed protectionist, insisting that both U.S. industry and agriculture had to be protect from low foreign wages (Hoover, 1952, 3: 290–294).

The importance of the Smoot-Hawley tariff in deepening the Great Depression is controversial. Hoover denied that it played the significant role Roosevelt attributed to it in the 1932 presidential campaign. Friedman and Schwartz (1963), with their all but exclusive emphasis on monetary policy, barely mention it. Kindleberger (1973) attaches large but mainly symbolic importance to it, as a sign of abdication by the United States from the world. Dornbusch and Fischer (1984) argue that in income expenditure terms, the tariff, plus the retaliatory actions it provoked but not counting the bank failures it may have induced, could have explained at most 3 percentage points of the 16 percent drop in U.S. GNP between 1929 and 1931; they put far greater weight on macroeconomic policies. No doubt there is ample blame to spread around. For our purposes the importance attributed to it by key policy-makers—Roosevelt, Hull, and Truman—is what is important.

7.4 Multilateral Trade Liberalization, 1934–1985

The Roosevelt administration tried to turn the tariff picture around in 1934, but even Roosevelt at first emphasized the need to reduce tariffs in order to raise U.S. exports rather than for the general value of commerce to harmonious relations among nations. He pointed to the threat of other nations negotiating agreements disadvantageous to the United States. His secretary of state from 1933 to 1944, Cordell Hull, represented a notable exception to the relative inattention statesmen have paid to economic and trade issues in framing foreign policy. Faced with the responsibility of picking up the foreign policy pieces left by the Great Depression, Hull felt that the ground rules of international trade played a critical role in determining whether the world lived in peace and harmony. In reflecting on his role in his memoirs, Hull stated:

Toward 1916 I embraced the philosophy I carried throughout my twelve years as Secretary of State. . . . From then on, to me, unhampered trade dovetailed with peace; high tariffs, trade barriers, and unfair economic competition, with war. If we could get fewer discriminations and obstructions [to trade] so that one country would not be deadly jealous of another and the living standards of all countries might rise, thereby eliminating the economic dissatisfaction that breeds war, we might have a reasonable chance for lasting peace. (Hull, 1948, 1 : 81)

In supporting the Trade Agreements Act of 1934, Hull wrote, "Nations cannot produce on a level to sustain their people and well-being unless they have reasonable opportunities to trade with one another. The principles underlying the Trade Agreements Program are therefore an indispensible cornerstone for the edifice of peace" (Hull, 1948, 1 : 364).

Roosevelt was not so singlemindedly a devotee of liberal trade as was his secretary of state. He strongly attacked Hoover and the Smoot-Hawley tariff in the presidential campaign of 1932 but backed off somewhat late in the campaign. He scuttled the London Economic Conference but supported the Trade Agreements Act. Then in 1935 he tentatively agreed to a bilateral countertrade agreement with Nazi Germany, pressed by trade adviser George Peck, backing off only under strong remonstrance from Hull (Hull, 1948, 1: 370–374). This backing and forthing reflects Roosevelt's ambivalence and the cross-cutting advice he was getting from his domestic economic advisers with respect to the incompatibility of such experiments as the Agricultural Administration Act and the National Recovery Act with liberal trade. By early

1940, however, Roosevelt, in support of extension of the Trade Agreements Act, said that the act "should be extended as an indispensible part of the foundation of any stable and durable peace.... I emphasize the leadership which this nation can take.... Such an influence will be greatly weakened if this government becomes a dog in the manger of trade selfishness" (quoted in Hull, 1948, 1: 747).

By 1945 Roosevelt was a thorough convert to Hull's perspective. In his message to Congress requesting a strengthening of the Trade Agreements Act in March 1945, Roosevelt said,

Trade is fundamental to the prosperity of nations, as it is of individuals. All of us earn our living by producing for some market and all of us buy in some market most of the things we need. We do better, both as producers and consumers, when the markets upon which we depend are as large and rich and various and competitive as possible. The same is true of nations. We have not always understood this, in the United States or in any other country.

He closed by quoting his message of the previous month on the Bretton Woods proposals:

The point in history in which we stand is full of promise and of danger. The world will either move toward unity and widely shared prosperity or it will move apart into necessarily competing economic blocks. We have a chance, we citizens of the United States, to use our influence in favor of a more united and cooperating world. Whether we do so will determine, as far as it is in our power, the kind of lives our grandchildren can live. (Quoted in Ratner, 1972, pp. 151–153)

President Truman took a similar view. He had taken the affirmative side of a high school debate on tariffs for revenue only and persuaded himself; thereafter he was a liberal trader: "The lesson in history, I said, was plain. Freedom of international trade would provide the atmosphere necessary to the preservation of peace" (Truman, 1956, 2: 112).

This history is relevant because the U.S. approach to trade policy since 1934 arises directly out of the economic and political disasters of the 1930s, which induced the United States to take a systemic view of trade and to see trade as intimately related to foreign policy in the widest sense. The Hull-Roosevelt-Truman view led to the negotiation of an international trade organization (ITO). Even before that controversial treaty failed at the hands of the Republican Senate, still protectionist, President Truman entered into the GATT as an executive agreement, an authority formally disputed by Congress until 1979. (For a discussion of Anglo-American cooperation on the postwar trading system and Anglo-American frictions over the question of imperial preference, see Gardner, 1956, especially chaps. 1–2.)

The present international trading system of nondiscrimination based on MFN treatment, multilateral trade liberalization, and international dispute resolution arises out of the most elemental foreign policy concerns: war and peace and the need for allies to be economically prosperous. But the framework itself was designed to insulate imports of foreign goods from manipulation for reasons of foreign policy or domestic economic policy. Foreign trade was put on its own track and was dealt with as a more or less isolated issue of foreign policy (see Cooper, 1972–1973).

This does not mean that manipulation of trade policy for broader foreign policy purposes has ceased. But such manipulation has been limited largely to the determination of club membership (who should benefit from nondiscrimination) and controls over exports. Trade policy has been fundamentally guided by foreign policy concerns, and these broad foreign policy concerns have probably been more important in the eyes of successive presidents than has the efficiency case for trade liberalization, although Truman's views on the foreign policy importance of liberal trade were reinforced by his strong animus against domestic special interests that sought tariff protection. The key point was that the prosperity of other countries, and especially of Europe and Japan, was linked to their ability to export, and that in turn was linked to the willingness of the United States to open its markets. The assumption was that they would be sound and secure allies if they were economically prosperous. The history of world affairs since 1945 cannot gainsay this proposition.

The remainder of this chapter will take as given the underlying foreign policy rationale for the main thrust of U.S. trade policy: to support a regime of nondiscriminatory trade along with a continuing effort to reduce the actual barriers to trade. The liberalizing effort was focused on balance of payments restrictions in the late 1940s and early 1950s, then on tariffs, and more recently on a host of nontariff distortions to trade. This broad strategy was driven in part by the desirability of the end result: a more efficient allocation of world resources and a consequential increase in standards of living. But it was driven even more by the perception that motion toward trade liberalization was necessary to avoid a reversion to protectionism—just as a bicycle must keep moving in order to remain upright—and that protectionism was in neither the economic nor the foreign interests of the United States.

In addition to this main theme, there have been a series of subplots relating trade policy to foreign policy in various ways. The first concerns membership in the club of countries whose trade is to enjoy nondiscrimination, for that membership does not come automatically if a country is strongly disapproved. The second concerns exceptionally favorable treatment with respect to trade, going beyond MFN status, for reasons of foreign policy. The third concerns the manipulative use of trade policy to influence the behavior of other countries. Because of the broad commitment to a nondiscriminatory, liberal trading world, this manipulation could not generally be undertaken with respect to imports into the United States. Rather it has relied largely on the selective and manipulative control of U.S. exports. Indeed one could offer the generalization that interference with imports results largely from domestic policy or political pressures within the United States, whereas interference with exports results largely from reasons of foreign policy.

7.4.1 MFN Treatment

While the United States since 1922 has favored the unconditional interpretation of the MFN clause, it has made an exception of those regimes—all communist—of which it strongly disapproved. The United States did not recognize the new bolshevik government in Russia until 1933, and it did not extend MFN to the Soviet Union until 1937.

The United States withdrew MFN treatment, which means that the high Smoot-Hawley tariffs apply, from all communist countries (except Yugoslavia) in 1951, following a mandate from Congress in the wake of Chinese entry into the Korean War. MFN was withdrawn from North Vietnam in 1954, following the division of that country; from Cuba in 1961, following Castro's revolution; and from Poland in 1982 following the declaration of martial law. The granting of MFN was also used to confer approval and to contribute toward the diversification and perhaps the dissolution of the East bloc. It was given to Poland in 1960, to Rumania in 1975, to Hungary in 1978, and to the People's Republic of China in 1979. It is worth noting that these extensions and withdrawals are unrelated to GATT. The United States has extended MFN treatment to many countries that do not adhere to GATT, such as Mexico and more recently China, and has withdrawn MFN treatment from countries that are adherents to GATT, such as Poland. The technical basis for withdrawing MFN treatment from Poland in 1982 was that Poland had failed to comply with its undertaking when it was given admission to GATT to increase its imports by 7 percent a year. The United States threatened to withdraw MFN from Rumania over human rights in the early 1980s, especially over the question of emigration. MFN treatment was offered to the Soviet Union in 1972 as part of a comprehensive foreign policy package, loosely called détente, but that faltered over the Jackson-Vanik amendment to the Trade Act of 1974 concerning the question of emigration of Soviet Jews.

7.4.2 Favorable Trade Discrimination

The United States has conferred trade privileges on countries despite its commitment to a nondiscriminatory trading world. Apart from Hawaii and Cuba of the pre-1914 era, the United States accorded preferential treatment to Philippine goods until 1974 under the Laurel-Langley agreement, to provide a transition for the Philippine economy following independence in 1946. (Philippine goods had been accorded favorable treatment in the U.S. market when the Philippines was under U.S. administration.)

More recently the United States has accorded duty-free treatment to automobiles and automobile parts from Canada under the U.S.-Canadian Automotive Agreement. Automobiles and parts also enter Canada duty free provided they are imported by firms that have more than a specified amount of production in Canada. The automotive pact began in 1966 to head off a nasty trade dispute. Canada had introduced new regulations that allowed Canadian firms, all foreign owned, to import automobile parts duty free if they exported a certain fraction of their output. The United States threatened to impose countervailing duties on automobiles from Canada on the grounds that the Canadian measures represented a bounty. To avoid serious trade friction, the duty-free pact was introduced. The Canadian version was technically MFN because it was limited to automobile firms operating in Canada. The United States sought and got a GATT waiver for its part in the agreement.

In the late 1960s the developing countries made a major plea in UNCTAD and elsewhere for duty-free treatment of their products in the markets of the industrialized countries. Under concerted political pressure, the industrialized countries responded, although with schemes far less generous than the developing countries had envisaged. The United States accepted the principle of preferential treatment for developing countries in 1967 in a speech by President Johnson at a meeting of the Organization of American States in Punte del Este, Uruguay. But the United States did not achieve implementing legislation until the final days of 1974. This conferred duty-free treatment on most manufactured goods from developing countries, with the notable exception of textiles and some leather products, but subjected all imports under the generalized system of preferences (GSP), as it was called, to a competitive need formula that linked continuing GSP treatment to the actual trade preformance of each developing country, product by product. If a country became strongly competitive in a product, as measured by exports to the United States exceeding an absolute threshold related to U.S. GNP (around $57 million today) or if it accounted for more than 50 percent of all exports from developing countries of that product, then GSP treatment was withdrawn in the following year.

There was a general GATT waiver for all GSP schemes, so it is perhaps more accurate to think of this as an amendment to the GATT rather than a derogation. It responded overwhelmingly to foreign policy concerns and represented a political gesture toward the aspirations of developing countries, as the forum for U.S. announcement suggests. This scheme was no doubt well intended by its supporters, but the politics of preferential treatment was not carefully thought through, so its contribution to economic development may well have been negligible or even negative insofar as the political price paid for GSP treatment was much stiffer application of escape clause or safeguard rules against products from developing countries (Cooper, 1971). But the political gesture was made nonetheless, and it did serve for a while to remove trade in manufactured goods as a contentious issue in the so-called North-South dialogue, as the G77—the label for the Caucus of Developing Countries—shifted its priorities to commodity price supports, debt, and general mechanisms for resource transfers to developing countries.

The U.S. provisions for GSP ran for only ten years. They were renewed in 1984 with some new conditions. Most of these are closely related to trade, but one makes GSP treatment conditional on the treatment a country gives such intellectual property as copyrights and trademarks and is directed at curtailing the production of counterfeit products, especially in the more advanced developing countries. Another, added by Congress despite reservations expressed by the Reagan administration, concerns each country's compliance with fair labor standards—a vague but possibly mischievous provision because of the opportunity it provides for harassment of imports from the country in question. This provision was no doubt well meant by some of its supporters to improve labor conditions in developing countries. In this respect it represents the U.S. use of trade policy, in this case the carrot of GSP treatment, to influence the domestic policies of other countries, a feature it has in common with the Jackson-Vanik amendment.

Yet another derogation from MFN treatment was the Caribbean Basin Initiative (CBI) designed to give economic support to an area politically sensitive to the United States. The CBI extends duty-free treatment to all products coming from the Caribbean area except for textiles, some leather goods, and petroleum products. Sugar imports are limited under a quota system associated with U.S. domestic sugar price support, but Caribbean sugar enters duty free. The net gain provided by the CBI over the GSP already in effect is in fact limited, the additional coverage involving mainly beef, tobacco products, and some electronic goods, plus more favorable tax treatment for U.S. conventions that take place in the area. But the scheme was introduced when the extension of GSP beyond 1984 could not be taken for granted and for the political symbolism involved in having a special program for the area. CBI is to last until the end of 1995, versus mid-1993 for the extension of GSP that was finally enacted. Apart from sugar, the incremental coverage of CBI over duty-free treatment already available to Caribbean countries through GSP or the duty-free list amounted to well under 10 percent of their exports in 1984, but with the stimulus of duty-free treatment that share may well grow in the future.

During 1984 and early 1985 the United States negotiated a free trade area between the United States and Israel, another derogation from MFN treatment although one that will probably be covered by article 24 of GATT concerning customs unions and free trade areas. The initiative for this arrangement seems to have come from Israel during a time when GSP extension was in doubt. The United States embraced it in large part for its political symbolism at home and abroad. The welfare effects for the United States are likely to be negligible. The negotiations are authorized by the 1984 Trade Act, which was explicit on Israel but also contains general language that seems to encourage the administration to pursue free trade areas with other countries as well, subject to congressional approval.

7.5 Manipulative Trade Policy

As was the case early in U.S. history, trade policy has been used during the last thirty-five years with some frequency to influence the behavior of other countries in particular circumstances. For this objective the trade actions must in principle be reversible. For the reasons already suggested, the manipulative use of trade policy has relied mainly, but not exclusively, on controls on exports, although in a few cases imports have also been embargoed.

Full embargo on trade represents the extreme case. Total or all but total trade embargoes have been directed at the People's Republic of China (1950–1972), North Korea (1950–present), North Vietnam (1954–present), Cuba (1960–present, medicines excluded), Rhodesia (1965–1978, chromium partially excluded), Uganda (1978–1979), and Nicaragua (1985). A trade embargo against Iran was threatened concretely in early 1980, to take effect in stages, and it was threatened in vague and general terms against Nicaragua in 1983 and implemented in 1985. The purpose of total embargo is to weaken or even destabilize a regime by isolating the country economically. Sometimes a specific change in behavior is desired, as in the threat against Iran, directed at release of the hostage diplomats. Sometimes there is no hope at effective isolation, especially when other countries will not go along with the embargo but the United States wants to show extreme disapproval and/or to show

Table 7.1
U.S. economic policy toward Cuba, 1959–1963

January 1959	Castro assumes power; U.S. recognizes new regime
February 1959	Cuba imposes stiff exchange controls
May 1959	Agrarian reform: all property over 1,000 acres is nationalized, with compensation in twenty-year bonds; U.S. and Cuban owners protest
February 1960	Cuba makes sugar-for-oil deal with Soviet Union
March 1960	U.S. embargoes arms sales to Cuba, and Eisehower asks Congress for authority to reduce Cuba's sugar quota
May 1960	U.S. ends economic aid to Cuba
July 1960	Cuba nationalizes Texaco and Standard Oil refineries for refusing to refine Soviet crude oil
July 1960	Sugar bill passes; U.S. virtually eliminates imports of Cuban sugar for remainder of year
August 1960	Cuba nationalizes American property in Cuba
October 1960	U.S. embargoes all exports to Cuba
December 1961	U.S. extends sugar embargo
February 1962	U.S. embargoes all imports from Cuba (about $15 million)
March 1963	U.S. restricts all financial dealings with Cuba

Source: Adler-Karlsson (1968, pp. 209–210).

strong support for a threatened country, as in the case of the embargoes against North Korea after the 1953 cease-fire and against North Vietnam after the fall of Dienbienphu. In the case of Rhodesia the embargo followed a United Nations resolution invoking chapter 7 of the UN Charter, under which a country that represents a threat to the peace can be embargoed. This provision represents a carryover from the League of Nations, which in turn reflected Woodrow Wilson's view that peaceful methods of coercion and demonstration of disapproval should be substituted for the use of force. The United States also invoked this UN provision in the Iranian case, but the Soviet Union vetoed the operative part of the UN resolution in early 1980.

It is interesting to look at the sequence that leads to an embargo because such extreme measures seldom come all at once; rather they typically are the result of a sequence of action and reaction. For example, the Castro revolution in Cuba was initially welcomed by many Americans; the United States recognized the new regime at once, and only gradually did relations cool to the point of frigidity and total embargo (table 7.1). The most consequential action the United States could take against Cuba in the economic arena was to cut its sugar quota into the United States. Sugar has long been subject to import quotas in support of domestic sugar price-support programs. Sugar in turn was (and still is) Cuba's largest export, and the United States was Cuba's largest markets, so an elimination of the sugar quota could be expected to exert great hardship, at least temporarily, on the Cuban economy. The official reason for eliminating the quota was that Cuba had committed so much of its sugar to the Soviet Union that Cuba had become an unreliable supplier.

A similar early sequence can be observed in the case of Nicaragua. The United States was at first cautiously friendly toward the Sandinista regime that replaced Somoza, and U.S. economic aid continued in 1979 and 1980. In 1981 a new, more hostile U.S. administration came into power, but there had also been important changes within the Sandinista group. Most of the social democrats had either left or been driven out of the regime, and a substantial military buildup (relative to Central America's history in these matters) had already begun. In 1983 the United States removed Nicaragua's sugar quota under the revived U.S. sugar program and reallocated it to other countries in the Caribbean. It also threatened to isolate Nicaragua economically. An arms embargo was introduced. Nicaragua did not ask for and did not receive benefits from CBI treatment. In May 1985 U.S. administration announced a total embargo on trade with Nicaragua, not with much hope of influencing Nicaraguan behavior, it seems, but largely to express its continuing disapproval of Nicaragua in the face of congressional disapproval of financial assistance to Nicaraguans fighting against the Sandinista regime and, it was informally admitted, to deflect public attention from an ill-conceived presidential commitment to visit a German military cemetery that interred some former S.S. officers.

7.5.1 Arms Exports

A full embargo is an extreme measure. Far more often, manipulation of trade is limited in scope. Probably the most frequent, indeed almost routine, instrument is exports of military equipment and associated training, which now amounts to over 5 percent of total U.S. merchandise exports. All exports of military equipment require license for national security and foreign policy reasons. Approval or denial of an export license request is therefore an act of foreign policy. Exports are routinely permitted to NATO countries and to Japan, but exports to any other area of the world occasions active consideration within the State and Defense departments. For example, it was U.S. policy not to encourage introduction of high-performance military equipment, especially aircraft, into Latin America, and until the Reagan administration's agreement to sell F-16s to Venezuela, the U.S. government not only denied export of high-performance equipment from the United States but strongly discouraged such sales from other arms suppliers as well. This was a broad foreign policy objective.

In contrast, under the Nixon Doctrine to rely on friendly regional powers around the world to reduce direct U.S. military involvement, President Nixon instructed that Iran was to have any nonnuclear military equipment it desired. Under this doctrine sales of the very high-performance F-14 and Phoenix missile system were made to Iran. Once again such sales were clearly part of a broad foreign policy strategy. (The sale of equipment or material that may be used for nuclear weapons has always been treated in a separate, more restrictive category, covered by separate legislation.)

Approval of particular arms requests is often taken as a test of the degree of U.S. political commitment to a country. Thus Saudi Arabia in the late 1970s asked for F-15s, the most advanced fighter then available, less because they needed F-15s than because they wanted to test the extent of the rhetorically strong U.S. commitment to Saudi Arabia. More recently the electronically formidable Airborne Warning and Control System (AWACS) has been in something of the same category, although occasional Iranian air attacks lent some military justification to the sale. The same issue arose with sales of F-16s to Israel in the late 1970s, less over the airplane so much as the particular performance package that was to be included in it. China continually probes the limits of U.S. willingness to license advanced materials to it, less, on the evidence, because it wants to buy than to test how far the United States is willing to go. Indeed arms sales can become such an important part of foreign policy that in 1981, the first year of the Reagan administration and following a sharp reversal of President Carter's attempt to restrain exports of arms, *Le Monde* could report that all U.S. diplomatic activity seemed to be concentrated in the section of the State Department that deals with security assistance (Pierre, 1982, p. 65).

Where arms sales have occurred before, denial of sales also becomes an act of foreign policy. The United States has imposed total arms embargoes a number of times in the last quarter-century. The Dominican Republic was covered in 1960, along with elimination of its sugar quota, to disapprove and perhaps destabilize the Trujillo regime after its attempted assassination of Venezuelan President Betancourt. Arms sales to South Africa were banned in 1962, following a UN resolution against apartheid. They were banned to Indonesia in 1963 to discourage Sukarno's "Crush Malaysia" policy, and to India and Pakistan in 1971 when those countries went to war. Arms sales were banned to Chile in 1979 over that country's unsatisfactory judicial handling of the suspects in the Washington murder of Letelier, a former Chilean foreign minister. More recently there has been a partial embargo on arms sales to Taiwan as part of a 1982 agreement with China to phase out such sales over time and in the meantime to improve Taiwan's military forces neither quantitatively nor qualitatively.

The United States has also tried to influence the behavior of countries through the control of U.S. exports other than munitions. The now-classic case is that of Japan in 1940 and 1941. In July 1939 the United States had terminated the thirty-year-old Friendship, Commerce, and Navigation Treaty with Japan, and in April 1940 the U.S. Pacific fleet was ordered to Hawaii (from its home bases on the West Coast of the United States) indefinitely. Both moves reflected growing alarm with Japanese actions in China. In July 1940 after the fall of France to the Nazi German armies and strong pressure by Japan on Britain and France with respect to supplying China, the United States embargoed export of aviation gasoline and high-grade scrap to Japan. In September 1940 Japan occupied northern French Indochina (now North Vietnam) in order to increase its pressure on China. The United States extended its embargo to all scrap. In July 1941 Japan, despite warnings from Roosevelt, occupied southern Indochina with troops and planes. At that point the United States froze Japan's assets in the United States, which meant that any transaction with Japan had to be licensed.[1] Apparently the intention was to license sales to Japan, but the policy was ambiguous and subordinates were not sure of the intention of the policy. Few licenses were issued. In the presence of this uncertainty, Japan in August withdrew its merchant ships from U.S. trade, and by November there were virtually no transactions with the United States (Acheson, 1969, pp. 23–27). The effect of the asset freeze was an embargo on exports of petroleum products, vital to the Japanese military forces. Britain and the Netherlands (covering the Dutch East Indies) had followed the U.S. freeze. The attack on Pearl Harbor ensued.

Export controls were widely used during World War II, not only as a consequence of the allocation of strategic materials but also occasionally to put pressure on neutral countries such as Sweden and Switzerland. Export controls were enshrined in peacetime legislation in the Export Control Act of 1949, which authorizes the president to prohibit or curtail exports in furtherance of three objectives: "(A) to protect the domestic economy from the excessive drain of scarce materials and to reduce the inflationary impact from abnormal foreign demand, (B) to further the foreign policy of the United States and to aid in fulfilling its international responsibilities; and (C) to exercise the necessary vigilance over exports from the standpoint of their significance to the national security of the United States." The first two provisions were taken over from wartime legislation, and the third was added in 1949 (Adler-Karlsson, 1968, pp. 25, 217). The Export Control Act has been renewed periodically at three- to four-year intervals, most recently in 1979, sometimes routinely and sometimes with important changes. The act expired in 1983, and Congress has been unable to agree on the terms of a renewal, so export controls have continued under the president's emergency powers. In principle all exports from the United States are subject to license, but most products are not controlled, and they can take place under general license without regard to destination. Items administratively controlled require a specific license for export, usually with the exception of NATO countries and Japan.

The United States has attempted to coordinate its control over exports of sensitive products to communist countries through an organization called COCOM (Coordinating Committee), a committee shrouded in semisecrecy because of the political sensitivity of export controls in many European countries for products other than munitions. COCOM was established in late 1949 to help control the export of strategic materials to the Soviet Union and its allies and extended in 1951 to China. Its purpose is a broad one concerning national security: to deny to the Soviet Union important materials and equipment, such as high-speed computers and microelectronic production technology, that are of potential military significance. It is strategic rather than manipulative. Indeed Europeans have expressed great concern over the U.S. proclivity to manipulate export controls for short-run foreign policy gains rather than to stick to the strict criterion of potential military significance. The fact that the U.S. export control list, requiring specific licenses, is much longer than the (unpublished) COCOM list—four times as long in 1969—has been a source of continuing complaint by U.S. business firms, which see themselves losing export sales with no corresponding benefit to national security. At present the U.S. control list, including controls instituted for foreign policy as well as national security reasons, is about 50 percent longer than the COCOM list.

7.5.2 Diverse Objectives

The United States pursues several general objectives of foreign policy through export controls, and the president normally has the authority to control additional exports for unanticipated foreign policy reasons in the light of unfolding events. Congressionally mandated objectives concern discouragement of the proliferation of nuclear weapons, encouragement of human rights, and discouragement of international terrorism.

The United States has always been sensitive to the export of nuclear materials and has required a bilateral agreement for most sales since the Atomic Energy Act of 1954. It has opposed the spread of technology and equipment for uranium enrichment and for reprocessing spent fuel from nuclear reactors as a matter of foreign policy. In 1974 major suppliers of enriched uranium agreed to coordinate their exports, with the objective of inhibiting proliferation of nuclear weapons. In 1975 the United States suspended sale of enriched uranium to South Africa because of that country's efforts to develop its indigenous enrichment capacity. In 1978 Congress passed the Nuclear Nonproliferation Act, despite reservations over some features by the administration. Subsequently Argentina, Brazil, and India have been denied enriched uranium (even low percentage, reactor grade uranium, which is far from being bomb-grade material) because those countries have refused to agree to full-scope safeguards in their nuclear reactors. More recently U.S. export of nuclear materials to China has been held up pending a satisfactory agreement from that country on the handling of nuclear materials.

Human rights in other countries have also become an objective of U.S. foreign policy. In the 1973 Mutual Assistance Act Congressman Donald Fraser introduced a "sense of Congress" statement that the United States should reduce or eliminate its security assistance to countries that engage in gross violations of human rights. This statement was strengthened to become the "policy of the United States" later, and it was made mandatory in 1978. Technically the act covered only security assistance, but in congressional eyes it was closely linked to arms sales and to sales of police and riot control equipment. President Carter accepted this link, but President Reagan dropped it in 1981. Congress in 1977 prohibited sales of police equipment to Uruguay and Argentina, and many countries have been denied U.S. products selectively on grounds of human rights violations. In 1978 the United States denied sale of a computer to TASS in the Soviet Union over that country's trials of the dissidents Ginzberg and Shcharansky.

Opposition to internationally supported or condoned terrorism has also become an objective of U.S. foreign policy. Senator Abraham Ribicoff sponsored an omnibus antiterrorism bill in 1977, which was opposed by the Carter administration on the grounds that it left too little discretion to the president. But Congresswoman Millicent Fenwick successfully amended the Export Administration Act of 1979 to require that the administration notify Congress of exports in excess of $7 million in value to countries supporting terrorism if such exports would add to their military potential or their capability for supporting international terrorism. The Fenwick admendment therefore served to make a public issue out of every consequential sale to countries on the terrorism list. In 1980 this list included Libya, Syria, South Yemen, and Iraq. In 1982 Iraq was deleted, and Cuba was added. And in 1984 Iran was added to the list. In 1980 the United States denied sales of commercial aircraft to Iraq on grounds of that country's support for Palestinian terrorists. The foreign policy complications that can arise under this policy are illustrated by the tension between the United States and Italy that arose over the proposed sale by Italy to Iraq of naval frigates, which included U.S. engines exported to Italy.

Some idea of the operation of this kind of policy can be illustrated by the recent history of U.S. exports to Libya. The United States banned military sales to Libya in 1978 while the antiterrorist bill was still under debate in Congress, but it agreed to sales in 1979 of commerical aircraft (Boeing 727s and 747s). It also agreed, after much controversy, to the sale of Oshkosh heavy trucks to Libya but only after receiving a written guarantee that they would be used solely for nonmilitary purposes. Libya subsequently used the Boeing 727s to land troops in Uganda in support of Idi Amin. In 1981 the United States banned the sale of small aircraft, helicopters, and parts and avionics to Libya. In 1982 it was reported that Libya had rebuilt the Oshkosh trucks to enable them to carry tanks across the desert, despite written assurances. Shortly after the United States embargoed U.S. oil imports from Libya, invoking a provision of the Trade Expansion Act of 1962 and drawing on the same national security finding as was used to ban imports of oil from Iran following the taking of the diplomatic hostages in November 1979. The ostensible reason for both actions was to signal that the United States would not be subject to oil blackmail by those countries. The United States also restricted exports of sophisticated oil and gas equipment and technology to Libya, provided it was not available from other sources. In late 1982 the United States barred the sale of twelve commercial jet aircraft to Libya. Following Libya's invasion of Chad in 1983 the administration debated refusing to license the sale of any irrigation or refining equipment or indeed any other equipment that would materially help the Libyan economy, but no action was taken.

Occasionally there are foreign policy linkages to trade policy that do not fit comfortably into the categories discussed. Three cases illustrate the point, involving Britain, Japan, and the Soviet Union.

The first concerns the U.S. desire to see the United Kingdom join the emergent EEC in the early 1960s. Britain had been involved in the original discussions over creation of a European customs union but opted out of the Rome Treaty and led an alternative arrangement, the European Free Trade Association (EFTA), limited to trade in manufactures. The United States did not want Europe divided economically, had been very cool to the formation of EFTA, and continually urged Britain to join the EEC, which began to function with the six original members in 1958. What was thought to be an enticement was included in the Trade Expansion Act of 1962. This act provided presidential negotiating authority for what became known as the Kennedy Round of tariff reductions concluded in 1967. The act authorized a reduction in U.S. tariffs of up to 50 percent. But a dominant-supplier provision was included in the act under which tariffs could be completely eliminated on products for which the United States and the EC together accounted for 80 percent or more world exports. Apart from civil aircraft, in which the United States dominated the world market, coverage of this provision was negligible in 1962, but it would become consequential if Britain joined the EEC. Britain did not then take the bait, and the provision remained a dead letter.

A second example of foreign policy linkage involves Japan and represents an attempt to use a foreign policy issue to influence trade policy, as had been common in U.S. policy in the latter half of the nineteenth century. As World War II receded in time, Japan chafed increasingly at the U.S. jurisdiction of Okinawa, an island group south of Japan and traditionally Japanese, which the United States had built up as its major military base in the Far East. This issue became a source of friction between the United States and the Japanese public, and it increasingly interfered with broader common purposes of the two countries. At the same time Japanese textile imports were portrayed as flooding into the U.S. market, creating major adjustment problems for the U.S. textile industry. (In fact, Japanese textiles provided less than 3 percent of U.S. textile consumption in 1969.) President Nixon conceived the idea that he would trade Okinawa reversion for Japanese textile restraint, and he posed this exchange, delicately, in his 1970 meeting with Prime Minister Sato. The sensitivity of this kind of exchange and the incapacity for specialized bureaucracies in both countries to span political-defense issues and economic issues meant that the groundwork had not been laid for such a deal. Sato inadvisedly made commitments to Nixon with respect to textiles that he should not have made in the context of Japanese decision making and that he could not keep, thereby weakening Nixon's confidence in Japan (Kissinger, 1979, pp. 325–38; Destler, Fukui, and Sato, 1979, chap. 5).

The third issue involves linkage in the opposite direction, with the United States holding out more trade and MFN treatment to the Soviet Union in exchange for greater political restraint by that country in Berlin, Vietnam, and elsewhere in the world. Many Americans were eager to trade more with the Soviet Union, and Russians were eager to get more goods and credits in the West, especially grain and high-technology products. The Nixon-Kissinger approach was to dangle increased trade, credits, and MFN treatment as a carrot in part of a larger strategic bargain that ultimately involved the strategic arms limitation talks (SALT) and the Helsinki Accords as well. This form of linkage, imposing political conditions on improved trade relations, was widely criticized at the time. Senator Henry Jackson, however, was fundamentally opposed to improved relations with the Soviet Union because he did not trust the Soviet regime and he thought détente would lull the American public into

Table 7.2
Jewish emigration from the Soviet Union

1969	2,902	1977	16,736
1970	1,044	1978	28,864
1971	13,022	1979	51,320
1972	31,681	1980	21,471
1973	34,733	1981	9,447
1974	20,628	1982	2,670
1975	13,221	1983	1,315
1976	14,261	1984	896

Source: U.S. State Department *Bulletin*, various issues.
Note: Arrivals in Vienna.

a false sense of security. He seized on a Soviet imposition of an export tax on emigrating Jews—a puzzling action in the context of improving U.S.-Soviet relations in 1972 and explained by Soviet Ambassador Drobrynin as an independent action by a low-level minister—to propose what became the Jackson-Vanik amendment to the Trade Act of 1974, then wending its way through Congress. This amendment made the granting of MFN to any communist country conditional on an explicit undertaking by that country that it would follow a liberal emigration policy. This issue would be regarded by most countries, including the United States and notably the Soviet Union, as preeminently a question of domestic policy, not the proper subject of negotiation between countries. The Soviets were willing to give private but not public undertakings with respect to emigration. The amendment passed— what congressman could seem to oppose Jewish emigration from the Soviet Union?—administration opposition, thus effectively killing MFN for the Soviet Union. Since the provision, while apparently general, was really aimed at the Soviet Union, the standards applied to other communist countries were less rigorous because they were less controversial. Rumania, Hungary, and the People's Republic of China received MFN despite the Jackson-Vanik amendment, although their emigration practices are subject to periodic review.[2]

The actual course of Jewish emigration from the Soviet Union is shown in table 7.2. It had been the subject of quiet diplomacy before 1972 and was allowed to rise, presumably to improve the political climate for détente within the United States. When it became clear that the Jackson-Vanik amendment could not be stopped, emigration dropped sharply in 1974–1976 and then rose again in the hope that the Carter administration, whose position on human rights was subject to less doubt in the eyes of the Congress than was Nixon's, could either have the Jackson-Vanik amendment repealed or could find a formula acceptable both to the Soviet Union and to Senator Jackson. When that failed and U.S.-Soviet relations cooled dramatically after the Soviet invasion of Afghanistan, emigration plummeted again. These figures suggest that it is plausible that a realistic prospect of getting MFN treatment allowed many Jews to emigrate, but we cannot be sure of this motivation without access to Russian archives, nor can we be sure what would have happened if MFN treatment had been granted. (On the episode, see Kissinger, 1979, chap. 26, pp. 270–72; Kissinger, 1982, pp. 246–255, 985–998).

7.5.3 Congress

Throughout the last decade, the role of Congress in insinuating trade policy into foreign policy, and foreign policy into trade policy, has been significant. The Jackson-Vanik amendment of 1972, the Ribicoff bill (1977), and the Fenwick amendment (1979) on terrorism have already been mentioned. Congress also took the lead on human rights (1973) and in the embargo against Uganda (1978), and it went further than the incumbent administration wanted to with respect to limitations on arms sales (1976) and nonproliferation (1978). This increasing direct congressional involvement with respect to the foreign policy aspects of trade policy reflects a lower willingness since Vietnam and Watergate to leave foreign policy to the executive branch.

7.6 Evaluation and Conclusion

Any particular course of action cannot be evaluated definitively without addressing two questions, well known to economists in other areas: (1) What would the world have been like without the action under examination? and (2) What alternative courses of action with respect to the same objective were available to the authorities? Economists have come to build complex interactive models to simulate counterfactual situations with respect to the absence of one action and with respect to the taking of alternative actions. Practitioners in this art know that these models involve a lot of judgment in their creation and use, although their formal structure sometimes conceals that to nonspecialists. Political science has not progressed to the point at which persuasive formal models of counterfactual scenarios can be drawn upon. The judgment required in evaluating foreign policy actions is all out in the open, yet judgment is inevitably necessary.

Moreover, given the sweep of actions and the wide diversity of contexts in which U.S. trade policy and foreign policy have interacted, any overall evaluation is virtually impossible. Furthermore it is necessary to distinguish between the impact of trade sanctions on trade and the impact of this in turn on the desired objective. Actions by American colonists in the 1760s and 1770s clearly affected British trade. They almost effected their objectives. But in the end they did not because of George III's determination to show the colonists who ultimately was in charge. The result was the Revolutionary War.

In the early nineteenth century the 1808–1812 embargoes also clearly affected trade, and they also almost effected their objective of stopping British harassment of U.S. shipping and seamen, but due to communication and other delays, the War of 1812 was not avoided. The early embargo of 1807 has gone down in history as having been unsuccessful. Frankel (1982) has recently argued that the embargo was in fact effective in throttling trade and worsening Britain's terms of trade, but it was abandoned because of political disagreements within the United States before the British responded to it.

With respect to the second long period of U.S. history, in which foreign policy went largely in pursuit of opening export markets, trade agreements did avoid union with Canada and fostered the ultimate absorption of Hawaii into the United States, both consonant with the aims of their supporters. But who is to say that history would have been markedly different in this respect if the trade agreements had not been made?

As for the most recent period, it is hard to dissociate the enormous success of post–World War II U.S. foreign policy from Cordell Hull's vision, embodied in the GATT, of a liberal, nondiscriminatory trading world. This success is marked by the fact that not only has there not been world war in the intervening forty years, but war between the traditional European antagonists, France and Germany, is virtually unimaginable today. West Germany has been fully integrated into a cooperative community of nations. Futhermore democratic values have been firmly implanted not only in Germany, Japan, and Italy but also, it seems, in Spain and elsewhere in Western Europe. Of course it is difficult to separate these unquestionable successes from many nontrade measures as well: the Marshall Plan, NATO, the many conscious U.S. efforts to heal the wounds of World War II as rapidly as possible, and above all the use of active monetary and fiscal policy in the United States and elsewhere to avoid the serious and politically disruptive economic slumps of earlier periods.

When it comes to the manipulative, as opposed to the strategic, aspects of trade policy, the task of evaluation is only somewhat easier. For instance, in his study of arms sales and their use for foreign policy purposes, Andrew Pierre writes, "A key question must be whether the restrictions on arms sales have been effective in altering the human rights practices of the would-be purchasers. There is little evidence that the curtailments, of themselves, have had the desired impact" (Pierre, 1982, p. 251). He goes on to argue, however, that a

Table 7.3
Effectiveness of trade sanctions

Contribution of sanctions[a]	Success in attaining objective[a]				
	1	2	3	4	Total
U.S. actions					
1	10	2			12
2		9	3	1	13
3		1	1	3	5
4		1	3	2	6
Actions by other countries					
1	11	1			12
2		4	1	3	8
3			4	7	11
4				1	1

Source: Compiled from Hufbauer and Schott (1985)
Note: Many cases also include other economic sanctions as well.
a. 1 = failure; 4 = significant.

strong signal on the question of human rights of U.S. disapproval probably did influence the behavior of the Argentine and Chilean governments, ameliorating their human rights violations and helping to restore the tarnished image of the United States throughout Latin America (Pierre, 1982, p. 252). In short, we are told that the manipulative use of arms sales probably was not effective in influencing human rights, but maybe it was after all.

A major study of the use of economic sanctions has recently been completely by Hufbauer and Schott (1985). The authors consider some five dozen cases in which trade sanctions played at least a partial role (other forms of economic sanctions were also used in many of these cases). They score on a scale of 1 to 4 the degree of success in achieving the objectives of the sanctions and, separately the role of the sanctions in achieving that result. Table 7.3 summarizes their findings. If the objective was not achieved, the sanctions were judged ineffective, so the scorings with respect to attainment of objectives show a somewhat higher degree of success than the contribution of the sanctions toward attaining the objectives. What will be a surprise to many economists, Hufbauer and Schott find that economic sanctions were either moderately or very successful in about a third of the cases. In another third they were completely ineffective, and in the remaining third they were slightly effective.

To underline the difficulty in evaluating the use of economic sanctions in complex foreign policy environments, however, I would reverse sharply three of their findings: that concerning the contributions of economic sanctions against Rhodesia in 1965, which they score with a 3, and the U.S. sanctions against the Soviet Union in 1980, and against Japan in 1940–1941, to both of which they award a 1, completely ineffective. It is true that eventually, after fourteen years, black rule was established in Rhodesia (now Zimbabwe); it is true that the Soviets remain in Afghanistan, still fighting five years after they started; and it is true that U.S. sanctions against Japan in 1941 did not prevent the attack on Pearl Harbor. But in evaluating the sanctions it is necessary to ask if, given the same circumstances but somewhat greater knowledge about what the future would bring, we would take the same actions again. My answer in the case of Rhodesia is negative, and my answers with respect to the Soviet Union and Japan are positive. It comes back to the questions posed earlier: What would the world be like in the absence of the actions, and what were the alternatives available? In the case of Rhodesia, it took fourteen years and a major civil war to result in majority rule. For a variety of reasons the embargo was predictably largely a symbolic one since South Africa refused to cooperate. That does not mean that Rhodesians did not feel the effects of the embargo, as Hufbauer and Schott show, but it does mean that the embargo was not able to cripple the Rhodesian economy. I believed at the time, and subsequent conversations with British officials have strengthened the belief, that the Ian Smith regime of Rhodesia could have been brought down by sending promptly a small force of British commandos in 1965. The embargo would have been unnecessary, and the subsequent civil war could possibly have been avoided. From that point of view, if my judgment is correct, the embargo was the wrong policy to pursue in that it resulted in a much higher cost to attain the objective.

In the case of economic sanctions against the Soviet Union following its invasion of Afghanistan, it was clear that there was nothing the United States and its allies could do, short of war, to induce the Soviets to withdraw from Afghanistan. That was known and understood at the time, although public officials understandably had some reticence about stating publicly that the United States could not get the Soviets to leave Afghanistan. The purpose of the embargo was quite different: to present a strong remonstrance at the Soviet actions to the Soviet Union and, even more important, to the rest of the world, especially to other countries in southern Asia and the Middle East, on whom the Western world depends much more heavily than it does on Afghanistan. The economic sanctions, and particularly the grain embargo, had the desired effect. Paradoxically the louder that American farmers complained about the grain embargo, the more effective it was as a serious statement of U.S. concern about Soviet actions to foreign ears. More conjecturally it is possible to argue that Afghan resistance would have been greatly weakened if the United States had seemed to acquiesce in the Soviet invasion, confining its protestation to speeches and diplomatic notes. Also more conjecturally it is possible to argue that Soviet restraint with respect to Poland in the next few years was conditioned by the strong U.S. reaction to the Soviet invasion of Afghanistan, a country that was far more remote and far less threatening to direct Western interests than was Poland. There is not much leverage that the United States has with respect to the Soviet Union, but the 1980 embargo showed that the United States was serious in its concerns, short of going to war.

Similarly Hufbauer and Schott score as completely ineffective the U.S. oil sanction on Japan in 1941 since (presumably) it did not prevent the Japanese attack on Pearl Harbor. But was this the objective in freezing Japan's assets? We do not know what President Roosevelt thought. We do know, however, that the two leading agencies advising him, the State Department and the U.S. Navy, were quite confident that an oil embargo would lead to war—not an attack on Pearl Harbor, which was not foreseen, but an attack on the Dutch East Indies that would almost certainly involve the Philippines and might well draw the United States into war.

Formal restrictions on U.S. exports to Japan in fact came in a series of steps, starting in July 1940 with a ban on the sale of all arms and munitions, critical and strategic raw materials, airplane parts, optical instruments, and metal working machinery. Later in the month aviation gasoline and number 1 heavy iron and steel scraps were added to the list. These export restrictions seem to have been motivated mainly by domestic shortages in the face of the need to mobilize for war, combined with strong moral disapproval of Japan's bombing of civilians in China and a desire to dissociate from it. After Japanese troops moved into Tonkin in August, the export ban was extended to all iron and steel scrap as a reproof, signaling that the United States was serious. The ban was specifically not extended to oil, on the ground that that would provoke Japan to war and the United States was not yet ready for it (Feis, 1950, pp. 74, 92–93, 106).

The following summer the United States warned Japan not to move troops and aircraft into South Vietnam (from where it would be possible to attack the British base at Singapore and reach the oil wells in Sumatra). Japan ignored the warning, whereupon the United States froze Japanese assets, in effect putting all exports to Japan under license. In fact only a few licenses were given, but the U.S. government maintained an ambiguity about licensing policy and never formally banned the sale of oil, known to be a political touchstone in Japan.

By this time U.S. policymakers were gravitating toward the view that war with Japan was inevitable since the United States would not alter its principles and Japan seemed unwilling to alter its behavior. The task therefore was seen to be to play for time while U.S. forces could be built and positioned—especially the new B-17 long-range bomber to the Philippines—and to inhibit Japan's preparations for war. The embargo of critical materials, iron and steel scrap, oil (de facto), and rubber and tin from the Philippines and Malaya played a role by weakening Japan's stocks of critical materials and conserving those in the United States. Japanese stocks of iron and steel scrap and petroleum fell consequentially during 1941, as Japanese consumption ran ahead of reduced imports, in contrast to previous years in which stocks had been built (Feis, 1950, pp. 109, 268–269).

Feis, the historian of U.S.-Japanese relations immediately before U.S. entry into the war, concludes that "the [scrap] embargo failed as a lesson, since it was taken up as a challenge" (Feis, 1950, p. 109). But his own evidence suggests that the principal purposes of the series of restrictive steps the United States took between July 1940 and July 1941 were less to provide a lesson than to conserve scarce materials at home (and make them available to Britain, which was at war with Germany) and to deny crucial materials to Japan. In this the restrictions were at least a partial success.

Judgments may and do differ on these points. I cite these examples simply to illustrate how difficult it is to evaluate even after the fact the impact of a given course of action in a complex situation.

In concluding, I will quote two statesmen on the overall relationship between trade policy and foreign policy. In his famous Farewell Address, George Washington said in September 1796 (Commager, 1958, p. 174):

The great rule of conduct for us in regard to foreign nations is, in extending our commercial relations to have with them as little *political* connection as possible. . . .—Harmony, liberal intercourse with all nations are recommended by policy, humanity, and interest. But even our commercial policy should hold an equal and impartial hand, neither seeking nor granting exclusive favors or preferences.

And nearly two hundred years later Henry Kissinger observed:

The vulnerability of American policy to protectionist pressures . . . remains a serious weakness of the American system. . . . Protectionism is above all an untenable posture for a nation that seeks to be the leader of the alliance of industrial democracies. (Kissinger, 1979, p. 340)

References

Acheson, Dean. *Present at the Creation.* New York: W. W. Norton, 1969.

Adler-Karlsson, Gunnar. *Western Economic Warfare, 1947–1967.* Stockholm: Almquist and Wiksell, 1968.

Ball, George W. *The Past Has Another Pattern*. New York: W. W. Norton, 1982.

Bemis, Samuel Flagg. *A Diplomatic History of the United States*. 4th ed. New York: Henry Holt & Co., 1955.

Brzezinski, Zbigniew. *Power and Principle*. New York: Farrar, Straus, Giroux, 1983.

Commager, Henry Steele, ed. *Documents of American History*. 6th ed. New York: Appleton-Century-Crofts, 1958.

Cooper, Richard N. "Third World Tariff Tangle." *Foreign Policy* 4 (Fall 1971): 35–50.

Cooper, Richard N. "Trade Policy Is Foreign Policy." *Foreign Policy* 9 (Winter 1972–1973): 18–36.

Destler, I. M., Haruhiro Fukui, and Hideo Sato. *The Textile Wrangle: Conflict in Japanese-American Relations*. Ithaca: Cornell University Press, 1979.

Dornbusch, Rudiger, and Stanley Fischer. "The Open Economy: Implications for Monetary and Fiscal Policy." NBER Working Paper, no. 1422 (August 1984).

Feis, Herbert. *The Road to Pearl Harbor*. Princeton, N.J.: Princeton University Press, 1950.

Frankel, Jeffrey A. "The 1807–1809 Embargo against Great Britain." *Journal of Economic History* 42 (1982): 291–308.

Friedman, Milton, and Anna J. Schwartz. *A Monetary History of the United States, 1867–1960*. Princeton, N.J.: Princeton University Press, 1963.

Gardner, Richard N. *Sterling-Dollar Diplomacy*. Oxford: Oxford University Press, 1956.

Hoover, Herbert. *The Memoirs of Herbert Hoover*. Vol. 2, *1920–1933*, and vol. 3, *The Great Depression, 1929–1941*. New York: Macmillan, 1952.

Hufbauer, Gary Clyde, and Jeffrey J. Schott. *Economic Sanctions Reconsidered: History and Current Policy*. Washington, D.C.: Institute for International Economics, 1985.

Hull, Cordell. *The Memoirs of Cordell Hull*. Vol. 1. New York: Macmillan, 1948.

Kennan, George F. *Memoirs, 1925–1950*. Boston: Little, Brown, 1967.

Kindleberger, Charles P. *The World in Depression, 1929–1939*. Berkeley: University of California Press, 1973.

Kissinger, Henry A. *The White House Years*. Boston: Little, Brown, 1979.

Kissinger, Henry A. *Years of Upheaval*. Boston: Little, Brown, 1982.

Lake, David A. "International Economic Structures and American Foreign Economic Policy, 1887–1934." *World Politics* 35 (1983): 517–543.

Pierre, Andrew J. *The Global Politics of Arm Sales*. Princeton, N.J.: Princeton University Press, 1982.

Ratner, Sidney. *The Tariff in American History*. New York: Van Nostrand, 1972.

Stimson, Henry L., and McGeorge Bundy. *On Active Service in Peace and War*. New York: Harper & Brothers, 1947.

Taussig, Frank W. *Some Aspects of the Tariff Question*. Cambridge: Harvard University Press, 1915.

Taussig, Frank W. *The Tariff History of the United States*. 8th ed. New York: G. P. Putnam & Sons, 1931.

Temin, Peter. *Did Monetary Forces Cause the Great Depression?* New York: W. W. Norton, 1976.

Truman, Harry S. *Memoirs*. Vol. 2 Garden City, N.Y.: Doubleday, 1956.

Notes

1. In 1940 the United States froze the assets in the United States of European countries that had been overrun by the Nazis to prevent the Nazis from seizing those assets. It did not freeze German assets until June 1941, after Hitler's invasion of the Soviet Union.

2. When the delicate issue of emigration was raised with Deng Xiaoping during his 1979 visit to the United States and his attention was drawn to this condition for MFN under U.S. law, Deng is reported to have exposed U.S. hypocrisy on the issue by asking, "Fine. How many do you want: 10 million?"

Comment on "Trade Policy as Foreign Policy"

Gary Clyde Hufbauer

Since World War II, the great triumphs of U.S. foreign policy have largely been economic: the postwar renaissance of Europe and Japan, much assisted by the Marshall Plan and basic structural reforms; the spread of development along market-oriented lines to such diverse nations as Malaysia, South Korea, India, and Pakistan, with large doses of bilateral aid and World Bank loans; the spectacular growth of world trade flourishing under the umbrella of the GATT system; the spread of multinational corporations; and the creation of an enormously resilient international banking system. Together these achievements add up to the successful marketing of an economic system on a grand scale in a very short time.

By comparison with these economic triumphs, U.S. foreign policy in the field of military and political contests has experienced many frustrations: the seemingly permanent division of Europe; a divided Korea; defeat in Vietnam; Soviet occupation of Afghanistan; an unfriendly government in Cuba; Soviet parity in nuclear weaponry; thirty years of turmoil in the Mideast.

But as Cooper notes, economic policy receives decidedly less attention than military and political affairs in the memoirs of leading statesmen. Indeed a functioning international economy is seen as part of the landscape, rather like the lawns of the Oxford and Cambridge colleges. The economy, like an Oxbridge lawn, is most noticed when torn up—for example, by the 1973 and 1979 oil shocks. Seldom do international economic events involve the clash of personalities or the intricate play of alliances that make good memoir material. But when the authoritative history of the U.S. role in shaping world events over the years 1945–2000 comes to be written, the economic story should receive a good deal more attention than it was given by Acheson, Kissinger, or Brzezinski.

Cooper identifies three phases in the interaction between trade policy and foreign policy. In the period 1765–1820 trade policy served as instrument of foreign policy, with boycotts and embargoes a major feature. In the period

1820–1934 trade policy became a leading objective of foreign policy, in the sense that export promotion was a key theme. After 1934 trade policy once again became an instrument of foreign policy: open trade became a device for cementing the Western alliance, while trade sanctions were used to deny strategic goods to the Soviet Union and China (usually with little effect) and to shape the policies of numerous smaller powers (often with success) (Hufbauer and Schott, 1985). In this third period public and private flows of capital came to be seen as coequal instruments with trade in the overall management of foreign relations.

Can the post-1934 phase last for the foreseeable future—say to the year 2000? I think not. It seems to me that we are entering a fourth phase where trade and finance once again become an objective of foreign policy.

In a *forthcoming* book I. M. Destler (1986) spells out the decline of the post-1934 approach to trade policy. This decline is important because it was Franklin Roosevelt's liberal approach that enabled successive administrations to use trade as an instrument of foreign policy. The post-1934 regime had at least three key features:

1. Congressional delegation of extensive trade negotiating powers to the president.

2. The design of elaborate legal mechanisms—the escape clause, the countervailing duty, the antidumping duty, and the omnibus section 301—meant to depoliticize pressure in unfair trade cases and in fair but injurious trade cases.

3. A general faith that an open, nondiscriminatory trading system would serve U.S. commercial interests and that macroeconomic policies—fiscal policy, monetary policy, and since 1971, floating exchange rates—would serve to ensure a rough balance between imports and exports.

In recent years these elements of the liberal order have come under increasing attack. After seven GATT rounds average tariff levels have reached quite low levels, and Congress has not been inclined to delegate authority to the president to negotiate nontariff barriers. Indeed in the Kennedy Round, congressional sensitivities were rubbed the wrong way over administration attempts to bargain away the American selling price system and certain features of the U.S. antidumping law. As a result, in the legislation that ushered in the Tokyo Round, the Trade Act of 1974, Congress gave the president only talking room on nontariff barriers, with instructions to report back for implementing authority. A similar short leash will likely characterize the Reagan Round of trade negotiations. Close congressional guidance affords the administration less scope to use trade negotiations as an instrument of foreign policy.

As for the depoliticization of trade in hard luck cases, since the 1930s, successive presidents have responded to congressional pressure with long-lasting quota regimes to protect major industries: sugar (1934), dairy (1953), meat (1965), and petroleum (1959–1973). More recently this style has spread to important industrial sectors, beginning with textiles and apparel (1957), steel (1969), and automobiles (1981). In big trade cases, as Cooper (1972–1973) observed, the legal mechanisms of the countervailing duty law, the antidumping law, and the escape clause have been used not as a vehicle for statutory relief but as a fast ride to political solutions. Learning from this experience, important congressional blocs have come to view trade policy as an instrument of industrial policy: as a device to protect those declining sectors that can mount sufficient congressional pressure to catch a presidential eye.

Meanwhile a broad spectrum of business leaders have increasingly come to doubt that the GATT system will ensure fair access to export markets. It is not only Eastern Europe, China, Brazil, and numerous other developing countries that are seen as practitioners of controlled trade. Japan is viewed as the star example of a country that closes its markets to foreign goods using a formidable array of administrative and cultural barriers. In most countries of the world, power plants, civil and military aircraft, and public telephone systems are seen as objects of diplomacy first and commerce second. The view is widely gaining ground that market access must be traded for market access on a country-by country or even sector-by-sector basis. The institutional counterpart to these ideas is that, within the executive branch, the management of trade policy has gradually shifted away from the State Department to the U.S. Trade Representative and the Commerce Department, agencies that are far more attentive to domestic interests.

Finally, faith that macroeconomic forces will bring about a balanced current account position and a competitive exchange rate has been badly shaken. In recent years the automatic stabilizers seem to have disappeared. When capital flows drive trade flows, rather than responding passively, enormous tensions are set up between the free flow of capital and the free flow of goods. This tension has erupted in Congress with considerable talk of an import surcharge. Meanwhile a Republican administration has embraced the concepts and nuances of managed trade.

As a consequence of forces that are eroding support for a liberal approach to trade policy, a troubling discordance has emerged between U.S. politico-military relationships and its economic relationships. In the politico-military sphere the NATO countries and Japan are seen as U.S. allies; countries such as Israel, Saudi Arabia, and Pakistan are regarded as friendly; Sweden, Switzerland, India, and many others are seen as neutral; and Eastern Europe is viewed as the enemy. In the economic sphere Canada, Israel, and the Caribbean basin are the allies; Europe and Japan are at best friendly; much of Latin America is barely neutral; and Eastern Europe remains the enemy. The discordance between the high standing of Europe and Japan in politico-military terms and their far lower standing in economic terms says a great deal about the executive branch's current difficulties in using trade policy as an instrument of foreign policy.

Emphasis on using trade policy to cushion the decline of weak industries and to open markets for strong industries will likely continue for a good many years. In the forthcoming Reagan Round of trade talks, the United States will ask for reciprocal concessions from Brazil and Mexico, as well as Canada and Europe. In the case of Japan, the United States will probably ask for advance implementation of concessions. Indeed the NTT affair is merely a prologue for future U.S.-Japan trade battles. The new hard-headed approach means less scope for using international economic policy as an instrument of Pax Americana. Whether the new approach will cause Pax Americana to unravel is an interesting question that I leave for a later occasion.

References

Cooper, Richard N. "Trade Policy Is Foreign Policy." *Foreign Policy* 9 (Winter 1972–1973): 18–36

Destler, I. M. *System under Stress: The Politics of American Trade*. Washington, D.C.: Institute for International Economics 1986. Forthcoming.

Hufbauer, Gary C., and Jeffrey J. Schott. *Economic Sanctions Reconsidered: History and Current Policy*. Washington, D.C.: Institute for International Economics, 1985.

Comment on "Trade Policy as Foreign Policy"

Stephen D. Krasner

Cooper presents a set of relationships between commercial policy and foreign policy goals and illustrates these possibilities with reference to the historical experience of the United States. To summarize briefly, he argues that trade policy was an instrument of foreign policy during the early years of American independence aimed at establishing nationhood, that export promotion was an objective of trade policy from 1820 to 1934, and that promotion of a general environment conducive to full employment, growth, political development, and international harmony has been the primary goal of commercial policy since 1934.

These three possibilities can be placed in a larger descriptive framework that distinguishes commercial policy according to its objectives. At least five possible goals of commercial policy can be described: sovereign autonomy, power maximization, specific political objectives, specific economic objectives, and milieu goals.

1. Sovereign autonomy. In the present international system the ability of a state to control its commercial policy (although not its consequences) is regarded as a basic attribute of sovereignty. In the eighteenth century the resistance of the American colonies to commercial and other economic policies established in England was part of the basic struggle to achieve political independence. Similarly a major objective of Japanese policy at the end of the nineteenth century was to regain control of the right to set tariff levels, a right that had been denied Japan through unequal treaties imposed by Europe and the United States. China sought to reassert sovereignty over commercial policy that it had lost through Britain's victory in the Opium Wars. Various Western Hemisphere states pressed to reverse the consequences of gunboat diplomacy, which at times included foreign control of their customs houses. Concerns about sovereign control have largely disappeared as a consequence of decolonization. In the contemporary environment they are echoed, albeit faintly, in issues such as the debate over the legitimate scope of IMF conditionality.

Any political entity aspiring to independence will make sovereign control over commercial policy a basic objective. This control is a necessary condition for using commercial policy for other purposes.

2. Power maximization. Commercial policy may be used to promote the relative power position of the state in the international system. This may imply attempting to enhance relative growth, especially in militarily relevant sectors, guarding against dependence on critical imported materials, or avoiding situations of asymmetric relative opportunity costs.

A state that aims at power maximization is likely to regard trade as a zero-sum situation. Such a state is concerned with the relative, not the absolute, gains from trade. This does not necessarily imply protectionism. If free trade provides proportional benefits for two states, they may have liberal commercial policies even if they are interested in power maximization. If one state is concerned with power maximization but others are not, liberal policies may also prevail. But if openness would result in asymmetric benefits and both states are concerned with power maximization, trade will be restricted.

In the contemporary environment the best example of concerns with power maximization involves U.S. relations with the communist bloc. The United States has tried to block Soviet access to commodities that could have military value. Some U.S. officials have also argued that trade should be restricted to weaken the overall capability of the Soviet economic system, although this policy has never been consistently implemented. In the 1930s Nazi Germany adopted a trade policy designed to maximize its power relative to the smaller states of Central Europe by enmeshing them in a set of trading relationships from which they could not extricate themselves except at great cost, relationships that imposed at least short-run economic costs on Germany (Hirschman, 1945). The mercantilist policies of the seventeenth and eighteenth century that are generally associated with export promotion, import restrictions, and efforts to accumulate bullion were formulated to increase the power of the state. Although the specific tactics of the mercantilists now appear to be ill informed, if not quaint, their policy objective of power maximization has hardly become obsolete.

3. Specific political objectives. Commercial policies may be aimed at specific political goals rather than the overall power capability. Hirschman (1945) offers an elegant analysis of the conditions under which such coercion can be implemented. A state can effectively use a pattern of international transactions for political purposes when the opportunity costs of change are asymmetric. If state A gains far more in economic terms from a set of trading relations than state B, state B can credibly threaten to alter those relations if state A does not accept state B's policy preferences. If, however, state A can find new markets

for exports or imports or if factors of production within state A can easily shift to different sectors with limited income loss, state A cannot be subject to external coercion based on international economic transactions.

Small or undeveloped states are not likely to be able to use trade policy to achieve specific political objectives. But large, developed states with alternative markets, relatively low involvement in the world economy, and mobile factors may be able to implement economic coercion.

Political scientists and economists have generally dismissed the efficacy of economic statecraft. Deardorff and Stern argue in chapter 2 that embargoes are more likely to "generate resistance" than compliance. In chapter 8 Srinivasan, referring to findings in a study by Hufbauer and Schott (1985), states that the "lack of success ... is evident." Cooper is more open-minded. He writes, "What will be a surprise to many economists, Hufbauer and Schott find that economic sanctions were either moderately or very successful in about a third of the cases." Since economic sanctions are likely to be used only when other policy instruments fail, this level of success is indeed surprising.[1] Policymakers who have frequently resorted to economic statecraft may be wiser than conventional academic views suggest. If commercial policies can be used for specific economic objectives, trade issues cannot be kept on a separate track.

4. Economic objectives. The most extensive analysis and debate about commercial policy has been concerned not with political goals but with economic ones. Neoclassical trade theory demonstrates that everyone can, with effective redistributive mechanisms, be better off with free trade. The exceptions to this conclusion, primarily related to variants of optimal tariff and infant industry arguments, are few and generally regarded as being subject to great abuse by misguided, venal, or pusillanimous (weak-willed) policymakers.

Despite the elegance of trade theory, policymakers have rarely been willing to allow the international movement of goods to be solely determined by a free market. As Cooper points out, the promotion of exports was a basic goal of U.S. trade policy from 1820 to 1934. What distinguishes more recent activities from the nineteenth century is the clear recognition, embodied in GATT, of the need for reciprocity. Since World War II no state has been able to assume that tariff policy is merely a matter of domestic concern.

On the import side, U.S. restrictions have, as Cooper accurately notes, been primarily a result of protectionist pressures. Since the 1930s the executive branch, especially the White House and the Treasury and more recently the Office of the U.S. Trade Representative, has eschewed protectionism. Congress has, not surprisingly, been more responsive to specific constituency needs, although the propensity of Congress to support import restrictions should not be exaggerated. Since the beginning of the century, when the Tariff Commission was created, the legislature has been sympathetic, to varying degrees, with efforts to delegate discretionary control to the executive branch lest individual congressmen be overrun by particularistic pressures. (The classic treatment is Schattschneider's 1935 analysis of Smoot-Hawley.)

Trade policy has also been used frequently to promote industrial development. In the postwar period Japan is the premier example. The Japanese imposed substantial tariff barriers on the import of targeted manufactures through the 1960s. When tariff barriers began to be removed, nontariff barriers were sometimes erected in their place. Japanese companies were encouraged to import foreign technology, not foreign products. Only in the late 1970s did Japan dismantle most formal barriers. By that time a wide range of Japanese industries was able to compete effectively on world markets (Krasner and Okimoto, 1985). Catch-up industrialization and infant industry protection have not, of course, been limited to Japan. Virtually all of the latecomers in the nineteenth century (all states except Britain) protected their nascent manufacturing industries behind tariff barriers (Gerschenkron, 1962).

The general view of economists is that these countries succeeded despite protection. Since World War II many developing countries have imposed restrictions and failed to accomplish their economic objectives. The empirical evidence on the relationship between infant industry protectionism and growth is murky. Theoretical issues are also unresolved. Recent claims (Zysman and Cohen, 1983) about created comparative advantage in which intervention is explained as an effort to alter factor endowments reject the conventional Heckscher-Ohlin assumption that endowments are exogenous. Discussions of economies of scale, imperfect competition, and externalities as justifications for protection or subsidization do not address this issue.

5. Milieu objectives. Commercial policy can also be used to promote long-term political ideological, and security, as well as economic, objectives by attempting to create a particular global environment. Such milieu goals ignore clearly identifiable short-term benefits. As Cooper accurately notes, the United States placed great emphasis on milieu goals in formulating and implementing its trade policy in the postwar period.

The exceptional U.S. commitment to global liberalism since World War II has not been motivated by a desire to provide cheap Toyotas. Rather liberalism is, as Cooper notes, identified with a much broader and more ambitious set of foreign policy objectives related not only to global prosperity but also to world peace. An open international economic system has been seen as conducive to economic growth and prosperity, economic growth and prosperity to domestic political stability and democracy, political stability and democracy to nonaggressive foreign policies, and nonaggressive foreign policies to world peace. Conversely protectionism is associated with economic stress, economic stress with political instability and autocratic regimes, and instability and autocratic regimes with aggressive foreign policies and war (Packenham, 1973).

The use of trade policy to achieve general milieu goals is unusual; the postwar U.S. experience may even be unique. The British did pursue an open trading system in the middle of the nineteenth century, and British foreign policy was influenced by the Manchester school, which associated economic involvement with understanding and peace. But British efforts were not as intense or single-minded as those of the United States (McKeown, 1983; Stein, 1984).

In sum, commercial policy can be aimed at least five objectives: sovereign autonomy, power maximization, specific political objectives, specific economic objectives, and general milieu goals, especially global liberalism. These policies are not mutually exclusive. As Cooper notes, for the postwar United States, it is possible to identify specific policies with all but the first objective, and this because the establishment of sovereign control has not been an issue. There are, however, modal tendencies, and what distinguishes U.S. behavior since 1945 is the great effort directed to promoting a liberal and open international trading system.

How can this behavior be explained? What accounts for the variance in the objectives associated with commercial policy with regard to the weights given to different aims within a single country and variations across countries and over time? In particular, what accounts for the unusual postwar U.S. emphasis on milieu goals? Cooper offers two arguments: the lessons of history and of economic analysis.

The 1930s and World War II continue to hold great sway over the perceptions and beliefs of U.S. policymakers, as well as influencing the institutional environment within which policy is made. Cooper argues that "the most disastrous single mistake any U.S. president has made in international relations was Herbert Hoover's signing of the Hawley-Smoot Tariff Act into law in June 1930." The 1930s seemed to show that protectionism led to depression, autocracy, aggression, and war. Furthermore neoclassical economic analysis provided a powerful rationale for free trade, although the Heckscher-Ohlin-Samuelson model was an extension to, not a departure from, Ricardo's demonstration more than a century before that both parties could benefit from free trade. Thus the decisive explanation offered by Cooper for the U.S. adoption of milieu objectives for foreign commercial policy is the lesson of the 1930s.

Are there alternative explanations? Are the lessons so clear? Let us deal with
the lessons first. Put in more general terms the question is, Is there a systematic
relationship among high tariffs, economic breakdown, international disorder,
autocracy, and war? These relationships are more problematic than Cooper
suggests. These conditions did coexist to an unusual extent during the 1930s.
But consider the other great war of the twentieth century, World War I. This
war occurred during a period of relative economic growth and prosperity. The
depression of the latter part of the nineteenth century had ended. International trade and the ratio of trade to GNP was growing for most major
countries. Internal tensions were high in the Austro-Hungarian Empire, and
Germany and Russia as well, but these tensions were the result of ethnic
conflicts in Austria-Hungary and the consequences of economic growth in
Germany and Russia, not of economic breakdown and failure. (For some
general arguments, see Olsen, 1983. For a discussion of Germany, see Gordon,
1974.)

In general the relationship between economic distress and political autocracy is problematic even for the 1930s. The political response to the 1930s,
and to other periods of global depression such as the 1870s and the 1970s, has
not been uniform across countries. Economic difficulties did contribute to the
rise of the Nazi regime in Germany; however, they also led to the Democratic
coalition in the United States and to the dominance of the Labor party in
Sweden, both governments committed to democracy and equity. While Cooper is certainly right in noting that political science does not have the tools to
construct systematic counterfactual analyses, consider for a moment a U.S.
polity without the Great Depression and even without World War II. Would
such a polity be more democratic? Would, for instance, the position of
minorities be worse or better?[2]

In general the way in which states have responded to externally generated
economic pressures has been a function of their existing institutional structures and the political coalitions that form in response to new circumstances.
Major crises do weaken old patterns of behavior. They undermine the legitimacy of prevailing policies and beliefs. They lead specific interest groups to
rethink their self-interest and pattern of alliances. They prompt policymakers
to explore new institutional arrangements. The consequences of these efforts,
with regard to democracy, peace, and prosperity, have not been uniform
across countries (Gourevitch, 1977, 1984).

The relationship between economic performance and international peace is
also much more problematic than conventional U.S. views would suggest. In
fact, war has more often occurred during periods of increasing global prosperity than during periods of recession. A study by Vayrynen (1983) of major wars

(defined by battle deaths and duration) since 1815 found that seven occurred during periods of accelerated growth in the world economy and only two during periods of decelerated growth (the Soviet-Japan War of 1939 and World War II). Major wars have most frequently been associated with power transitions when relatively rapidly growing states try to alter existing boundaries and institutional arrangments (Doran, 1983; Organski and Kugler, 1980; Gilpin, 1981). If an open, liberal, global economy provides greater benefits for relatively weaker states, it may make war more rather than less likely.

Thus although Cooper's positive arguments concerning the perceptions of U.S. policymakers are convincing, his tacit acceptance of these arguments is not. U.S. policymakers have associated economic breakdown with autocracy and war, and this has influenced the commitment they have made to milieu objectives. But the historical evidence does not support this analysis.

Are there other explanations for the prominence the United States has given to milieu goals in the postwar period? Let me suggest one: a state will pursue milieu goals only when it is unconstrained by pressures emanating from the international system. Only very powerful states will be relatively free of constraints either political or economic. As these constraints increase, milieu goals will be subordinated to more specific political and economic concerns.

Consider U.S. behavior in the postwar period. The United States emerged from the war in a power position unparalleled in the history of the modern state system. Its GNP was three times larger than that of the Soviet Union and six times larger than that of Great Britain, its nearest rival in the noncommunist world. The industrial facilities of all of the other major countries had been damaged by the war. Through the mid-1950s the United States had a trade surplus in virtually all manufacturing sectors, including products such as shoes and textiles. As international competition increased, protectionist pressures grew, and U.S. policymakers resorted with somewhat greater frequency to directing commercial policy toward specific economic objectives rather than general milieu goals. I do not want to exaggerate this tendency because the ideological commitment to free trade and the institutional arrangements related to this commitment (the concentration of commercial policymaking in the executive branch) did moderate protectionist outcomes (see Goldstein, 1984).

Relations between the West and the Soviet bloc, dominated by concerns with relative power, were never included in the liberal trading system. U.S. policymakers were not willing to allow commercial activity to be guided by market principles. U.S. export controls and COCOM are the institutional manifestation of this policy. Confronted with a political threat, milieu goals were subordinated to other considerations.

As Cooper notes, there are also a number of departures from the liberal regime associated with specific political objectives rather than relative power capability. These include the free trade agreement with Israel, the Caribbean Basin Initiative, the GSP, and various examples of economic sanctions. It is, however, only fair to admit that the number of cases in which commercial policy has been directed toward specific political objectives are quite small in absolute terms, especially given the kind of leverage the United States had during the postwar years.

In sum there is an alternative explanation for U.S. commitment to liberal milieu goals in the postwar period. Rather than simply being motivated by the perceived lessons of the 1930s and the persuasiveness of neoclassical economic doctrine, U.S. policymakers were liberated from the normal concerns of statesmen by the extraordinary power position of the United States. In areas where U.S. power was not overwhelming, relative power capabilities and specific political objectives always dominated commercial policy. In areas where the constraints imposed by the international system increased, especially growing economic competitiveness, economic protectionism increased. The pursuit of general milieu goals by states is a luxury, not a natural or modal characteristic of international behavior. U.S. policy in the postwar period is an abnormal, not a typical, pattern. As U.S. power declines, central decision makers will confront more international constraints; as the number of constraints increases, policymakers will place more emphasis on specific economic and political objectives as opposed to milieu goals. This does not necessarily imply that the United States will move toward protectionism. It does, however, suggest that general principles will become less important; that the United States will more frequently demand reciprocity; that variations across different issue areas will increase; and that specific deals will become more important than general principles. While this tendency may disturb professional economists committed to the market and global economic efficiency, it may provide more political stability in a multipolar world in which the United States is unwilling to tolerate free riders and incapable of providing effective leadership. Shortly before the outbreak of World War I, Sir Norman Angell argued that the level of economic interdependence would preclude a general war. He was wrong. After World War II, U.S. policymakers concluded that protectionism led to general economic breakdown and breakdown to major international conflict. They were wrong too. The relationship between economic performance and global stability is highly attenuated. Without the luxury of overwhelming power, ideological commitments will give way to self-interested calculations of clearly identifiable short-run interests.

Notes

1. I am indebted to Robert Keohane for this point. See also Baldwin (1985) for similar conclusions about the efficacy of economic statecraft.

2. I confess to some discomfort with the suggestion of Olsen (1983) that a good catastrophe now and then is just what is needed for economic efficiency.

References

Baldwin, David. *Economic Statecraft: Theory and Practice*. Princeton: Princeton University Press, 1985.

Doran, Charles. "War and Power Dynamics: Economic Underpinnings." *International Studies Quarterly* 27 (1983): 419–442.

Gerschenkron, Alexander. *Economic Backwardness in Historical Perspective*. Cambridge: Harvard University Press, 1962.

Gilpin, Robert, *War and Change in World Politics*. Cambridge: Cambridge University Press, 1981.

Goldstein, Judith. "A Domestic Explanation for Regime Formation and Maintenance: Liberal Trade Policy in the U.S." Paper presented at the American Political Science Association meetings, Washington, D.C., September 1984.

Gordon, Michael. "Domestic Conflict and the Origins of the First World War." *Journal of Modern History* 46 (1974): 191–226.

Gourevitch, Peter. "International Trade, Domestic Coalitions, and Liberty: Comparative Responses to the Crisis of 1873–96." *Journal of Interdisciplinary History* 8 (1977): 281–313.

Gourevitch, Peter. "Breaking with Orthodoxy: Europe in the 1930s." *International Organization* 38 (1984): 95–130.

Hirschman, Albert. *National Power and the Structure of Foreign Trade*. Berkeley: University of California Press, 1945.

Huntington, Samuel P. *Political Order in Changing Societies*. New Haven: Yale University Press, 1968.

Krasner, Stephen, and Daniel Okimoto. "Japan's Trade Policy: From Mercantilism to Cooperation?" Mimeo. Department of Political Science, Stanford University, February 1985.

McKeown, T. "Hegemonic Stability Theory and the 19th Century Tariff Levels in Europe." *International Organization* 37 (1983): 73–92.

Olsen, Marcus. *The Rise and Decline of Nations*. New Haven: Yale University Press, 1983.

Organski, A. F. K., and J. Kugler. *The War Ledger*. Chicago: University of Chicago Press, 1980.

Packenham, Robert. *Liberal America and the Third World*. Princeton: Princeton University Press, 1973.

Schattschneider, E. E. *Politics, Pressures and the Tariff: A Study of Free Enterprise in Pressure Politics as Shown in the 1929–1930 Revision of the Tariff*. New York: Prentice-Hall, 1935.

Stein, Arthur A. "The Hegemon's Dilemma: Great Britain, the United States, and the International Economic Order." *International Organization* 38 (1984): 355–386.

Vayrynen, Raimo. "Economic Cycles, Power Transitions, Political Management and Wars between Major Powers." *International Studies Quarterly* 27 (1983): 389–418.

Zysman, John, and S. Cohen. "Open Trade and Competitive Industry." *Foreign Affairs* 61 (1983): 1113–1139.

8

The National Defense Argument for Government Intervention in Foreign Trade

T. N. Srinivasan

8.1 Introduction

The arguments for intervention in foreign trade on national defense grounds could be classified broadly into two categories. The first category is based on the perception that the existence and continued operation (at specified levels of output) of certain industries is deemed vital from the perspective of national defense. In the absence of intervention such industries may either go out of existence or operate at inadequate levels. If such is the case, there is the further issue of the form of intervention—in particular, whether intervention is called for in foreign trade is to be established. The second category arises at one level from an extension of the dictum of Clausewitz that war is the pursuit of diplomacy through other means, with strategic use of foreign trade substituting for the more violent instruments of war to achieve political objectives in international relations. More recently Cooper (1973) has gone so far as to characterize trade policy as foreign policy. At another level it reflects concerns that unfettered trade with adversaries in certain commodities and services will only strengthen their military (offensive and defensive) capability. In what follows the arguments under each of these categories will be described and analyzed from an economic point of view. Issues relating to the spillover effects from defense to the civilian sector of the economy are not addressed.

8.2 National Defense as a Noneconomic Objective

8.2.1 Production Expansion

It has long been argued that the viability of certain industries (particularly manufacturing industries) and of the availability of certain factors of production are vital from the point of view of national defense. From Alexander Hamilton who suggested in 1791 that the independence and safety of a country

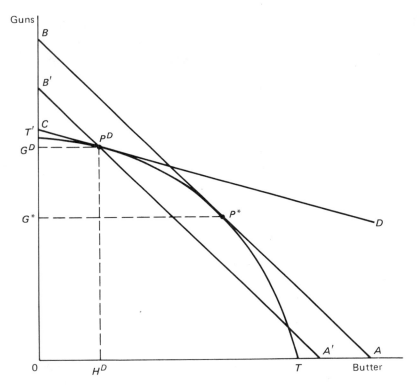

Figure 8.1
Optimality of an output subsidy to increase defense production.

were materially connected with the prosperity of its manufactures to General
Slay who is quoted by Seabury (1983) to have said in 1980 that the United
States cannot maintain its position as a first-rate military power with a second-
rate industrial base, it is a recurring theme. A case can be made for market
intervention based on this viability consideration. One of the simplest models
for demonstrating this is the standard static model of international trade in its
two-commodity version. Consider a country that can produce two commodities (with due apologies), guns and butter, in any combination lying inside or
on the boundary of the area OTT' in figure 8.1, the area being determined by
the availability of primary factors and the technology of production of guns
and butter. Suppose further that this country can trade with the rest of the
world, exchanging guns for butter at a fixed price represented by the slope of
the straight line AB. By producing the combination P^* (where the production
possibility curve $T'T$ is tangential to the international price line AB) and
trading with the rest of the world, our country can consume any combination

in the larger area bounded by OA, OB, and the line AB as contrasted with those in the area bounded by $T'T$ and the two axes available from domestic production alone. Suppose now that the domestic output OG^* of guns at P^* is deemed inadequate from a national defense point of view and an adequate output is OG^D. It is clear that an efficient way to achieve the output OG^D is to produce the combination P^D and trade along the line $A'B'$ through P^D parallel to AB. In other words, given that at least OG^D of guns is to be produced, relying only on domestic production will enable the country to consume any combination in the area $OH^D P^D T'$—but producing at P^D and trading allows consumption of any combination lying in the larger area bounded by OA', OB', and the line $A'B'$. The cost to the economy of achieving the national defense objective is the foregone opportunity of consuming any combination in the region lying between the two parallel lines AB and $A'B'$.

In this simple analysis although the mechanism by which resource allocation and production decisions are implemented was not spelled out, it is nevertheless clear that once at P^D, not availing the opportunity to trade along the line $A'B'$ cannot but hurt the economy. Hence the policy intervention to attain the needed shift in production, given that the defense objective has been defined in terms of production level of guns, will not involve intervention in foreign trade, if by intervention is meant the restriction of the choice of combination of guns and butter to some proper subset of those available by freely trading from the desired production point.

In order to go beyond this analysis, one has to spell out the institutional arrangements in which production and consumption decisions are taken in such an economy. For instance, in a command economy, the authorities decide that production will be at P^D and consumption at some point on $A'B'$. In the polar opposite case of a perfectly competitive economy, atomistic producers decide what and how much to produce (given commodity and factor prices that they assume will be unaffected by their own decisions) on considerations of their profit. Given the relative price of guns in terms of butter as represented by the slope of the line AB (or $A'B'$), production at P^* (and not at P^D) is consistent with profit maximization. A government wishing to shift production to P^D from P^* has to provide the needed incentives to private producers; that is, it has to ensure that the prices faced by the producer makes their profit maximization consistent with production at P^D. From figure 8.1, it is clear that such a price is the slope of the production possibility curve at P^D (that is, the slope of line CD), making guns relatively more expensive, compared to the slope of line AB. Since the objective is to shift production and not necessarily to restrict consumption choices, consumers will be allowed to choose from any combination achievable through trade at prices represented by $A'B'$ through trade from P^D. In other words consumer prices are the same whether production is at P^* or at P^D, while producer prices are different. A policy intervention that will achieve this wedge between producer and consumer prices is an output subsidy to producers of guns or equivalently an output tax on producers of butter. One can think of other equivalent taxes or subsidies on factor use (Bhagwati and Srinivasan, 1969). But the important point is that the intervention affects production and does not restrict trade. As such, an import tariff (which is equivalent to an output subsidy and a consumption tax at the same rate on the importable) is ruled out as an instrument to achieve the objective of national defense.

If we relax the assumption that the country faces fixed terms of trade (the slope of AB in figure 8.1) but instead it has market power in the sense that its trading volume affects its terms of trade, an influence not perceived and hence not taken into account by atomistic domestic producers and consumers, the traditional argument for the use of import tariff for exploiting its market power holds. However, the introduction of a national defense objective defined in terms of the level production of guns in such a context will call for the use of an output subsidy for gun producers (or its equivalent) in addition to a tariff to exploit market power. Although the level of the optimum tariff could be affected once such an objective is introduced, the relevant policy intervention associated with the objective is still the output subsidy. In any case, since producers have to be induced by the subsidy to produce what is deemed adequate rather than rely on the market forces to achieve without intervention, the defense objective can be termed noneconomic.

8.2.2 Consumption Expansion

One could have stated the national defense objective in terms of consumption rather than production of guns. Imagine, for instance, that guns could be used for private recreation as well as for national defense. While each consumer takes fully into account the recreational value to him of his gun, being one among a large number of consumers, he ignores the fact that his purchase of a gun contributes to national defense by adding to the total volume of gun purchases in the economy. Assuming as before that the economy can trade with the rest of the world at fixed terms of trade and representing private preferences (for simplicity assuming that all individuals are alike) by an indifference map, one can depict the nonintervention equilibrium in figure 8.2, with production at P^* and consumption at C^*.

Clearly the fact that private consumption of guns contributes to national defense as well means that a point other than C^* from among those available

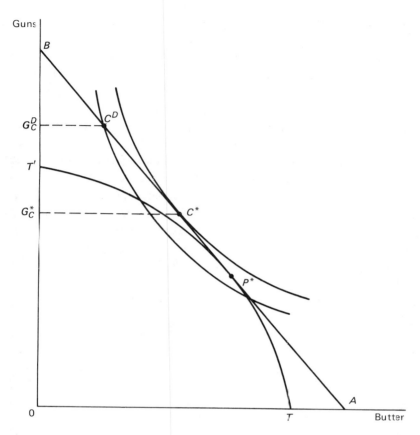

Figure 8.2
Optimality of a consumption subsidy to increase consumption of defense goods.

through production and trade will be socially desirable. Since producing at any point other than P^* and then trading (at terms represented by the slope of AB) will only shrink the set of available consumption points, adding the defense consideration will not dictate any change in production plans. Once its contribution to defense is accounted for, private consumption of guns ought to be higher than at C^*—say, at G_c^D. The consumers have to be induced to consume at C^D. This can be achieved by making consumers face a relative price of guns equal to the slope of their indifference curve through C^D (that is, making guns relatively cheaper than at C^*). This involves a consumption subsidy equal to the difference between the producer price (slope of AB) and consumer price (slope of indifference curve through C^D). Once again it is not optimal to intervene in trade through tariffs or quotas. With national defense considerations manifesting themselves as a consumption externality, a consumption subsidy is the appropriate form of intervention. Again such a subsidy will be in addition to an optimum tariff to exploit any market power that the country may have.

8.2.3 Export (Import) Restriction

An alternative formulation of the national defense or security objective is in the form of restricting the volume of exports, particularly of commodities (such as, computers) that have both civilian and military uses or of imports. Seabury (1983, p. 13), for instance, argues that "the fact that manufactures critical to U.S. defense needs may be made more cheaply abroad is a small comfort to anyone who would commonsensically conclude that the resulting dependence (on imports) would entail unacceptable risks." In the context of the institutional assumptions of the previous examples, private producers and consumers responding to the prevailing prices in the international market decide on their privately optimal production and consumption levels, thereby leading to an export (or import) level that may be too large from a national security perspective. In figure 8.3 the privately optimal production and con-

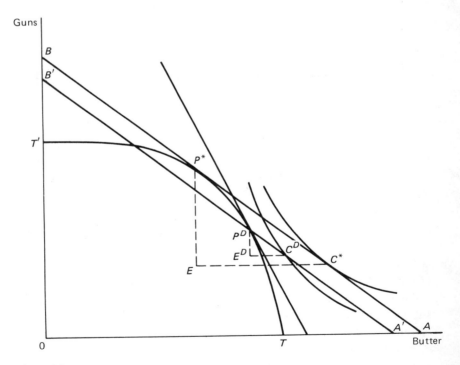

Figure 8.3
Optimality of an export tax to restrict exports of defense goods.

sumption points are P^* and C^*, respectively, resulting in an export of P^*E guns. To reduce the export to the level $P^D E^D$, it is natural to impose a tax on the export of guns (or equivalently a tax on the import of butter). Such tax being an output tax and a consumption subsidy on guns (both at the same rate) simultaneously reduces the output and raises the domestic consumption of guns, thereby reducing the export level. Clearly with the trade level, in this case the level of exports of guns, being the target of policy, the appropriate instrument is a trade tax: an export or import tariff. It can be shown that for achieving a specified reduction in exports, a production tax by itself (or a consumption subsidy by itself) is inferior to an export tax in that it leads to greater welfare loss to consumers compared to the situation of no intervention (Bhagwati and Srinivasan, 1969).

8.2.4 Employment Expansion

It is sometimes suggested that neither the level of output nor the level of consumption of a specific commodity (say, guns) is of interest from the point of view of national defense but the skills of the workers involved in its production are. One can view this consideration as requiring that employment in the production of guns should not be allowed to fall below some specified level. It is easy to show that the optimal policy instrument to achieve this is an employment subsidy (or equivalently an employment tax) to producers of guns (or producers of butter).

In sum, except in the case where national defense and security objectives directly involve the restriction of foreign trade, trade taxes (or equivalently quantitative restrictions in the form of trade quotas) are not the optimal policy instruments to achieve the objectives. This conclusion, however, does not in general hold if the policy intervention in the form of taxes (on production, consumption, employment or trade) or quotas involves the use of resources in their implementation or diverts resources to lobbying activities by private citizens to appropriate the revenues (rents) generated by the taxes (quotas). Under some circumstances, for instance, an import tariff, which is the optimal instrument to restrict imports in the absence of any lobbying for the disposition of the tariff revenue, may become inferior to a consumption tax on importables once the resources diverted to lobbying are taken into account. Similarly a production or consumption tax may not be the optimal policy instrument for achieving national security objectives defined in terms of domestic output or consumption once allowance is made for lobbying (Anam, 1982; Bhagwati, 1984; Bhagwati and Srinivasan, 1982, 1984). The intuitive explanation of this phenomenon is that resources diverted to lobbying or for enforcing the chosen policy not only shrink the production possibility set but also distort the production possibility frontier. Thus with lobbying there are two distortions: the distortion due to the policy instrument that triggered the lobbying in the first place and the lobbying-induced distortion. The net effect of the two distortions may vary depending on the policy instrument used.

8.3 Defense as an Externality

Consumption of certain commodities may not only generate welfare to private consumers but contribute to national defense as well. A consumption externality arose when in private consumption decisions, its contribution to national defense was not reflected. As contrasted with this static argument, Thompson (1979) develops two other dynamic national defense arguments that could also generate externalities. In his model defense expenditures are necessary social expenditures to prevent one nation from acquiring the assets (capital stock) of another. National defense expenditures are set at a level that ensures that the expected gains for a successful aggressor net of the resources he spends in his aggression are zero. It is reasonable to assume that defense expenditures so determined are an increasing function of capital stock and that private investors in their investment decisions that affect the capital stock will not take into account the effect of their investment on defense expenditures. Obviously an externality (in this case an external diseconomy) arises. A suitable ad valorem tax on capital will be needed to internalize such an externality in private investment decision profitability calculus. Thompson generalizes the model to allow for two opposing tendencies. First, private capital accumulation increases the defense expenditures needed to deter aggressors because an increase in capital stock ceteris paribus increases the return to successful aggression. Second, it increases the nation's defense capacity because, given any level of defense expenditures, the larger is the private capital stock, the greater are the resources available for mobilization in the event of aggression. Seabury (1983) makes a similar point: the United States as a guarantor of Western security has to have an adequate industrial capital that can be mobilized during a war. He adds that the U.S. industrial base (capital stock in industry) should include industrial assets readily fungible in case of major international crises and conflicts. Ignoring the issue of the composition of domestic capital stock, whether the appropriate form of intervention is a capital tax or subsidy depends on which of the two tendencies dominates. Thompson's empirical analysis based on data from a cross-section of countries leads him to conclude that in fact the first effect dominates, so that a capital tax rather than a subsidy is called for on national defense grounds.

Thompson's second argument is based on the fact that in war and other national emergencies, price ceilings and quantity rationing are often imposed. To the extent they cannot be evaded, they result in rational private investors' undervaluing their peacetime investment in capital stock that is producing such goods. Thus a capital subsidy raising its peacetime private value to its social value is called for. Many examples of possible private undervaluation of investment can be given. For instance, if individuals with particular skills are drafted into service in the armed forces (without an option to buy out of one's draft obligation) for a wage below market wage, then human capital investment in the acquisition of such skills in peacetime may be undervalued. Indeed generous military retirement plans have often been justified on the grounds that they compensate for underpayment during service. Investment in petroleum exploration in peacetime may be undervalued if, during wartime, price ceilings and rationing of petroleum supplies are certain to be imposed.

It is clear that peacetime tariff protection against the import of goods subject to wartime price controls would be an inefficient instrument compared to capital subsidy. Although a tariff would attract capital resources to the production of such goods in peacetime, it does not encourage investment needed to augment their output in wartime to the same extent as a capital subsidy. If, however, the country is a sufficiently large importer of capital as to affect its import price, under the usual assumptions there is a case for an optimum tariff in order to exploit the country's market power. To the extent that imports are restricted during wartime and price controls on outputs apply as well, the optimum tariff substitutes in part for the capital subsidy since it increases the domestic production of import-competing capital goods in peacetime as well as wartime.

In the case of goods (other than capital imports) that are wholly or largely imported, wartime rationing and price controls at home lead to undervaluation of peacetime foreign investment in foreign production of such goods. Since investment subsidy to foreigners is infeasible, domestic peacetime stockpiling of such goods and/or encouraging a foreign cartel are alternatives to capital subsidy.

Thompson also argues, citing Kahn (1960), that credibility of a nation's defense posture requires that the nation be willing to commit itself to punishing an aggressor even if it costs more than capitulating once aggression has taken place. In a system of majority voting, goes Thompson's argument, the citizenry will vote just enough resources to defense that will ensure that the expected net gain to an aggressor is zero. But in wartime when the nation's precommitment is being tested, the citizenry will not find it in its interest to devote more resources to fighting the war than its assets are worth. Thus credible commitment dictates that the military be assured a level of resources above what the citizenry will be willing to vote for. Since the military cannot tax the citizenry directly, the ability to purchase goods and services at controlled prices enables them to achieve the required level of real defense expenditure levels given the level of nominal expenditures voted by the citizenry. This rationale for wartime price controls also implies that the political process will not eliminate the peacetime undervaluation of investment that price controls generate. Thus a corrective fiscal intervention to offset the undervaluation is needed.

Thompson's interesting empirical analysis, though casual by the canons of econometrics, leads him to conclude that the actual fiscal policies in the United States turn out to be close to what would be optimal under his theory of national defense. In his view this occurred because the U.S. political system is guided by a compensation principle that meant that any Pareto-dominated policy has no chance of being approved.

8.4 Response to the Threat of Trade Embargoes and Sanctions

Yet another rationale for intervention arising from broad national security grounds is based on the possibility that a trade embargo might be imposed once hostilities break out. Indeed even a disruption of imports short of an embargo may have serious consequences in an emergency. The embargo threat is another aspect of the fear of excessive import dependence. A partial equilibrium analysis of the implications of a trade embargo is provided by Tolley and Wilman (1977). Mayer (1977) and Bhagwati and Srinivasan (1976) provide general equilibrium analyses. The following discussion is based on the latter. Consider a two-period model in which in the first period (peace) there is no threat of an embargo and in the second period (war or national emergency) with probability P an embargo will be imposed by the adversaries. Suppose the maximum national welfare achievable in the second period with (without) an embargo is $\underline{U}$ ($\bar{U}$) so that the expected welfare in the second period is $P\underline{U} + (1 - P)\bar{U}$. It is clear that as long as P, $\underline{U}$, and $\bar{U}$ are not affected by any action taken in the first period, there is no argument for intervention in the first period.

There are two possible but not mutually exclusive ways in which actions in the first period could affect the outcomes in the second. First, the production possibilities in the second period could be influenced by actions in the first, either through investment in capacity creation or because the first-period output (capacity) levels in various sectors of the economy restrict the choice of output levels in the second due to, say, adjustment costs. Second, the probability P may depend on the choices made in the first period, for instance, on the level of imports. It is plausible to argue that the level of a country's imports may be taken by its adversaries as an indicator of the vulnerability of its economy, and as such it is natural to assume that P is an increasing function of the level of imports. It should be stressed, however, that even if either circumstance prevails, there will be no case for intervention if private agents anticipate and allow fully for the dependence of outcomes in the second period on actions in the first.

Taking the case of investment first, it can be shown (see the chapter appendix) that if a risk-neutral private investor correctly anticipates the expected return to investment given that an embargo may be imposed, there is no need for intervention. If, on the other hand, the investor either ignores the possibility of an embargo or while correctly assessing the probability of an embargo nevertheless does not allow for the possibility that the marginal product of capital with embargo in place may differ from that in the absence of an embargo, intervention in the form of an investment subsidy (assuming that the difference in marginal products is positive) will be called for. If the first-period choice of production levels constrains those in the second period, once again an intervention in the form of an appropriate production tax (or subsidy) in the first period will be necessary if private production decisions do not anticipate and appropriately allow for the relevant effects. Last, if the probability of the imposition of an embargo is an increasing function of the level of imports in the first period and this effect is not allowed for in private decisions regarding imports, an import tariff is the appropriate form of intervention.

8.5 Strategic Use of Trade Restraints, Embargoes, and Economic Sanctions

The threat and, less often, the imposition of economic sanctions by one country against another in pursuit of mainly noneconomic goals such as foreign policy objectives are of ancient origin. From Pericles' Megarian decree of 432 B.C. that may have played a role in triggering the Peloponnesian war (Hufbauer and Schott, 1983) to the U.S. trade embargo on Nicaragua and the serious consideration allegedly being given to imposing some economic punishment on New Zealand for the latter's refusal to let U.S. naval vessels carrying nuclear weapons into its ports, economic sanctions have been viewed as an alternative to the use of force in the pursuit of policy objectives. The offer of economic concessions linked to changes in the policies of the recipient nation in directions desired by the offerer is another aspect of the same phenomenon. The literature, originating mainly from political scientists and political economists writing on East-West relations generally and U.S.-Soviet relations in particular, has been concerned with issues relating to the significance of East-West trade in increasing the military as well as economic capability of the East. Another example of the strategic use of international trade is the policy of accumulation of and release from stocks of certain commodities. The well-known recent example is the strategic petroleum reserve policy initiated by the United States after the first oil shock. Stockpiling of certain nonferrous metals is of longer standing. Even stocks of agricultural commodities that were compiled mainly to serve domestic policy objectives have come to have strategic significance in the pursuit of security objectives. Among the economic punishments being considered against New Zealand, apart from withdrawing the preferential treatment given to its lamb exports by the United States, is the possibility of releasing butter and other dairy products from U.S. stocks to the international market in order to hurt New Zealand's export earnings from the same products.

8.5.1 Strategic Stockpiles

Thompson's (1979) analysis suggested the accumulation of stocks of imported goods during peacetime as an alternative to an infeasible policy of subsidizing foreign investors for their peacetime undervaluation of investment for wartime exports reflecting price controls and rationing. Tolley and Wilman (1977) also examine the role of stockpiling in preembargo times as a way of responding to the threat of a future embargo. In the absence of any externalities, private storage activities will bring about the right amount of storage in response to an embargo threat. If, however, externalities arise, either government subsidization of private storage or government storage itself may be called for. Neither of these two analyses views stockpiling from a strategic perspective. Eaton and Eckstein (1984), on the other hand, develop a model in which the petroleum reserve policy is examined in a strategic context that takes into account that petroleum is an exhaustible resource so that imports for stock accumulation in any period not only affect equilibrium prices in that period but in all future periods as well.

   The model postulates a two-period world in which a single good in each period is produced with capital stock and oil as inputs. In the first period the output of the single good is allocated between current consumption and addition to capital stock. Oil can be extracted from the ground for current use and for storage. While all the oil left in the ground in the first period is available for extraction in the second, only part of the oil put in storage above the ground becomes available for use in the second period, thus reflecting cost of storage. Total amount of oil available in the ground may be known by all agents with perfect certainty in period 1, or alternatively it is uncertain in period 1 but becomes known at the beginning of period 2. It follows that in a world of perfect foresight in which markets for claims contingent on any possible stock of oil to be revealed in period 2 (in case it is uncertain) exist in period 1 and all agents behave competitively, no government intervention is necessary to sustain an intertemporally Pareto-optimal allocation of resources.

From a competitive world Eaton and Eckstein move to a world of bilateral monopoly in which a monopolistic seller of oil (OPEC) faces a monopsonistic buyer (the United States). OPEC's strategy variables are oil prices in the two periods and its investment in U.S. capital markets in the first. The U.S. government's strategy variables are import tariffs in the two periods, the tax rate on OPEC's investment in the United States, and the level of strategic petroleum reserve accumulated in the first period. Private agents behave atomistically, correctly anticipating U.S. and OPEC policies but treating them parametrically. Alternative rules of the game between OPEC and the United States are considered. One dichotomy is between open-loop policies, in which strategies for both periods are chosen in the first period, and feedback policies, in which the strategy for the second period is contingent on the outcome of the first period and the choice for the first period is made taking into account its influence on the second-period choices. Open-loop policies may result in time inconsistency; once the first-period component of the policy is implemented and its outcome known, one or the other of the players may not have an incentive to implement the second-period component of the open-loop policy. Thus open-loop policies may not be credible. Within each of these categories, two types of behavior can be distinguished: (1) one of the players acts as a (Stackelberg) follower in choosing his strategy given the strategy of the other player. While the latter, acting as a leader, sets his strategy, taking full account of the follower's reaction to his choice, (2) both choose their strategies simultaneously, acting as noncooperative Nash players with each taking the other's choice as given. In the case of feedback policies, the Stackelberg or Nash behavior applies to each period separately, while in the case of open-loop policies, it applies to the choice of strategies made in the first period but applicable for both periods. All agents are assumed to have perfect foresight. U.S. and OPEC policymakers correctly anticipate the effect of their policies on private behavior.

Although Eaton and Eckstein are able to characterize the optimal strategies of the players, they are unable to evaluate the overall welfare effects without making particular assumptions about functional forms that describe technology and preferences. They find that the strategic petroleum reserve policy in their model can have both desirable and undesirable consequences for U.S. welfare depending on technology, preferences, and rules of the game. In one scenario in which OPEC sets its prices taking into account U.S. response to its prices, a price-contingent U.S. inventory policy can improve U.S. and even world welfare. The authors suggest that the reason for this is that the optimal U.S. inventory policy makes U.S. demand more elastic in each period, thereby reducing the consequences of the distortion due to OPEC monopoly. Be that as it may, their main conclusion is that the case for establishing strategic reserves is rather limited.

8.5.2 Gains from Trade versus National Security and Global Political Influence

The traditional argument in favor of voluntary trade is that it will take place only if it leads to gains to both parties to the exchange. In international trade a country gains by pursuing its comparative advantage. With the opening of trade, it exports those commodities and services it produces relatively cheaply compared to its trading partner prior to trade and imports those that were relatively more expensive to produce. The distribution gains from trade (measured by using some metric such as the Hicksian equivalent variation) will depend on how far the posttrade equilibrium prices deviate from the pretrade prices of each partner. And anything that has the effect of reducing the prices that a country obtains for its exports or raising the prices it pays for its imports reduces the gains from trade.

By viewing conflict between two countries as having the effect of reducing export and raising import prices in their trade, Polachek (1980) tests the hypothesis that a negative relationship between conflict and trade exists, using ten-year, thirty-country cross-section data. Conflict is quantified by analyzing yearly events reported in forty-seven newspaper sources and coding them on a fifteen-point scale representing different kinds of conflict and cooperation. Between any pair of countries, a measure of net conflict is obtained by computing the difference between the frequency of conflictual events (categories 9–15) and cooperative events (categories 1–7). Since the direction of causality can run both ways (less conflict can lead to more trade, and greater trade can lead to less conflict), Polachek estimates a simultaneous equation model in which exports, imports, and conflict are endogenous and several exogenous variables are included. He finds (p. 55) that "a doubling of trade on average leads to a 20% diminution of belligerence." In a later application of similar ideas to the East-West trade during the period of détente, Gasiorowski and Polachek (1982) postulate that incentives to reduce conflict are related to the desire to protect gains from trade. If the distribution of gains is skewed toward one partner, the other can use it as a lever to obtain political concessions. They find a strong inverse relationship between trade and conflict. With the Warsaw Pact members having relatively more to gain from trade with the United States, trade leads to a greater reduction in conflicts directed from the Warsaw Pact to the United States than in conflicts directed from the United States to the Warsaw Pact. Granger causality tests suggested that the direction of causation is far stronger from trade dependence to conflict than vice-versa. The authors also report correlations between conflict and trade in specific commodity groups. They find that capital goods exports from the United States and imports of industrial supplies into the United States from the Warsaw Pact countries have much higher (negative) correlation coefficients than trade in other commodity groups. They view this finding as confirming that the dependence of Warsaw Pact countries on the West for technology imports and their comparative advantage in supplying industrial raw material to the West tend to moderate their conflicts with the United States.

The perceived trade-off between gains from trade with the East and security interests of the West has led to the imposition of formal controls on such trade (including controls on investment and technology transfer) through COCOM, consisting of all NATO countries except Iceland and Japan. Sweden and Switzerland, though not members of COCOM, nevertheless broadly conform to COCOM decisions. There is a vast literature on East-West economic relations in general and the functioning of COCOM-imposed controls in particular (Agnelli 1980; Hanson, 1981; Holzman and Levgold, 1975; Roosa, Matsukawa, and Gutowski, 1982). Root (1984) provides a succinct exposition of the rationale of trade controls, the inevitable conflict of interests among members of COCOM arising from unequal incidence of the economic cost of controls in individual countries, and other internal contradictions. The following discussion is based on his analysis.

The basic agreed objective of COCOM control was to prevent Western goods and technology from adding significantly to the military potential of the East. The United States, however, favored the further use of selective export restrictions for political purposes not directly related to Western security interests and indeed attempted it unilaterally on several occasions. The other COCOM members were opposed on the grounds that such selective controls could not be defined clearly, let alone equitably administered, and in any case they were unlikely to alter Soviet behavior. The U.S. position was based on the belief in the White House that the gains from East-West trade accrued almost entirely to the East and as such, "given Soviet needs, expanding trade without political quid pro quo was a gift. Our strategy was to use trade concessions as a political instrument, withholding them when Soviet conduct was adventurous and granting them in measured doses when the Soviets behaved coopera- tively" (Henry Kissinger as quoted in Agnelli, 1980, p. 1020). Other branches of the U.S. government, on the other hand, favored liberalized trade: the State Department on the belief it would improve the political climate for negoti- ations in other areas such as arms control and the Commerce Department on traditional grounds that it would improve U.S. business prospects. While the executive branch attempted to link trade to external behavior of the Soviets, the Congress went even further and linked it to Soviet treatment of some of its own citizens, in particular Soviet policy toward emigration of Jews.

Even the argument that controls limited to export of items of potential military use are sensible has been challenged on the grounds that the Soviet Union would not let itself become critically dependent on Western suppliers for running its military machine and, further, controls would merely accele- rate Soviet development of indigenous technology to substitute for Western imports. In the absence of peacetime controls, it is argued, the Soviets would refrain from actions that would reduce their dependency and thus make themselves vulnerable during crises or wartime. This argument is without merit. The same behavioral response of the Soviets to peacetime controls by the West—accelerated import substitution—would be elicited if instead of peacetime controls they expect embargoes to be imposed during crisis. Indeed this is what the analysis of the threat of embargoes in section 8.4 would lead one to expect.

The essential point of peacetime controls or embargoes in crisis is to impose an opportunity cost (perceived or actual) on the Soviets. This cost is the foregone gains, both static and dynamic, from trade. The static gains arise from resource savings in having a production and trade pattern that conforms to static comparative advantage, and the dynamic gains arise from resource savings in having an investment (human and physical) pattern that conforms to dynamic comparative advantage. The dynamic gains would also include any favorable impact on the rate and character of resource productivity, raising technical change that trade in goods and services, particularly equipment, brings about. The gains could be modest or large, but whether the gains in productive capacity would be used for augmenting military strength or consumer welfare depends on Soviet policymakers' objectives.

There are diametrically opposite views expressed in the literature on Soviet policymakers' objectives and response. Those opposed to controls argue that the cost imposed on the Soviets by the controls would be shifted entirely to the consumer or civilian part of the economy with no appreciable effect on the military. Those in favor of controls argue that even the Soviets could not impose a full shift and the military would have to bear at least part of the cost. Another strand in the arguments about the use of gains from trade relates to the influence of trade with the West on economic reform within the Soviet Union. Some believe that with the import of equipment and its installation, the Soviets would get an opportunity to observe the technological superiority of Western equipment and the efficiency of their contractors over their domestic analogs and would then initiate and/or accelerate economic reform. Others believe that by importing Western technology and employing Western contractors to install it, the Soviets would be able to postpone the badly needed but politically risky reform of the system. This debate about Soviet policymakers' responses sometimes degenerates into imagining two opposing camps in the highest echelons of the Soviet policymaking apparatus: the doves committed to détente, consumer welfare, and peaceful policies and the hawks inexorably pursuing global domination and arguing whether Western controls strengthen the doves or the hawks.

Root (1984) correctly argues that it would be simplistic to assume that gains from East-West trade accrue entirely to the East, and, as such, there is a cost to the West as well of trade controls. For instance, the loss of potential profits from sales to the East could affect the resources devoted to research and development in the West and hence slow down the pace of technical change. Also freedom of scientific exchange that is inhibited by the controls could dampen fundamental research.

An example of Western gain from sales to the Soviets is in oil and gas equipment and technology. Such sales, by enabling the Soviets to develop their Siberian natural gas and oil resources for sale to Western Europe and Japan, would have helped the latter countries to diversify their source of energy imports. The strategic significance of an assured supply of energy is obvious. The Europeans correctly perceived this, and diversifying Western sources of energy had been a U.S. objective as well. Yet the United States, by attempting to achieve political objectives that related to the Soviet trial and conviction of dissident Anatoly Schcharansky in 1978, Soviet invasion of Afghanistan in 1979, and imposition of martial law in Poland 1981, periodically suspended licenses for the export of such equipment. Eventually these export controls were extended to exports by U.S. subsidiaries abroad and of foreign-made products using U.S. technology irrespective of whether such technology transfer had taken place prior to the imposition of U.S. restrictions. Other Western nations rejected the U.S. policy, and finally the Reagan administration bowed to allied pressure.

8.5.3 Security and Gains from Trade: A Simple Model

Many of the arguments of section 8.5.2 can be sharply illustrated by the following two-country model. Each country produces three goods, two are traded internationally, and the third, called security or defense, is a nontraded good. The welfare of each country's citizens depends on the consumption of the two traded goods. Consider the decision problem of one of the countries. Let C_i denote its consumption of good i $(i = 1, 2)$ and Q_i the production of good i $(i = 1, 2, 3)$. The production possibility frontier (PPF) of this country (given its resource endowment, not explicitly shown) is given by:

$$F(Q_1, Q_2, Q_3) = 0 \tag{8.1}$$

with the domain of (Q_1, Q_2, Q_3) being determined by the resource endowment. Assuming the production possibility set of this economy to be convex implies that F is concave.

Suppose consumer welfare can be represented by a quasi-concave Samuelson (direct) social utility function $U(C_1, C_2)$. Let the corresponding indirect utility function be $v(p, Y)$ where p is the relative price of good 2 in terms of good 1 and Y is consumer expenditure in terms of good 1. Given any p and given any level $\overline{Q}_3$ of the output of the defense good, maximization of consumer welfare is equivalent to maximizing consumer expenditure Y, which in turn equals the value of output of the two traded goods. Thus

$$Y \equiv Q_1 + pQ_2. \tag{8.2}$$

The first-order condition for an interior maximum is

$$F_2 = pF_1. \tag{8.3}$$

Equations 8.1 and 8.3 yield the optimum values of Q_1^* and Q_2^* as functions of $\overline{Q}_3$ and p. The maximized value Y^* of Y is also a function of $\overline{Q}_3$ and p.

It is obvious that $\partial Y^*/\partial \overline{Q}_3 < 0$, as increasing $\overline{Q}_3$ shrinks the production possibilities for Q_1 and Q_2. By the envelope theorem $\partial Y^*/\partial p = Q_2^*$. Substituting Y^* for Y in the indirect utility function, we get the maximized welfare as

$$v(p, Y^*) = v(p, Y^*(\overline{Q}_3, p)) \equiv V(\overline{Q}_3, p). \tag{8.4}$$

It can be seen that $\partial V/\partial \overline{Q}_3 = v_2(\partial Y^*/\partial \overline{Q}_3) < 0$ since $v_2 > 0$, and $\partial V/\partial p = v_1 + v_2(\partial Y^*/\partial p) = -v_2(C_2^* - Q_2^*)$ using Roy's identity where C_2^* is the consumption of good 2. Hence welfare V decreases as p increases as long as $C_2^* > Q_2^*$, or good 2 is being imported. Let us denote by p^A the price at which net imports $C_2^* - Q_2^*$ are zero; p is the autarky price. Thus in the region $0 < p < p^A$, welfare V is decreasing in p.

Suppose one viewed the country depicted as the Warsaw Pact facing a NATO-determined p either because NATO is large relative to the pact in the markets for the two commodities or because a NATO embargo results in the pact's facing a costlier source than NATO for its imports, the alternative source being large as well. Since even in socialist countries, the market is used for the allocation of consumer goods, the use of the utility maximization subject to a budget constraint for depicting consumer decisions is not too unrealistic, though the assumption that effective consumer prices do not differ from world prices is not. Also the assumption that international prices influence production decisions is questionable. Nevertheless for the purposes of this analysis, the additional welfare loss imposed by price distortions in consumer and producer decision is not central.

Suppose initially there were no trade restrictions. Let the pact's initial defense output and terms of trade be $\bar{Q}^0$ and p^0, respectively. A NATO imposition of trade controls raises the import price to p^1. If the pact kept its defense output unchanged at $\bar{Q}_3^0$, consumer welfare would go down by $V(\bar{Q}_3^0, p^0) - V(\bar{Q}_3^0, p^1)$. The pact's response to the imposition of controls could be either to maintain consumer welfare by reducing defense output to $\bar{Q}_3^1$, such that $V(\bar{Q}_3^0, p^0) = V(\bar{Q}_3^1, p^1)$, or maintain defense output at $\bar{Q}_3^0$, let the consumers bear the cost of NATO controls, or reduce defense output to a level between $\bar{Q}_3^0$ and $\bar{Q}_1^1$ so that both the military and the consumers bear some of the costs.

The allocation of costs between consumers and the military may be determined, say, by postulating that the decision makers in the pact maximize a welfare function W that is additively separable in consumer welfare and security. Security is assumed to be a function $S(\bar{Q}_3, Q_3^*)$ of the pact's and NATO's defense output Q_3^*. It is natural to assume that S is an increasing and concave function of $\bar{Q}_3$ and $\bar{Q}_3^*$. Thus W can be expressed as

$$W = \alpha V(\bar{Q}_3, p) + (1 - \alpha)S(\bar{Q}_3, Q_3^*), \tag{8.5}$$

where $0 < \alpha < 1$. Maximization of W with respect to $\bar{Q}_3$ given Q_3^* leads to the first-order condition

$$\alpha \frac{\partial V}{\partial \bar{Q}_3} + (1 - \alpha) \frac{\partial S}{\partial \bar{Q}_3} = 0. \tag{8.6}$$

The assumptions that consumer preferences are convex, both goods are normal in consumption, and the transformation function $F(Q_1, Q_2, Q_3)$ is concave ensure that V is concave in $\bar{Q}_3$. By assumption S is concave in $\bar{Q}_3$ as well. Thus the second-order condition for a maximum is satisfied. Some unsurprising comparative static results can be easily established using equation 8.6, assuming that its solution $\bar{Q}_3^0$ is unique. First $\partial\bar{Q}_3/\partial\alpha < 0$; that is, an increase in the weight placed on consumer welfare reduces optimal defense output $\bar{Q}_3^0$. Second, if an increase in NATO defense output Q_3^* increases the marginal security product $\partial S/\partial\bar{Q}_3$ of the pact's defense output (once again a reasonable assumption), $\bar{Q}_3^0$ will increase as Q_3^* increases. Third, an increase in p brought about by NATO controls will increase (decrease) $\bar{Q}_3^0$ as $\partial^2 V/\partial p\partial\bar{Q}_3 > (<)0$; that is, as the marginal welfare impact $\partial V/\partial\bar{Q}_3$ defense is increased (decreased) by the price increase. In principle it can be of either sign depending, as it does, on the substitution possibilities in production as well as consumption. It could be zero as well. For example, let preferences be represented by the log linear utility function $\beta \mathrm{Log}\, C_1 + (1 - \beta) \mathrm{Log}\, C_2$ and let $F(Q_1, Q_2, Q_3)$ take the form $Q_1^2 + Q_2^2 + Q_3^2 - \bar{R}^2 = 0$, where $\bar{R}$ is the resource endowment. Then it is easy to show that $V(\bar{Q}_3, p) = \frac{1}{2}\mathrm{Log}(\bar{R}^2 - Q_3^{-2}) + \frac{1}{2}\mathrm{Log}(1 + p^2) - (1 - \beta)\mathrm{Log}\, p + \beta \mathrm{Log}\, \beta + (1 - \beta)\mathrm{Log}(1 - \beta)$ so that $\partial^2 V/\partial p\partial\bar{Q}_3 \equiv 0$. In such a case NATO price controls have no effect on the pact's defense expenditure $\bar{Q}_3^0$.

In the discussion Q_3^*, the defense output of NATO, was assumed given. One could postulate a Cournot-Nash equilibrium determination of $\bar{Q}_3$ and Q_3^* by using equation 8.6 as the reaction function of the pact. A reaction function of NATO could be derived by postulating a NATO security function $S^*(Q_3^*, \bar{Q}_3)$. It is reasonable to assume that S^* is an increasing concave function of Q_3^* and $-\bar{Q}_3$. If, for simplicity, we assume that consumer welfare in NATO is insensitive to p, the a NATO welfare function W^* analogous to W for the pact can be postulated:

$$W^* = \alpha^* V_3^* (Q) + (1 - \alpha^*) S_3^*(\bar{Q}_3, Q_3^*). \tag{8.7}$$

The NATO reaction function is implied by the following first-order condition for the maximization of W^*:

$$\alpha^* \frac{dV^*}{dQ_3^*} + (1 - \alpha^*)\frac{\partial S^*}{\partial Q_3^*} = 0. \tag{8.8}$$

The assumptions that S^* is increasing and concave in Q_3^* and $-\bar{Q}_3$ and $\partial S^*/\partial Q_3^*$ is increasing in $\bar{Q}_3$ imply that Q_3^* is an increasing function of $\bar{Q}_3$. Equations 8.6 and 8.8 together determine the Cournot-Nash equilibrium expenditures $(\bar{Q}_3^*, Q_3^*)$. Since by assumption NATO's reaction curve is unaffected by changes in p, while the pact's curve can shift up or down or remain unchanged, the Nash equilibrium defense expenditure of the pact can go up, down, or remain unchanged as NATO imposes trade controls.

Table 8.1
Success and failure of sanctions, pre-1973 and 1973–1983.

Policy goal	Pre-1973 Success	Pre-1973 Failure	1973–1983 Success	1973–1983 Failure
Modest policy changes	7	1	8	15
Destabilization	8	6	1	3
Disruption of military adventure	5	7	1	2
Military impairment	2	4	0	2
Other major policy changes	0	9	1	1
Total	22	27	11	23

Source: Hufbauer and Schott (1983, p. 75, table 5.2).

8.6 Embargoes and Sanctions in a Historical Context

Several studies of the historical experience with embargoes and sanctions are available (Carswell, 1982; Doxey, 1980; Losman, 1979; Hufbauer and Schott, 1983). The sanctions reviewed included unilateral as well as multilateral sanctions, involved trade in goods as well as financial investment, and applied to only a limited set of goods or to all goods except food, medicines, and others excluded on humanitarian grounds. By and large the success of sanctions in achieving the objectives of those imposing them seems to be modest. By scoring success on a scale of 1 to 4 (from failure to success) and the contribution of sanctions to success again on a scale of 1 to 4 (from zero to a significant contribution), Hufbauer and Schott constructed an overall success index by multiplying the scores. Their review of seventy-eight cases by policy goal and the period of imposition of sanctions is summarized in table 8.1 (success means an overall index of 9 to 16). The lack of success of sanctions, particularly in the period 1973–1983, is evident. The reasons for lack of success were also fairly obvious. The authors cite the following as the major ones: (1) sanctions imposed were often inadequate in relation to the objectives, which were themselves elusive; (2) sanctions created their own antidotes in terms of unifying the target country and in successfully initiating a search for commercial alternatives by it; (3) allies of the target country often offset the effects of sanctions with their support; and (4) sanctions created backlash in the imposing country itself from lobbies of export interests affected by the sanctions. Besides, the imposing country's allies may not share its goals, and their trade with the target country may offset the effect of sanctions.

Losman's (1979) review of the cases of Cuba, Israel, and Rhodesia supports the findings of Hufbauer and Schott. He concludes that partial sanctions covering only some goods have no hope of success, and embargoes against affluent countries with large economies are not likely to succeed either. The cost of sanctions may fall mostly on a politically powerless group in the target country (for example, black Africans in Rhodesia and the middle class in Cuba) and thus has little influence in changing government policy. In sum he found that "political success has not been forthcoming in any of the embargo studies, despite sanctions having some very damaging economic results" (Losman, 1979, p. 124).

In contrast Carswell (1982) argues that the U.S. sanctions against Iran imposed after the taking of hostages, in particular the blocking of Iranian assets in the United States, were effective. He attributes the effectiveness to the unique circumstances of the case. "First, the blocking was keyed to an event (the hostage seizure) that could be quickly resolved, and the blocking itself was therefore destined to have the same resolution. Second, by accident of history a very large amount of Iranian assets was under U.S. control, far larger than the U.S. assets under Iran's control. Third, the principal U.S. allies also had vital interests to protect in Iran. Thus the U.S. had extraordinary leverage, a condition that did not exist in the China-Cuba-Vietnam situations and is not likely to be repeated" (Carswell, 1982, p. 260). In this he agrees with Doxey (1980) who points out that the effectiveness of sanctions "must be judged on a case by case basis, and although authorized sanctions may have more symbolic value, the absence of authorization for collective measures does not necessarily rob them of efficacy. The crucial factors will be the nature of objectives sought, their value to both coercor and coerced and the resources they are prepared to invest in them, as well as the target's ability to withstand pressure on its own, or with outside help. In a divided and economically interdependent world such help is often forthcoming—except in the hypothetical cases of extreme vulnerability amounting to total economic dependence on the states imposing sanctions, or of universal ostracism, the coercive properties of economic sanctions are limited" (Doxey, 1980, p. 131).

8.7 Conclusions

Economic theory suggests that a case can be made for intervention in a market economy on national defense or security grounds whenever national defense requirements create some production or consumption externality. Many of the forms of intervention were in terms of domestic economic policy instruments and not in terms of restrictions of foreign trade. Even when trade policy is viewed in a strategic context, theory does not lead to any unambiguous conclusions regarding its efficacy in furthering security objectives. The

review of economic sanctions that have been applied in the past also points
to their limited effectiveness.

Appendix: Response to the Threat of Trade Embargoes and Sanctions

For simplicity assume that (1) there are two goods, which can be traded
internationally at a fixed term of trade p in the first period as well as in the
second period in the event that there is no embargo; (2) the embargo, if
imposed, is total in the sense of eliminating all trade; (3) the probability of the
embargo's being imposed is P; (4) the economy lasts only two periods, and as
such there is no scrap value to capital stock remaining at the end of the second
period (capital does not depreciate); and (5) one of the goods can be consumed
or invested in addition to capital stock that becomes available for productive
use at the end of the second period.

Case 1: Investment Decision

Let $\bar{K}_1$ be the inherited capital stock at the beginning of period 1. If I is
investment in period 1, the capital stock available for use in period 2 is $\bar{K}_1 + I$.
The production possibilities in either period (assuming that the choice of
output levels in period 1 does not affect similar choices in period 2) can be
represented by the transformation function $Q_1 = F(Q_2, K)$ where Q_1 is the
output of commodity i and K is the available capital stock at the beginning of
the period. For simplicity, it has been assumed that labor available for production is exogenous and is the same in each period. It is therefore not shown
explicitly as an argument of the transformation function. Let good 2 be used
for investment as well. Let us assume that production and consumption
decisions are taken in period 2 after the uncertainty about the embargo has
been resolved. Also since there is no scrap value for capital left at the end of
period 2, there is no investment in period 2 regardless of the embargo threat.
Let the welfare of citizens in each period be represented by a quasi-concave
Samuelson social utility function $U(C_1, C_2)$.

Consider first the case where an embargo is imposed in period 2. Since the
embargo precludes trade, the consumption of each good is the same as its
production. Hence, given I, the maximum welfare under an embargo is
$\underline{U} \equiv \text{Max } U(F(Q_2, \bar{K}_1 + I), Q_2)$. The first-order condition for an interior maximum is $-F_1 = U_2/U_1$, where the subscript i denotes the partial derivative of a
function with respect to its ith argument ($i = 1, 2$). Under the usual neoclassical assumptions about production functions, F is concave and U is quasi-
concave, so that the second-order conditions for a maximum are satisfied.

Under well-known conditions about the behavior of marginal products and marginal utilities, as output Q_2 and consumptions C_i approach zero, a unique interior maximum can be shown to exist. The first-order condition states that the marginal rate of transformation $-F_1$ in production equals the marginal rate of substitution U_2/U_1 in consumption. This will be met in a competitive equilibrium in period 2 under an embargo without any intervention other than lump-sum transfers among individual consumers that are needed to justify the use of the Samuelson social utility function representation of consumer welfare. For concreteness let the dependence of $\underline{U}$ on $\bar{K}_1 + I$ be indicated by $\underline{U}(\bar{K}_1 + I)$. By the envelope theorem, $\underline{U}_1 \equiv d\underline{U}/dI = U_1 F_2$ where U_1 and F_2 are evaluated at the optimum value of Q_2.

Similarly $\bar{U}$, the maximum welfare in period 2 when there is no embargo, is given by $\bar{U} \equiv \text{Max } U[C_1, C_2]$ subject to $C_1 + pC_2 = F(Q_2, \bar{K}_1 + I) + pQ_2$. The first-order conditions for an interior maximum are $U_2/U_1 = p = -F_1$, these having the interpretation that the marginal rate of transformation in production $(-F_1)$ and the marginal rate of substitution in consumption (U_2/U_1) both equal the fixed terms of trade p. No intervention other than lump-sum transfers is called for in supporting this allocation. $\bar{U}$ can be written as $\bar{U}(\bar{K} + I)$, and once again $\bar{U}_1 = \bar{d}U/dI = U_1 F_2$, where U_1 and F_2 are evaluated at the optimal value of C_1, C_2, and Q_2.

The choice problem in the first period can be viewed as maximizing (with respect to C_1, C_2, and Q_2) the expected welfare $W = U[C_1, C_2] + \beta[\underline{U}(\bar{K}_1 + I)P + \bar{U}(\bar{K}_1 + I)(1 - P)]$ where β represents the discount factor applicable to period 2 welfare, subject to the constraint $C_1 + p(C_2 + I) = F(Q_2, \bar{K}) + pQ_2$. The first-order conditions can be written as $U_2/U_1 = p = -F_1$ and $\beta[P\underline{U}_1 + (1 - P)\bar{U}_1] = U_1 p$.

The first set of conditions has the same interpretation as in period 2 under no embargo and once again shows that no intervention in product markets or trade is called for. The left-hand side of the second condition represents the marginal gain in expected welfare of an additional unit of investment in period 1, and the right-hand side represents the welfare cost of that investment. If consumers ignore the threat of embargo, they will be equating $\beta\bar{U}_1$ to $U_1 p$ if there is no intervention and the first-order condition will be violated. An investment subsidy (tax) raising the return (in welfare units) by $\beta P(\underline{U}_1 - \bar{U}_1)$ will rectify the situation as long as $\underline{U}_1 > (<) \bar{U}_1$. If consumers correctly perceive the probability P but nevertheless ignore the possible difference between $\underline{U}_1$ and $\bar{U}_1$ and assume it to be $\bar{U}_1$, once again they will wrongly equate $\beta\bar{U}_1$ to $U_1 p$, and an investment tax or subsidy will be needed to correct it.

Case 2: Adjustment Costs

To make this case dramatic, let us ignore investment possibilities and assume that the production choices made in period 1 cannot be altered in period 2. In this case $\underline{U} \equiv U(F(Q_2^1, \bar{K}_1), Q_2^1)$ where Q_2^1 is the output of good 2 in period 1 and $\bar{U} = \text{Max } U(C_1, C_2)$ subject to $C_1 + pC_2 = F(Q_2^1, \bar{K}_1) + pQ_2^1$. The first-order condition for this maximization is $U_2/U_1 = p$. Thus in period 2 no intervention is called for. For concreteness denoting the dependence of $\underline{U}$ and $\bar{U}$ on Q_2^1 by $\underline{U}(Q_2^1)$ and $\bar{U}(Q_2^1)$, by the envelope theorem we get $\underline{U}_1 = U_1 F_1$ (evaluated at Q_1^1) and $\bar{U}_1 = U_1(p + F)$ (evaluated at Q_2^1 and optimal values of C_1 and C_2). The first-period problem is to maximize $U[C_1, C_2] + \beta[\underline{U}(Q_1^2)P + \bar{U}(Q_1^2)(1 - P)]$ subject to $C_1 + pC_2 = F(Q_1^2, \bar{K}_1) + pQ_1^2$. The first-order conditions for a maximum are $U_2/U_1 = p$ and $\beta[\underline{U}_1 P + \bar{U}_1(1 - P)] = U_1(p + F_1)$. If producers ignore the fact that they have the choice of output levels only in the first period, even though they know P they will behave as if the left-hand side of the latter equality was zero and equate p to $-F_1$. To rectify this, one needs a production tax to the extent of $\beta[\underline{U}_1 P + \bar{U}_1(1 - P)]/U_1$ so that the marginal rate of transformation $-F_1$ is equated to the tax-inclusive price $p - \beta[\underline{U}_1 P + \bar{U}_1(1 - P)]/U_1$. It is easy to see that if producers ignore P (assume that it is zero) but allow for the effect of the production constraint, they will wrongly equate $\beta\bar{U}_1$ to $U_1(p + F_1)$. Once again a production tax, this time to the extent of $\beta(\underline{U}_1 - \bar{U}_1)P/U_1$, will be needed to rectify the situation.

Case 3: Endogenous Embargo Probability

Let us ignore investment and adjustment costs; however, let the probability P of an embargo's being imposed be an increasing function $P(M)$ of imports M of good 2 in period 1. Then in period 2 the welfare levels under an embargo and no embargo are obtained by setting $I = 0$ in the functions $\underline{U}(\bar{K}_1 + I)$ and $\bar{U}(\bar{K}_1 + I)$ derived in case 1. As was shown there, there is no case for any intervention in period 2. Now the problem in the first period is to maximize $U(C_1, C_2) + \beta[P(M)\underline{U} + (1 - P(M))\bar{U}]$ subject to $C_1 = F(Q_2, \bar{K}_1) - pM$ and $C_2 = Q_2 + M$. In this formulation, good 2 is imported, and M is the level of imports. By assumption $P(M)$ is increasing in M. The first-order conditions for a maximum can be written as $U_2/U_1 = -F_1$ and $\beta P_1(M)(\bar{U} - \underline{U}) = U_1(-p + U_2/U_1)$.

Since by construction $\bar{U} > \underline{U}$, if $P_1(M) = 0$ (if the probability of embargo is unaffected by level of imports), $U_2/U_1 = -F_1 = p$, and no intervention is called for. If $P_1(M) > 0$ and consumers (producers) fully take it into account by equating their marginal rate of substitution U_2/U_1 (their marginal rate of transformation $-F_1$) not to P the terms of trade, but to $p + \beta P_1(M)(\bar{U} - \underline{U})/U_1$, no intervention is called for. If producers and consumers ignore the probability of embargo, they will be wrongly equating U_2/U_1 and $-F_1$ to p. Then an intervention in the form of an ad valorem import tariff at the rate $\beta P_1(M)(\bar{U} - \underline{U})/U_1$ is called for to satisfy the first-order condition.

Note

I thank Jagdish Bhagwati and Michael Intriligator for drawing my attention to some relevant references. Thanks are also due to Lois Van de Velde for editorial assistance and to Joann Young for her patience in processing several drafts.

References

Agnelli, G. "East-West Trade: A European View." *Foreign Affairs* 58 (1980): 1016–1033.

Anam, M. "Distortion-Triggered Lobbying and Welfare: A Contribution to the Theory of Directly-Unproductive Profit Seeking Activities." *Journal of International Economics* 13 (1982): 15–32.

Bhagwati, J. N. "Tariffs and DUP Theory." Presented at the Annual Meetings of the American Economic Association, December 1984.

Bhagwati, J. N., and T. N. Srinivasan. "Optimal Intervention to Achieve Non-Economic Objectives." *Review of Economic Studies* 36 (1969): 27–38.

Bhagwati, J. N., and T. N. Srinivasan. "Optimal Trade Policy and Compensation under Endogenous Uncertainty: The Pheonomenon of Market Disruption." *Journal of International Economics* 6 (1976): 217–236.

Bhagwati, J. N., and T. N. Srinivasan. "The Welfare Consequences of Directly Unproductive Profit Seeking Activities." *Journal of International Economics* 13 (1982): 33–44.

Bhagwati, J. N., and T. N. Srinivasan. "DUP Activities and Economic Theory." In D. Collander, ed., *Neoclassical Political Economy*. Cambridge, Mass.: Ballinger Publishing Company, 1984.

Carswell, R. "Economic Sanctions and the Iran Experience." *Foreign Affairs* 61 (1982): 247–265.

Cooper, R. N. "Trade Policy Is Foreign Policy." *Foreign Policy* 9 (1973): 18–36.

Doxey, P. *Economic Sanctions and International Enforcement.* 2d ed. New York: Oxford University Press, 1980.

Eaton, J., and Z. Eckstein. "The U.S. Strategic Petroleum Reserve: An Analytic Framework." In Robert E. Baldwin and Anne O. Krueger, eds., *The Structure and Evolution of Recent U.S. Trade Policy.* Chicago: University of Chicago Press, 1984.

Gasiorowski, M., and S. W. Polachek. "Conflict and Interdependence." *Journal of Conflict Resolution* 26 (1982): 709–729.

Hanson, P. *Trade and Technology in Soviet-Western Relations*. New York: Columbia University Press, 1981.

Holzman, F. D., and R. Levgold. "The Economics and Politics of East-West Relations." In F. Bergsten and L. B. Krause, eds., *World Politics and International Economy*. Washington, D.C.: Brookings Institution, 1975.

Hufbauer, G. C., and J. J. Schott. *Economic Sanctions in Support of Foreign Policy Goals*. Washington, D.C.: Institute for International Economics, 1983.

Kahn, H. *On Thermonuclear War*. Princeton: Princeton University Press, 1960.

Losman, D. *International Economic Sanctions: The Cases of Cuba, Israel and Rhodesia*. Albuquerque: University of New Mexico Press, 1979.

Mayer, W. "The National Defense Argument Reconsidered." *Journal of International Economics* 7 (1977): 363–377.

Polachek, S. W. "Conflict and Trade." *Journal of Conflict Resolution* 24 (1980): 55–78.

Roosa, R., M. Matsukawa, and A. Gutowski. *East-West Trade at a Crossroad: Economic Relations with the Soviet Union and Eastern Europe*. New York: New York University Press, 1982.

Root, W. "Trade Controls That Work." *Foreign Policy* 56 (1984): 61–80.

Seabury, P. "Industrial Policy and National Defense." *Journal of Contemporary Studies* 6 (1983): 5–15.

Thompson, E. "An Economic Basis for the 'National Defense Argument' for Aiding Certain Industries." *Journal of Political Economy* 87 (1979): 1–36.

Tolley, G. S., and J. D. Wilman. "The Foreign Dependence Question." *Journal of Political Economy* 85 (1977): 323–347.

Vernon, R. "Apparatchiks and Entrepreneurs: U.S.-Soviet Economic Relations." 52 *Foreign Affairs* (1974): 249–262.

Vernon, R. "The Fragile Foundations of East-West Trade." *Foreign Affairs* 57 (1979): 1035–1051.

Comment on "The National Defense Argument for Government Intervention in Foreign Trade"

Michael D. Intriligator

Srinivasan provides a valuable summary and elaboration of the national defense argument for government intervention in foreign trade. He develops classical static and dynamic approaches to this question, using partial and general equilibrium arguments. His particular concerns are with the possibility that national defense requirements create a production or consumption externality and whether such an externality creates a justifiable basis for restrictions on foreign trade in the form of tariffs or some other type of intervention. He finds that although there are some cases in which such intervention may be warranted, in many other cases in which an externality exists it can be treated not by trade intervention but by various alternative domestic economic policy instruments.

In my comments I will extend some of Srinivasan's arguments and discuss some additional issues concerning trade and national defense and some broader issues. I do so from a complementary viewpoint to Srinivasan's. He looks at how national defense issues impinge on foreign trade, and he argues that, wherever possible, national defense should not be used as a justification for interfering with the gains from free trade, recognizing that there are some special situations in which such intervention is warranted. I will be looking at the issue from the other direction: how foreign trade affects national defense issues. My comments will consider national security as a goal, defense and trade, and the implications of modern weapons, trade, and global interdependence.

National Security as a Goal

It is perhaps only natural that economists treat economic welfare as the primary goal of a social system, whether one is dealing with a household, firm, or nation-state. But there are other goals, a preeminent example being national security. Srinivasan starts with the traditional economic analysis of ignoring this other goal and proceeds in stages by allowing first for a requirement to produce (or consume) certain minimum quantities of defense goods (guns in the standard guns versus butter example). He then extends the argument in his formal model of security and the gains from trade by allowing trade-offs between economic welfare and security. He treats a welfare function, which is a weighted average of economic welfare, measured by the indirect welfare function evaluated at the optimum, and security, which is assumed to depend on the defense output of both sides.

The argument could, however, be made the other way around, and it is in fact usually done so in the literature on arms races.[1] In this alternative way of looking at the problem, national security becomes the primary goal, and economic welfare becomes the secondary goal. The first step is the opposite side of the coin of the international economic argument that ignores national defense as a goal. Instead it ignores economic welfare as a goal, focusing only on national security. When each of two countries has the goal of national security, using the instrument of arms production, the dependence of national security on arms levels in both countries leads to an arms race. The next step, comparable to that of allowing for a requirement to produce a given minimum level of weapons in the international trade approach, is to allow, in the defense economics approach, for an explicit or implicit requirement to consume a given minimum level of consumption. The third step, again comparable to that of Srinivasan's approach, is to allow for explicit trade-offs between economic welfare, as measured by consumption, and national security. An example, in the context of a dynamic model of an arms race, is the Brito welfare function for country A at time τ,

$$W_A(\tau) = \int_\tau^\infty e^{-rt} U_A[C_A(t), D_A[M_A(t), M_B(t)]]dt,$$

where $\dot{M}_A = Z_A - \mu_A M_A$ and $C_A = Y_A - Z_A$. Here r is the discount rate, U_A is the utility function in country A, $C_A(t)$ is consumption in country A at time t, D_A is a measure of defense in country A, M_A is the level of armaments ("missiles") in country A, M_B is the level of armaments in country B, $\dot{M}_A$ is the arms increase in country A, Z_A is the arms procurement in country A, μ_A is the depreciation rate for arms in country A, and Y_A is the (given) national product in country A.[2] This welfare function, used by Brito to derive a pair of reaction functions that imply an arms race, is a dynamic variant of the Srinivasan welfare function in which there is additive separability over time but not necessarily between economic welfare and defense at each instant.

Clearly there is a process of bridge building here, with international economists reaching out to include explicit consideration of national defense as a goal and with defense economists reaching out to include explicit consideration of economic welfare as a goal. This process of synthesis is valuable because both economic welfare and national defense are important influences on trade policy and arms policy. In fact, given trade-offs between economic welfare and national defense, the classical prescription of free trade, which ignores national defense, need not be valid.

Defense and Trade

Some important trade issues stem from defense considerations, in particular, the major role of the defense sector that involves government intervention, some of which are not treated directly by Srinivasan.

One such issue, discussed by Srinivasan, is the perceived need to support or protect certain key industries that could be important in war mobilization, such as basic metals, automobiles, aircraft, machine tools, chemicals, and electronics. The support or protection of these industries includes trade intervention in the form of various types of protection.

Another such issue is the perceived need to have inventories or stockpiles of certain critical materials, minerals, and other items, resulting in some cases in government purchases abroad or promotion of imports of these critical materials. Government intervention in foreign trade can take the form of direct purchases or import subsidies, as well as the more frequently discussed tariffs and quotas.

A third such issue discussed by Srinivasan is export controls for certain sensitive items that could have military use, such as controls of sales of computers and avionics, to East bloc nations and controls of transfers of nuclear materials, facilities, technology, and training to nations that may be developing nuclear weapons. In the latter area, the United States and the Soviet Union cooperate in various ways to restrict such exports as part of a nonproliferation regime, but second-tier suppliers, such as Argentina, Brazil, China, India, Israel, and Taiwan, are becoming increasingly important in such nuclear shipments.[3]

A fourth area is the growing significance of conventional arms shipments, the role of such arms transfers as an instrument of foreign policy for East and West, and the growing importance of new arms supplier nations, such as Brazil and North Korea, in this market.

A fifth area is trade policies regarding allies or perceived opponents, which are significantly affected by national defense considerations.

Other areas could also be cited, such as military R&D, but what is important is that it is not enough to look at the issue solely from the vantage point of a trade economist. Looking at the issue from the vantage point of defense economics opens up additional aspects of the role of national defense in leading to government intervention in foreign trade.

Implications of Modern Weapons, Trade, and Global Interdependence

The only criticism I have of Srinivasan is that he does not take account of salient features that are affecting defense and trade. He analyzes traditional problems and uses traditional tools, but the changes that have occurred, particularly in the last twenty-five years, call for studies of new problems and the use of newer tools, some of which have yet to be developed.

Starting with the question of modern weapons, Srinivasan deals with the question of guns but ignores the implications of nuclear weapons with long-range delivery systems, which raise additional issues of deterrence, defense, proliferation, the role of alliances, and others, all with implications for government intervention.

Another issue is the nature of trade. Classical arguments largely deal with trade in goods with some further discussion of services, but the late twentieth century has witnessed the growth of trade in weapons, information, technology, and training, all of which require further treatment and analysis.

Finally, there is the issue of global interdependence, usually interpreted in terms of growing economic linkages among different nations. This is a proper interpretation, but global interdependence also involves growing political, military, and other linkages, and in a deeper sense it involves the fact that these various linkages are themselves connected and interdependent. It is impossible to separate out and treat economic issues independently of political, military, and other issues. These concepts of global interdependence have yet to be analyzed in a fundamental way, but one important aspect of such an analysis would be the interrelationships between international trade and national defense. To analyze these linkages calls for new tools of analysis. Srinivasan's analysis proceeds from partial equilibrium analysis, in which other markets are fixed, to general equilibrium analysis, in which other markets can change but the basic institutions are fixed. The next logical step would be that of generalized general equilibrium in which basic institutions can change, and changes in political, military, and other institutions can be treated along with changes in economic institutions.

Just as a new type of analysis is called for in treating global interdependence, a new concept of time is called for in treating such interdependence. Srinivasan's treatment of time proceeds from a static to a dynamic treatment.

The next logical step would be that of generalized dynamics in which the conventional dynamics of trends and cycles is augmented by the possibility of discontinuous change through war, economic collapse, political change, and so forth. It is conceivable that global interdependence, while an extremely productive system that can take advantage of the gains from trade, comparative advantage, and others, is also extremely fragile, small disruptions in one sphere, possibly even in a remote corner of the globe, could have significant consequences world-wide. These disruptions could be economic, such as in the 1973 and 1979 oil shocks or the more recent international debt crisis; they could be military, such as the United States in Vietnam or the Soviet Union in Afghanistan; they could be political, such as the return of democracy to several Latin American countries; or they could be environmental, such as El Niño or drought in Africa. All have important consequences in other dimensions and in other regions, involving complex dynamics.

In addition to a new type of analysis and a new concept of time, it will be necessary to extend game-theoretic concepts to treat global interdependence. Just as general equilibrium must be extended to generalized general equilibrium and dynamics must be extended to generalized dynamics, so too must game theory be extended to generalized game theory. Most studies of trade treat only bilateral and multilateral situations. These two are natural for economists. Our basic paradigms of exchange are either that of two players—buyer and seller—or that of a perfectly competitive market, involving many players. Reinforcing this tendency to either two or many players is game theory's focus on two-person or many-person games and the presence of international institutions involving either bilateral negotiations or multilateral organizations, such as the GATT and the IMF. But many issues involve three, four, or five players, requiring further theoretical developments in game theory and a change in the way of thinking about international trade. A case in point of the latter is Japan. The Japanese have announced major planned increases in their automobile exports to the United States. The reaction in the media, among politicians, and others has been that the United States should force Japan to open its market to U.S. goods. These reactions are examples of bilateralism and the failure to think in broader terms. The Japanese import raw materials from the Middle East, China, and Australia and use these materials to produce finished goods that they export to the United States. Thus the solution may not be a bilateral one but rather a trilateral one—that of completing the last leg of the triangular trade by having the United States export to the Middle East, China, and Australia.[4] More generally, we need newer game theory concepts to study problems of multiplayer non-zero-sum games that are part of global interdependence.

These last several points have a much wider impact than just defense and trade. The linkages between these two, however, suggest the need for newer theoretical tools, such as those of generalized general equilibrium, generalized dynamics, and generalized game theory, to study global interdependence in its many dimensions that constitute major problems now.

Notes

1. For a review of arms race models, see Intriligator and Brito (1976, 1982, and 1985). For a broader review of the literature on conflict theory, including arms races, organized by analytic approach and area of application, see Intriligator (1982).

2. See Brito (1972).

3. The issues of U.S.-Soviet cooperation on nonproliferation and nuclear exports are major areas of concern to the UCLA Center for International and Strategic Affairs. See, for example, Brito, Intriligator, and Wicks (1983), Potter (1985), and Jones et al. (1985).

4. It is somewhat surprising that international trade economists, who are familiar with triangular trade, have not emphasized this potential solution.

References

Brito, D. L. "A Dynamic Model of an Armaments Race." *International Economic Review* 13 (1972): 359–375.

Brito D. L., M. D. Intriligator, and A. E. Wick, eds. *Strategies for Managing Nuclear Proliferation-Economic and Political Issues.* Lexington, Mass.: Lexington Books, 1983.

Intriligator, M. D. "Research on Conflict Theory: Analytic Approaches and Areas of Application." *Journal of Conflict Resolution* 26 (1982): 307–327.

Intriligator, M. D., and D. L. Brito. "Formal Models of Arms Races." *Journal of Peace Science* 2 (1976): 77–88.

Intriligator, M. D., and D. L. Brito. "Arms Races: Behavioral and Economic Dimensions." In J. A. Gillespie and D. A. Zinnes, eds., *Missing Elements in Political Inquiry: Logic and Levels of Analysis.* Beverly Hills: Sage Publications, 1982.

Intriligator, M. D., and D. L. Brito. "Theoretical Models of the Arms Race." In C. Schmidt, ed., *Military Expenditures and Economic Growth and Fluctuations.* London: Macmillan, 1985.

Jones, R., J. Pilat, C. Merlini, and W. C. Potter, eds. *Nuclear Suppliers and Nonproliferation.* Lexington, Mass.: Lexington Books, 1985.

Potter, W. "U.S.-Soviet Cooperation on Nuclear Nonproliferation." *Washington Quarterly* (1985).

Comment on "The National Defense Argument for Government Intervention in Foreign Trade"

Elhanan Helpman

T. N. Srinivasan has written a broad review of the arguments for policy intervention on national security grounds, relying on economic and political considerations. With the aid of an appealing taxonomy, he has been successful in presenting complicated issues in a simple way. What I find lacking is a critical evaluation of the implied policies. Which are the more relevant? How likely are these policies to work in practice? How difficult is it to design successful policies? Srinivasan seems to believe that the arguments are rather weak, and I tend to agree. They are weak on theoretical grounds and become even weaker when considering the difficulties involved in their implementation. Moreover there is little in these arguments that can justify intervention in foreign trade; they can at most justify the targeting of very specific activities.

The main arguments for policy intervention that emerge from the chapter are the following:

1. The need to secure a minimal size of certain industries.

2. The need to secure a minimal consumption level of certain good.

3. The need to preserve certain skills in the economy.

4. A country's assets, and in particular its capital stock, invite aggression in order to take it over, with more wealth inviting more aggression. On the other hand, the larger is the stock of capital, the larger is the defense capability.

5. Private investors undervalue capital investments because the private return on the stock during wartime is limited by price controls, rationing schemes, and drafting.

6. There are foreign trade disruptions and embargoes during wartime. They are related to the extent of foreign trade.

7. Foreign trade affects the military capability of one's adversaries both directly, through the imported goods and technology, and indirectly through its shift of resource allocation between military and civilian use.

As Srinivasan makes clear, the first five arguments do not call for intervention in foreign trade. In order to secure a desired size of certain industries, it is most efficient to subsidize their output; in order to secure desired mimimal consumption of certain goods, it is most efficient to subsidize their consumption; in order to preserve certain skills, it is most efficient to subsidize the acquisition and maintenance of these skills; and in order to equate the private return on capital to the social return, it is most efficient to subsidize investment. None of these remedies calls for intervention in foreign trade.

By probing deeper into the first five arguments for policy intervention, one cannot avoid the conclusion that even in those cases in which they are valid in principle, their practical applicability is highly questionable. Take, for example, the first one: that certain industries should be subsidized in order to secure a minimal size. What is the nature of an industry to which it applies? A case in point might be an agricultural sector that produces perishable products. Since these products cannot be stored, supply in emergencies during which a country is cut off from foreign sources (as in wartime) can be assured only by maintaining a desired level of productive capability. In this case the perishability property is essential for the validity of the argument, for if a commodity is not perishable, supply during emergencies can be secured by stockpiling. This raises a question concerning the length of the emergency. For short emergencies, stockpiling will do, but for long emergencies, we may want to secure a minimal level of productive capacity. In the latter case there will typically be particular activities of the industry that require subsidization, which makes this case fall squarely into category 3. Consequently in order to pursue such a policy, it is necessary to identify the precise source of market failure and engage in corrective taxation or subsidization of this source; across-the-board subsidization of the industry will not be an optimal policy.

Another point about the targeting of activities on national security grounds concerns the structure of firms in such industries. These firms are typically multiproduct firms. Some of their products may embody a large share of the activities that need to be subsidized, while other products embody a small share of these activities. Some of their products may be used by the military, while other products may be marketed for civilian use. If one subsidizes the industry at large, all types of products and all the activities within the industry get subsidized, which is wasteful. One way to deal with this difficulty is to apply a government procurement policy for the proper items. This method can be efficiently used to generate the desired output levels in those cases in which the targeted output is used by government agencies, which happen to apply in some cases but not in others.

I find it difficult to think about examples in which one would like to secure a minimal level of consumption by the private sector because only in this case can one justify a consumption subsidy. Clearly if the minimal consumption concerns government agencies, there is no need for subsidies, and the desired level can be achieved by direct purchases.

Arguments 4 and 5 for intervention, concerning the valuation of the assets and in particular the capital stock, are probably not important in most countries. Thompson, the originator of these arguments, concluded that the former—concerning the effect of assets on the desire of a potential aggressor to take them over and the effect of their size on deterrence—is weak. The case is further weakened by the observation that many assets are typically destroyed during wartime. He expressed also a belief that the latter argument—concerning the undervaluation of investment due to wartime controls—is significant. It is clear, however, that the degree of significance of this argument depends on the probability of occurrence of a war that will be severe enough to require internal controls like those used during World War II but were not used in the United States during, say, the Vietnam War. It also depends on the probability distribution over other war characteristics such as its duration; short wars weaken the argument. One would think that for these reasons the second argument would be insignificant for most countries. It also seems very difficult to come up with a good estimate of the degree of subsidization of investment that might be required on the basis of this policy. Incorrect degrees of policy implementation can be more harmful than a lack of intervention.

The next argument, concerning trade disruption during wartime, including embargoes, does not justify intervention in foreign trade as long as the probability of a disruption does not depend on the extent of foreign trade. If, however, the probability of disruption depends on the volume of imports, then one can improve resource allocation by taxing imports at a rate equal to the marginal social cost induced by their effect on the probability of disruption. This is the Bhagwati-Srinivasan justification of a tariff on the assumption that larger imports increase the probability of an embargo. It is not clear to me that larger trade volumes have to increase the probability of an embargo. When there exist gains from trade that are secured by both parties, an embargo will be harmful to both. In fact the evidence from Polachek's study that Srinivasan reports indicates that more trade reduces belligerence, which would suggest that this is indeed the case. If so, one may argue for the need for import subsidies rather than tariffs. Again empirical estimates of the desired policy are not available.

Second, this argument, as well as the previous ones, is based on the identification of an externality that calls for Pigouvian corrective taxation, which in this case is a tax on foreign trade, the source of the externality. As we know from the public finance literature, externalities of this type typically generate nonconvexities in the relevant commodity space, and the problems at hand are no exception. In such cases Pigouvian taxes may fail to achieve the first-best allocation, and there is therefore a need to take a global view of the policy implications, which is hard to do in practice. This is, of course, not to say that one should not try, but it does call for extreme caution in the implementation of such policies.

The last argument, concerning the effects of foreign trade on military capability, has many conflicting facets that Srinivasan has brought out clearly; they have to do mainly with political considerations. He shows that in the presence of a trade-off between private consumption and national security, trade restrictions may lead the potential adversary to increase military spending rather than reduce it. Hence here too no clear message emerges concerning the desirability of intervention in foreign trade.

It seems to me, however, that the most important source of market failure in the context of the national defense argument is the lack of private instruments for risk pooling and risk spreading. Private markets provide reasonable insurance opportunities for individual risks, but they fail to provide adequate opportunities for the insurance of large, nonindividual risks. In particular there is hardly any insurance available in private markets for very large nonindividual risks such as macroeconomic fluctuations or wars. If one takes the view, however, that incompleteness of financial markets is the major source of market failure, one runs into the well-known problem that in such circumstances there are no robust Pigouvian policy conclusions.

One may summarize by saying that there exist some arguments for intervention in foreign trade on national security grounds but that they make a rather weak case for such policies. One may come up with arguments that are related to national security but in which the reason for policy intervention is rooted in a different aspect of the problem. A case in point might be the desirability to restrict exports of secret weapons. In this case export restrictions preserve the (military) monopoly power of the country owning the weapons, and it can be justified on the same grounds as the preservation of other types of monopoly power is justified.

Postscript to "The National Defense Argument for Government Intervention in Foreign Trade"

T. N. Srinivasan

I thank Michael Intriligator and Elhanan Helpman for their valuable discussion of my chapter. I found that Intriligator's discussion of foreign trade from the perspective of a defense economist complements my discussion from an economist's standpoint. It is natural for a defense economist to view national defense as the objective to be maximized with economic welfare as a side constraint, while the economist may interchange the roles of the two. But either way of looking at the problem at hand normally leads to the same result: the characterization of the efficiency frontier representing the trade-off between defense and economic welfare, as the level of one of them is continuously varied.

I am also grateful to Intriligator for bringing Brito's work to my attention. While Brito's model is dynamic, his production structure is very simple: a constant level (or alternatively an exogenously specified time trend level) of national product is divided between consumption and accumulation of missiles, thus making consumption and missiles perfect substitutes in production. My model is static, but with its richer production structure, it allows consideration of production responses to terms of trade changes induced by trade controls. Both of us make additive separability assumptions though different ones: Brito's welfare function is additively separable over time, while mine is between economic welfare and national security. His dynamic formulation is natural for studying an arms race, while my static analysis is adequate for my purpose of analyzing the impact of trade controls. This is not to deny that a dynamic version of my model can yield additional insights.

Intriligator argues for a grand unified theory that in one fell swoop will tackle international trade in information and technology (and weapons) and feedback dynamics characterizing the evolution of political, military, administrative, and economic institutions in a world of exogenous uncertainty, as well as strategic uncertainty arising from viewing defense and trade issues as a dynamic game among a few with reputation effects lurking in the background.

Although I am sympathetic toward such an approach, to the best of my knowledge none of the subdisciplines he mentions—general equilibrium theory, dynamics of institutions and economies in an uncertain and strategic environment, and game theory—is at a stage that an attempt at unification is likely to be fruitful.

Helpman complains that I am not sufficiently critical of the several approaches to defense and trade that I discuss. I thought that there were so few rational national defense arguments for trade intervention that they ought to be presented without excessive criticism. He also raised the point that the anticipated duration of hostilities ought to enter into the calculations relating to strategic stockpiles. I entirely agree. Yet for analytical convenience one may have to assume that duration is exogenous though uncertain—an assumption I find inappropriate. Another point Helpman made is that it was hard to think of commodities whose domestic consumption level may be of interest from a defense perspective. What I had in mind when I discussed consumption as a defense objective were commodities that have dual-use capabilities (for defense and civilian consumption), such as computers. At the level of aggregation of the trade model I was using, it is not at all unrealistic to assume dual use.

I cannot subscribe to the post-hoc ergo propter-hoc logic implicit in Richard Cooper's defense of the ban on sales of strategic commodities and weapons to the Soviet Union and its allies. According to him, the ban contributed to deterrence by imposing a sufficiently high cost of circumventing it. And of course everybody knows that deterrence has been successful since there has been no war between the United States and Soviet Union!

9

Multilateral and Bilateral Negotiating Approaches for the Conduct of U.S. Trade Policies

John H. Jackson

9.1 Introduction

I have been asked to address multilateral and bilateral negotiating approaches for the conduct of U.S. trade policies. This is one facet of a much broader, and I feel more serious, question about trade policy generally: the question of whether the current institutions for implementing trade policy, such as the GATT or the U.S. trade statute framework, are adequate to cope with the increasingly complex and difficult problems being raised by advancing economic interdependence of the world.[1] Thus although here I will focus primarily on the question of whether the United States would be better off continuing its preference for multilateral approaches to managing international trade problems, as compared to bilateral or other preferential approaches, nevertheless to evaluate multilateral or bilateral approaches, one has to be concerned with the broader context of the institutional infirmities of today's trading system.[2]

The principal multilateral institution for managing international trade problems today is the GATT. Therefore part of this chapter will focus on it. In that context I would like to point out that there are at least three policy issues that often become confused with each other: nondiscrimination or MFN treatment, multilateralism, and the institution of GATT. One can envisage an MFN-type structure for managing trade without the GATT. Indeed the original intention was to have a different institution than the GATT. One can also envisage an essentially bilateral agreements system of managing world trade that nevertheless embraces MFN. So persons may really mean criticism of the GATT when they talk about criticism of multilateralism, or they may mean criticism of the MFN approach when they really mean criticism of multilateralism. We should be cognizant of the differences of these three concepts. We could, for example, conclude that the GATT as an institution needs to be abandoned or replaced and yet feel that what replaces it should be based on both MFN and multilateralism. We could also envisage a multilateralism that did not depend on MFN, such as a "rich man's club" of like-minded nations. (Of course, there are a number of other multilateral institutions in the world that relate to economic matters, including the World Bank, the International Monetary Fund, the OECD, UNCTAD, and commodity agreements. I will not be dealing with those here for practical reasons of space.

What I say has important current implications for U.S. policy. In the fall of 1984 we witnessed the passage of the Trade and Tariff Act of 1984.[3] In many ways this is the most striking departure from the pattern of trade legislation of Congress since the 1934 Reciprocal Trade Agreements Act. To my knowledge, the 1984 act is the first broad general policy enactment concerning trade that is not based primarily on a comprehensive legislative proposal sent to the Congress by the executive branch. Parts and pieces of the 1984 act were derived from suggestions from the executive branch, but the 1984 act is truly a congressional enactment and not an executive branch enactment, although the executive branch had great influence. The implications of that bit of history are yet to be fully revealed. Does this history stem from the unwillingness of the current administration to give leadership to the government and to Congress about an overall trade approach? Does it, on the contrary, indicate a continuing increasing assertiveness by the Congress of its historical constitutional preeminent role with respect to the regulation of international trade? These issues are part of the background scenery of this book, although it is probably premature to try to answer the questions I have just posed.

9.2 U.S. Attitudes toward the GATT and Multilateralism in International Trade

If one were to sum up U.S government attitudes toward the GATT and multilateralism during the forty-year period since World War II, I believe the word that would most prominently come to mind is *ambivalence*. There has always been a love-hate relationship between the United States and the GATT as exemplar of the multilateral approach in trade. This is partly an understandable result of the circumstances of the U.S Constitution, with its sharp division of responsibilities between the executive branch and the Congress. There is also a time line characteristic of U.S. attitudes. In the early decades of the GATT, the United States was in a position of some hegemony in world economic matters and consequently could more easily prevail in multilateral discourse on trade matters. As the decades wore on and U.S. postwar economic policies, particularly toward Europe and Japan, proved so successful, U.S. hegemony was broken, so that the United States increasingly found itself in the position of necessarily treating other parts of the world as having a more equal status in the multilateral councils of world trade management. To a certain extent the United States may not have yet adjusted to this new world condition, although its policy leaders usually stoutly maintain that they have adjusted and do take this into account. Nevertheless one witnesses in a variety of circumstances involving relations with other countries, particularly Japan, sets of attitudes on the part of U.S. government and political leaders as well as business leaders that in certain ways seem to be more appropriate for circumstances of earlier decades.

9.2.1 History of the U.S. Relationship to GATT and Multilateral Trade

The GATT, as we know it today, was never intended by its originators.[4] At the end of World War II the United States and primarily its European allies, tried to establish an international trade organization (ITO) as a counterpart to the IMF and the World Bank. The GATT, as such, was designed merely to be another in a series of reciprocal trade agreements authorized under the 1934 Reciprocal Trade Agreements Act and its extensions from time to time. But the ITO failed to come into being, largely as a result of the U.S. Congress. The GATT was then forced to fill the vacuum created in world economic institutions. That it has been able to fill that vacuum so well, despite its infirm constitutional base, is perhaps one of the wonders of postwar international economic history. Nevertheless these odd circumstances of birth for the GATT as an institution have left it with certain defects that continue to plague its efficient performance.

In the years 1946 through 1948 and immediately after there was an obvious ambivalence within the U.S. government about the GATT and multilateral trade institutions. The negotiations for an ITO, and for GATT, were carried forward by the executive branch, which strongly favored these approaches. But the executive branch increasingly received criticism from the congressional branch, and ultimately the congressional concerns led to the failure of the ITO.[5] The GATT at that point was not subject to approval by the Congress, having been negotiated under the statutory authority granted to the president by the 1945 extension of the Reciprocal Trade Agreements Act. This fact annoyed many members of Congress, who found many occasions to criticize the GATT. Indeed for many years there was no explicit statutory authority even for the government to pay its annual financial contribution to the GATT, and in some statutory language, the Congress more or less disavowed the GATT: "The enactment of this Act shall not be construed to determine or indicate the approval or disapproval by the Congress of the Executive Agreement known as the General Agreement on Tariffs and

Trade."[6] Furthermore in the 1950 Agricultural Adjustment Act, section 22 would have required the United States to take action that would violate its GATT obligations. The United States was able to obtain a 1955 waiver from the GATT for the requirements of Section 22.[7] The waiver, however, was not costless to the United States or to the international trade system.

In the mid-1950s the Congress once again failed to approve a mini-ITO labeled the Organization of Trade Cooperation (OTC), which would have helped correct or cure some of the defects of the original GATT.[8] After the Kennedy Round negotiations were completed in 1967, there was an acrimonious dispute between the executive branch and the Congress on two GATT matters. In one circumstance the negotiators had completed a subsidiary agreement to the tariff agreement regarding particularly the relinquishment by the United States of its system of American selling price valuation of certain goods for customs purposes, in exchange for certain concessions by European countries regarding particularly chemical goods. The Congress failed to ratify this side agreement, just as it had failed in connection with the ITO and then the OTC.[9] In addition the executive branch negotiated and entered into an agreement regarding antidumping duties, which it felt it was authorized to accept on the behalf of the United States. Many members of Congress felt the contrary, and the Congress even enacted a clause in 1968 that cast considerable doubts on the legality and enforceability of the 1967 Antidumping Code in U.S. law.[10] Even in the Trade Act of 1974, certain vestiges of these congressional attitudes can be seen, although in this act (section 121(d)) for the first time the Congress explicitly authorized appropriations for U.S. financial contributions to GATT, and the typical disowning phrase of congressional language was somewhat modified: "This authorization does not imply approval or disapproval by the Congress of all articles of the General Agreement on Tariffs and Trade."[11]

Given the rest of the structure of the 1974 act and its intimate dependence on and recognition of the rules of GATT, it would be fair to say that the 1974 act finally was a congressional recognition (perhaps grudging) of GATT as a binding international treaty obligation and institutional mechanism for world trade policy. Nevertheless worry and concern were expressed in that statute and in the congressional committee reports for that statute about certain characteristics of the GATT as an institution and of multilateralism. The statute, for example, worried about the free-rider problem and imposed some explicit conditions on presidential actions to try to ensure that the United States would not be extending the benefits of certain international obligations to important industrialized countries that refused to reciprocate adequately in the course of the newly launched Tokyo Round negotiation.[12] Otherwise language in the statute called for the reform of various GATT rules, including dispute settlement, and balance of payments measures.[13] A procedure was included in that statute (section 301) by which the executive branch found itself under increased pressure to assert GATT rights vigorously against other countries on behalf of U.S. business and broader economic interests.[14]

9.2.2 U.S. Views on MFN and Multilateralism

Despite these reservations and hesitations about GATT and some of its rules, in general the United States has been a strong supporter of the principles of multilateralism and nondiscrimination as embodied in the unconditional MFN clause of GATT. These were pillars of U.S. policy during the drafting and formation years of the GATT. Through the 1960s, for example, the United States continued to express skepticism and hostility toward the proposal of developing countries to carve out an exception to MFN so as to allow a GSP to provide particularly favorable conditions of trade for developing country exports. The United States was the last major industrialized country to implement the GSP policy, which had been called for by international and multilateral institutions, including the GATT.[15] And although the United States had tolerated and perhaps even favored the formation of the EEC, partly for broader strategic reasons, the United States found itself increasingly skeptical about the benefits and directions of that and other regional trade groups in international trade well into the 1970s. The United States particularly viewed the series of agreements between the EC and about four dozen developing countries in the world, the so-called Lomé Conventions and their predecessor, as detracting from MFN principles of GATT. The Congress specified certain conditions regarding this convention in its 1974 legislation, refusing to extend GSP benefits to developing countries that afforded preferential treatment to developed countries (so-called reverse preferences).[16]

At the same time one can discern a drifting away from MFN and multilateralism in U.S. policy: nevertheless, with respect to the GATT as an institution, one thing that we find in U.S. government statements, even recent statements, is extraordinarily strong support for the GATT and its multilateral institutions. Statements by Ambassador William Brock, as well as statements in congressional committees, support this.[17] In enacting the 1979 Trade Agreements Act, the Congress also took elaborate care to avoid any statutory provision that would result in a violation of its obligations in the GATT or any MTN agreements.[18]

9.2.3 U.S. Trade: A Trend toward Bilateralism?

Despite its general longer-range policy support for multilateralism and MFN, it is clear that during the last decade U.S. policymakers have been seriously tempted by bilateral approaches.

One of the earliest post-1945 departures from MFN by the United States was its exclusion of communist countries from such treatment in 1951.[19] In the 1960s, however, the United States began a series of moves that related to its more traditional trading partners, with the development and 1965 implementation of the U.S.-Canada Automotive Products Agreement. The United States obtained a GATT waiver from its MFN obligations for this agreement, and there was at least some comment at the time that the agreement and waiver efforts helped undermine U.S. advocacy of MFN and multilateralism in connection with other GATT exercises such as GSP.[20]

In the Tokyo Round (1973–1974), the United States took some steps that departed from unconditional MFN. The Congress mandated in the 1974 Trade Act that the United States try to offset the free-rider problem, at least of industrial countries, by withholding MFN treatment from certain countries if they did not provide reciprocal advantages in the results of a negotiation. In addition, in the development of the so-called codes (special side agreements that resulted in the Tokyo Round negotiation), the United States has refused to give unconditional MFN status to all GATT members in connection with the obligations of three of those codes.[21] As to two of those three, there are probably GATT legal arguments that justify the U.S. stance. Clearly, however, the United States was again concerned about the free-rider problem and the need to provide an incentive for countries to enter into the discipline of the codes.

More recently one of the most visible and acrimonious trade relationships has become that of the United States and Japan. The United States has essentially dealt with this on a bilateral level, rarely going to a multilateral forum, possibly partly because it distrusted the effectiveness of that forum. At the end of the Tokyo Round, the United States entered into bilateral negotiations with Japan for additional and special concessions under the Government Procurement Code for purchases by the Japanese telephone company, NTT.[22] Subsequently bilateral meetings between the United States and Japan have occurred frequently, and certain institutional mechanisms have been set up to try to ameliorate their problems.[23] Europe also has had similar difficulties with Japan. Yet there does not seem to be an inclination on the part of either the United States or Europe, or for that matter Japan, to focus these troubled bilateral relationships in the multilateral forum of GATT, although some specific cases and representations have been made in GATT about the "Japan problem."[24]

From the beginning of the Reagan administration in 1981, statements by the U.S. Trade Representative and his deputies have hinted at a willingness of the administration to consider the potential of bilateral actions, at least where multilateral activities seem to be ineffective. For example, in April 1981 Ambassador Brock said:

Our objective of obtaining a freer and fairer and more open trading system can best be achieved, in my judgment, by being very frank, very open, very honest, very strong and very fervent in our dealings with trading partners. It is a fact that we intend to treat our friends as friends, and that those who would describe themselves otherwise will be treated otherwise. We will take into account the actions of other nations when they seek special privileges and special access to this market. I think that is something that needs to be understood and needs to be stated. I don't know how else to encourage other countries to participate as responsible members of the community. If people seek preferential access to our markets, then I think it is somewhat unbecoming of them to suggest that they should impose absolute and categorical barriers to the importation of our products. We will take those actions into account in our dealings with them.[25]

At the same meeting, Ambassador Brock's deputy, David MacDonald, said, "I think he [Brock] feels that we may have pressed multilateralism to the limits. . . . I think he means that our reactions will be somewhat quicker and somewhat more bilateral and reciprocal than perhaps they previously have been."[26] More recently additional statements by high administration officials have hinted at a growing impatience by the United States toward multilateral approaches.[27] Congressional efforts to promote reciprocity also seemed to be a tilt away from multilateralism toward bilateralism in many respects.[28]

Even when ostensibly carrying out an MFN policy, sometimes a close examination detects a strong bilateral defect. On the escape clause case on motorcycles, for example, the quotas that were actually implemented seem to affect Japan and very few other countries.[29] And during the massive group of countervailing duty cases on steel brought in 1982, the United States found it convenient to negotiate extensively with the EEC. In many ways the EEC and the United States bypassed the GATT in working out their conflicts in the context of that series of cases.[30]

In 1983 the United States proposed and subsequently implemented a free trade area for the Caribbean basin.[31] This was the first free trade area exercise by the United States (the U.S.-Canada Automotive Products Agreement was a sectorial free trade area but not an across-the-board one). This may have represented a major watershed in U.S. policy, although it was not particularly noticed to be such at the time. Today we are familiar with negotiations concluded with Israel for the formation of a free trade area between the United States and that country.[32] Other such possibilities have been mentioned, such as Canada, Mexico (or more broadly a North American free trade area), or countries belonging to the Association of Southeast Asian Nations, although there seems to be considerable resistance to those ideas.[33]

In sum there are conflicting sets of evidence about the future direction of U.S. policy, but there are ample situations that have occurred, particularly during the last decade, that suggest the possibility that the United States has gradually moved substantially away from its earlier rather adamant support for MFN and multilateralism toward a more pragmatic (and some might say ad hoc) approach of dealing with trading partners on a bilateral basis and rewarding friends.

9.3 The GATT: A Troubled Institution

I want to turn away from a focus on U.S. policies and instead look at the GATT as the principal multilateral institution regarding trade. In particular I want to examine some of the problems that many see in the context of GATT as an institution.[34] Many of these problems of GATT are particularly troublesome to the United States and help cause it to turn toward bilateral alternatives.

The GATT has defects. In fact, when one recalls its troubled origins, it is more surprising that it has lasted so long and performed so well. Nevertheless it is easy to see a number of problems, institutional and more substantive. Indeed it is fair to raise the question whether the GATT system can effectively cope with the myriad of complex new problems engendered by the increasing international economic interdependence of the world.

For convenience the problems of GATT can be divided into two sets: those dealing with procedures and institutional problems and those dealing with substantive norms and coverage of GATT.

9.3.1 Procedures and Institutions of the GATT System

Every effective ongoing legal system needs a procedure for norm making so as to keep rules up to date and effective in the face of constant change and a procedure for effectuating those rules through a dispute settlement mechanism or otherwise. The GATT leaves a great deal to be desired as to both.

The GATT amending process is so unsatisfactory that in general governments deem amendment impossible. In the Tokyo Round the approach to norm making was to develop side codes, stand-alone treaties, with a more limited membership than GATT. One particular aspect of GATT has been troublesome: the voting structure, or lack thereof. Unlike the IMF, with a weighted voting structure that at least arguably has some efficiency in reflecting real world power situations, the GATT has been largely addicted to a one-nation, one-vote structure. Indeed in a number of side codes, nothing is mentioned about voting, so that if circumstance pushed matters to a vote, the one-nation, one-vote structure would undoubtedly be presumed by GATT and international custom.[35]

Sometimes statements are made that voting procedures do not matter because decisions in GATT are arrived at by consensus. In my view, this is a shallow stance. A consensus always involves considerable give and take and negotiation with an eye toward what would happen if the situation broke down. Thus a voting structure (explicit or implicit) will influence the negotiations toward a consensus. As the GATT membership increases and many smaller and less economically powerful countries join the GATT, the trend toward decisions that are out of touch with the reality of economic power in the world accentuates.

In this context a word must be mentioned about the role of the EEC in GATT. The EEC as such is not a contracting party to GATT, but under the EEC basic treaty (Treaty of Rome), GATT matters are commercial policy, which the treaty delegates to the EEC common institutions. This means essentially that the EEC commission represents the ten member states of the EEC, all of them GATT contracting parties, in the GATT meetings. Effectively, then, the EEC has ten votes. In addition the EEC is allied with a number of countries through free trade agreements and the series of Lomé Conventions, and the number of GATT contracting parties that are included in one or another of these alliances is over forty (out of ninety total). Thus although it would be too simple to say that the EEC can exercise multiple votes, nevertheless the EEC has a considerable presence in the GATT, which geographical proximity and language often increase. Too much cannot be made of this because the EEC sometimes (almost paranoically) seems to feel that the United States has too much power in the GATT. Nevertheless because the EEC is currently going through a major constitutional evolution, which has led many EEC statesmen to fear for its continued existence, there has been some tendency by the EEC to take a sort of fend-off position in GATT. That is, some EEC officials try to prevent the GATT contracting parties from narrowing or constraining the variety of options available to EEC officials to use in their complex internal negotiations for compromise on a variety of issues so as to hold the EEC together.[36]

In addition to these major problems the GATT has a comparatively small secretariat, partly traceable to its infirm constitutional origins. Also the GATT for most of its history has been troubled by a so-called grandfather rights issue, originating in the protocol of provisional application. Even if this issue's importance has been fading, nevertheless it has been a source of acrimony and feelings of asymmetry, particularly by the Europeans as they view certain U.S. privileges. Related to that is the 1955 waiver granted to the United States for agricultural goods, which although not a grandfather right nevertheless plays a similar role.

The results of the Tokyo Round of multilateral trade negotiations ending in 1979 added great stress to the GATT system. That negotiation probably more than tripled the scope of trade rule operation and the detail required. Contracting parties find their missions stretched thin, and so does the GATT secretariat. Since inadequate attention was given to the institutional problems in the Tokyo Round negotiations, the one effect of the GATT codes has been a certain balkanization of the GATT, contributing to a centrifugal force of divisiveness.[37]

Finally reference must be made to the troublesome developments in the dispute settlement procedures of GATT. In the last few years some dispute settlement processes have raised exceedingly troublesome issues, including problems of delay, problems of national government improper interference with panel deliberations, and a certain shoddiness of expression in the rationale as published in panel determinations.[38] One can detect a growing feeling in the United States that the dispute settlement processes of GATT have not operated in a way that contributes to even the long-range enlightened interests of U.S. trade policy.

The so-called DISC case (concerning a US tax statute that allowed a domestic international sales corporation certain advantageous tax deferrals on export profits), for example, damaged both GATT and U.S. political perceptions of it. The EEC complained against DISC in 1972, and the United States countered that territorial tax practices of Belgium, the Netherlands, and France were so similar in their effects that they should be considered at the same time. GATT panels ruled in 1976 (incorrectly in my opinion) that all four practices were inconsistent with GATT. After much delay the GATT in 1981 finally took action, which was muddled, ambiguous, and inconsistent but essentially let the European nations off the hook while demanding U.S. law changes.[39] The U.S. government, at considerable political cost, managed to obtain a revision of the DISC to a FSC (foreign sales corporation) patterned largely on the European territorial tax system. Although the revision was not completely without criticism, it was a major change done solely for the purpose of making U.S. law compatible with GATT—a remarkable attempt by a superpower to comply with an international ruling. Yet despite this effort and despite the likelihood that the DISC (or FSC) has little real impact on trade, the EEC has continued to assert its complaint against the United States in GATT, partly for tactical reasons to fend off U.S. complaints on other unrelated EEC practices.[40]

9.3.2 Substantive Problems of the GATT

Almost from the beginning several important problems of the substantive rules of GATT manifested themselves. The whole segment of the world economy relating to agricultural products almost proved the undoing of GATT. This was partly a result of the U.S. Congress's enacting section 22 of the Agricultural Adjustment Act of 1950, which threatened to force the United States to violate its obligations and thus compelled the executive branch to obtain from the GATT a waiver for actions under that statutory section. This agricultural waiver became a sort of precedent to which other nations could refer in deviating from GATT obligations with respect to agricultural matters. Obviously other forces were at work, including the political needs of many governments that were tied to agricultural interests. For whatever reason the result has been largely an exclusion of agricultural sector products from the discipline of GATT.[41]

In the early 1960s, a similar development began for textiles. Subsequently a series of side agreements concerning textiles has resulted in a situation today where textiles largely escape the discipline of GATT and are ruled by these side agreements instead.[42]

Even for products that are traditionally and effectively under some GATT discipline, GATT rules have failed to keep abreast with the rapidly changing world economic developments. The ingenuity of government officials, sometimes needing quick solutions for various problems for national political reasons, has led to a number of protectionist-like devices that are not easily brought within the discipline of relatively ambiguous GATT rules. The variable levy and the import deposit come to mind. Among the most prominent of protectionist devices in recent years has been the rapidly spreading use of export restraints, formal or informal. These VRAs or orderly marketing arrangements have been tempting to government officials since they often evade national legal and constitutional problems, as well as GATT discipline.[43] An increasing reliance on these devices can be witnessed, such as the 1984 development of a worldwide cartel-like arrangement for export limitations in steel.[44] Before that automobile exports had been similarly restrained.

These events highlight the problem in GATT of safeguards. The GATT escape clause of article XIX was originally the central point for safeguards, but in the last decade this article has been increasingly irrelevant as governments

turn more and more to a variety of other safeguard devices. At a time of
growing capacity of developing countries to become new entrants to world
markets of a number of commodities—steel, textiles, and even electronics—
the problem of the desirability and need of structural adjustment of some of
the older industry sectors of industrial economies has been noted. Yet by
escaping the GATT discipline, or for that matter any other international
discipline, a variety of the safeguard devices, including the export restraints,
are effectively avoiding the necessity of facing up to the realities of structural
adjustment.

Finally, as to the existing rules of GATT, the area often labeled unfair trade
practices must be mentioned. The GATT has rules concerning dumping and
subsidization of goods that move in international trade, and these rules have
been evolving with the assistance of side codes into a complex set of norms. To
some extent the norms relating to antidumping duties may be working reasonably effectively. But with respect to the use of subsidies in international trade
and responses to them of countervailing duties, the GATT system is very
troubled indeed. In the Tokyo Round one of the most important negotiations
concerned the development of the subsidies/countervailing duty code.[45] The
code was completed and has been accepted by several dozen nations; however,
its implementation and operation have been the subject of a great deal of
criticism. One of the reasons for this, not surprisingly, is that there was in fact
relatively little real agreement among nations that drafted it and agreed to it. A
careful examination of the code reveals considerable ambiguity. Knowledge of
the negotiating context of many portions of the code reveals at least a dozen
important instances where fundamental disagreements between negotiating
parties were papered over by words that were often deliberately vague or
contradictory.[46] Yet the problems of subsidies and international trade increase
as the world becomes more interdependent.

Apart from the subjects that have traditionally been considered subject to
GATT discipline, there are a number of new areas in today's interdependent
world for which at least some governments feel international discipline is
essential. One can easily identify the question of trade in services, as well
as a number of the issues connected with intellectual property and high-
technology trade.

9.4 MFN Policies and Multilateralism

We now turn to look more deeply into the fundamental policy arguments for
MFN and multilateralism. I will do this primarily in the context of MFN as
such, since that is often identified as the essential of multilateralism, although

there is a distinction between the two. Certainly the policies favoring MFN also favor multilateralism. It is possible to have multilateral approaches that do not depend on MFN, but the reverse seems relatively unlikely although not impossible (for example, an MFN policy in the context of only bilateral agreements). In addition we should look at the question of how bilateralism coexists in the multilateral context of the GATT system.

9.4.1 General Policy Reasons Concerning MFN Obligation

At least two groups of arguments buttress the policy of MFN: some arguments that we can loosely call economic reasons and a group of political or not-so-economic arguments.[47]

With respect to the first category, several economic policy arguments in favor of MFN can be stated. To begin, nondiscrimination can have a salutory effect of minimizing distortions in the market principles that motivate many arguments in favor of liberal trade. When governments apply trade restrictions uniformly without regard for the origin of goods, the market system of allocation of goods and production will have maximum effect. Lamb meat will not be shipped halfway around the world when nearby markets could just as easily absorb that product.

A second economic argument is that MFN often causes a generalization of liberalizing trade policies, so that overall more trade liberalization occurs.

Third, MFN concepts stress general rules applicable to all participating nations, which can minimize the costs of rule formation (such as the difficulty of negotiating a multitude of bilateral agreements). Some theoretical arguments incidental to the Prisoners' Dilemma suggest that an optimum approach to avoid mutually destructive actions is to enter into an agreement that effectively restrains attempts by any party to engage in exploitative behavior. When many parties are involved (such as the ninety nation members of GATT), a generalized rule seems the best approach. In addition attention must be given to making the rule effective.[48]

Finally, MFN helps minimize transaction costs since customs officials at the border need not ascertain the origin of goods to carry out their tasks.

Turning to the second group of arguments, the political side of MFN policies, we can note that without MFN, governments may be tempted to form particular discriminatory international groupings. These special groupings can cause rancor, misunderstanding, and disputes because those countries that are left out resent their status. Thus MFN can form a function of lessening tensions among nations and inhibiting temptations for short-term ad hoc government policies that could be tension creating in a world already too tense.

There are, however, certain counterpolicies, and certain categories of nations hold a view with respect to some of the MFN policies that are contrary to a full implementation of MFN obligations. In recent decades this has been particularly true of the nonindustrialized developing countries, which have argued that the GATT world trade system operates in such a manner as to inhibit the economic development of many societies that have a weaker economic status in the world. In the view of these countries, preferences should be arranged to compensate for the operation of this system and generally for charitable reasons to assist the poorer nations to develop faster. Obviously these arguments are not without merit. The risk always is that these arguments will be used to rationalize preferential systems that do not have the intended function of promoting economic development but rather are used to assist national governments in certain short-term nationalistic political objectives not materially related to overall economic development. In addition the experience of the GSP in the GATT system during the last fifteen years or so is that each of the preference-granting national entities (the industrialized countries) succumbs often to the temptation to use the preference systems as part of the bargaining chips of diplomacy for a number of different reasons.

A second set of counterarguments stresses the risks of a unilateral unconditional MFN approach. These are the foot-dragger and free-rider arguments. To negotiate a general rule applicable to all nations in a system that stresses unanimity and consensus often means that a hold-out nation can prevent agreement or cause it to be reduced to the least common denominator. This can greatly inhibit needed improvement in the substantive or procedural rules.

On the other hand, for like-minded nations to go ahead with reforms and agreements without the foot dragger but to grant (as unconditional MFN requires) all the benefits of the new approach to the nonagreeing parties gives the latter unreciprocated benefits without any of the obligations. This furnishes an incentive to nations to stay out of the agreement. It was this that led the United States to require nations to accept the subsidies code obligations as a condition to receiving beneficial U.S. treatment in countervailing duty cases, as specified in the code.[49]

9.4.2 Bilateralism in the GATT Multilateral Context

Although GATT is identified with MFN and the first article of GATT sets out the MFN obligation, nevertheless it is widely recognized that there are substantial departures from MFN in GATT. Some of these departures were contemplated in the original agreement of GATT, at least implicitly. It has been recognized for many decades, if not centuries, prior to the GATT, for example, that although a tariff may be established on an MFN basis, classifications of tariff items can operate to discriminate between the goods of various countries.[50] If one country primarily ships alloy steel while another primarily ships ordinary steel, a tariff classification that imposes a higher tariff on the alloy steel discriminates effectively against the former country.

In addition when the GATT was drafted, there were a number of preferential systems in existence, most prominently the Commonwealth Preference System. The GATT recognized that some of those preferential systems could continue as sort of a grandfather exception to the GATT, with the view that in due time the effect of those preferences would phase down. Thus, annexes to GATT explicitly provide for such exceptional treatment from MFN.[51]

One of the most prominent and difficult problems engendering exceptions to MFN and GATT is that of article XXIV, which provides an exception for customs unions, free trade areas, and interim agreements leading to either. This article has furnished a very large loophole for a wide variety of different kinds of preferential agreements.[52] A recent GATT case may have even opened this loophole further.[53]

Later in GATT history, other types of preference exceptions to MFN developed, including the treatment by the United States of the codes that resulted from the Tokyo Round. These provide, in the U.S. viewpoint, a sort of conditional MFN, whereby advantages are extended only to those countries that sign and accept the obligations of the particular code.

Another area concerning exceptions to nondiscrimination obligations of GATT is the general problem of article XIX known as selectivity. In the exercise of an escape clause action or, indeed, other safeguard actions, the question of whether such an action can be selective and discriminate in its application against imports from particular countries has provided considerable grounds for dispute within the GATT system. During the ill-fated safeguard negotiations of the Tokyo Round, this issue became one of the rocks on which part of the negotiation foundered. There is a major debate over the legal obligations of article XIX as to whether they require safeguard-escape clause action on a nondiscriminatory basis.[54]

In a similar context the explosion of use of export restraint arrangements in world trade provides one of the most significant recent challenges to the whole MFN principle of GATT history. Quotas themselves, whenever used, are to a certain extent discriminatory. Nevertheless there is a certain modicum of obligation in the GATT (particularly article XIII) and in practice on which one can base arguments that even the use of quotas is subject to MFN-type obligations. In the widespread current addiction to the use of VRA orderly market arrangements, however, the typical application is on a bilateral basis and often provides de facto discrimination. Thus countries that have proved most successful in rapidly expanding their exports of particular products become the target of importing country governments' pressure to adopt export restraints. Japan and the automobile restraints, with respect to the U.S. market, come immediately to mind.

This brief inventory of at least some of the discriminatory or non-MFN activities within the context of the current world trading system is not complete without noting the real difficulty of this problem in the context of nonmarket economies. Where the enterprises that do the trading, either importing or exporting, do so not on the basis of market principles but on the basis of government commands, it is very hard to police any notion of MFN nondiscrimination. A government can always argue that it is not discriminating, and can often conceal the noneconomic motivations that have led it to command differential orders for imports or treatment for exports (such as price). In this connection the problem of reconciling the form of economic organization of nonmarket economies with the particular obligations of GATT designed for market economies is not unique.[55] This problem comes up in a number of different types of obligations of the GATT.

9.5 U.S. Government Institutions

We have been speaking of the problem of MFN and multilateralism in connection with the world trading system revolving around GATT; however, national government institutions—legal, constitutional, and otherwise—also play a prominent role in affecting the issues of concern. A brief overview of some of the problems of U.S. institutions should be useful to remind readers that the U.S. system, as it relates to the GATT multilateral system, can profit from some scrutiny and suggestions for change as well.

Clearly the checks and balances system of the U.S. Constitution, with its attendant tension between the executive and the Congress, poses considerable difficulty for the execution of foreign policy of the United States, particularly economic foreign policy. This is not to say that the constitutional protections embodied in the checks and balances system should be abandoned; they have an important function.[56] But there is also a price, and it may be necessary for the government to consider modes and methodologies for handling these division-of-powers problems that would put less strain on the international institutions relating to economic affairs. At one point a legislative veto was considered a potential way to deal with some of the problems, but the Supreme

Court seems to have largely eliminated that pathway. An alternative to the legislative veto is the fast-track legislative approval technique, embodied in the 1974 Trade Act and utilized for congressional approval of the Tokyo Round results in 1979.[57] There may be other procedures that should be considered, both to help U.S. negotiating tactics and to give clearer and more predictable guidance to foreign governments.

One important problem that lurks in the background is the effect of U.S. government institutions on certain international institutional procedures. Among the most criticized, and many would say the most important, of the GATT institutions are the dispute settlement procedures. The United States has consistently pressed for improvement in those procedures; however, it is not entirely clear that the United States is prepared to accept the consequences of a more meaningful international dispute settlement process. Particularly with recent actions by the United States regarding the International Court of Justice in the Nicaragua case, foreign governments could be understandably skeptical of the real depth of U.S. dedication toward international dispute settlement.[58] In the context of GATT it is not entirely clear to foreign governments or international statesmen that the United States would always be prepared to accept the result of an international dispute settlement process that went against it. The United States has, by and large, accepted the unfortunate consequences for it (and for the GATT) of the messy DISC case, although it took many years for that to occur. There have been other GATT dispute settlement findings against the United States, however, that have not induced U.S. activity to bring itself into conformity with its international obligations.[59] On the other hand the U.S. record may not be any worse than any other major nation in the GATT, and there is considerable evidence of U.S congressional and executive branch activity to try to minimize any inconsistency between U.S. actions and international obligations.

One of the problems possibly inherent in the U.S. constitutional system is the degree to which fairly narrow and parochial interests can make themselves felt in the legislative processing in Congress. Occasionally such narrow interests succeed in obtaining an amendment or rider to broader legislation, almost without scrutiny of its relation to broader policy perspectives. In the Trade and Tariff Act of 1984 a number of such provisions crept into the legislative proposals. Fortunately many were stricken out before final enactment.[60] These kinds of provisions make foreign governments nervous about the effective commitment of the United States toward an international system of rules regarding international trade and other economic matters.

One of the current important problems is the degree to which Congress will participate in what now appears to be a firm executive branch decision to try to get a new major trade negotiation launched.[61] A president and his officials can negotiate on almost anything without explicit authority from Congress. In many instances, however, the product of the negotiation cannot be implemented without the approval of Congress. This sometimes renders an international negotiation relatively meaningless since foreign government negotiators may appropriately challenge the negotiating credibility of U.S. government officials when all results have to be submitted to a body as large, and arguably unpredictable, as the Congress. In particular foreign nations hesitate to negotiate in a procedural context in which they feel the United States gets two bites to the apple. By this they mean that after difficult compromises are achieved in the international negotiation, the result is taken back to the Congress, where certain interests are able to prevent approval unless foreign negotiating partners come forward with even more concessions. Thus an important question for the United States and its international trade partners is whether the executive branch has adequate negotiating authority delegated to it from the Congress for the United States to be able to launch and participate meaningfully in a new round of international negotiation.

One implication of this brief questioning of U.S. institutions is to raise (but not answer) the question of whether the U.S. system lends itself better to multilateral or MFN approaches or, on the other hand, to bilateral approaches. The enormous costs of obtaining congressional approval of each of a series of bilateral initiatives suggest an added reason for multilateralism in U.S. diplomacy. And the enormous diversity of U.S. society (with many interest groups with special affinities to one or another foreign nation) suggests the value of U.S. multilateral approaches since in that context the Congress can thrash out the various trade-offs and compromises that may be impossible if bilateral cases come up one at a time.

On the other hand one is entitled to question whether U.S. political and governmental institutions are sufficiently integrated into an international multilateral system to allow the United States to play an appropriate constructive role. The Congress likes to tie the hands of the executive, and that makes it harder for U.S. diplomacy to seek appropriate multilateral consensus on a number of issues.

9.6 Conclusions

Some of the problems I have discussed are endemic and will never be totally resolved and possibly never satisfactorily controlled. There are certain tensions between competing objectives of the international and national institutions concerned with international economic affairs, as there are also in connection with substantive rules. In short, no one is entitled to expect a tidy world.

Clearly, however, a number of institutional questions need considerable attention, particularly in connection with a new round of multilateral trade negotiations. In the context of growing international economic interdependence, many national leaders are finding it increasingly difficult to manage the problems presented to them. Going it alone with national policy measures designed to alleviate economic distress or to promote growth in an economy is no longer as feasible as it was even as recently as several decades ago. If one nation uses monetary or fiscal policies to promote its economic growth, for example it may find that a good portion of the cost it has incurred has gone to benefit foreign countries and not its own economy. And in a myriad of relatively picayune details, such as particular targeted subsidies, what one nation does for legitimate national policy reasons may have a damaging effect on another nation.

For these reasons nations join together to establish international rules and international institutions, which are essential to effective rules. Dispute settlement, norm formulation, and a number of other procedures are essential ingredients to designing techniques that can effectively manage interdependence in today's complex world. Techniques for accomplishing this can include multilateral and bilateral approaches, yet one wonders whether the risks of bilateralism have been adequately assessed. As frustration with the multilateral approach increases, the temptation to turn to bilateral approaches increases. We would not expect that GATT as an institution would suddenly expire, but we have already witnessed a gradual decline in its effectiveness to accomplish some of the goals that nations feel are important but cannot be accomplished by unilateral or even bilateral means.

Despite arguments for multilateral or MFN approaches, however, clearly there are also detriments. Foot dragging and free riders (with incentives to remain unobligated) have been mentioned. When a preferred multilateral approach comes up against these detriments, a strong case can be made for at least a tactical departure from MFN. A bilateral or minilateral approach may then prove the next best way to proceed and if done sensitively could even endure later, more widespread participation so that ultimately multilateral goals are reinvigorated.[62]

Over the next several years we shall have the opportunity to observe whether statesmen and political leaders have the capacity, imagination, and perseverance to improve the multilateral and bilateral institutions that can help the world's leaders to manage interdependence.

Notes

I express appreciation for comments and contributions of the conference participants. This chapter has been revised in the light of those comments. I also wish to thank Karin Seifert, a student at the University of Michigan Law School, for her able assistance in the final preparation of the notes for this chapter.

1. For works dealing with this broader question and GATT generally, see Jackson (1969, 1977, 1980) and Jackson, Louis, and Matsushita (1984).

2. See Jackson (1983).

3. Trade and Tariff Act of 1984, P. L. 98-573, 98 Stat. 2948 (1984).

4. Jackson (1969, chap. 1).

5. See Jackson (1967).

6. Jackson (1977, p. 408).

7. GATT, *Basic Instruments and Selected Documents* (1955, pp. 3, 32).

8. Jackson (1969, chap. 2).

9. See Evans (1971, pp. 227–229, 272–273, 285–286, 301–305).

10. Agreement on Implementation of article VI of the General Agreement on Tariffs and Trade, GATT Document L/2812 (July 12, 1967); Long (1969); Renegotiated Amendments Act of 1968, Title II, sec. 201, P. L. 90-634, 82 Stat. 1347, 19 U.S.C. sec. 160.

11. Trade Act of 1974, P. L. 93-618, 88 Stat. 1978 (1975); Trade Act of 1974, Title I, sec. 121(d).

12. Ibid., sec. 26.

13. Ibid., sec. 121, 122.

14. Ibid., sec. 301–302, subsequently amended in the Trade Agreements Act of 1979, P. L. 96-39, 19 U.S.C.A. sections 2501 et seq., 93 Stat. 144 (July 26, 1979), and the Trade and Tariffs Act of 1974, supra note 3. See also Jackson et al. (1984, pp. 174–175).

15. McCulloch (1974, p. 217) ; Jackson (1977, pp. 1018–1019); Customs Tariff Amendment Act, 1973, Canadian Statutes, c. 10, as. 2, 3—July 1, 1974.

16. Trade Act of 1974, sec. 502(b) (3).

17. ITIM, December 19, 1984, p. 774.

18. "Trade Agreements Act of 1979," Committee on Finance, U.S. Senate, 96th Cong., 1st sess., S. Rep. 96-249 (July 17, 1979), p. 36.

19. "Briefing Materials Prepared for Use of the Committee . . . on the Subject of Foreign Trade and Tariffs," Committee on Ways and Means, U.S. House of Representatives, 93d Cong., 1st sess. (1973), pp. 189–190.

20. Canada/United States Agreement on Automotive Products, Report of the Working Party, GATT, 13 BISD 112, 119 (1965); United States—Import of Automotive Products, GATT, 14 BISD 181, 185 (1965).

21. In particular the United States so limited its application of the countervailing duty code, the government procurement code, and the technical barriers or "standards" code. See Trade Agreements Act of 1979, P. L. 96-39, 93 Stat. 144 (1979)—Title IV (Standards Code), Title III (Government Procurement Code), Title I (Countervailing Duty Code); and Jackson et al. (1984, pp. 171–172).

22. Jackson et al. (1984, pp. 116–120).

23. Annual Report of the President of the United States on the Trade Agreements Program, 27th issue, April 1984.

24. Japanese Measure on Imports of Leather, Report of Panel, GATT, 26 BISD 320 (1979); EC GATT Complaint against Japan, 401 ITEX 768 (March 30, 1982); 8 ITIM 136 (April 27, 1983).

25. In Macrory and Suchman (1982, p. 2).

26. Ibid., p. 135.

27. ITR, November 21, 1984, p. 625.

28. Reciprocal Trade and Investment Act of 1982, amendment to the Trade Act of 1974, S. 2094, 97th Cong., 2d sess. (1982); "Reciprocal Trade and Investment Act of 1982," Committee on Finance, U.S. Senate, S. Rep. 97-483, 97th Cong., 2d sess. (June 30, 1982).

29. Heavyweight Motorcycles and Engines and Power Train Subassemblies Thereof, Investigation No. TA-201-47, USITC Pub. No. 1342 (1983); Presidential Action, 8 ITIM 5 (April 6, 1983).

30. Tentative Steel Agreement Reached by U.S. Commerce Department and European Community Negotiators, August 5, 1982, 141 ITIM 628 (August 18, 1982).

31. Caribbean Basin Economic Recovery Act of 1983, P. L. 98-67, 97 Stat. 384 (1983); Schultz (1985, pp. 1–5); Stokes (1985, pp. 206–210).

32. ITR, October 31, 1984, p. 540, November 21, 1984, p. 624.

33. Trade Agreements Act of 1979, Title XI, sec. 1104, P. L. 96-39, 93 Stat. 144, 310 (1979).

34. With respect to some of the problems of GATT, see Jackson (1969, 1978, 1980) and Jackson et al. (1984).

35. Jackson (1980).

36. See Patterson (1983).

37. See Jackson (1980, n. 34).

38. See Ministerial Declaration of November 29, 1982, GATT, 29 BISD 9 (1982); Understanding Regarding Notification, Consultation, Dispute Settlement and Surveillance, GATT, 26 BISD 210 (1979); Trade Organizations, 128 ITIM 206 (May 19, 1982). See also Hudec (1980) and Jackson (1978, n. 53).

39. GATT Document C/M/154, of January 28, 1982, Minutes of Council Meeting of December 7–8, 1981. The panel reports of 1976 are contained in GATT Documents L/4422, 4423, 4424, and 4425.

40. Deficit Reduction Act of 1984, Title VIII—Foreign Sales Corporations, P. L. 98-369, 98 Stat. 494, 985 (1984); Jackson (1978); Harwood (1981).

41. Curzon (1965, pp. 166–208, 331); Dam (1970, p. 257).

42. Textiles and Clothing in the World Economy, Study by GATT Secretariat (Geneva: GATT, 1984).

43. Committee on Trade and Development Report, GATT, 30 BISD 72 (1983), p. 75; Safeguards, Chairman's Report, GATT, 30 BISD 216 (1983); Director General of GATT, (1979, p. 90).

44. White House Statement on Steel Import Relief Decision, 1 ITR 11 (September 19, 1984), p. 330, Steel, p. 296.

45. Director General of GATT (1979, pp. 53–56).

46. Agreement on Interpretation and Application of Articles VI, XVI and XXIII of the General Agreement of Tariffs and Trade, GATT, 26 BISD 56 (1979). These ambiguities include the following (references are to article followed by paragraph number): 4:1, amount of a countervailing duty to be permitted; annex paragraph (1) and 9:1 and 9:2, question of bilevel pricing; 14:2, commitments of developing countries; 11:2, domestic subsidy obligations; question whether definitions in part 2 of the agreement applied also to part 1; 10:1, 10:2, and 10:3, are processed agricultural goods primary; 18, aspects of the dispute settlement procedure, particularly power of the Committee of Signatories; 6:1, note 1, effect of the nature of subsidy in question (export subsidy?); 10:1, "equitable share"; in general, definition of subsidy, particularly nullification or impairment. See also Tarullo (1984).

47. Jackson (1983).

48. See especially chapters 2 and 6 to this book. See also note 34 above.

49. See note 21 above and Jackson et al. (1984).

50. The classical instance of this, often cited, is the Swiss-German 1904 Treaty, specifying lower German tariffs on the importation of "large dapple mountain cattle or brown cattle reared at a spot at least three hundred meters above sea level and having at least one month's grazing each year at a spot at least eight hundred meters above sea level." See Curzon (1965, p. 60) and the references in note 1 above.

51. GATT Agreement Annexes A through E.

52. See especially Dam (1963) and Jackson (1969, chap. 26; 1977, chap. 9, sec. 9.4).

53. GATT Document L/5776 of February 7, 1985, Report of the Panel: *European Community—Tariff Treatment on Imports of Citrus Products from Certain Countries in the Mediterranean Region.*

54. See Director General of GATT (1979, pp. 90–95; 1980, pp. 14–16); Bronckers (1981, 1983, 1984); and Koulen (1983).

55. See Carbon Steel Wire Rod from Czechoslovakia and Poland, 49 FR 19370, 9 ITIM 967 (May 9, 1984); Report of Working Party on Accession of Poland, GATT, 15 BISD 109 (1967).

56. Jackson (1984).

57. See sec. 102 of the 1974 Trade Act, note 11 above. The U.S. Supreme Court in I.N.S. v. Chadha, 103 S. Ct. 2764, 77 L. Ed. 2d 317, 51 U.S.L.W. 4907 (June 23, 1983), affirmed a Ninth Circuit Court of Appeals ruling that the one-house veto provision in the Immigration and Nationality Act permitting an override of the attorney general's decision to suspend deportation of an alien is unconstitutional because it violates the separation of powers doctrine. See Smith and Struve (1983). A number of questions have been left open by the Supreme Court's decision.

58. See *New York Times*, January 19, 1985, pp. 1, 4, January 20, 1985, p. E22, and January 21, 1985, p. 17.

59. See note 40 above regarding the DISC case. The only case that involved the actual application of retaliation under article XXIII (dispute settlement provision) of GATT was the case brought by Netherlands against the United States in 1951. The Netherlands was authorized to limit U.S. exports to it of grains as a response to U.S. import restrictions on dairy products from the Netherlands. The Netherlands applied these restraints for several years, but they had no perceivable effect on U.S. policy. GATT, BISD 1st Supp. 32 (1953); Jackson (1969, p. 172; 1977, p. 429).

60. Trade and Tariff Act of 1984, Title II, sec. 207, P. L. 98-573, 98 Stat. 2948, at 2976 (1984); House Conference Report No. 98-1156, October 5, 1984, Congressional Record, vol. 130, no. 131—pt. II, p. 11560.

61. *New York Times*, February 7, 1985, p. 13.

62. See, for example, the statement by trade representative Michael Smith, quoted in "A Risky Shift in Trade Policy," *Business Week*, November 12, 1984, pp. 34—35: "Our preference still is [to bargain] multilaterally. But if that is not on, we will attack these issues . . . with any and all nations willing to move ahead on them." See also statements by assistant trade representative Cooper (1984, p. 3).

References

Bronckers, M. C. E. J. "The Non-Discriminatory Application of Article XIX GATT: Tradition or Fiction?" *Legal Issues of European Intergration* 2 (1981): 35—76.

Bronckers, M. C. E. J. "Reconsidering the Non-Discrimination Principle as Applied to GATT Safeguard Measures." *Legal Issues of European Integration* 2 (1983): 113—137.

Bronckers, M. C. E. J. "Controlling Selectivity in a New Safeguards Code." GATT 4/01, 1984.

Bureau of National Affairs, *International Trade Reporter's-U.S. Import Weekly* (ITIM), various issues.

Cooper, Doral. "Free Trade Areas: New Opportunities, New Risks." *International Business Review* 3 (1984): 3—6.

Curzon, Gerard. *Multilateral Diplomacy: The General Agreement on Tariffs and Trade and Its Impact on National Commercial Policies and Techniques*. London: Michael Joseph, 1965.

Dam, Kenneth W. "Regional Economic Arrangements and the GATT: The Legacy of a Misconception." *University of Chicago Law Review* 30 (1963): 615–665.

Dam, Kenneth W. *The GATT—Law and International Economic Organization*. Chicago: University of Chicago Press, 1970.

Evans, John. *The Kennedy Round in American Trade Policy: The Twilight of GATT?* Cambridge: Harvard University Press, 1971.

GATT. *Basic Instruments and Selected Documents (BISD)*. Geneva, various issues.

GATT. Director General. *The Tokyo Round of Multilateral Trade Negotiations*. Geneva: GATT, 1979.

GATT. Director General. *Tokyo Round of Multilateral Trade Negotiations*. Supplementary Report. Geneva: GATT, 1980.

GATT, Secretariat. *Textiles and Clothing in the World Economy*. Geneva: GATT, 1984.

Harwood, Judd. "The GATT, DISC Dispute." *Taxes International* 25 (1981): 3–12, 46.

Hudec, Robert E. "GATT Dispute Settlement after the Tokyo Round an Unfinished Business." *Cornell International Law Journal* 13 (1980): 145–203.

Jackson, John H. "The General Agreement on Tariffs and Trade in United States Domestic Law." *Michigan Law Review* 66 (1967): 249–332.

Jackson, John H. *World Trade and the Law of GATT*. Indianapolis: Bobbs-Merrill, 1969.

Jackson, John H. *Legal Problems of International Economic Relations—Cases, Materials and Text on the National and International Regulation of Transnational Economic Relations*. St. Paul, Minn.: West Publishing, 1977.

Jackson, John H. "The Crumbling Institutions of the Liberal Trade System." *Journal of World Trade Law* 12 (1978): 93–106.

Jackson, John H. "The Jurisprudence of International Trade: The DISC Case in GATT." *American Journal of International Law* 72 (1979): 747–781.

Jackson, John H. "The Birth of the GATT-MTN System: A Constitutional Appraisal." *Journal of Law and Policy and International Business* 12 (1980): 21–58.

Jackson, John H. "Equality and Discrimination in International Economic Law (XI): The General Agreement on Tariffs and Trade." *British Yearbook of World Affairs* (1983): 224–239.

Jackson, John H. "Perspectives on the Jurisprudence of International Trade: Costs and Benefits of Legal Precedures in the United States." *Michigan Law Review* 82 (1984): 1570–1587.

Jackson, John H., Jean-Victor Louis, and Mitsuo Matsushita. *Implementing the Tokyo Round: National Constitutions and International Economic Rules*. Ann Arbor: University of Michigan Press, 1984.

Koulen, Mark. "The Non-Discriminatory Interpretation of GATT Article XIX—A Reply." *Legal Issues for European Integration* 2 (1983): 87–111.

Long, Russell B. "United States Law and the International Antidumping Code." *International Lawyer* 3 (1969): 464–489.

Macrory, Patrick F. J., and Suchman, Peter O., eds. *Current Legal Aspects of International Trade Law*. Chicago: Section of International Law, American Bar Association, 1982.

McCulloch, Rachel. "United States preferences: The Proposed System." *Journal of World Trade Law* 8 (1974): 212–226.

Patterson, Gardner. "The European Community as a Threat to the System." In W. R. Cline, ed., *Trade Policy in the 1980s*. Cambridge: MIT Press for the Institute for International Economics, 1983.

Schultz, George. "Democracy and the Path of Economic Growth." *Department of State Bulletin* 2094 (January 1985): 1–5.

Smith, Richard B., and Guy M. Struve. "Aftershocks of the Fall of the Legislative Veto." *American Bar Association Journal* 69 (1983): 1258–.

Stokes, Bruce. "Reagan's Caribbean Basin Initiative on Track, But Success Still in Doubt," *National Journal*, January 26, 1985, pp. 206–210.

Tarullo, Daniel. "The MTN Subsidies Code: Agreement without Consensus." In Seymour Rubin and Gary C. Hufbauer, eds., *Emerging Standards of International Trade and Investment*. Totowa: Rowman and Allanheld, 1984.

Comment on "Multilateral and Bilateral Negotiating Approaches for the Conduct of U.S. Trade Policies"

Robert O. Keohane

Government policies toward international trade are in flux, and the GATT is, as Jackson says, a "troubled institution." Protectionist proposals are being advanced with increasing frequency and stridency in the United States; often their proponents call for general or discriminatory protection that would break decisively with the last fifty years of U.S. trade policy. Some pundits have declared 1986 the "year of trade" in U.S. politics.

In part this surge of protectionist sentiment reflects the recent overvaluation of the dollar and the resulting huge U.S. trade deficit. But its intensity, its rhetoric, and its focus on East Asian exporters suggest that protectionism also stems from the sense that principles of fair competition are being violated at the expense of well-managed and productive U.S. enterprises. Thus some of the pressures for protection seem to result from the fact that U.S. firms are competing with firms that operate, in their own national political economies, under very different rules. Although aggregate welfare in the United States may rise as a result of concerted government-business cooperation in Japan or the subsidization of exports by the Korean government, Americans may still seek to restrict such exports on the grounds of unfairness. For many people equity among firms may be more important than economic efficiency. As a result some of the recent pressures for protection may persist even after the dollar and the trade deficit fall, although they will surely become less intense.

Viewed within this political context, one of the great merits of Jackson's chapter is its attention to norms and principles rather than merely to the economic effects of trade. Jackson's concern with the maintenance of international cooperation and a pattern of international rules reminds us that fairness among competitors is not the only noneconomic principle to be considered in discussing trade policy. He points out that unilateral U.S. protectionism, or a reversion to bilateralism in trade policy, would have adverse consequences for international institutions and cooperation, as well as for the liberal international trading order. Thus the issue is not merely one of economic welfare and efficiency versus equity among competing firms; there is also the question of how to maintain some approximation to an orderly and fair international society in which weak countries are not discriminated against and in which mutually beneficial cooperation is maintained.

Jackson clearly regards liberal trade, and therefore the liberal trading order, as in the interest of the United States. Yet he recognizes that unconditional liberalism could provide incentives for other countries to act as free riders or foot draggers, penalizing the liberal countries and eventually producing a backlash against nondiscriminatory practices and liberal trade. He therefore shows that he is aware of the strategic considerations, elaborated by Dixit in chapter 6 that the United States must take into account in its trade policy—in part to deter others from adopting trade-distorting measures that would damage specific economic interests of this country. Strategic issues are also relevant to the more general objective of maintaining an open international economic system. For instance, threats to impose trade barriers as part of a strategy of reciprocity may, if successful, help to maintain a liberal trading system.

Strategies of reciprocity, however, raise the issue of discrimination, which Corden discusses in chapter 10. In the public debate reciprocity has positive connotations, presumably due to its association with equity and mutual benefit. It is therefore used by proponents of a variety of antithetical policies (Keohane, 1986). Discrimination, on the other hand, has negative connotations. Yet reciprocity, defined as a policy of cooperating only with those who cooperate with you, implies discrimination if some of one's partners act differently from others. One person's reciprocity is another person's discrimination. If we are to believe in the value of reciprocity, we will have to rethink our attitude toward discrimination.

Discrimination has often been viewed as antithetical to liberalization; indeed in the GATT system, liberalization of trade barriers and nondiscrimination are two of the central norms. Yet I wonder whether these norms are as mutually reinforcing as we often assume. From a bargaining perspective, threats to discriminate against those who fail to liberalize their own barriers may promote liberalization under some circumstances. Perhaps more important in practice, the ability of powerful governments to discriminate against certain suppliers may render general liberalization more tolerable than it would otherwise be; and conversely liberalization may lead to discrimination when unanticipated consequences (such as a surge of textile imports from China) ensue. At any rate it is a curious but little-observed fact that the period of greatest liberalization during the postwar period—since the mid-1960s—was also the period in which discrimination increased. In 1955 90 percent of GATT trade took place at MFN tariff rates, but by 1980 this had fallen to about 65 percent (Finlayson and Zacher, 1981, p. 569). This does not necessarily imply a causal connection between discrimination and liberalization, in one direction or another, but it certainly throws doubt on the assumption that nondiscrimination and liberalization necessarily go hand in hand.

Reconsideration of the relationship between liberalism and nondiscrimination is already evident in some of the literature on trade. Vernon (1982, p. 504) has asked "whether or not we have reached a point at which selective discrimination may generate more open international markets than the rule of nondiscrimination could produce." Citing Axelrod (1984), Goldstein and Krasner (1984, p. 282) declare that "the United States can best insure international cooperation by responding in kind to foreign practices." The core of these critics' argument is that nondiscrimination, by enabling countries to act as free riders, will discourage liberalization. Many countries that prefer general liberalism to protection but would prefer to protect while reaping the benefits of letting others do the liberalizing will behave as free riders, thus degrading liberalism in the system as a whole.

On the other hand experience with discrimination in international trade is hardly reassuring. Conditional MFN treatment in the context of bilateral negotiations led the Harding admininstration—hardly an exemplar of ideological liberalism—to adopt unconditional MFN in 1923. The combination of conditional MFN and sequential negotiation of bilateral agreements had led to negotiating chaos since each new agreement affected the value of previous concessions and potentially required renegotiation of all related earlier pacts. Thus strictly conditional reciprocity involved, as one contemporary observer put it, "unceasing and difficult negotiations which are quite unnecessary and often costly" (Sayre, 1939, p. 109). Such bargaining, according to one of Harding's advisers, "is at best complicated and dilatory and seldom, if ever, produces results which are commensurate with the irritation which it engenders among excluded nations" (Culbertson, 1937, p. 249).

The result of such practices is likely to be, at best, a series of discriminatory bargains that are continually subject to acrimonious revision. In the case of U.S. trade policy in the early years of this century, matters did not get even this far, partly because of the reluctance of the executive to make far-reaching agreements and of Congress to ratify them and partly because the trading partners of the United States became increasingly unwilling to grant the one-sided privileges that U.S. espousal of conditional MFN treatment implied (Viner, 1951).

It appears that neither strict reciprocity (discrimination) nor unconditional MFN treatment is entirely satisfactory. Discrimination can lead to acrimonious feuds; unconditional MFN treatment can generate free riding and unfairness, which may in turn contribute to the collapse of political support for trade liberalization. What we need to search for are mixed strategies that combine the openness to new or weak entrants of unconditional MFN treatment with the incentives to cooperate inherent in reciprocity. To achieve this, institutional innovations will be required.

In the past progress in international trade has often involved institutional innovations of precisely this type. The institution of multilateral trade rounds was one such innovation since it meant in practice that negotiations could combine the bilateral, conditional practice of reciprocity with a final simultaneous package deal negotiation to reach equilibrium. This avoided the infinite regress problem of sequential bilateral bargaining. Thus in the Kennedy Round a nominally multilateral negotiation became in practice a large and closely interrelated series of bilateral or plurilateral negotiations among principal suppliers of products, supplemented at the end by package deals in efforts to achieve overall reciprocity among concessions.

Three other rules or practices illustrate the importance of institutional innovation. The first is the principal supplier rule, which permitted conditional concessions among major suppliers while allowing small producers to act as free riders. Thus in the Dillon Round, "no participant would agree to reduce its tariffs on any product on which a non-participant supplied more than 10 percent of its imports" (Curzon and Curzon, 1976, 1: 173, quoted by Blackhurst, 1979, p. 224). The second innovation began in the Kennedy Round in the mid-1960s and continued in the Tokyo Round ending in 1979. Governments first negotiated on tariff-cutting formulas rather than engaging from the outset on item-by-item negotiations. These formulas created the presumption of large, across-the-board reductions in tariffs; if governments sought exceptions, they had to do so explicitly rather than simply by dragging their feet on negotiations for the relevant item. The third innovation appeared in the code negotiations of the Tokyo Round. The codes were negotiated separately. Within each negotiation reciprocity was demanded, but countries that did not wish to reciprocate could fail to sign one code or another without being excluded from other negotiations or blocking agreements to which they did not consent. Insofar as governments signing the codes could in practice discriminate against nonsigners, this arrangement protected the negotiations against the adverse incentives created by the presence of a number of potentially important free riders, yet this was done within the framework of rules.

These institutional innovations had one feature in common: they enabled governments to pursue liberalization by practicing reciprocity while providing a structure of rules that limited the abuse of reciprocity that has given discrimination such a bad name. Yet to devise these institutional innovations, practitioners had to make two distinctions, in addition to Jackson's useful distinction among multilateralism, MFN treatment, and the GATT. First, negotiators had to recognize that strategies of conditional concessions are not necessarily associated with bilateralism but that they may indeed be rendered more tolerable by multilateralism. The problems of having continually to renegotiate agreements made obsolete by conditional concessions were overcome only through the package deals inherent in multilateralism. Second, negotiators had to distinguish a regime based on conditional MFN from a system without rules of any kind.

The latter distinction is often missed. Indeed it is frequently argued or implied that unconditional MFN is a necessary condition for an international trading system based on clear and well-understood rules. Reciprocity is rejected on the ground that it leads to uncontrolled and discriminatory exercises of power. Yet this argument conflates the constitutional structure of the international trading regimes with its specific practices. What is obnoxious about conditional MFN as often practiced in the past is not that states demanded quids pro quo but that these demands have typically been enforced by the unconstrained exercise of power, including threats that may entail a high risk of trade wars. That is, what is really objectionable in such systems has been the absence of a clear set of rules that would be applied impartially to any country accepting the obligations of the regime itself.

What would be internally contradictory about an international trade regime with nondiscriminatory rules that allowed discrimination in trade under carefully specified conditions? In referring to nondiscriminatory rules, I mean that any member of GATT could receive the benefits open to any other member, provided that it agreed to specific obligations in a given area of trading activity. No country would be excluded from the benefits of liberalization on the grounds that it was too competitive. But countries that did not adhere to a set of rules themselves could demand the same privileges as those who did. In addition to its strategic benefits—limiting free riding and foot dragging—such a policy would be appealing to those who fear unfair competition between foreign and U.S. firms. The demand for fair trade is not just a preoccupation of the French, and those who have liberal trade at heart would be wise to consider how they could appropriate the symbol of fairness before it is identified with blind protectionism.

The Tokyo Round codes constitute an institutional innovation that seeks to combine openness to new joiners with fairness for countries and firms playing by the rules. Membership in the regime is open to all GATT members. Yet if some fail to adhere to the rules, they do not necessarily receive the benefits of the regime. The principle is defensible: those that fail to adhere to the rules have little basis for demanding the right to be granted all the benefits received by those who follow the rules. There may be legal, political, or admininstrative reasons that make it unwise to practice reciprocity too strictly, as Dixit suggests. There may be ethical or political reasons as well to provide certain countries, such as LDCs, with nonreciprocal privileges. Nevertheless we should pay more attention to the virtues of reciprocity, and therefore of discrimination, as means to preserve or extend liberalism. Supporters of liberal trade, cognizant of bargaining problems and of domestic pressures for fair trade should refrain from simplistic ideological defenses of liberalism but should reflect instead on the feasibility of devising institutional innovations that will respond to the international bargaining realities and domestic political pressures of our day. Jackson constructively leads us to begin thinking along those lines. So do the Tokyo Round codes, which permit tit-for-tat strategies to promote liberalization and fairness while retaining an open, multilateral structure of rules to which all participants in GATT may adhere.

References

Axelrod, Robert. *The Evolution of Cooperation*. New York: Basic Books, 1984.

Blackhurst, Richard. "Reciprocity on Trade Negotiations under Flexible Exchange Rates." In John P. Martin and Alasdair Smith, eds., *Trade and Payments Adjustment under Flexible Exchange Rates*. London: Macmillan for the Trade Policy Research Center, 1979.

Culbertson, William S. *Reciprocity: A National Policy for Foreign Trade*. New York: McGraw-Hill, 1937.

Curzon,, Gerard, and Victoria Curzon. "The Management of Trade Relations in the GATT." In Andrew Schonfeld, ed., *International Economic Relations of the Western World, 1959–1971*. Oxford: Oxford University Press, 1976.

Finlayson, Jock A., and Mark Zacher. "The GATT and the Regulation of Trade Barriers: Regime Dynamics and Functions." *International Organization* 35 (1981): 561–602.

Goldstein, Judith L., and Stephen D. Krasner. "Unfair Trade Practices: The Case for a Differential Response." *American Economic Review*, Papers and Proceedings 74 (1984): 282–287.

Keohane, Robert O. "Reciprocity in International Relations." *International Organization* (Winter 1986).

Sayre, Francis Bowes. *The Way Forward: The American Trade Agreements Program*. New York: Macmillan, 1939.

Vernon, Raymond. "International Trade Policy in the 1980s." *International Studies Quarterly* 26 (1982): 483–510.

Viner, Jacob. "The Most-Favored-Nation Clause." In his *International Economics*. Glencoe, Ill.: Free Press, 1951.

Comment on "Multilateral and Bilateral Negotiating Approaches for the Conduct of U.S. Trade Policies"

Gardner Patterson

I find it easy to agree with most of what Jackson has said; he understands these matters. But these are a few points where I differ or want to elaborate. My comments are largely limited to the institutional issues—and particularly international institutional and procedural matters—rather than theoretical or substantive ones.

Section 9.3 of Jackson's chapter is entitled "The GATT: A Troubled Institution." He is correct. My observations have led me to conclude that a large part of the problems and difficulties the GATT faces stem from two groups of developments since it was negotiated. First is the obvious one. The text of the General Agreement—while finding its raison d'être in the long-term economic benefits of a system of nondiscrimination, stable rules, and a gradual lowering of trade barriers—does recognize other economic and noneconomic objectives that must be accommodated. But it does not give these other national objectives anything like the importance they now have. I have in mind particularly the great place now given to subsidies and all that follows from that and, more generally, the assumption by many governments, and not just the developing countries, of direct responsibility for the pattern and structure of their economic development. Such a major reshuffling of priorities could not but create huge problems for the GATT.

Beyond those considerations the GATT system has been subjected to acute strains by the replacement of one giant, the United States, with three—the United States, the EC, and Japan—and the emergence of a very large number of small nations that are poor, want things the giants can but often do not want to give in the field of trade, and operate in an international environment where it is widely accepted as right and proper that these developing nations are entitled to preferential treatment and should be excused from most of the trade obligations the General Agreement imposes on the developed countries. The consequence is that the appeal of bilateral rather than multilateral negotiations is greatly increased, and the GATT seems to some a less attractive place for the United States to do business.

This is so for two reasons. First, it is much easier to negotiate on complex matters with one or two others than it is with twenty, or thirty, or fifty sitting around the table. This becomes strikingly clear when many of the others are more articulate about what they want, at least in general terms, than what they are prepared to offer. As one U.S. negotiator said during the Tokyo Round, "When the negotiations get serious, I want to talk only to those who know exactly what they want and who have some chips on the table. I want no kibitizers around." Second, because the markets of the three giants are large and interesting to each other, it is worthwhile to work out bilateral or trilateral deals. It is true that the developing countries' markets and trade policies, seen as a whole, may be more important to each of the giants than the markets in either or even both of the other two. But these developing country markets are fragmented, and no one is able to speak or negotiate for them as a group other than on the most general level of broad issues. This is not surprising given their diversity. But trade negotiations that lead to binding and operational commitments are about specific matters: What is to be the tariff rate on good C? What is to be the definition of an export credit subsidy that is to be restrained? It is not about the broad obligation to provide special treatment to developing countries.

The consequences are not only that it is tempting for the giants to approach trade problems bilaterally and outside the GATT framework but also that negotiations within that framework are often essentially bilateral. A common complaint, not only of the LDCs but even of such a power as Canada during the Tokyo Round, was that agreements were hammered out in negotiations taking place in Brussels, or Washington, or Tokyo rather than in Geneva and then put forward on a take-it-or-leave-it basis with some concern that if they left it, the giants would go ahead and apply the agreement among themselves and deny any benefits to nonsigners. And so the offer of the GATT as a negotiating forum is reduced for the smaller countries as well.

This touches on the voting procedures in the GATT, seen as a problem and defect by Jackson. Here I part company with him and share what he calls a shallow viewpoint by joining those who say the one-country, one-vote provisions do not really matter because decisions on almost all matters—including all the results of both the Kennedy Round and the Tokyo Round—are taken by consensus. In the GATT this means that a proposed action is approved unless any opposing it are either silent when the matter is up for approval or that those speaking against it are so few and so substantively unimportant in the trade involved that their participation is not needed for the decision to become effective. It also means that both the United States and the EC have an effective veto power in the GATT in the sense that it is hard to imagine a matter in which

either is strongly opposed that would be adopted by the contracting parties—
a dispute panel finding against either of them excepted—simply because of
doubt that any such arrangement or agreement could become effectively
operational, not because of any supporting votes that could be mustered were
the question to be put to a vote.

The real problem arising from the great increase in GATT members of
widely differing economic significance is not the voting structure of one-
nation, one-vote. It is, in a sense, just the opposite. Given the incentives for
bilateral negotiations, a major problem in making the GATT more effective is
how to provide for effective participation in negotiations by the smaller
countries that are so important in the trading system. Participation is especially important during the early stages when their needs might be accommodated but cannot be considered after the principles have already hammered
out among themselves many of the elements of an accord, a state of affairs, that
typically has incorporated a complex series of trade-offs whose balance could
easily be upset by any change in what has already been agreed. Indeed any
change that would require the big parties to go back to their own capitols and
seek approval is often seen as out of the question.

One of the major unsolved problems in maintaining a system based on a
multilateral approach to negotiations is how to bring the valid and important
concerns of the developing countries into the process. There is, to be sure,
another side: the need to find more effective ways to ensure that the developing countries assume more and more of their GATT obligations. On this
graduation issue I will hide behind Jackson's skirts. He did not deal with it,
and so I will not say anything either, but it does warrant major consideration.

I turn now to a few more specific of Jackson's points. Because it raises a more
important point about the operation of the system, I would note that he is in
error in saying that the GATT was among those that called for the introduction
of the GSP into the international trading system. This scheme was the creation
of UNCTAD. It received a cool reception indeed from many of the spokesmen
in GATT meetings when it was first broached, and it created serious problems
for the GATT. But once the negotiators in the UNCTAD, for the most part
representatives of the same governments that were members of the GATT, had
agreed to the policy in that forum, those same governments, though usually
different spokesmen, had to seek in the GATT a waiver to permit their
governments to do what their GATT obligations forbade them to do. This
affair highlights the continuing problem that can arise when a nation's spokesmen in one forum are looking primarily at the political aspects of an issue and
those in another at the economic aspects. Intragovernmental coordination is
apparently never easy in big governments.

The question of MFN treatment is on all trade agendas these days. In his brief catalog of economic arguments for the unconditional MFN rule, Jackson did not mention what some consider the most important consideration: if one is to have a system of negotiated rather than unilateral reduction of trade barriers, then it is the unconditional MFN commitment that provides the useful insurance that the benefits you have negotiated will not be taken from you by your partner's subsequently giving even more favorable treatment to someone else. I would, however, broaden the definition of unconditional MFN to permit the signatories of codes of behavior on nontariff matters to deny the benefits of each code to nonsignatories provided the codes are open to all on the same terms and the original signatories account for an important part of the trade affected by the codes.

In his discussion of discrimination, Jackson usefully draws attention to the nasty and still unresolved issue of whether the international rules should provide for the selective application of safeguard measures. Quite properly a great deal of attention has been given to the argument of the developing countries that such a policy would in practice mean it was their exports that would suffer the most because they are often the newcomers in the market and so would be identified as the troublemakers—a gross misapplication of the marginal principal in their, and my, eyes. But there is another important though less publicized argument against the selective approach: selectivity would create a vested interest in all those nations not being selected in supporting the maintenance of the restrictions against the unfortunate few. One of the advantages of the nondiscriminatory application of import restrictions as temporary safeguard measures has been that all exporters have joined in seeking their removal.

Jackson characterizes as troublesome several aspects of the dispute-settlement procedures of the GATT. Fortunately some of the problems he cites are now being tackled, with good prospects of improvement in this important facet of the international trading system. Establishment of a roster of persons willing and qualified to serve as panel members, which I am told is underway, should reduce the delays so often encountered in the past in constituting panels. The growing use in the last couple of years of nongovernmental persons should go some way toward solving the problem of delays and the improper interference by governments with panel deliberations. The current discussions in Geneva on how better to deal with the problem of procrastination in implementing panel recommendations are encouraging and long overdue. The GATT secretariat, which services the panels by providing a wide range of essential support, has recently been much strengthened. Incidentally, it is my personal observation that the GATT secretariat is not, as Jackson suggests, stretched so thin it is not up to its job. I know of no instance in recent years when the secretariat was responsible for failing to carry out tasks given it, and in good time. There have been many instances when there were delays because the contracting parties could not agree on the specific task to be given the secretariat or, much more frequent, when there were delays in the secretariat's completing a task because some of the member governments failed to meet the agreed deadline for submitting information.

There is much talk of a possible new round of multilateral trade negotiations. The difficulties in the way of reaching agreement even on the terms of reference for such an exercise are formidable, although most informed observers appear to agree that not to have such a negotiation will be very costly politically and economically. It would certainly mean a continuing increase in the resort to bilateral approaches and, I fear, to a surge in unilateral solutions.

It is already evident that the United States will have to provide the leadership in initiating and in pursuing it. It seems to be out of character for Japan to take the lead. And the EC does not seem to have either the political will or decision-making machinery to play that role. Both must be active participants in the preparations for and the actual negotiations, and both have indicated they will, as has Canada. The recently enacted Trade and Tariff Act of 1984 did not give the administration the authority to conclude any new major multilateral trade negotiation. Nor was such authority requested by the administration. But Congress did give the executive branch the authority to prepare for and to initiate such negotiations, and the administration is making a serious effort to get them underway.

One can hope they succeed and that the negotiating mandate finally hammered out specifies not only the substantive areas to be covered—including, Congress has already insisted, agriculture, services, and high-technology goods—but also a thorough review of the GATT, last attempted in 1955, although a partial review was done in the so-called framework part of the Tokyo Round. It is my guess that so far as the General Agreement is concerned, a review in the context of a new round will leave the agreement largely intact because most of the rules set out there have served the signatories well.

The results might be limited to removing some of the ambiguities, elaborating some of the articles to cover what the negotiators can agree to do about trade in services, and refurbishing the Tokyo Round codes and the related GATT articles in the light of the experiences since 1979. None of them would be an easy task. But if it were to come about, a truly major consequence should be that governments would no longer be able to use the argument that the GATT was out of date and largely irrelevant as a justification for reverting to bilateralism.

10 On Making Rules for the International Trading System

W. Max Corden

10.1 Introduction

What issues are involved in making rules for the international trading system? The issues are immediate. First, the existing set of rules seems to be breaking down, with countries bypassing GATT in numerous ways, and there is a general sense that this cannot continue. Second, the views of the Japanese and U.S. governments suggest that new multilateral negotiations may be initiated soon.

My approach will be somewhat taxonomic. I wish to sort out and highlight issues. While concluding with some particular recommendations, I aim to contribute to clarification rather than urge a particular point of view.

One might be concerned with the probable, the possible, or the desirable. Economists, who claim to be realists but are often idealists, devote much of their writing to the last in the hope that by doing so, it will become the first. Like most other economists, I have never been very good at long-term forecasts, so I shall be concerned with the second and especially the third.

10.2 On the Making of Rules

Should there be formal international trade rules, whether simple or complex, and, if so, how should they be made? The alternative to rules is a system of continuous negotiations and power play. Rules themselves have to be constructed through negotiations and power play, but the establishment of a rules-based system economizes on the amount of the latter required. In addition rules provide the benefit of certainty. On the other hand there is a loss of flexibility. These are trade-offs in choosing between a rules-based and a negotiations-based system. I need hardly add that since the early 1970s, the international trading system has been slowly moving from a rules-based system toward a negotiations-based one, but also that, for trade to continue at all, there must be some rules, even if implicit.

Let me begin by turning to the second question: how the rules should be made. They will, of course be made by negotiations, but what are the principles that negotiators should have in mind? Here I will focus on one issue highlighted in the theory of the social contract and of justice. One could argue that participants should establish a just system that each will find satisfactory in whatever relative situation they eventually find themselves. With hindsight, particular participants might have benefited from different rules, but rules are made at a time when participants cannot be sure about their eventual situations, so any participant should bear in mind the possibility of being at some stage in a relatively weak situation.

In practical terms negotiators should take a long-term view. They should not just try to forecast the actual situation their particular country will be in and then try to negotiate rules that will be favorable for that situation. They should bear in mind that their country may later be in quite a different situation, one they are not able to forecast. One can hardly take this to the theoretical (I think, Rawlsian) extreme and suggest that negotiators should imagine that they know nothing at all about the prospective situations of their countries—that the United States and New Zealand know nothing about their likely relative size or bargaining power in the future. But a country should not assume that because it is in a current account deficit now, it will always be so, or because it is a net exporter of primary products now, it will always be one.

This is not a minor point. Great and powerful nations, such as Britain, have become less powerful and more dependent on rules. the United States initiated the exemption of agriculture from the GATT rules and now finds its interests have changed. Some developing countries have become major exporters of manufactures, and others will no doubt move in that direction. There are certainly many other examples. The issue comes down to one that lies behind so much economic policy debate: the short-term versus the long-term view, economists usually favoring the latter.

The central issue is rules versus continuously negotiated or discretionary equilibria (or disequilibria). The key point is that there is a trade-off between the costs of continuous negotiations and continuous power play, with threats, possibly culminating in trade warfare and political crises, and the costs resulting from loss of flexibility. The more stable the underlying environment is believed to be—that is, the more the parties feel that they can forecast the future—the more they would be likely to choose rules. On the other hand, great uncertainty might also lead to a bias for rules, which might succeed in reducing the uncertainty.

One might argue that countries that expect to be weak (that is, small countries, including most or all developing countries) would favor rules. It is generally assumed that any rules that are now made for the international trading system (such as the existing GATT system, if it were enforced) will protect the weak. This may be one reason why the EC, which feels itself to be in a strong bargaining position, is not enthusiastic about a stricter rules-based system. This is also the reason why many people argue that the developing countries would benefit from a system where GATT was strengthened and properly enforced.

Yet one might note a qualification to this view. It seems to be assumed that the rules would actually protect the weak in the way in which a Rawlsian social contract would. But if countries likely to be weak in the future are also weak at the time the negotiations to frame the rules are made, there may be no net gain to them. The position of the United States is interesting. Presumably the United States can confidently expect to be very powerful for many years to come. Therefore it would not seem to have a strong incentive to support a rules-based system that protects the weak. The only incentive would be to move to such a system in order to economize on later negotiation (and related) costs. For the United States, and to a lesser extent other countries, it is a matter of weighing the short run versus the long run. Negotiating for rules is a form of investment: costly negotiations now are the investment, and fewer negotiations later are the returns. To repeat, the cost of negotiations includes the cost of breakdowns, power play, and so on, including the spillover of conflicts into areas outside trade.

In explaining U.S. attitudes, there is another consideration. Many ideas for tightening up and constructing rules, and indeed for constructing complex legalistic systems, seem to have come from the United States because, for various historical reasons, this is a legalistic country and, above all, a country that always thinks in terms of constitutions and rules because it is held together by a constitution. This is well known. But some other countries, notably Japan and Britain, are very different. Whatever system is constructed will have to be a compromise between different attitudes to rules versus discretion and negotiation. The interesting point is that insofar as rules protect the weak, other countries should welcome the U.S. bias toward rules.

10.3 Criteria for Judging Policies and Systems

Let us take as given that a system with rules will be constructed or that the existing system will be amended in various ways. Before discussing various detailed issues, there are some further general principles that have to be explored. I am concerned not with the probable or the possible but the desirable. In other words, I am concerned with welfare economics.

10.3.1 Efficiency and Long-term Mutual Gain

Economists' recommendations are usually based on the efficiency criterion, defined as Pareto efficiency. A policy is efficient if the gainers could compensate the losers and still have something left over. Actual compensation does not have to take place, but it must be possible. This is the basis of the argument for free trade, subject to the numerous qualifications (often second best or worse) that have been explored in the literature of international trade theory. In discussing the rules-versus-discretion trade-off, I referred to costs of both types of systems, and these were meant to be Pareto-efficiency costs.

The problem about this efficiency criterion that economists use so much—and politicians and others are often so reluctant to accept—is that efficiency is not optimality. How can one say that a policy represents an improvement if some people are made better off and some worse off and full compensation does not take place? This issue is important even within countries where there is often some element of compensation through the fiscal system (gainers pay more taxes, and losers may be the beneficiaries of more support from government) but where compensation is rarely if ever complete. But it must be a major concern in the international arena since there is no intercountry system of compensation, and no system of rules is likely to create it (other than possibly in a partial way). This problem led at one stage in the developement of welfare economics to a nonsolution: the nihilistic answer of the new welfare economics that economists can (in effect) make no prescriptions about anything. This was the orthodoxy in economic theory for a brief period, but it was an uncomfortable position for a profession to get itself into.

A way out, much used in cost-benefit analysis, implicit in a great deal of policy analysis, and formalized earlier by Samuelson, Meade, and others, is to attach welfare weights to different incomes and so combine the efficiency and the income distribution criteria. The welfare-weights approach encourages explicitness in policy recommendations, which economists normally regard as a virtue, but gives no criteria for agreement. A social welfare function is required to provide the welfare weights, and every person—or every government—can have his or her own. To get some generally agreed prescriptions, one must then look for some generally acceptable social welfare functions, or—put less formally—generally acceptable approaches to income distribution effects of policy changes.

Two kinds of social welfare functions must play some role. One is the egalitarian social welfare function, which gives more weight to the poor than the rich. It certainly influences my own thinking and policy proposals. In the present context it means that relatively more weight should be given to the interests of the developing countries, especially the least developed among them. This is, of course, an arbitrary judgment. The second is the conservative social welfare function, a concept that describes or rationalizes an approach that can be found to underlie policy advocacy in many countries. Severe adverse effects on incomes of any sections (though they may already be relatively well off) should be avoided, and, to prevent such effects, policy interventions are justified. Clearly this criterion underpins the numerous safeguard arrangements in trade policy (whether within or outside the famous GATT escape clause article XIX) and justifies, at least to politicians and the general public, so much protection. Economists cannot ignore this criterion, though they may realize that regular application of it will reduce national income. There is a moral hazard problem in systematically rescuing industries or people in trouble. The traditional position of economists is to argue against policies that reflect a conservative social welfare function and in favor of the efficiency criterion.

We are still left with the problem of justifying our traditional efficiency approach when compensation does not take place. Must we always take distribution effects, including intercountry distribution, into account when considering any policy? And does this not completely destroy the market-based noninterventionist rules that many of us favor? The answer must be in probability terms. It might be called the long-term mutual gain argument. I shall put it here in world rather than national terms, though it applies at both levels. It has to be conceded that any policy or set of rules that raises world national income (that is, that is favorable on the efficiency criterion) is likely in the short run to make some countries better off and some worse off. But if such policies are consistently followed over a longer period, it is probable that eventually everyone will be better off. This seems to provide some defense for advocacy of systematic efficiency and growth-oriented policies.

10.3.2 Restraining Governments for the Good of Their Countries

Should international rules restrain governments not for the sake of protecting other governments or countries as part of an international social contract but rather for the sake of protecting the peoples of individual countries from their own governments and protecting the governments from the continuous pressures that act upon them? Some advocacy of rules in international trade— or advocacy that international organizations or committees that themselves have discretion should have some authority in particular fields over governments—runs along these lines. To some extent the role of the IMF is seen in these terms. The idea is that we need international rules and international organizations to allow governments to resist pressure groups. But it is worth remembering that this implies that when the rules are made and the organizations are staffed, the governments are able to resist these pressures. Perhaps the idea is that it is possible to resist these pressures once (when the rules are made) but not continuously.

There is also the idea that politicians do not generally understand economists' efficiency-based arguments against protection, so somehow we should get some rules imposed that will enforce the desirable policies, possibly not just through enforcement procedures in the international system that is created but also through the policy inertia that convenient, simple rules allow.

One might then ask, If we cannot persuade politicians of our views, how can we get the rules established? I can think of an answer only in terms of economies of scale and efficiency. We have something to teach (the gains from trade and the efficiency arguments against protection) that is basically correct and of which we can convince people if only there is time and effort enough available. We can succeed once every twenty years or so, when a system of rules is established or revised, but we cannot succeed continuously other than at excessive cost. Thus one might use an efficiency argument for the establishment of proefficiency rules.

There are arguments against the view that international rules should be established that restrain governments from pursuing policies that (in the belief of economists or of other governments) are against their own countries' interests. One argument is that the presumption should be that each government knows best what is good for its citizens. People who believe in the need for a government to plan the economy, and believe their government would do so beneficially, are naturally opposed to international constraints. This was an element in the opposition by the left wing of the British Labour party to Britain's joining the EC. More generally it seems that one cannot just assume that international rules will impose better arrangements than would any particular government. For example, international trading rules imposed by majority vote in the United Nations might well be inferior to those imposed unilaterally by the United States.

My view is that there is still some presumption that governments are better judges of the possible trade-offs and appropriate equilibria in their countries than are centralized bureaucracies, intergovernmental committees, or other governments. This does not deny that governments may be unwise or ill intentioned, but there is a case for decentralized decision making between countries just as there is within countries.

Inevitably international rules will be made primarily by the powerful countries. The fact that they are big and powerful economically is some indication of the economic success of their policies. Thus the rules they make, influenced by the ideologies that have helped to make them successful, may also be good for other countries. Nevertheless other countries should be encouraged more by example than by international rules to follow in their footsteps.

10.3.4 Harmonious International System

One criterion should have a high place in setting up or reforming an international trading system, or indeed any other international system: one should aim to have a harmonious international system where political tensions generally are minimized and economic policy warfare is avoided. Countries should not feel aggrieved about each others' policies and not inclined to retaliate. This idea represents the idea of the conservative social welfare function interpreted across borders. Countries should not affect each other adversely in a marked way. The efficiency criterion (long-term mutual gain argument) should in general be the guiding star for setting the rules for an international system, but it should be qualified by this consideration. The advocacy of this approach rests on the eventual cost—not just economic but also political—resulting from lack of the required harmony. Rules should be devised that make for harmony, that minimize costly negotiations and conflicts, but also that do not place unnecessary restraints on governments.

10.4 Special Role of the United States

The United States will have the dominant role in any reconstruction of the rules for the international trading system. Nothing can happen without it, and a great deal can happen if both the administration and Congress want it to happen. The United States has inevitably inherited the leadership mantle from Great Britain. Japan has supported a new initiative but for good reasons is generally reluctant to take on a position of leadership. The EC lacks the ability to lead because of the decentralized nature of its decision making. The division of powers in the EC is much greater than in the United States. Furthermore if Europe did lead, it might well be in the wrong direction—wrong from the point of view of the economist's efficiency criterion, that is. The EC is racked by the central economic problem of excessive real wage levels and social security arrangements relative to productivity, which had led to unemployment beyond the power of orthodox macroeconomic policy to reduce, and this generates inflexibility, feelings of insecurity, and protectionist pressures. In addition, a key role, indeed a veto role, is played in its decision-making processes by France, a country where the belief in free or freer trade is somewhat less than in other major Western countries.

The major role of the United States must be as the successful market economy, which by its visible success sets an example to other countries and spreads the belief in some simple principles that should also guide the international trading system. Of course, the United States has been and is an offender against these principles. The examples are well known. But its militant proclamation of belief in the basic market principles should foster a more widespread commitment to efficiency-oriented and market-based policies. At the same time the United States must bear in mind the legitimacy of other ideologies—more interventionist and often with more emphasis on sectoral income conservation—prevalent in other countries.

10.5 Discrimination and Nondiscrimination

There are many specific issues relating to the making of international trading rules that one can and should discuss. Here I select two: the question of nondiscrimination and that of subsidies.

One of the central issues that will arise in any new negotiations is whether a new safeguards code, involving a revision of article XIX of GATT, should be negotiated and whether countries that subscribe to the new system should be compelled to use this article and not bypass it, as they do now, with VERs and other devices. The article insists on nondiscrimination, but the devices that are being used outside the GATT framework are always severely discriminatory, usually directed against particular developing countries or Japan. The notorious Multi-Fiber Arrangement is grossly discriminatory against developing countries and outside GATT rules.

The nature of the current problem is the following. Let us assume for the moment that discrimination is undesirable from the point of view of the international system but is seen as being in the national interest of particular major countries. Article XIX might be revised through negotiation of a new safeguards code that allows for discrimination, possibly subject to some limitations, subject to transparency, and so on. In that case countries might cease to bypass GATT. That would be desirable for the system. On the other hand, the force of antidiscrimination arguments within each country would be weakened if discrimination were made legal within the GATT system. It is the old issue of whether use of an undesirable but popular drug should be legalized. The EC has blocked negotiation of any new safeguards code that does not permit discrimination. Perhaps one must then explore the possibilities of permitting very limited and temporary discrimination within a new code or article XIX while trying to convert the Europeans to the virtues of nondiscrimination.

Nondiscrimination and the MFN clause have been at the center of the GATT system that emerged postwar, mostly as a reaction against the mutually destructive discriminatory and discredited policies of the 1930s, as well as the hostility of the United States to imperial preference. But in the last twenty-five years or so, nondiscrimination has broken down in three ways.

First, there has been the establishment of the European Common Market and its preferential arrangements for the associated territories. This has clearly had a trade diversion element in it, but it has been widely thought acceptable because it was, after all, associated with trade creation, and the usual presumption (with some empirical support) is that trade creation far outweighed trade diversion. In fact outsiders may have been net gainers as a result of the higher real incomes that resulted from the net beneficial effect within the EEC. Second, there has been the GSP in favor of LDCs. This has been seen as acceptable because it discriminated in favor of the poorer countries. But more important the effects have been so small, and the exceptions so large, that it has been no threat to the system. On the other hand, it has diverted the developing countries from pushing hard for universal nondiscrimination, which would be much more in their interests. Third, there has been the discrimination through the Multi-Fiber Arrangement and, more recently, through the widespread use of VERs in many other product areas. These developments are far more of a threat becase they are so widespread and because they are wholly associated with protection; they do not represent a partial movement to free trade. They represent a combination of trade destruction (negative trade creation) and trade diversion. It is this development that requires the current international trading system or nonsystem to be reviewed.

Let me now come to the more basic question. What really is wrong with discrimination? Who gains and who loses? The orthodox world efficiency approach, basing itself on Viner, gives the well-known answer: every act of discriminatory reduction of trade barriers has a favorable trade creation and an unfavorable trade diversion effect, and nondiscriminatory reduction of trade barriers would always be better. Going beyond this type of analysis, there seem to me three considerations.

One argument weighs in favor of permitting discrimination. Discrimination may be necessary as part of a process of moving to world free trade. For example, a group of countries might successfully negotiate a free trade area or customs union arrangement, but they might be unable to persuade some outside countries to join. For a variety of reasons they may not be willing to offer free trade unilaterally to these other countries. This unwillingness may be desirable, in any case, because it puts some incentive on the other countries to join the free trade area, hence removing their own barriers as well. A customs union or free trade area that is genuinely wide open to new members seems to me a highly desirable development, though it involves discrimination against outsiders and hence some (possibly short-term) trade diversion cost. If such a union begins, say, with the United States, the EC, and Japan, it may be the best way in which a movement toward the world freeing of trade can be revived. If fact proposals of this kind have frequently been made.[1]

Two other considerations count against discrimination. First, the opportunity for discrimination produces continuous opportunities for bargaining, which is costly. Partly as a result, it is conducive to international ill will, as the experience of the 1930s testifies. It does not contribute to a harmonious international system. Second, it is inevitable that it would damage those in a weak bargaining position, notably the developing countries. The fact that it tends to be particularly directed against developing countries, as evidenced by numerous VERs and the Multi-Fiber Arrangement, and that it is antiharmony leads me to favor strongly the nondiscriminatory approach other than that which is involved in the free trade area process.

10.6 On Subsidies

Optimal intervention theory tells us that well-chosen subsidies are almost always preferable to tariffs, and even more, to quotas. This does not mean that all subsidies are desirable but that particular objectives—such as fostering an infant industry or offsetting a distortion in the labor market that raises the cost of labor to an industry or throughout the economy—can be more efficiently achieved by subsidies than by trade intervention. Before this theory was developed, many economists preferred subsidies to tariffs because the former are more transparent. The cost is more visible, going through the annual budget, and there is therefore a built-in restraint on pressures for protection.

The general decline of tariffs and the willingness in OECD countries to allow government expenditures in relation to GNP to rise to unprecedently high levels has made subsidies relatively more important as instruments of intervention. Forms of subsidization are numerous and sometimes quite indirect. Some built-in restraint must still be there, but it is now frequently argued that subsidies, because they take so many forms and are not always measured on an equivalent basis to tariffs, are less transparent. Surprisingly there is a hankering for tariffs, and sometimes it even seems to be suggested that the replacement of subsidies by tariffs would be desirable. I suspect that this is mainly explained not by any change in the nature of either device but by the fact that tariffs have been reduced over the years.

A subsidies code has emerged out of the Tokyo Round of multilateral trade negotiations, and it is widely proposed that all subsidies that might affect trade should be brought within the GATT framework. The principal feature of present arrangements is that GATT allows countries to impose countervailing duties on imports in cases where the suppliers of imports have benefited from export subsidies, while the subsidies code (to which not all members of GATT have subscribed) prohibits export subsidies completely, other than in agriculture and when imposed by developing countries. The code is somewhat vague on other kinds of subsidies, but there is pressure, particularly in the United States, to restrict them further and to allow countervailing action.

The GATT opposition to export subsidies has often been queried. Export subsidies may well benefit the importing country (by having a favorable national effect in terms of the efficiency criterion) because of improved terms of trade. The adverse effect will be sectoral. From a world efficiency point of view, if the export subsidies offset tariffs and quotas, the net effect may, on second-best grounds, also be efficient. If country A subsidizes exports on a long-term basis, from the point of view of country B the effect is no different than when there has been a sectoral productivity improvement in country A that cheapens particular exports and so changes the conditions of comparative advantage. Thus the concern with export subsidies cannot be based either on the efficiency (long-term mutual gain) argument or on the conservative social welfare argument. It rests on the fairness argument, whereby any unfavorable comparative advantage change brought about by policy is considered to be unfair to the adversely affected parties. Only if the adverse effect is sudden and severe would some temporary protection be justified on conservative-social-welfare-function grounds.

Subsidies in general cannot be prohibited by international rules or be used as a justification for permitting other countries to impose trade restrictions. Subsidies can fulfill many social purposes, including the provision of adjustment assistance, encouraging the training of labor, and regional development. And what is a subsidy? Is the United States subsidizing technological development through its military budget, for example? Surely the United States would not agree that this be placed within the ambit of international trade negotiations. This is just one example, but numerous other items of public expenditure can be described as subsidies to someone or to something. Proposals to maintain or strengthen the rule of law in international trade will be bound to fail if it is attempted to extend the scope of the law so widely that it digs deep into the sovereignty of governments.

It would seem to me much wiser to allow full subsidy freedom, including export subsidies. If country A wants to protect its own industry against the consequences of country B's subsidies on exports or production of a competing product, let country A countervail with a subsidy of its own. In both cases there is the built-in constraint of the cost to the budget. Both governments will have some incentive to negotiate to reduce their subsidies if they find that they are getting too expensive. But this might be supplemented by a scheme to encourage transparency. Perhaps each country should be required to produce an annual subsidies report and to supply statistics on subsidies to GATT.

10.7 Conclusion

So many considerations have been introduced here that one can hardly claim that a clear-cut policy recommendation inevitably emerges. Nevertheless starting from some simple presumptions, it seems that one can arrive at a set of recommendations for a new system that may not be probable but is just posssible and would certainly be desirable.

The presumptions are that the major negotiating nations, in particular the big three, broadly accept the long-term mutual gain argument for free trade, that they accept the relevance of the concern with sectoral income maintenance, that they wish to have as far as possible a harmonious international system, and that they see some virtues in policy openness and in decentralization of decision making.

This leads me to the following package, at least as a long-term target at which the negotiating nations should aim.

1. Complete free trade (no tariffs or quantitative import restrictions among the countries that agree to participate). This should include both agriculture and textiles. With all trade restrictions completely ruled out, there should be no incentive for exporting countries to accept VERs.

2. This may be qualified by a safeguards code that allows for temporary, nondiscriminatory tariffs, the rules being similar to those of article XIX. This qualification is meant to take some account of the sudden injury problem (that is, the concern with the temporary conservation of sectoral incomes or, at least, avoiding sudden declines).

3. Developed countries that do not participate do not get the benefits of free trade or the safeguards code, so discrimination against them is permitted. But they should be free to enter the system without any negotiations.

4. There shall be subsidy freedom.

5. With regard to protection imposed under safeguards and protection imposed against those outside the agreement, there shall be complete transparency, including regular international examinations along OECD lines.

6. There will be no restrictions on imports from developing countries other than those imposed under the same safeguards code, but developing countries will not be required to join the scheme until they have reached particular levels of income per head or exports per head. These should not be set too low, roughly drawing the line where it is now drawn in United Nations and World Bank categorizations. When they reach these levels ("graduate"), they will be invited to join the scheme, with transitional arrangements lasting some years to allow for infant industry protection and gradual dismantling of trade barriers. They will retain their subsidy freedom, as the others do. If they do not join the scheme when they graduate, they will gradually lose the privilege of free entry into the free trade area.[2]

It seems to me that all this is desirable, little of it is probable, but some of it is at least possible.

Notes

This chapter provided the basis for the keynote address at the conference.

1. The *Annual Report of the Council of Economic Advisers* (1985, pp. 125–26) suggests the free trade area approach as a secondary strategy for trade liberalization if fully multilateral negotiations do not succeed. The correct point is made that free trade area negotiations "tend to reverse the usual incentives in international trade negotiations by making countries more eager to be among the first to agree to liberalise trade rather than among the last" and "as the number of countries joining an FTA grows, the incentives for outsiders to join increase."

2. At the conference the recommendation to allow free entry for imports from developing countries, even when they themselves still have trade restrictions, was queried. The issue is not whether the markets of the developed countries should be wide open to imports from developing countries, for given trade restrictions in the developing countries, whether positive or zero, this is clearly desirable from an efficiency point of view and if one agrees that developed countries' trade policies should generally help, rather than discriminate against developing countries. The issue is whether pressure should be put on developing countries to reduce their own restrictions, possibly moving to complete free trade, in their own interests. Is it asking too much from their policymakers, or is the carrot of open markets in the developed countries what is needed?

One consideration to bear in mind is that there are some conceivably valid arguments for tariffs at modest levels, at least on second-best grounds, in developing countries, primarily on infant industry grounds or for the raising of revenue. (such a view must be stated with careful qualifications.) Probably more important, given that protection levels are high in many developing countries, the adjustment problems involved in moving rapidly to free trade in order to gain the benefits of open markets in the developed countries may be perceived as too great. On balance many of the developing countries may then decline to join, possibly because they incorrectly perceive the adjustment problems to be too great or because their decision makers are not intellectually convinced of the case for free trade.

Participants

Gardner Ackley
University of Michigan

William James Adams
University of Michigan

C. Michael Aho
Council on Foreign Relations

Sven Arndt
American Enterprise Institute

Robert Axelrod
University of Michigan

Deane Baker
University of Michigan

G. Paul Balabanis
U.S. Department of State

Thomas O. Bayard
Ford Foundation

Miloslav Bernasek
University of Michigan

W. Michael Blumenthal
Burroughs Corporation

William H. Branson
Princeton University

Drusilla Brown
Tufts University

John Campbell
University of Michigan

Richard N. Cooper
Harvard University

W. Max Corden
Australian National University

William J. Davey
University of Illinois College of Law

Alan V. Deardorff
University of Michigan

Robert Dernberger
University of Michigan

J. Kimball Dietrich
University of Southern California

Avinash Dixit
Princeton University

Rudiger Dornbusch
MIT

Richard Drobnick
University of Southern California

Ronald Findlay
Columbia University

Jeffrey A. Frankel
University of California

Edward M. Gramlich
University of Michigan

Elhanan Helpman
Tel Aviv University

Nancy Hennigar
Michigan Office of International
Development

Marsha Herring
Office of Senator Carl Levin

Robert S. Holbrook
University of Michigan

Ann Hollick
U.S. Department of State

Candace Howes
International Union, United Auto
Workers

Gary Clyde Hufbauer
Institute for International Economics

Kent Hughes
Joint Economic Committee

Michael Intriligator
University of California, Los Angeles

John H. Jackson
University of Michigan

Ronald W. Jones
University of Rochester

Robert O. Keohane
Brandeis University

Carol Keyes
Michigan Department of Agriculture

Stephen D. Krasner
Stanford University

Mordechai Kreinin
Michigan State University

Paul Krugman
MIT

Vernon L. Lacy
American Motors Corporation

Edward E. Leamer
University of California

Jay H. Levin
Wayne State University

Susan S. Lipschutz
University of Michigan

Helene C. McCarren
University of Michigan

Rachel McCulloch
University of Wisconsin

Stephen P. Magee
University of Texas

Keith Maskus
University of Colorado

James Melvin
University of Western Ontario

Allan I. Mendelowitz
U.S. General Accounting office

Jeff Miron
University of Michigan

J. Peter Neary
University College, Dublin

Neal D. Nielsen
University of Michigan

Gardner Patterson
Washington, D.C.

Lee Price
United Auto Workers

Alan Rapoport
National Science Foundation

Edward J. Ray
Ohio State University

Alfred Reifman
Congressional Research Service

J. David Richardson
University of Wisconsin

Howard Rosen
Institute for International Economics

Marc Santucci
Michigan Office of International
Development

Gary Saxonhouse
Center for Advanced Study in the
Behavioral Sciences

Gregory K. Schoepfle
U.S. Department of Labor

Partha Sen
University of Michigan

Harold T. Shapiro
University of Michigan

Ronald Silberman
General Motors Corporation

Murray Smith
C. D. Howe Institute

T. N. Srinivasan
Yale University

Robert M. Stern
University of Michigan

Wolfgang Stolper
University of Michigan

Joe Stone
Council of Economic Advisers

Niara Sudarkasa
University of Michigan

John W. Suomela
U.S. International Trade Commission

Mary Ann Swain
University of Michigan

David Tarr
Federal Trade Commission

Adrian Tschoegl
University of Michigan

Marie Thursby
Ohio State University

Steven Wecker
National Bank of Detroit

Marina v. N. Whitman
General Motors Corporation

Ernest J. Wilson III
University of Michigan

S. Bruce Wilson
Office of U.S. Trade Representative

L. Alan Winters
World Bank

Ian Wooton
University of Western Ontario

Alexander J. Yeats
United Nations Conference on Trade
and Development

Evans Young
University of Michigan

Leslie Young
University of Texas

Subject Index

Name Index